W9-DHU-145

THE TIMES THEY WERE A-CHANGIN'

Also by Robert S. McElvaine

Down & Out in the Great Depression:
Letters from the "Forgotten Man"
The Great Depression: America 1929–1941
The End of the Conservative Era: Liberalism after Reagan
Mario Cuomo: A Biography
What's Left?—A New Democratic Vision for America
The Depression and New Deal: A History in Documents
Eve's Seed: Biology, the Sexes, and the Course of History
Franklin Delano Roosevelt
Encyclopedia of the Great Depression (editor-in-chief)
Grand Theft Jesus: The Hijacking of Religion in America

THE TIMES THEY WERE A-CHANGIN'

1964

THE YEAR THE SIXTIES ARRIVED AND THE BATTLE LINES OF TODAY WERE DRAWN

ROBERT S. McELVAINE

ARCADE PUBLISHING · NEW YORK

First Edition

Arcade Publishing books may be purchased in bulk at special discounts for sales promotion, corporate gifts, fund-raising, or educational purposes. Special editions can also be created to specifications. For details, contact the Special Sales Department, Arcade Publishing, 307 West 36th Street, 11th Floor, New York, NY 10018 or arcade@skyhorsepublishing.com.

Arcade Publishing® is a registered trademark of Skyhorse Publishing, Inc.®, a Delaware corporation.

Visit our website at www.arcadepub.com.
Visit the author's site at robertsmcelvaine.com.

10 9 8 7 6 5 4 3 2 1

Library of Congress Cataloging-in-Publication Data is available on file.
Library of Congress Control Number: 2022930527

Cover design by Erin Seaward-Hiatt
Cover photography: Fannie Lou Hamer image © Warren K. Leffler and Adam Cuerden; John Lewis image © Bettmann / Getty Images; Lyndon Johnson image © Keystone / Stringer / Getty Images; Nashville protest image © Bettmann / Getty Images; Textures © duncan1890 / Getty Images and Olga_Z / Getty Images

ISBN: 978-1-950994-10-6
Ebook ISBN: 978-1-950994-12-0

Printed in the United States of America

for

Brett

a child of the sixties

born in 1988

"1964 threatens to be the most explosive year America has ever witnessed. . . . You let that white man know, if this is a country of freedom, let it be a country of freedom; and if it's not a country of freedom, change it."
—Malcolm X
(April 1964)

"If the young people of the South—young black people, young women, young men—could change the world then, then we can do it again now."
—John Lewis
(March 2020)

"Today, old battles have become new again."
—Representative Terri Sewell (D-AL)
(August 2021)

CONTENTS

PREFACE

A SCENE FROM THE NIGHT calendar 1964 began illustrates how the times they were a-changin' in that momentous year of upheavals that continue to reverberate in so many ways today:

Lyndon Baines Johnson had been president for twenty-nine days. He was home in Texas for the holidays after an extraordinarily successful start to his administration. Almost immediately after John F. Kennedy's assassination, Johnson had hired as his personal secretary a woman named Geraldine Whittington. On New Year's Eve, Johnson chose to go party-hopping in Austin. The exhausted First Lady decided to stay home, so the president took some of his staff with him on a helicopter to the state capital. One of the parties was for the birthday of Horace Busby, a longtime associate and aide to LBJ, at the Forty Acres Club. When the presidential party arrived, Johnson took Whittington's arm and they walked in.

What of it? you ask.

Gerri Whittington was African American (her hiring by Johnson a few weeks earlier was itself a milestone), and the Forty Acres Club was rigidly segregated. But when they walked in, no one said a word. The next day, a University of Texas professor called the club to ask if he could bring black guests. All such requests in the past had been summarily rejected. This time, the professor was told, "Yes, sir. The president of the United States integrated us on New Year's Eve."[1]

Now, it was 1964.

♦♦♦

"The United States is now," historian Nancy MacLean wrote in her 2017 book, *Democracy in Chains*, "at one of those historic forks in the road whose outcome will prove as fateful as those of the 1860s, the 1930s, and the 1960s."[2] Her book details "the deep history of the radical right's stealth plan" for the "tearing up of the social contract on a scale never attempted in a democracy,"[3] and the overturning of a nation "of the people, by the people and for the people."

As I complete this book in late 2021, the inflection point MacLean described has become much more apparent. President Joseph R. Biden Jr. has undertaken an effort "to rewrite the American social compact . . . a fundamental reorientation of the role of government not seen since the days of Lyndon B. Johnson's Great Society."[4] Simultaneously, his opponents have amped up to an extraordinary degree their efforts to undermine democracy in order to regain and then retain power.

Those who seek to turn us back appreciate that control over how the past is perceived goes a long way toward gaining control over the present and future, and today they are engaged in an all-out effort to misrepresent the American past.

It was in the extended 1964 that the social contract and the inclusive democracy they are working to undermine came to fruition. A careful examination of the time when the battle lines of today were drawn is of substantial value in understanding the present.

♦♦♦

It was different then.

For one thing, the only notable Nazi in 1964 America was Dr. Strangelove.

There was hi-fi, but no one had yet heard of Wi-Fi. People still listened to music on AM radio. The latest technological advance in this area was the transistor radio, which made reception of the music on those AM stations portable. At home, people listened to music on phonographs that played discs that were decidedly non-compact. The newest versions provided stereophonic sound.

People tended to know several of their neighbors well, talk with them regularly, and even have them over of an evening. Far more kids played pickup games of baseball, football, and basketball on vacant lots in the neighborhood and driveway courts than participated in various organized Little Leagues and such. The number of American kids playing what the rest of the world calls football was scarcely above nil.

Interracial marriage was illegal in a third of American states.

People—a term that was then widely taken by white people as a synonym for whites—generally felt safe in their hometowns, even after dark. Howard Johnson's reigned as king of highway food. McDonald's still charged fifteen cents apiece for its hamburgers.

It made a difference what season it was, especially in a grocery store. Apples and pears were to be found only in the fall and early winter; strawberries were confined to late spring; peaches, plums, and tomatoes to the summer. Although air-conditioning was no longer so unusual that it commanded comment, it was far from ubiquitous.

Razor blades had two edges, on opposite sides of the blade.

People could—and did—argue endlessly about all sorts of things, with no easy resort to the correct answer on the internet via their phones.

Google was the name of a comic strip character that had inspired a 1920s song, "Barney Google (with the Goo-Goo-Googly Eyes)."

"On line" was a New York colloquialism for "in line," and "in line" was where people stood waiting for something; it was not an adjective placed before *skates*.

The web was something spiders wove; the internet was not yet even a glint in Al Gore's eye. Cells were components of plants or animals or spaces that housed prisoners—or groups of clandestine Communists. All phones were dumb, large, had rotary dials, and were tethered to a wall by a cord. There was only one telephone company.

In 1964, most people still read daily newspapers—and considered what was in them, a day or more after the events had occurred, to be news.

Most women, who had no reason to think they should try to decrease the appearance of the size of their waist, wore girdles. The purpose was to hold up their hose, which were separate, one for each leg. Women were expected to wear sheer nylon stockings, particularly if they were in the business world—a male preserve into which a hose-less female was unlikely to gain admission.

Young males, no matter how poor they were as students, were bilingual. They spoke one language around parents, other adults, and females of all ages. When among male friends, they spoke another language that had an expanded vocabulary. Today, this bilingualism is all but forgotten. There is little difference between the words used among the guys and those spoken in what was then termed "polite company."

In 1964, a comedian—Lenny Bruce—could be arrested for using obscenities in his act and sentenced to four months in prison in New York City.[5]

Sex was much more of a mystery. The Pill had been put on the market only four years earlier, and its effects on female sexuality were just beginning to ripen. Television depicted married couples as sleeping in separate beds, and even the mildest sexual references were removed by censors.

At the beginning of 1964, references to sex in popular music were subtle. If you wanted to hear "dirty" words in songs, you had to play a record at the wrong speed. Or transfer it to tape and play it backward. Or so it was said.

Today we know that JFK had turned the White House into a personal brothel and the man who succeeded him in November 1963 had previously used a private chamber in the United States Capitol as his "nooky room."[6] But then reporters—almost all male—kept the public blissfully ignorant of such matters.

Before the internet, there were no easily accessible views of naked women to help young males learn about the mysteries of female human anatomy. *Playboy* offered a look at uncovered female breasts, but in still-repressed middle-class households, Hugh Hefner's anatomy lessons weren't that easy for boys to obtain—and the magazine wouldn't go to full-frontal nudity until 1972. The only ready source of at least slightly titillating illustrations was that old standby, the Misses' underwear section of the Sears, Roebuck catalog, where both the underwear and the women wearing it were uniformly white. And the only place to see any parts of the female body that differed significantly from those of curious young males was *National Geographic*, which sometimes carried photographs of topless "native" women, as they were then called. Unlike the Sears models, these women were all black or brown. Apparently, the elite, scientific minds of the editors of the magazine thought of these women as in a category so close to animals that there was no expectation of privacy for their "private parts."

Divorce was still remarkable—and people remarked at length about it when it happened in their neighborhood, although they generally did so in hushed tones. Unwed pregnancies were the stuff of tragedy.

Abortions were illegal, dangerous, done clandestinely, and usually remained unspoken of.

Almost all OB/GYN practitioners were male.

Until the Supreme Court's 1965 decision in *Griswold* v. *Connecticut*, a law in that state prohibited the use of "any drug, medicinal article or instrument for the purpose of preventing conception."[7] In an attempt to skirt such laws in that and other states and the anti–birth control stance of the Catholic Church, manufacturers placed on condom packages statements along the lines of "Sold for the prevention of disease only."

Gay was a synonym for happy or fun-loving. Homosexuals were referred to as "queers," "faggots," "fairies," or "homos" and generally considered to be beneath contempt. In 1964, sexual acts between consenting adults of the same sex were classified as felonies in every state except Illinois. Punishment for those who were convicted ranged up to life imprisonment.

Most colleges and universities in 1964 were "coeducational," but that term applied to classrooms and social events, not to living arrangements. Dormitories were strictly segregated on the basis of sex. At almost all times, males could go no farther than a lobby in a female dorm, and vice versa. On the rare occasions when—a Sunday afternoon once or twice a semester, perhaps—members of one sex were permitted for an hour or two to visit the dorm room of someone whose twenty-third chromosome differed from theirs, there were strict rules: The room's door must be left wide open; the feet of both students must be touching the floor, and so on.

These rules were part of a policy known as in loco parentis, which placed the school in the legal position of acting as a parent to the students on its campus. Students were not considered to have the freedom to do as they pleased. And freedom was what 1964 would be all about.

And then there's this, perhaps the greatest difference of all between 1964 and today, and one of the most important ways in which that time relates to ours: In 1964, 77 percent of Americans said they believed that the government in Washington could be trusted to do what was right always or most of the time. And, given a choice between whether they thought the government is "pretty much run by a few big interests looking out for themselves or that it is run for the benefit of all the people," 64 percent chose "for the benefit of all the people."[8] In 2019, the figure on trusting the government was down by 60 points, to a paltry 17 percent.[9]

The person most responsible for initiating the precipitous decline in public trust that ensued after 1964 was the man who assumed the presidency when our story begins. It was in 1964 that Lyndon Johnson made the fateful decisions and uttered the lies that would lead the country into the abyss of the Vietnam War and so destroy Americans' trust in their government.

It is both highly ironic and tragic that it was Johnson, a man who believed more completely than anyone else who has ever been president—with the possible exception of Franklin Roosevelt—that government can be a powerful instrument for good in helping people, who set off the collapse in Americans' trust in government that would, over the ensuing decades, bring much of the populace to adopt the anti-government outlook championed by his 1964 opponent in the presidential election, Barry Goldwater.

Had it not been for the collapse of faith in government that began under LBJ and accelerated through his presidency and that of his successor, Richard Nixon, it is highly unlikely that the move to the right that brought Ronald Reagan and later, more disastrously, Donald Trump to power would have occurred.

The belief that government cannot work for the benefit of all the people became self-fulfilling and helped to fuel the selfish desires of the very rich to be free from government intervention to rein in their efforts to acquire ever-larger portions of the nation's income and wealth for themselves. "The nine most terrifying words in the English language," Reagan said in the 1980s, "are: I'm from the Government, and I'm here to help."[10] In the next decade, even a Democratic president, Bill Clinton, felt the need to proclaim: "The era of big government is over."[11]

Surely, we continue to face today the consequences of that misbegotten offspring of 1964. Just maybe, though, as the daring agenda President Biden enunciated in 2021 proposed, we'll be able in the 2020s to restart what was attempted then: to begin again the effort to remake the reality of America into something closer to the vision of America. That hope is what characterized so much of 1964. Optimism abounded: we can conquer poverty, racism, and wrongs of all sorts.

◆ ◆ ◆

Bob Dylan's "The Times They Are a-Changin'" was released as the title track on his third album thirteen days into calendar 1964. Its lyrics foretold the significance of the year in which the sixties arrived:

> *As the present now*
> *Will later be past*
> *The order is rapidly fadin'*
> *And the first one now will later be last*
> *For the times they are a-changin'*[12]

The period discussed in this book—from November 1963 through mid-1965, which I call the "Long 1964"—takes America from a time, prior to the assassination of John F. Kennedy, of persisting innocence among the nation's white youth, when the most "radical" student actions on campuses were "panty raids" (a group of male students gathered outside a girls' dorm shouting for the girls to throw underwear out their windows to them), to young whites joining with African Americans to risk their lives for the freedom of others in Mississippi;

FROM a time when more than half of all Americans said they had never heard of Vietnam to when President Johnson was given carte blanche to conduct war there and had begun massively to do so;

FROM a time when it was still legal to refuse on the basis of race to serve people or provide them with public accommodation to when such discrimination was prohibited by federal law;

FROM nonviolent resistance to racial injustice in the South to violent resistance to racial injustice in the North and California;

FROM when the civil rights movement was characterized by "We'll walk hand in hand" and "black and white together" to deepening friction and distrust between African American activists and white liberals;

FROM a time when hardly anyone was seeing a similarity between the oppression of black people and the treatment of women to one in which that connection was beginning to ignite radical feminism; from "Wives and Lovers" to "You Don't Own Me";

FROM a time when the music charts were topped by Bobby Vinton and the Singing Nun to one in which the Beatles were dominant and, within a span of six weeks in June and July 1965, the two best rock songs of all time, the Rolling Stones' "(I Can't Get No) Satisfaction" and Bob Dylan's "Like a Rolling Stone" were released[13]—along with Dylan going electric at the Newport Folk Festival.

The pages that follow explore and interpret this extraordinary transitional period that took Americans from what was, President Kennedy's inspiring words notwithstanding, still the pre-sixties to what we can readily recognize as "the sixties"—a time in which clashing conceptions of freedom had emerged to create one of the most tumultuous and significant periods in American history.

THE TIMES THEY WERE A-CHANGIN'

INTRODUCTION

1964 IN THE CONTEXT OF THE HISTORY OF "THE LAND OF THE FREE"

Mississippi Freedom Democratic Party members on Atlantic City boardwalk, August 1964.

Oh, freedom
Oh, freedom
Oh, freedom over me, over me
And before I'd be a slave,
I'd be buried in my grave
And go home to my Lord and be free.
　　　　　—African American spiritual

Freee-dom! I say Free-ee-ee-dom
Freedom's comin' and it won't be long.
　　　　　—Chant and song at Greenwood,
　　　　　　Mississippi Freedom House
　　　　　　(August 1964)

FREEDOM IS WHAT AMERICA has always been about. But what sort of freedom, how much, and for whom—for *us* but not *them?* Such questions, along with related concerns about the implications of freedom for individualism, community, responsibility, equality, power, the economy, the distribution of wealth, and an ethnically diverse society, have been the fundamental issues around which American history has revolved. *Freedom* and *society*, *individual freedom* and *community*, are in constant tension, and radically differing conceptions of what *freedom* means are central to understanding what was going on in 1964 and the subsequent sixties as they are today.

The American experiment has centered on how much—and what kind of—freedom is compatible with the maintenance of society. How far could self-seeking individuals go in "the pursuit of happiness" before the centrifugal forces took over and society flew apart?

From the time of the earliest settlements Europeans established in America, it was apparent that unlimited freedom in an environment of seemingly limitless resources could pose danger to community and such virtues as responsibility. Their settlements were at the same time "unsettlements," in the sense that their migration left behind the settled society of the Old World, and it was not clear what would replace that old order. In the "virgin" environment of America, the ultimate land of opportunity, *freedom* could spread so rapidly that it had the capacity to overwhelm everything else.

American Freedom:
From Merry Mount to the Merry Pranksters

John Winthrop spoke in 1630 of a community in which "All the partes of this body being thus vnited are made soe contiguous in a speciall relation as they must needes partake of each other's strength and infirmity; joy and sorrowe, weale and woe,"[1] but from the earliest days a struggle has raged between that sort of community and the temptations of escaping the bonds of civilization and responsibility entirely, to live free, like "primitive men" or "savages," who were always symbolically represented by people of color. Even before Winthrop and his followers established the Massachusetts Bay Colony, Thomas Morton in

Merry Mount was trying to become what he apparently imagined was a "White Indian," in much the same way that the hipsters about whom Norman Mailer wrote shortly before the dawn of the 1960s sought to be "White Negroes."[2]

By the time Winthrop arrived in Boston in 1630, Puritans were alarmed over excessive freedom in the form of Morton and the Maypole he erected. "The men of whom we speak," Nathaniel Hawthorne wrote more than two centuries later of the revelers at Merry Mount, "after lo[o]sing the heart's fresh gayety, imagined a wild philosophy of pleasure, and came hither to act out their latest daydream."[3] That description of the outlook of the free spirits of Merry Mount in the 1620s could readily be applied across the centuries to those on a "freedom high" in the 1960s, such as Ken Kesey's Merry Pranksters, who traveled across America from California to New York in a school bus painted in psychedelic colors in the summer of 1964. Their physical goal was the New York World's Fair, but they named the bus "Furthur" (sic), indicating that their desired destination was not the fair's Unisphere but an expanded universe that could be reached only by freeing the mind through hallucinogenic drugs. The assessment of one of Merry Mount's fervent opponents, William Bradford of Plymouth, would also fit the Merry Pranksters and the hippies who followed the path they blazed. He wrote in 1628 that Morton and his band had fallen "to great licentiousness, and led a dissolute life, powering out them selves into all profaneness." He accused them of having revived "the beas[t]ly practieses of the madd Bacchinalians."[4]

The first Africans had arrived in Virginia in 1619, the year before the Pilgrims reached Plymouth and more than a decade before Winthrop and the Puritans set foot on Massachusetts soil. Of course, the territories to which the English migrants were laying claim were already occupied by a wide variety of indigenous peoples. And migrants from many other parts of Europe and, later, the rest of the world, were also attracted to the vast "unclaimed" resources in the lands that would become the United States. The result was a society in which understandings of freedom were complicated by the presence of numerous "Others." The struggle to create a unified society, an "us" that would include all of "them"—*e pluribus unum*, "out of many, one"—and to do it in such a way that people are "free" has been and continues to be the essential project of America.

Profoundly, the struggle for a unified society intersected from the beginning with the complete opposite of freedom—should all people be free, or should some be free to own or otherwise subordinate others?

Questions about the meaning and application of freedom have kept the people of the land that became the United States in a kind of cold civil war since 1607. In the 1770s, 1860s, and 1960s, the frictions heated to the combustion point. They again approached ignition from 2016 through 2020 and have a growing potential to burst into flame as I write in 2021.

The first major American conflagration over freedom established one vague and open-ended definition of *freedom* as "the pursuit of happiness." The War for Independence also brought to the fore the contradiction between the professed American ideals of freedom and equality and the actual denial of access to these benefits to large fractions of the population. Benjamin Franklin, Thomas Jefferson, and many others saw the incompatibility between the declared principles of the revolutionaries and the enslavement of black people. Thomas Paine and, especially, Abigail Adams, were among those who pointed to similar disparities between an ideology of equality and the subordination of women. Then there was the tension between the emerging free market economics (it is an entirely appropriate coincidence that Adam Smith's *Wealth of Nations* was published in the same year in which the Declaration of Independence was written) and the democratic objectives of equality and community. All these incongruities remained unresolved nearly two centuries later, in 1964. And, though there has been substantial progress since then, they are still the cracked foundation beneath America's conflicts today. The basic nineteenth-century attempt to deal with the incompatibility of conflicting notions of freedom, competition, community, democracy, and equality was segregation. There was, of course, both before and after enslavement was officially ended, a vicious segregation based on race, in which all traditional notions of freedom were denied to the vast majority of Americans of African ancestry. There was also a geographical segregation of some of the ideals of freedom, with the North increasingly subscribing to the free market, individualist model, while the South continued to operate much more on the premodern paradigm of an organic community—seeing society as an organism in which different types of people were the organs: white males, the head; white women, the heart; and enslaved black people as the hands and muscles. The rubbing along these two fault lines of American freedom became sufficiently intense in the middle of the century that it produced the most massive social earthquake in the nation's history.

The war resulting from the rebellion of enslavers intent on continuing to treat humans as property did not resolve or end the two forms of segregation of concepts of freedom that produced it. Anyone who doubts that there remains some level of geographic segregation of conflicting visions of the meaning of America and conceptions of freedom should consider the current division of the nation into what have come to be called "red states" and "blue states." Red and blue are in fact more states of mind than geographical states, with often substantial minorities of the populations of a state of one color adhering to the views represented by the other hue. But they also still have an undeniable geographical component.[5]

One of the nineteenth-century means of dealing with—or avoiding—the contradictions inherent in the American ideology of freedom was a sexual segregation of spheres: brutal, Darwinian, free market, individual competition in the man's world outside the home and, ideally at least, a nurturing, community-oriented refuge in the woman's world of the home.[6]

Although this "solution" of segregation of conflicting ideals by sex continued far into the twentieth century and enjoyed a powerful late-autumn blooming in the 1950s, another form of freedom segregation was becoming increasingly important.

The Protestant work ethic provided a means of confining freedom within acceptable bounds from the colonial era through the production-oriented phases of the Industrial Revolution. As the economy matured, however, industry became so prolific that the economic focus had to shift to increasing consumption. A population schooled in the virtues that maximize production had to be persuaded to shift its attention to consumption and spend like there was no tomorrow. Since the 1920s, interrupted only by the years of the Great Depression, advertisers carried the message of this different conception of freedom to the American public.

As necessary as the encouragement of buying was from an economic perspective, it also held the capacity to produce socially disastrous side effects, as Daniel Bell explained in the mid-1970s in *The Cultural Contradictions of Capitalism*: Promoting consumption meant endorsing self-indulgence. What was to stop acceleration along this vector before it reached hedonism?[7]

One result of this growing contradiction between the needs of the economy and the moral codes that had contained freedom within acceptable limits was that the traditional racial segregation of freedoms was magnified. American society continued to consider economic and political freedom as white, while sexual freedom was identified as black. This was, to be sure, not a new division in the twentieth century. White people had long promoted a loosening of their professed code of sexual morality among African Americans. That was "freedom" of a peculiar kind for black people, because almost always when a white man crossed the color line in search of that sort of freedom, the black woman on whom he exercised it was anything but free in her sexuality.[8] In the twentieth century, this traditional American segregation of freedom was intensified as large numbers of African Americans moved into cities outside the South. The redoubled racial segregation of freedom constituted an attempt, however unconscious, to quarantine the ill effects of the growing culture of consumption.

By the years following World War II, mainstream America was pursuing a domestic agenda that paralleled the nation's Cold War foreign policy of "containment." Much as the goal internationally was to contain communism within the areas it already held; the goals on the home front were to contain sexuality within the African American population and to contain white women within the domestic sphere.

Ironies abounded in this setup. Urban black people were largely "free" to be hedonistic but denied access to most of the material means of hedonism. Many whites were increasingly prosperous but much more constrained by conventional definitions of acceptable behavior. An even greater irony is that African Americans, the least free group in traditional meanings of *freedom*, came to be seen, at least from the 1920s onward, as the avant-garde of freedom by successive generations of young middle- and upper-class white people, who have followed black leads into the musical forms of blues, jazz, rhythm and blues, rock and roll, and hip-hop/rap and at least portions of the lifestyles associated with them. An appreciation of this extraordinary irony is the essential starting point for a successful effort to unravel the meaning of the era that arrived in 1964.

Black Freedom, White Freedom

The key to understanding 1964 and the era it spawned is the interplay of a variety of competing notions of *freedom*, among them two very different conceptions related to America's long history of racial division. Those seeking change in this tumultuous time—in civil rights, by ending the Vietnam War, in liberation from societal constrictions on behavior—have generally been lumped together as "the movement." In fact, they were motivated by contrasting conceptions of freedom.

Large portions of the United States remained segregated in 1964, and segregation also extended to forms of freedom. Black people, most of whom were at that time still far from free in the usual senses of the word, had become symbols of freedom to a growing number of white people. This phenomenon was evident in two important cultural landmarks that had appeared in 1957, Jack Kerouac's novel *On the Road* and Norman Mailer's essay "The White Negro."[9] African Americans appeared to some whites to be free because they were largely outside of or on the periphery of the consumer culture that had come to dominate twentieth-century America. They didn't have money, but they seemed to know how to get "kicks." Their freedom looked to be in the areas where many white youths felt deprived, most significantly, sex. Circa 1964, sex, drugs, and rock and roll were all seen as "Negro things."

While the sort of freedom that African Americans were imagined to have was attractive to many young white people who did not have it, many black people sought precisely the kinds of freedom that white Americans had—political participation, a degree of material abundance, and freedom to patronize restaurants, hotels, and other public establishments. Freedom to some of those who had grown up in economic security might consist of "nothing left to lose," as Kris

Kristofferson put it a few years later,[10] But to those who had little or nothing, freedom consisted in part of obtaining access to material things as well as material well-being. To those looking out from mainstream white America and those who were outside looking in, freedom appeared to be freer on the other side of the wall that separated them.

To be *a part of* or *apart from* mainstream America, that was the question of the sixties that was coming into focus in 1964.

Two principal ideals of freedom—one social and political, the other cultural and personal—were like two strands of a double helix that twisted around each other. They were usually not distinguished because both answered to the same name. The wide philosophical divide between the two strands of "the movement" is suggested by the early emphasis of the sociopolitical side on *civil* rights and the persistent calls by the cultural radicals, whose forebears were the Beats of the fifties and who would become the hippies of the later 1960s, for *individual* rights. Civil rights indicate rights *as citizens* and carry with them obligations to the community; they are rights inextricably bound up with responsibilities and they are the rights of people who are members of a community, not free-floating "selves." Civil rights are entirely compatible with traditional values; indeed, they are rooted in those values. Individual rights, in contrast, entail no necessary connection with anyone else, and so no responsibilities. This ideal meshes with the "every man for himself" doctrine of the modern, consumption-ethic economy.

There was a critical, but often overlooked, difference between the African Americans the white political-social and cultural radicals attempted to emulate. The political and social side took the black civil rights activists of the rural South as their model. The ways of the early civil rights movement were southern, rural, religious, "brotherly," and oriented toward family and community. Significantly, the anthem adopted by this early phase of the movement was the old union song, "We Shall Overcome." The southern civil rights movement was one that came from a social environment in which it was still possible to think in terms of *we*, rather than the modern *me*.

Outside the South, the modern social and economic atmosphere with its disintegrative, nonreligious, atomistic anomie infected the lives of black Americans, as it did of white Americans. It is telling that, with the shift to the urban environment, which began with scattered uprisings in the summer of 1964 and burst into full national attention in Los Angeles the following summer, the movement's goal began to shift from integration to black separatism and its means from nonviolence to violence. Separatism was in keeping with the disintegrative forces of the modern economy.

Not only were the two halves of "the movement" associated with the youth of the sixties philosophically incompatible, but the real, though unacknowledged, affinity then and later was more between the cultural radicals and the economic "conservatives." Before the decade began, such corporate consultants as Ernest Dichter were urging their clients to promote hedonism as moral.[11] Though Barry Goldwater presumably didn't have hedonism in mind, his 1964 pronouncement that "extremism in the defense of liberty is no vice," clearly promoted extreme individualism.[12]

In 1976, Tom Wolfe coined the term "Me Decade."[13] The 1930s had in many ways been a "We Decade."[14] Like those years of the Great Depression, 1964 was a time when the personal pronoun that exhibited the dominant cultural, social, political, and economic outlook, was the first-person plural subjective, *we*. The "we" feeling, though, didn't much outlast the extended 1964. The operative personal pronoun in the later sixties became the first-person singular objective, *me*. The later sixties were largely about being free to "do your own thing" and "if it feels good, do it!"

Wolfe's characterization of the 1970s had been applicable to the last years of the 1960s and became even more accurate after 1980. A striking example of the continuation into the 2020s of the extreme notion of "freedom" that concerns only *me* and not *we* was the extraordinary right-wing opposition to vaccination, masks, and other efforts to contain the COVID-19 pandemic and protect the lives of others.

The "We Long Year" of 1964 was followed by a "Me Half-Century."

◆ ◆ ◆

In 1964, two other categories of people were slowly coming to realize that they were on the outside when it came to important parts of freedom. White women had achieved the right to vote and many had the economic benefits of middle-class status, but some were beginning to realize that they were very much on the outside in other ways and began to seek the full equality of the freedoms men had: "male freedom."

At first blush it might seem outlandish to suggest that some men were trying to get "female freedom," but there were males who were beginning to seek freedom from the requirement to live up to masculine stereotypes. A man who advocated nonviolence or opposed war was likely to be mocked as "womanly." In a spring 1965 presentation at Rutgers, literary critic Leslie Fiedler spoke of nonviolent resistance as an aspect of a "revolt against masculinity"—"the possibility of heroism without aggression, effective action without guilt." Fiedler argued that, in their quest to become "other," the young people to whom he referred as the new barbarians "identified with woman." "To become new men, these children of the future seem to feel," Fiedler said, "they must not only become more Black than White, but more female than male."[15]

Almost everyone, it seemed, was talking about *freedom* in 1964. African Americans sought to be free *from* discrimination. White segregationists wanted to be free *to* discriminate. Liberals sought to free people from the fear of poverty, hunger, and illness. Free Market conservatives sought to free businesses from government regulation. Growing numbers of women were beginning to push for freedom from subordination to men and male-defined institutions. Some men were yearning to break free from society's definition of masculinity. The American government sought to free people around the world from the threat of communism. Vietnamese people sought to be free of foreign domination.

Does freedom include people whose skin is not white? Does freedom apply to women? Does freedom of speech include political speech on university campuses? Does it include obscene speech? Does freedom mean that people have a right to eat at restaurants and stay at hotels, or does it mean that the owners of those establishments have the right to deny people entrance to them? Does freedom in other countries mean being free from communism or free from foreign domination?

Nineteen sixty-four was, as Ronald Reagan said in October in what would come to be known by conservatives simply as "The Speech," "A Time for Choosing." The choosing was among widely varying conceptions of *freedom*.

"A Change Is Gonna Come"

1964 AND THE BATTLE LINES OF TODAY

Bob Dylan and Lyndon Johnson in 1964.

The chance won't come again . . .
For the loser now will be later to win
For the times they are a-changin'.
　　　　　　　—Bob Dylan, "The Times They
　　　　　　　Are a-Changin'"[1]

S AM COOKE'S HOPEFUL MESSAGE in his 1964 song "A Change Is Gonna Come"—that change had been far too slow, but he knew it would come—was timely. [2] Change, massive change, was about to come at a stunning pace. It was in that year that what we think of as "the sixties" arrived. "The differences between 1963 and 1969 were dramatic," as Kurt Andersen notes in his 2020 book, *Evil Geniuses*: "The clothes, the hair, the sound, the language, the feelings—and the changes happened insanely fast."[3]

In the chapters that follow, I argue that 1964 was the key year in the shaping of modern America. It launched the most intense, meaningful, and—on balance—positive period of change in American history. Moreover, the changes that occurred then still define the political, social, cultural, and economic battle lines along which Americans contend today. The "culture wars" that have been so prominent in the divisions of the nation since the 1980s center largely on the remarkable transformations that began in 1964. To appreciate what is at stake in the political and cultural conflicts of the 2020s, it is essential to understand the pivotal year explored in this book.

But history is not mathematics. Decades in culture, politics, and attitudes often don't match calendar numbers. What comes to mind when we hear "the sixties" went from the closing days of 1963 well into the early 1970s. Similarly, a year in history doesn't necessarily equate to 365 or 366 calendar days. Nineteen sixty-four, or what I call in this book the "Long 1964," began in late 1963 with the assassination of President John F. Kennedy and the arrival in America, albeit not yet in person, of the Beatles in November and December 1963. It continued through the summer and early fall of 1965, with Lyndon B. Johnson's major escalation of the American war in Vietnam, the release of "(I Can't Get No) Satisfaction" and "Like a Rolling Stone," the Voting Rights Act, the Watts uprising, and key portions of Johnson's Great Society legislation. When I refer to 1964 in what follows, it should be understood as shorthand for that extended period.

Here's a useful way to look at how that time relates to now:

Nineteen sixty-four was a time of righting wrongs. Today, one of the two major political parties is fully dedicated to wronging rights— reversing the progress initiated in the period I explore here. The once Grand Old Party has defined itself as both anti- and ante-1964.

♦ ♦ ♦

One of the prominent battle lines in the politically inspired culture wars emerged in 2019 when the *New York Times* introduced "The 1619 Project," which identified the introduction of slavery into the English colonies in North America four centuries ago as one of the defining moments shaping American history. Opponents swiftly countered with arguments supporting the traditional view that Enlightenment ideals underlying the Declaration of Independence in 1776 are central to the meaning of America, and the question became a culture-war litmus test.[4] In fact, 1619/1776 is not an either/or choice. Americans have always been, in a variety of ways, in historian Michael Kammen's accurate designation, a "people of paradox."[5] Surely, the greatest of all American paradoxes is that, from the start, the new land of freedom was also a land of enslavement. Much of American history can be seen as a tension between these two facts. Those who have attacked the 1619 Project have conveniently ignored that, in her introduction to it, Nikole Hannah-Jones wrote, "the year 1619 is *as important* to the American story as 1776. [emphasis added]"[6] That assertion should not be controversial.

The paradox that is the United States took bodily form in Thomas Jefferson. He enunciated the radical vision, with its majestic ideals of freedom and equality, but failed miserably to live up to those ideals. Yet the promise of America has rightly inspired even those people who have been excluded from it. African American poet Langston Hughes may have said it best in 1936: "America never was America to me / And yet I swear this oath— / America will be!"[7]

It was in the Long 1964 that the full promise of 1776 was for the first time opened to those for whom the legacy of 1619 had for so long defined America. Through the Twenty-fourth Amendment outlawing the poll tax, the Civil Rights Act banning racial discrimination, and the Voting Rights Act opening the vote to all, the United States for the first time became a full democracy.[8] As of this writing in 2021, the Republican Party is engaged in an all-out assault on that democracy. While the radical right seeks to make political capital out of insisting that 1776 is what America is *all* about, they are plainly on the side of returning the nation to its 1619 inheritance as was in place prior to 1964.

Zeitgeist:
A Dylan-Johnson Duet

History is punctuated by discontinuities that alter its trajectory. The key to the occurrence of such watershed moments is less the leaders than a sociopolitical environment that is receptive to change. Though Lyndon Johnson's vision and ability to get things done in Congress were clearly important in the change that occurred in 1964, more essential was that Johnson found himself, to use an evolutionary metaphor, in an environmental niche for which progressive approaches were adaptive. That is apparent in the dramatic cultural change that took place during the same period.

On January 13, 1964, Columbia Records released Bob Dylan's third album, *The Times They Are a-Changin'*. It seems to have gone unnoticed, both then and since, but the messages in Johnson's State of the Union speech in which he declared war on poverty and Dylan's song that provided the album's title in the first two weeks of 1964 were, while drastically different in tone and approach, parallel in the thrust of what they were saying about the times.

When Dylan sang about the chance not coming again and the loser later becoming the winner because the times were a-changin',[9] he could have been channeling the new president. These words almost exactly reflect how Lyndon Johnson saw the situation and the opportunity he had to change America for the better. Dylan and Johnson—the poet and the president—almost seemed to be singing a duet. This synchronicity was, of course, entirely unplanned. Dylan had written the song in September and October 1963, while JFK was still alive, and he was reflecting the sense of hope that Kennedy had provided but not fulfilled and, even more, the bold actions of civil rights workers.

The sort of convergence that happened with Dylan and Johnson is usually referred to as mere coincidence. Coincidence it certainly was, but was it *mere*? When two things coincide chronologically, it may be meaningless, or it may reflect something meaningful about that time. When Dylan's friend Tony Glover picked up a typed copy of the song's lyrics in Dylan's apartment in September 1963 and read aloud the line, "Come senators, congressmen, please heed the call," he asked, "What's this shit, man?" Dylan shrugged his shoulders and responded, "Well, you know, it seems to be what the people like to hear."[10] Precisely. Such a coincidence of a musician's words with the arguments of an activist president suggests that something was "in the air." And one of the things in the air—or "blowin' in the wind"—in 1964 was a desire to improve the conditions of society's "losers."

This interpretation is important when considering Bob Dylan's work. While he was deemed the voice of protest, the spokesman for his generation who, as Zora Neale Hurston said of her protagonist in her 1937 novel *Their Eyes Were Watching God*, put the "right words tuh our thoughts,"[11] Dylan has long denied that he had any such intention. Always fiercely refusing to be pigeonholed and frequently reinventing himself, he reacted against the embrace in which the civil rights and anti-war movements tried to hold him.[12] "The left tried to lionize him," Pete Seeger wrote in a letter to his father in 1967; "he reacted violently against this, saying fuck you to them all."[13] Dylan's answer to the claims that he was the leading voice of protest may have been contained in a song on his next album, *Another Side of Bob Dylan*, which was released seven months later, in August 1964: "It Ain't Me Babe."[14]

It is difficult to believe that Dylan was not authentic when he wrote the powerful words of protest and social justice contained in so many of his songs in 1963 and '64. But if we look at the songs and their reception as reflections of the spirit of the time, Dylan's purposes and sincerity don't matter. He was a major voice of his generation, even if he didn't want that role. And, speaking of sincerity, the same is the case with LBJ's words at this time. He wanted to uplift the downtrodden, but regardless of his candor or lack thereof, the enthusiasm with which many Americans greeted his calls for fundamental change indicates that, like Dylan, Johnson was voicing sentiments that were "in the air" and "what people want[ed] to hear" in 1964. This odd couple calling for changing times in January 1964 would have had a hard time singing in harmony, but growing numbers of those who formed their audiences were eager to harmonize with them. If the duet of Bob Dylan and Lyndon Johnson were to be given a name, the most appropriate one would be Zeitgeist.

One part of Lyndon Johnson might have wanted to sing along with the sentiments in another song on Dylan's January album, the powerfully antiwar ballad "With God on Our Side."[15] To do so, though, would have required LBJ to overcome his manhood insecurities, and, as I'll discuss later in the book, that wasn't in the cards. It was over the issues addressed in "With God on Our Side" and the question of the Vietnam War that the duo of Dylan and Johnson split apart. The majority coalition of Americans that came together in 1964 in support of the ideal of "for the loser now will be later to win" would be torn apart over the war. One result would be that the big winner in 1964, Johnson, would be "later to lose."[16] Another consequence would be a shortened life span for the spirit of the times of 1964.

The motto of the 1868 Democratic presidential ticket on the above poster directly raised the basic issue of American history: The question of whether America can and will be a free, diverse, inclusive democracy or "a *white man*'s country" has been with what became the United States since 1607, when English settlers arrived in a land already occupied by people who had skin of a color different from theirs.

It was central at the Constitutional Convention in 1787, in the virulent sectional disputes of the 1850s and the enslavers' rebellion, during Reconstruction and the "restoration" of white rule in the South, through the Jim Crow era, and in the civil rights and women's movements, and it is fundamental to the bitter confrontation today between progressives who advocate for the continued advance toward the ideals of America and those who are *regressive*—the sort of people Russian writer and artist Svetlana Boym categorizes as "restorative nostalgics."[17] They seek, British journalist Nick Bryant says in *When America Stopped Being Great*, "refuge in a misremembered past."[18] They want, as Anne Applebaum puts it in *Twilight of Democracy*, "the cartoon version of history" and "they want to live in it right now." They long to return to an imagined golden age before some conspiracy "perverted the course of history and reduced the nation to a shadow of its former self."[19] In the contemporary United States, they are striving to go back to when there seemed to be no serious question that it was a white man's country.

Nineteen sixty-four was the year in which the Democratic Party under the leadership of Lyndon Johnson unequivocally proclaimed, through the Civil Rights Act, that the United States is not a white man's country. The hostility of many white people to racial equality opened the way for the Republican "Southern Strategy." But the Voting Rights Act of 1965 provided a possibility of overcoming the defection of white racists by expanding the electorate—and it has done just that since the early 1990s. In 2014, Bill Clinton accurately said that "the Civil Rights Act and the Voting Rights Act made it possible for Jimmy Carter, Bill Clinton, and Barack Obama to be president of the United States."[20] Joe Biden can now be added to that list, as could, by virtue of winning the popular vote, Al Gore and Hillary Clinton.

Nineteen sixty-four was also the year the Republican Party first took on the appearance it has today. Delegates to the national convention rejected, by a margin of more than two to one, a proposed amendment to the party platform endorsing the Civil Rights Act of 1964.[21] And it was in that year that the party of Lincoln first openly embraced the sort of right-wing extremists who dominate it in the early 2020s. In 1964, state Ku Klux Klan branches in Georgia and Alabama widely publicized their unqualified endorsement of Barry Goldwater. Republican National Chairman Dean Burch's reaction to the KKK approval was: "We're not in the business of discouraging votes."[22] At the 1964 GOP National Convention, delegates rejected a proposed amendment to the platform to repudiate "the efforts of irresponsible extremist groups, such as the Communists, the Ku Klux Klan, and the John Birch Society." Words New York governor Nelson Rockefeller used to denounce the "radical right" that sought to take over the Republican Party then would fit exactly what has happened to that party since 2016: "the tactics of totalitarianism," the use of "ruthless, rough-shod intimidation."[23]

Lady Bird Johnson campaigned through the South in October 1964 and was harassed by vicious crowds of Goldwater backers. In Charleston, South Carolina, the First Lady was greeted with signs reading, JOHNSON'S A NIGGER LOVER and BLACK BIRD GO HOME. The crowd wouldn't stop booing long enough to allow her to speak. Louisiana congressman Hale Boggs called the Charleston mob "a Nazi gathering."[24]

As those events exemplify, there were many signs of the taking up of racism among the backers of Goldwater in 1964, but as a whole the party of Lincoln did not yet identify itself with white supremacy. The party's whole-hog adoption of the "this is a white man's country" position has occurred only in recent years, as the entire nation has been rapidly becoming what portions of Mississippi, Alabama, South Carolina, Louisiana, and other Deep South states were in 1964: a place where the population of people of color could, if allowed to participate in politics, outvote whites. It is the accelerating trajectory of the United States toward the status of a "majority minority" nation that has so terrified large numbers of white Americans and prompted them to seek to return the country to the "undemocracy" it was prior to 1964. The four states I just listed, which constituted two-thirds of those Goldwater carried in 1964, were then the only ones with populations less than 70 percent white. The 2020 census found that the population of the United States as a whole is only 58 percent non-Hispanic white, down from 89 percent in 1960—which was essentially unchanged from 1910—and 69 percent in 2000. In the 2010s, for the first time in history, the nation's white population declined, not just as a share of the total population but in absolute numbers, by 2.6 percent.[25] Those facts help "explain why so many whites outside the South turned into crypto-Southerners," Kurt Andersen rightly points out. "As their communities got more racially and ethnically diverse, they got more *consciously* white and defensive and racist."[26]

Reforms in 1964–1965 played a major role in decreasing the percentage of whites in the American population. The Immigration and Nationality Act of 1965 removed the quotas that had been aimed at keeping the country predominantly of northern and western European descent. As was his wont, Donald Trump confirmed the desire of many of his followers to go back to what the United States was before that change when he blurted out in 2018, "Why do we want these people from all these shithole countries [referring to Haiti and African nations] here? We should have more people from places like Norway."[27]

At least some Republicans have long understood voting barriers to be a necessity if they are to have any chance of winning elections. "I don't want everyone to vote," Paul Weyrich, a cofounder of such right-wing organizations as the Heritage Foundation and the Moral Majority, declared shortly before Ronald Reagan's election in 1980. "As a matter of fact, our leverage in the elections quite candidly goes up as the voting populace goes down."[28] In 2020, Trump concurred. Denouncing provisions to facilitate voting that were in a COVID-19 relief bill, he said, "They had things, levels of voting that if you'd ever agreed to it, you'd never have a Republican elected in this country again."[29]

In the early 2020s, the Republican Party came out foursquare for undermining democracy. Within less than a year following Trump's defeat in the 2020 election, and with his constant repetition of the Big Lie that the election had been stolen from him as background, Republican-majority legislatures in nineteen states had passed voter suppression laws making it more difficult to vote, with the transparent purpose of reducing Democratic votes. Many of these measures had provisions clearly targeting people of color. Some promoted voter intimidation.[30] Even more ominous, according to a report released in September 2021 by the nonpartisan Voting Rights Lab, Republican-controlled legislatures in eleven states had enacted seventeen *election suppression* laws: transferring "control of elections or reporting results from nonpartisan officials to [Republican] political operatives," Republican state officials taking over the powers of local election officials in heavily

Democratic counties, partisans counting ballots and doing recounts, and even empowering legislatures to override the state's voters in a presidential election and appoint to the Electoral College a slate for the defeated candidate.[31]

The ongoing full-frontal assault on voting rights and inclusive democracy is among the clearest illustrations of how the battle lines of today were drawn in the Long 1964. It is plain that a major objective of those on one side of the political lines of the 2020s is to overturn the accomplishments made then. On the right to vote, the contrast between where the Republican Party was in the period examined in this book and where it is now is stunning. In 1965, 83 percent of House Republicans and 94 percent of Senate Republicans voted for the Voting Rights Act.[32] As recently as 2006, an extension of the Voting Rights Act was supported by all Senate Republicans.[33] In October 2021, all fifty Republicans in the Senate voted not even to allow discussion of a bill titled the Freedom to Vote Act, which would restore voting rights protection.[34]

A more far-reaching effort to overturn the progress of the Long 1964 would be difficult to imagine, and the forces seeking to preserve and extend those gains find themselves needing again to fight the battles of six decades earlier.

The Ghost of Campaigns Yet to Come:
The Concept Sketch for Today's Republican Party

The concept sketch for what has happened in the Republican Party in recent years was created in 1964. A remarkable half-hour film produced for the Goldwater campaign eerily put forward an outline for reshaping the Republican Party into what it would become by 2020.

On Columbus Day 1964, with President Johnson holding a huge lead over Goldwater, one of the Republican candidate's strategists, F. Clifton White, wrote a memo contending that the big issue that could turn the election around was "the moral crisis in America today." That crisis was, White said, multidimensional, including "crime, violence . . . the [racial] backlash . . . the breakdown of law and order, immorality and corruption in high places, the lack of moral leadership in government, narcotics, pornography." Taken together, he declared, these concerns painted a "picture of a society in decay." The strategist proposed the creation of a front group, "Mothers for a Moral America," to sponsor a documentary film on American society in decay that would "attempt to bring the onus of this right to the steps of the White House." The film should, White said, be shown in swing-state markets during the last week of the campaign.

The next day, Goldwater responded: "Agree completely with you on morality issue. Believe it is most effective we have come up with. Also agree with your program. Please get it launched immediately."[35]

The hastily assembled national committee of the front group included a few women who were known in their own right, such as Hedda Hopper and Dale Evans, but most of them were the wives of important men and were listed as "Mrs." followed by the first and last names of their husbands: Mrs. Ronald Reagan, Mrs. Willis H. DuPont, Mrs. William F. Buckley Sr., and so on.

The result was a remarkable film, titled *Choice*, that had no impact on the 1964 election but is of great significance as a concept sketch for reshaping the Republican Party into the anti-sixties party at the time when "the sixties" were beginning. The outline of the argument for virtually all Republican campaigns for the next half century and more is to be found in this 1964 production.

Choice used some of the same images as Goldwater's television spots, to which it added scenes of race riots, drug dealing, other crime, and sex. It said people were afraid to go out after dark and complained of the open availability of "smut." What *Time* magazine referred to as "striptease babes, wild Twisters, [and] Negro riots" were "interlaced with shots of a black Lincoln Continental limousine careening madly along a country road, with beer cans being tossed out of the driver's window."[36] Viewers were intended to identify the driver as the president of the United States, who, it had been reported earlier in the year, liked to drive his Continental at extraordinary speeds on Texas country roads while holding a beer can in his hand.

The film then cuts to a large number of nice-looking white kids reciting the Pledge of Allegiance,[37] intercut with images of an American flag, the Capitol Dome, and the Statue of Liberty. A voice-over (actor Raymond Massey) says that there are now two Americas. Pictures of the Founding Fathers appear on the screen. "The other America, the other America, is no longer a dream but a nightmare." Images of African Americans fighting with police are accompanied by the narrator saying, "Our streets are not safe; immorality begins to flourish; violence pits American against American. We don't want this."

Unmistakably, the "other America" was intended by the makers of the film to be identified by white viewers as the *Others'* America—*our* America being taken over by *them*.

As *Choice* continues, images of the putative moral decay in 1964 America grow more startling—a woman dancing with her crotch positioned above a man; a topless woman with her arms around a man . . . a virtually naked man with a woman; a bare-bottomed woman; a woman with a lock on her vagina . . . books with such titles as *Call Me Nympho* and *Male for Sale*.

The film tells viewers that it is no longer safe to go out at night and shows scenes of riots and black people looting. "Demoralization. Chaos. ... In the streets, the mob—mobocracy." The camera zooms in on single words in newspaper headlines: FEAR, RIOT, BRUTAL, SMUT, FIEND, ASSAULT, DEAD. A long series of rioting scenes is followed by the statement: "By new laws, it is not the lawbreaker who is handcuffed; it is the police."

And, remarkably for a film shot a year before the Immigration and Nationality Act of 1965, *Choice* shows a border crossing with the sign MEXICO. The voice-over intones: "Over the borders: Dope! Narcotics trafficking setting a new, depraved record." It also features a kid raising his middle finger at a cop, one nearly naked woman spanking another, and . . . well, you get the picture.

John Wayne appears, with a rifle on the wall behind him, to close the sale: "You've got the strongest hand in the world—that's right, the hand that marks the ballot; the hand that pulls the voting lever. Use it, will ya!" Then photos of Goldwater and his voice come on, speaking of restoring "high morality" and stating, "I look forward to a time and a republic under God." Back to the Duke: "It's in your hands: Which America?"[38]

Journalist and historian Theodore White characterized the ad by saying, "naked-breasted women, beatniks at their revels, Negroes rioting and looting in the streets succeeded each other in a phantasmagoric film."[39] NBC refused to run the ad unless several of its more risqué scenes were excised.[40] At this point, Goldwater vetoed it, saying, "I'm not going to be made out as a racist. You can't show it."[41]

Other Republicans would prove to have no such qualms. The film is the prototype for the strategy and tactics Republicans would use from 1968 (and in some state campaigns, such as Ronald Reagan's in California, 1966) onward to the present.

"What *Choice* really did was establish the power of television to communicate American myths, values and beliefs," said political advertising professor Kathleen Watters in 1996. "Its use of visual symbols was unique at that time. Its power came visually. And that power was reinforced by positing two different images of America."[42]

The basic message of the film[43] was almost identical to what Reagan and Trump would use: "Make America Great Again!" by returning to the days when white men ruled without question, minorities and women knew their place, there was little crime, everyone was patriotic, and so on: the imagined time before 1964—before the sixties arrived.

Ending an Age of Ignorance of Guilt

"It is hard, now, to grasp just how profoundly the tectonic plates of American politics have shifted between 1964 and today," historian Rick Perlstein wrote in 2001.[44] That was even more the case during the Trump years, which can accurately be seen as the anti-sixties. Yet the echoes from the dramatic social, cultural, and political upheavals of 1964 continue to reverberate all around us in the present. What happened then shapes us today in numerous ways, some obvious, others less so. Many of the accomplishments that constituted the change that arrived in the year "A Change Is Gonna Come" was released were at least partially reversed from 1980 onward, four decades that have constituted a "long time waiting" for positive change to come again.

It is clear that 1964 marked a major discontinuity. In his 1999 book on the year, journalist Jon Margolis called it *The Last Innocent Year.*[45] Historian James T. Patterson included the last months of 1964 in his 2012 book, *The Eve of Destruction: How 1965 Transformed America.*[46] A year that can be seen both as the end of the previous era and the beginning of a new one clearly was an historical inflection point.

His book's title notwithstanding, Margolis doesn't see the time leading into 1964 as innocent. He rightly says that there was a "delusion
of innocence" about what America was.[47] The way I would put it is
that, rather than being a time of innocence, the period before 1964
was one of ignorance of guilt—the guilt of a nation founded on an
extraordinarily inspiring set of ideals that had expended much effort in
overlooking how far short of those ideals it has fallen through much
of its history. American history as it was taught in the 1950s and into
the 1960s was whitewashed.[48] The focus was on how the West was
won, with no consideration of the people who were losing it. The
existence of slavery was mentioned, but then the "peculiar institution"
was abolished and apparently all black people apart from Booker T.
Washington and George Washington Carver vanished from the American story. The United States had never done anything wrong and had
always stood for "truth, justice, and the American way."

Here is a striking example of just how distorted and perverse the
view of the past was then: In a 1963 collection of documents relating
to the career of Christopher Columbus, Samuel Eliot Morison, one
of the most prominent historians in mid-twentieth century America,
included a letter written by Michele de Cuneo, a Genoese nobleman
who accompanied Columbus on his second voyage. It is a startling
document, in which the writer recounts an incident in which Columbus
"gave" him a "beautiful Carib woman." Cuneo relates that he "conceived desire to take pleasure" with her, she resisted forcefully, digging
her fingernails into him, he "took a rope and thrashed her well," and
forced her to act like a harlot. The account is highly revelatory and
certainly worthy of inclusion in the book, but at least as horrifying as
the boastful account of a rape is the way Morison described the per-
petrator. Cuneo was, Morison reported without a hint of disapproval,
a "cultured ... Italian gentleman of the Renaissance, savoring life and
adventure, full of scientific curiosity"—a "jolly dog" who loved to
have "a good time, which obviously he did."[49]

Although President Johnson gave Professor Morison the Presidential Medal of Freedom in 1964,[50] it was in that year that both his sort
of casual acceptance of horrible truths about the American past and
the willful ignorance of them began to be replaced by an awareness on
the part of a much larger slice of the American population of some

of those facts. In that year, songwriter and folk singer Tom Paxton recorded a song, "What Did You Learn in School Today?" It is a biting satirical attack on the misinformation that was still being taught about the American past. The son in the song responds to his father's question by saying he learned that everyone in the United States is free, our country is always right and just, the police are always our friends, the wars America fights are always good, and so on.[51] Paxton's lyrics again seem tailor-made for the "guilt-free" mythology that Republicans today are imposing on school curricula and calling it "history."

Such nationalistic myth-history is, to be sure, not unusual in countries around the world. Nor was it absent in the United States prior to the Civil War. "The History of our Revolution will be one continued Lye from one End to the other," John Adams complained in a bitter private letter in 1790. "The Essence of the whole will be *that Dr Franklins electrical Rod, Smote the Earth and out Sprung General Washington. That Franklin electrified him with his Rod—and thence forward these two conducted all the Policy Negotiations Legislation and War* [emphasis in original]."[52]

But a distorted view of the American past was expanded in an unusual way after a combination of white terrorism and the removal of federal troops from the South as the rest of the country turned its attentions to other matters allowed for the "restoration" of white rule across the South between 1877 and the 1890s.[53]

"The Losers Now Will Be Later to Win"?

It is often said that history is a story told by the winners. Yet, stunningly, by a few decades after the Civil War and for well over a half century thereafter, it came to be the losers' stories of "a land of Cavaliers and cotton fields," moonlight and magnolias, kindly masters and happy slaves, a glorious "Lost Cause," and a horrible period of "Black Reconstruction" that were widely accepted as accurate history.

In the late nineteenth and early twentieth centuries, the nation was reunited on the basis of a tacit armistice in which the South accepted that the Union is indissoluble and much of the rest of the white country accepted the southern belief in the innate inferiority of people of African ancestry. That acceptance was facilitated by the popularity of the pseudoscience of social Darwinism and a fabricated story that Reconstruction had been a monstrous time of rule by ignorant black people, rather than the largely successful progressive period that it was.

This inverted history had an enormous impact on the lives of at least three generations of Americans that, though diminished, continues down to the present. The most consequential telling of it is D. W. Griffith's 1915 film, *Birth of a Nation*. The movie represents enslavers as benevolent caretakers for a lower life-form. The enslaved are shown singing and dancing during the "two-hour interval given for dinner." Reconstruction is painted as a time in which the "natural order" of white superiority was turned upside down. Griffith presents a frightening picture of "crazed negroes," with the necessary restraints of slavery removed, making "helpless whites" their "victims." As for "restoration," one of the title cards in the silent movie depicts the restoring of white man's rule as a glorious event and describes it as "the former enemies of North and South are united again in common defence of their Aryan birthright."[54]

The view that Reconstruction was a period of terrifying "black domination," and restoration the reaffirmation of the United States as "a white man's country" was prevalent throughout the nation from the 1890s into the early 1960s. Pushed by followers of early twentieth-century Columbia University historian William Dunning, this interpretation was routinely taught in schools. It was also reflected in popular culture, notably in Margaret Mitchell's hugely successful 1936 novel *Gone with the Wind* and its 1939 film adaptation.

It is a safe assumption that the adoption of the losers' view of slavery, race, the war, Reconstruction, and restoration by the winners in that war against the enslavers' rebellion is not what Bob Dylan meant when he wrote, "The losers now will be later to win."

◆◆◆

"A Shadow Stretched Across Our History for a Hundred Years," read a *New York Times Book Review* headline on September 13, 1964.[55] That shadow, cast by the acceptance of the losers' false history, which continued its pernicious effects through the Jim Crow era of segregation, was finally being lifted. It was during the Long 1964 that newer scholarship presenting a very different view of Reconstruction—and some older but largely ignored scholarship, notably W. E. B. Du Bois's 1936 *Black Reconstruction*[56]—was brought to a wider public attention.[57] Even more important in overturning the whitewashed history that had held sway for so long was the impact of the civil rights movement in awakening many Americans, particularly the young, to the fact that they had been spoon-fed a distorted version of the nation's past.

In our own time, the calls to "Make America Great Again" and "Take Back America" are partly about restoring the age of ignorance of guilt that existed before 1964. Those slogans mean to take America *back* in two senses: back *from* those who are not white or not male and back *to* the time when straight white males were in charge. It should not have been surprising that, as part of this overall quest to effect a second restoration of white man's rule, those who want to regress proposed to restore the ignorance of American history that had prevailed before 1964. The sociopolitical heirs of the 1865 losers are again attempting to rewrite the American past of the nineteenth century as a lie—and they are doing the same with the recent past, most notably by rewriting the January 6 Insurrection as a lie.

In October 2020, Donald Trump announced that he would create a 1776 Commission to combat "anti-American historical revisionism" and promote "patriotic education."[58] It was, as writer Konstantin McKenna put it, "a desperate search for the right enemies."[59] The commission's report was published on January 18, 2021. Among President Biden's first actions on the afternoon of his inauguration two days later was to disband the commission.[60] That action, however, did not deter states under right-wing control from enacting laws restricting what may be taught in their schools, especially about racism.

The Republican-controlled Texas state legislature enacted a law in 2021 specifying exactly what should—and should not—be taught to students about their nation's past. Excluded were the Fifteenth Amendment, which prohibits the federal government and states from denying or abridging the right to vote "on account of race, color, or previous condition of servitude," the 1965 Voting Rights Act, "the history of Native Americans," and documents on the separation of church and state, and the women's, Chicano, and labor movements.

Existing standards calling for teaching about the ways in which white supremacy, slavery, eugenics, and the Ku Klux Klan are "morally wrong" were removed.[61] The law is unmistakably a formula for again making Texas, where non-Hispanic whites are already a minority, what it was before 1964: a white man's state.

♦ ♦ ♦

The faux patriotism of the radical right, especially evident in the 2020s, connects with an underlying question in the sixties, from 1964 onward: Are bad things happening because America has abandoned its values and traditions, or are at least some of those values and traditions themselves bad?

In 1965, at one of the first anti–Vietnam War demonstrations, Carl Oglesby, president of Students for a Democratic Society, spoke eloquently on the question. "We have lost that mysterious social desire for human equity that from time to time has given us genuine moral drive," he said. Some people, he noted, would contend that he sounded "mighty anti-American. To these, I say: Don't blame me for that! Blame those who mouthed my liberal values and broke my American heart."[62]

Four years later, George Hanson, the Jack Nicholson character in the 1969 film *Easy Rider*, also questioned America and what had happened to it. "You know, this used to be a helluva good country," George says to Wyatt and Billy at his last campfire. "I can't understand what's gone wrong with it."[63]

Nineteen sixty-four was, on the whole, a time when the United States was becoming more of a "helluva good country," but also when it began once more to go wrong.

2

Death and Rebirth:
An Early Start to a
Long Year

JFK Departs; the Beatles Arrive

November 1963–February 1964

John F. Kennedy's casket, November 1963.   *The Beatles departing for New York, February 1964.*

The President had made "Real Freedom" a hope.
       —Anne Moody (November 1963)[1]

I'd like to take a fucking bomb and blow the
fucking state of Texas off the fucking map.
       —JFK aide Ted Reardon after the
       assassination[2]

W E'RE HEADING INTO NUT country today," President John F. Kennedy said to his wife on the morning of November 22, 1963, as he showed her an ad, bordered in black like a funeral announcement, that a right-wing extremist group, the John Birch Society, had placed in the *Dallas Morning News,* indicating that the Kennedys were pro-communist. "But, Jackie, if somebody wants to shoot me from a window with a rifle, nobody can stop it, so why worry about it?"[3] Jack Kennedy had long been a fatalist and remained so on his fatal day.

"There's something rotten in Dallas," leading psychologist Charles G. Osgood wrote to Robert Kennedy a few months after the assassination.[4] The city was the home of retired general Edwin Walker, who had been charged with insurrection against the United States during the riot over the integration of the University of Mississippi more than a year before. "Kennedy is a liability to the free world," Walker said not long before the president's scheduled trip to his city.[5] As far back as the 1960 campaign, a "mink coat mob" of right-wing high-society Dallas women joined with Congressman Bruce Alger, then the only Republican in the Texas delegation, to give native Texan Lady Bird Johnson a hostile reception at the Adolphus Hotel in Dallas. Alger led the mob holding a sign reading LBJ SOLD OUT TO YANKEE SOCIALISTS, swinging it close to Mrs. Johnson's head. One of the "ladies" pulled Lady Bird's white gloves out of her hands and threw them into a gutter. Then the well- and high-heeled thugs encircled the vice-presidential candidate and his wife, jeering, cursing, and spitting. Primal rage was unmistakable on their faces.[6] Nut country indeed.* The disgraceful behavior of those Dallas extremists occurred four days before the 1960 election, and political analysts concur that it turned embarrassed Texans away from the Republican ticket, making it possible for Kennedy and Johnson to carry the state and thereby the national election.[7]

Early on the afternoon of November 22, 1963, as the presidential motorcade moved through Dealey Plaza in Dallas, gunshots rang out and John Kennedy, who was riding in an open car, was hit

---

* It should be noted that this first violent, hate-filled political mob of the calendar 1960s was not composed of scruffy young left-wing antiestablishment "reds"; it was made up of "mature," neatly dressed "conservative" women of the Texas establishment who probably shopped at Neiman Marcus and wore red, white, and blue.

by two bullets, the second of which tore off part of his head. His car rushed to a nearby hospital, where he was pronounced dead. At least some of the gunfire came from the sixth floor of the Texas School Book Depository, where a shadowy character named Lee Harvey Oswald shot a rifle from an open window above the street as the president's car was passing. Oswald fled the building, later shot a Dallas policeman, and was apprehended as the prime suspect in the murder of the president. Two days later, while in police custody and being taken to a court hearing, Oswald was shot and killed by a local nightclub owner, Jack Ruby, as a national television audience watched in stunned disbelief. A week after Kennedy's murder, the new president, Lyndon B. Johnson, established a commission, headed by Chief Justice Earl Warren, to investigate the assassination. In September 1964, the Warren Commission announced its findings, the key one of which was that Oswald had acted alone in killing Kennedy. In 2007, Vincent Bugliosi completed a monumental examination, *Reclaiming History*, based on twenty years of research, in which he concluded that it is beyond a reasonable doubt that Oswald acted alone.[8]

There are many reasons why a majority of the American people has never accepted the Warren Commission's lone gunman conclusion, beginning with the fact that that conclusion was preordained by Johnson. The commission's purpose was not to find the truth but to put down rumors of a conspiracy that might involve the Cuban or Soviet government.

Lyndon Johnson, who was personally adept at shaping events in secret backroom meetings, was a man given to seeing conspiracies behind any negative occurrence.[9] He believed that his predecessor's death had been the result of a conspiracy involving Fidel Castro, in retribution for CIA attempts to assassinate the Cuban leader. "President Kennedy tried to get Castro," Johnson told his aide Joe Califano, "but Castro got Kennedy first."[10] "We had been operating a damned Murder, Inc. in the Caribbean," Johnson told CBS news anchor Walter Cronkite in 1969. LBJ knew that it was JFK's brother who had been pushing anti-Castro activities, and surely Johnson's eagerness to believe this scenario was enhanced by his loathing for Bobby Kennedy. But the target of Johnson's abhorrence shared his view that the plots to kill Castro had led to the Cuban dictator turning the tables and having JFK killed. "Though [Robert] Kennedy gave lip service to the single-gunman explanation, he never quieted his own doubts," biographer Evan Thomas points out.[11]

The new president saw it as imperative to convince the American people that Oswald had acted alone. Johnson told Chief Justice Warren that, "because it involved both Khrushchev and Castro," the rumor of a conspiracy "might even catapult us into a nuclear war." "I was afraid of war," Johnson later recalled having told Warren. "The nation cannot afford to have any doubt this time. You can imagine what the reaction of the country would have been if this information came out."[12] He made clear to Warren that the commission's conclusion must be that Oswald acted alone.

This action may not have been Lyndon Johnson's first presidential lie—he had, after all, already been in office for a week—and it was thousands of lies from his last, but it may have been the one with the best motivation. If Kennedy had avoided nuclear annihilation by restraining the shoot-first-ask-questions-later proclivities of his military and civilian advisers during the crisis thirteen months before, when it was discovered that Soviet missile bases were being constructed in Cuba, Johnson sought to avoid nuclear war by not allowing the American populace to see a reason to give in to their similar tendencies.

That the Warren Commission's finding that Oswald acted alone was preordained does not necessarily mean it was wrong, but Johnson's directing of that outcome led to an investigation and report that ultimately increased rather than calmed suspicions of a conspiracy. Over the next several years, the decline in the public's trust of the government as the American war in Vietnam both escalated and deteriorated contributed to skepticism concerning the official story of the assassination. By 1967, two-thirds of the respondents to a nationwide poll said they believed the murder was the result of a conspiracy.[13] In 1988 the same portion of Americans (66 percent) believed that there was a conspiracy to kill President Kennedy as had held that view in 1967, and merely 13 percent thought Oswald acted alone.[14]

"An Incalculable Loss of the Future": Camelot, the First Kennedy Assassination, and the Course of the Sixties

Don't let it be forgot, that once there was a spot,
For one brief shining moment that was known
as Camelot. There'll never be another Camelot
again.

> —Jacqueline Kennedy
> (November 29, 1963), quoting
> Alan Jay Lerner, *Camelot*[15]

Wherever one comes down on the matter of who killed John F. Kennedy, the more important aspect of the assassination for our purposes is its impact on the American people and on the development of what we think of as the sixties.

"9/11 changed everything," Vice President Dick Cheney and other members of the administration of the second George Bush repeated as a mantra through most of their time in office.[16] Regardless of whether the government and the American people should have let 9/11 change everything, the related question about the sixties is: Did 11/22 change everything?

The answer, I believe, is that it changed a great deal about the trajectory of the ensuing year and the remainder of the decade but far from everything. In the immediate aftermath of the assassination, the American people gathered around television sets for four days, experiencing the same events as if they were all one family in one immense national living room.[17] At that time, Ben Bradlee captured the view that 11/22 changed us, even if it didn't change everything. "John F. Kennedy is dead," Bradlee wrote in *Newsweek*, "and for that we are a lesser people in a lesser land."[18] What was lost was what Kennedy had seemed to provide: an "electrifying sense of hope and possibility."[19] One of the principal ways in which 11/22 changed the sixties was by taking on the role of "the Fall" needed to establish and perpetuate the myth of an Eden before everything collapsed.

Kennedy was nearly mythical in stature while alive; his death, particularly in the way it occurred, removed the *nearly*. The Thousand Days of JFK became the Paradise Lost of 1964 and the sixties. In the week after its fall, this mythical paradise was given another name that stuck and influenced the remainder of the decade by setting an imagined standard that could not be duplicated. In an interview with Theodore White a week after her husband's death, Jacqueline Kennedy referred to his time in office as "Camelot" because of JFK's fondness for the play about King Arthur, expressing the idea that President Kennedy had now become the fallen king.[20] White used the term publicly in reference to the Kennedy presidency in an article in *Life* magazine for the next week.[21]

The coupled ideas that the Kennedy presidency had been "one brief shining moment" and "there'll never be another Camelot again" became widespread and influential and played a major part in shaping the long year that followed as well as the rest of the sixties. In retrospect, it seemed that all things had been possible during that shining moment while the fallen king had been alive. Had it not been possible then, in the words of the signature song from another Broadway musical, 1964's *Man of La Mancha*, "to dream the impossible dream"?[22]

Initially, though, impossible dreams still seemed possible despite— and in part because of—Kennedy's murder. None of the major reforms JFK had proposed was passed while he was alive. Civil rights, antipoverty programs, and federal aid to education, among others, were enacted only after his death. Their passage was facilitated by the feeling, forcefully emphasized by his successor, that they should be passed as a tribute to the fallen leader, and they were pushed through by Johnson's far more effective abilities to get things through Congress.[23] In death, JFK became a much greater reformer and idealist than he had ever been in life.

But as time passed and everything, it seemed, started to deteriorate, "Camelot" came more and more to be seen as a paradise in which none of those bad things—such as the war in Vietnam, violent racial clashes, and bitter division—would have happened. To the millions who came to think in this way, 11/22 had indeed changed *everything*.

◆ ◆ ◆

The Cuban Missile Crisis in October 1962 had made the prospect of nuclear annihilation palpable and taken a toll on the innocence and optimism of young people of the era, but the death of the nation's young president was a much greater blow. Kennedy was part of a new generation, as he emphasized when he declared in his inaugural address, "the torch has been passed to a new generation of Americans." He didn't seem like the old politicians and government leaders. Like the other products of the youth culture, from Davy Crockett coonskin caps and hula hoops to commercialized rock 'n' roll, Kennedy was made for the young. He was their friend and future.

Barack Obama, who was born the year after Kennedy was elected, captured the importance of JFK to the sixties—and this particularly applies to 1964 and 1965—and to American memory when he wrote in 1995 of "a spirit that would grip the nation for that fleeting period between Kennedy's election and the passage of the Voting Rights Act: the seeming triumph of universalism over parochialism and narrow-mindedness, a bright new world where differences of race or culture would instruct and amuse and perhaps even ennoble. A useful fiction, one that haunts me no less than it haunted my family, evoking as it does some lost Eden that extends beyond mere childhood."[24]

"A useful fiction." That's exactly the way Lyndon Johnson saw the Kennedy myth. He believed it to be a galling fiction, but he made remarkable use of it during the period that is our subject.

Daniel Patrick Moynihan, then an assistant secretary of labor in the Kennedy administration, may have put it best on the day of the assassination. When journalist Mary McGrory said to him, "We'll never laugh again," Moynihan responded, "No, Mary, we'll laugh again, but we'll never be young again."[25]

Despite this sentiment of loss, the young in 1964 managed with the help of music to restore their youth, albeit with less innocence than had been the norm before. Prior to John Kennedy's assassination, most young white Americans of the post–World War II generation had experienced tragic, early death only through fiction, in films such as *Rebel Without a Cause* and in a spate of teen tragedy songs that were popular at the beginning of the 1960s, including most famously Mark Dinning's "Teen Angel." Now the young had to face a tragic early death that was real. "The Leader of the Pack" himself dies in the Shangri-Las' 1964 classic.[26]

"Countless individuals have noted that the president's death affected them even more deeply than the death of their own parents," Kennedy confidant Ted Sorensen remarked the month after JFK's assassination. "The reason, I believe, is that the latter situation most often represented a loss of the past—while the assassination of President Kennedy represented an incalculable loss of the future."[27]

The Beatles Arrive

"The world, it seemed, was a dark and malignant place," journalist Tom Wicker wrote of the aftermath of the assassination, "the chill of the unknown shivered across the nation."[28] The "desire to huddle together" that the public felt cried out for fulfillment. As young Americans grieved for their fallen young president, their trembling hands were held by four young men from England.

The Beatles' "I Want to Hold Your Hand" arrived on American airwaves and a huge portion of the nation's youth quickly turned its affections in a new, nonpolitical direction. In fact, the *CBS Morning News* aired a report from London on "Beatlemania" in Britain on the morning of November 22. Because of what happened later in the day, it was not used on the network's evening newscast until almost three weeks later.[29] In the background of the other events going on during 1964 were the sounds of the British Invasion.

The fallen president had been something like a teen idol himself. The first televised debate in the 1960 presidential campaign made Jack Kennedy the first political superstar of the new celebrity culture. In the days that followed, "jumpers"—young women who leaped in the air as JFK passed—began to appear along the Democratic nominee's motorcade routes.[30] In mid-October, Kennedy received what was described as an "orgiastic welcome" from as many as 1,250,000 people in New York City.[31] JFK was now the political Elvis: a celebrity sex symbol. By late in the campaign, Kennedy was, one southern senator said, a combination of "the best qualities of Elvis Presley and Franklin D. Roosevelt."[32]

Kennedy was a new kind of candidate. He was *hip.* "This man seeks the highest elective office in the world not primarily as a politician, but as a celebrity," one journalist wrote, disapprovingly but not inaccurately.[33]

In the parlance of a later time, *Kennedy rocked*.

His sudden removal left a void, not only in the nation's politics, but also in its popular culture. There was a great demand for a new idol (or group of idols) to fill the vacated place in the hearts of the young. The Beatles were perfectly positioned to become that replacement. In the wake of the assassination, an event that "sang the Blues," in the words of Don McLean's 1972 song "American Pie," Americans thirsted "for some happy news," some diversion, something new, yet familiar and reassuring. The Beatles fit on every count. And, coming from abroad, they could be silly and joyful at a time when it would have been difficult for any American performers.[34]

"I Want to Hold Your Hand" almost seemed like it had been written for Americans, especially young Americans, in this moment. By the time the Beatles arrived in New York on February 7, 1964, for their first American tour, Beatlemania had swept the nation. "I Want to Hold Your Hand" had surged to number one on the *Billboard* chart the week before.

If President Kennedy's assassination marked an end of innocence for the rising Baby Boom generation, the transition was not immediate. In this regard, too, the Beatles were perfect as the first platoon of the invading musical forces to come ashore. Although their mop-top hairdos horrified many parents, the Beatles were not at this point in their career threatening or revolutionary—far less so, in fact, than Elvis had been a decade before. The Fab Four provided a seemingly safe haven for young white Americans traumatized by the loss of JFK. "She loves you, yeah, yeah, yeah" was difficult to label as a secret message of communist subversion. That their parents saw the Beatles as a threat added to kids' attraction to the group, without posing any serious danger.

Or did they? A decade earlier, Elvis had crossed both racial and sexual lines. He was not only a white man singing black music but a man who liked to wear pink, had his hair done in a beauty salon, and wore eye makeup. He was not only musically biracial but also androgynous. In 1964, the Beatles were the latter, but not the former. They looked and sounded almost female. As Elvis had, they represented a blurring of the line between the sexes. "The Beatles set the tone for feminism," historian Elaine Tyler May has contended. "And that meant that they recognized in their own way that men had to change too in order for that revolution to happen."[35]

Almost all the songs on the Beatles' first American album were written by John Lennon and Paul McCartney. They were decidedly *not* the highly sexual songs of American R&B. They were singing about love, not sex. Yet once these four young Brits in their matching suits had established a landing zone on American shores, the invasion route was cleared for much more subversive British proselytizers of what I've called "black freedom,"* far and away most notably the Rolling Stones. Apart from their long hair, there didn't seem to be anything androgynous about *them*. Much more about all that as our exploration of 1964 unfolds.

---

* Though for the most part I won't continue to place quotation marks around "black free-dom," readers should understand that it always refers to a misunderstanding on the part of whites of the realities of African American life and its "freedoms."

3

THE COLOSSUS OF THE LONG 1964

LYNDON BAINES JOHNSON

1908–NOVEMBER 1963

*FDR shakes hands with young LBJ, Gov. Allred of Texas
in between. Galveston, Texas, May 1937*

I've just met the most remarkable young man. . . .
This boy could well be the first Southern President.
                    —Franklin D. Roosevelt on
                    meeting LBJ (1937)[1]

I was *meant* to be President. I was *intended* to be
President. And I'm *going* to be President.
                    —Lyndon B. Johnson (1958)[2]

He's a son of a bitch, but he's got talent.
                    —John F. Kennedy, on
                    Lyndon B. Johnson[3]

T HE LONG 1964 WAS Lyndon Johnson's triumphant time. As Shakespeare had Cassius say of Caesar 2,008 years earlier,[4] Johnson bestrode the world—or at least the American political and governmental world—like a colossus. As the protagonist in some of our most important stories, he deserves proper introduction.

Lyndon Johnson was, as his longtime aide George Reedy put it, "a combination of complexities and simplicities that bewildered all observers."[5] "He's thoughtless and thoughtful, cruel and compassionate, simple and immensely complicated," said another Johnson insider early in his presidency. "I don't know anyone who doesn't feel ambivalently about him."[6]

"He was an All-American president," his vice president, Hubert Humphrey, said of LBJ. "He was really the history of this country, with all the turmoil, the bombast, the sentiments, the passions. It was all there, all in one man, and if you liked politics, it was like being at the feet of a giant."[7]

LBJ: His Father's Son . . . Or His Mother's Daughter?

How children dance to the unlived lives of their parents.
—Rainer Maria Rilke[8]

Lyndon Johnson's relationships with his mother and father seem to have shaped what he would become and what he did in 1964 and subsequently far more profoundly than is ordinarily the case. Six major traits of LBJ—all molded by his experiences growing up—played important roles in shaping the sixties that arrived in 1964: lying, masculine insecurity, the need to feel loved, insistence on the total subservience of those around him, fear and envy of intellectuals, and a genuine desire to help people.

◆ ◆ ◆

One of the most important things to know about Lyndon Johnson is that he was a liar. Johnson lied far, far above and beyond the political profession's normal code of misconduct, though Donald Trump took presidential lying to an even more astonishing level.

"But Lyndon just had to lie," his college classmate Horace Richards said of him. "It just seemed like he had to lie about everything."[9] A firm believer in the power of "story truth," Johnson made up stories that served his purpose. Addressing troops in Korea in 1966, the president told them that his great-great-grandfather had died at the Alamo. In a 1968 book, *Time* presidential correspondent Hugh Sidey pointed out that the story wasn't true and suggested that LBJ had made it up to identify himself with fallen heroes.[10] When Doris Kearns (now known by her married name, Doris Kearns Goodwin) brought up the story while interviewing Johnson after he left office, the former president indignantly insisted that he was being unjustly attacked for nothing more than "a slip of the tongue." "The fact is," Johnson told Kearns, "that my great-great-grandfather died at the Battle of San Jacinto, not the Alamo." But that story, too, was a lie. Johnson's ancestor had been at neither of those events in Texas history and mythology; he had been a real estate dealer who died in his own bed.[11]

Johnson's mother was one of the few people who knew him who did not recognize his extraordinary penchant for fabrication. "All children tell stories," Rebekah Baines Johnson insisted. "My boy never lies."[12]

At Southwest Texas State Teachers College, he was known as "Bull" Johnson. The "bull" was, of course, short for "bullshit."[13] Reporters covering President Johnson liked to say: "How do you know when Lyndon Johnson is telling the truth?" The answer: "When he pulls his ear lobe, scratches his chin, he's telling the truth. When he begins to move his lips, you know he's lying."[14] It was funny because it was, unlike so much that was heard when LBJ moved his lips, close to the truth.

♦ ♦ ♦

Being in control was "manly," and, like so many men throughout history who have sought great power, Lyndon Johnson was insecure about his masculinity.[15] Growing up on the Texas frontier, the future president was pulled in opposing directions by his mother and father. As a young boy, he was close to his mother, a woman who thought of herself as intellectual and cultured and felt stranded in a frontier cabin with a husband she "considered vulgar and brutish." Rebekah Johnson attempted to mold her son into someone who would fulfill the unachieved dreams she had had for herself.[16] She treated him more like a daughter. By trying to make him a person of learning and culture, she placed him in a realm that society—especially the society of frontier Texas—classified as feminine. She read him books, bought him a violin, put him in a dance class, tried to keep him from getting dirty, kept his hair in long, yellow curls, and dressed him in a Little Lord Fauntleroy outfit and other "girlish" clothes. Other boys laughed at little Lyndon. His father was not amused. He wanted a son. "He's a boy," Sam Ealy Johnson would say to his wife, "and you're making a sissy of him. You've got to cut those curls." When Sam cut them himself, his wife was so angry that she wouldn't speak to him for a week.[17]

Lyndon Johnson's early experiences with his mother fixed in his mind, as Kearns put it, "the equation of femininity, intellectualism and paralysis—and the corresponding compulsions to move, keep control, stay in charge."[18] Johnson was constantly torn between his desires for his mother's love and his father's respect. The two were, to a large extent, mutually exclusive.

As he grew older, Lyndon increasingly identified with his father and felt the need to meet the older man's tests of "manhood." He frequently went hunting squirrels and rabbits with other boys and sometimes pointed his rifle at the animals to know, he said, that he could kill if he had to. But he never wanted to kill any of them. When his father finally asked him why he was the only boy who never shot anything and suggested that he was a coward, Lyndon went out the next day and shot a rabbit. Afterward, he attested in telling the story, he threw up.[19]

For all his felt need to demonstrate his manhood, Johnson was said by those who knew him when he was growing up to have been "an absolute physical coward" and to have acted "like a girl" when threatened with a fight.[20] People who knew him have described Johnson's reaction to even minor pain as "hysterical."[21] The root of that word suggests the fear he battled throughout his life.

Into his early teens, Lyndon idolized his father, who served three terms in the Texas state legislature, and tried to act like him. He loved being in the state capitol and out on the campaign trail with his father. Then, in the early 1920s, Sam Johnson went broke and the family became a laughingstock.[22] His father's failures left Lyndon humiliated and feeling contempt for him, but the fact that his father had failed as a "man" did not release LBJ from trying to live up to the masculine model his male parent had set for him. Indeed, his father's failure seems to have left Lyndon wanting all the more to prove that he was a *real* man.

Soon after taking office, the new president instructed holdover press secretary Pierre Salinger to paint a verbal portrait of him "as a tall tough Texan in the saddle."[23] In truth, LBJ wasn't a very good rider, but he seems to have felt constrained to live in John Wayne's world. Wayne was taken by most Americans at the time as the ultimate example of a "real man," but in truth he was a reel man. He *acted* like a man, and Lyndon Johnson did the same.

His father had put him through manhood tests, and the adult Lyndon Johnson liked to do the same to other males. When John Kennedy sent his brother Robert to see LBJ at the ranch in 1959 to try to find out whether Johnson, then the Senate majority leader, was going to run for president in 1960, Johnson insisted that Bobby go deer hunting with him. LBJ lent him a shotgun. When Bobby fired it, the recoil knocked him to the ground and cut his face above the eye. "Son, you've got to learn to handle a gun like a man," Johnson chided from his asserted position of superior masculinity.[24] As president, LBJ made his vice-presidential choice, Hubert Humphrey, kill two deer. Humphrey's reaction after carrying out the deed was similar to what young Lyndon's had been after shooting the rabbit.[25]

The equation of *man* with "superior" and *woman* with "inferior" goes back to before the beginning of recorded history,[26] so there was nothing unusual in LBJ's employment of it, but the extent to which he used it strongly suggests the extreme level of his insecurity.

When one member of his administration started to "go soft" on Vietnam, Johnson's response was to reclassify him as a woman: "Hell, he's got to squat to piss."[27] And when he learned that Vice President Humphrey had doubts about the wisdom of the war, Johnson said Humphrey "wasn't a real man, he cried as easily as a woman."[28] When someone mentioned JFK's womanizing, LBJ responded in a loud voice, "Why I had more women by accident than he ever had by design!"[29] Johnson's lips were moving.

One of the things about which he routinely lied was the size of his penis. He loved to show off his sexual organ and brag about its size. Sam Houston Johnson remembered several incidents when he visited his older brother at college and Lyndon came out of the shower naked, holding his penis and saying, "Well, I've gotta take ol' Jumbo here and give him some exercise. I wonder who I'll fuck tonight."[30] But, according to some of the many people before whom he exposed himself, Johnson's "johnson" was not, in fact, very big. "Johnson doesn't have a particularly big one," said Don Schanche, a *Saturday Evening Post* editor who had been at one of the president's naked pool gatherings. "If anything, it was a little smaller than average."[31]

Arthur Goldberg, Johnson's ambassador to the United Nations, vividly remembered a conversation Johnson had with reporters who were questioning him about why the United States was in Vietnam. Johnson answered by unzipping his fly, pulling out "ol' Jumbo," and proclaiming: "*This* is why!"[32] That was not an isolated incident. Following a Cabinet meeting in 1967, the president went into a tirade about *his* war and who the hell was Ho Chi Minh to think "he could push America around?" With Interior Secretary Stewart Udall and some of Johnson's top aides looking on, the president of the United States then unzipped his pants, pulled out his penis, and asked rhetorically, "Has Ho Chi Minh got anything like that?"[33]

Lyndon Johnson no more wanted to go to war in Vietnam than he had wanted to kill a rabbit when he was a boy. Then, he had done what he didn't want to do in order to show his father—and himself—that he was not a coward or a sissy. Doing it, though, literally made him sick to his stomach.

Johnson's social programs, which he called "the woman I really loved,"[34] had to be sacrificed in order to avoid the condemnation of men, who would see him as a coward if he chose the maternalist state over manly war.

Tim O'Brien's story "On the Rainy River" provides not only a riveting account of the struggle so many young American males faced over whether to go to war in Vietnam, but also serves as a metaphor for the torment Lyndon Johnson experienced over getting deeply involved in Vietnam. "I feared ridicule and censure," O'Brien writes, of being called a "damned sissy" and a "treasonous pussy." "I was ashamed of my conscience, ashamed to be doing the right thing." These words O'Brien's self-named character says of himself fit Lyndon Johnson like a surgical glove, as does the story's conclusion: "It's not a happy ending. I was a coward. I went to war."[35]

◆ ◆ ◆

Like many politicians, Lyndon Johnson appears to have sought the love of masses of people to compensate for a lack of dependable love on a personal level. Here again his mother played the crucial role. Her love was never unconditional. When Lyndon failed to do what his mother wanted him to do or in some way did not meet her expectations for him, she withdrew her affection, sometimes not speaking to or even looking at her son for days or weeks.[36]

Johnson's political life can be seen as a quest to secure the "steady love he had lacked as a child."[37] In the 1964 presidential election, Johnson experienced that love of the masses from the huge, cheering crowds. He won the largest percentage of the nationwide vote any candidate has ever obtained. "Look at them, just look at them!" Johnson would say of the people at his campaign stops. In their faces he saw the love he had always sought. He later told Kearns that on Election Day 1964 he could "picture everybody going into the voting booth and pulling a lever or writing an 'X' for him, and I think it really meant, 'They love me!'" "Millions and millions of people, each marking *my* name on their ballot—each wanted *me* for their president," Johnson gushed. "For the first time in *all* my life, I truly felt loved by the American people."[38]

But it was not to last. The public's love, like that of his mother, was conditional. By his last year in office in 1968, Lyndon B. Johnson was among the most hated people in America. It was said that one of the most popular pieces of graffiti across the country by that time was: "Lee Harvey Oswald, where are you now that your country needs you?"[39]

◆ ◆ ◆

Closely related to Johnson's never-ending quest for love was his demand that people be subservient to him. He wanted to do things to help people, but he insisted in return that he receive their gratitude. He never wanted associates; he wanted subordinates. "I want people around me," Johnson often declared, "who would kiss my ass on a hot summer's day and say it smells like roses."[40]

Ass-kissing was a subject Lyndon Johnson had studied carefully. During his college years, he ingratiated himself to the college president, administrators, and faculty. The same would be true throughout his pre-presidential political career. He was utterly obsequious to anyone above him who might be in a position to help him, but the moment he rose above that person, he would demand to receive the submissiveness he had previously given.

A story told by a man in his Secret Service detail illustrates what having power meant to Lyndon Johnson. The president stopped during one of his high-speed drives across open country in Texas to relieve himself. The Secret Service man standing close to him felt warm liquid running down his leg. "Mr. President, you're urinating on me," he said. "I know I am," Johnson responded. "It's my prerogative."[41]

LBJ famously said that the American war in Vietnam was about winning the "hearts and minds" of the people there. Dropping millions of tons of bombs, napalm, and defoliants on people from long range is about as likely to win their hearts as is pissing on them from close range.

Finally, always insecure about his rural background and the fact that he wasn't educated at a top university, Johnson had an enormous desire to be accepted by those who wouldn't accept him. Many of the "Harvards," as LBJ called the intellectuals around John Kennedy, had contempt for him. At Georgetown cocktail parties, Kennedy insiders laughed about the uninvited vice president and referred to him by such names as "Rufus Cornpone" and "freckle-belly."[42] Intellectuals hated him, Johnson believed, and the hatred of those who would interpret history would keep him from being recognized as the greatest president in history.[43] When he had the ultimate power, he could return the disfavor by being crude in their presence and forcing them to accept it.

◆ ◆ ◆

Yet, for all the negatives about Lyndon Johnson that are so readily enumerated, there can be no serious question that he wanted to help people. He had grown up surrounded by poverty and was sometimes impoverished himself. While in college, he dropped out for a year and taught in a poor Mexican American school district in south Texas. He knew abject poverty firsthand. While Johnson's quest for power was always tightly intertwined with his need for love and recognition, there was also a genuine desire to use that power for the good of disadvantaged people. He was a firm believer that government can be an instrument for good.

Johnson had had to hide his arch-progressive beliefs while in Congress in order to rise to the top of the government he wanted to utilize to help the people. Let us take a quick look at his rise to the point at which he was in line to reach the presidency.

"The Most Remarkable Young Man"

Lyndon Johnson was a young man in a hurry. He arrived in Washington as an administrative assistant to a new Texas congressman, Richard Kleberg, in 1931. His first day in the Capitol, December 7, 1931, was the day that Texans—John Nance Garner, Sam Rayburn, and others— took control of the House of Representatives.[44] Johnson has been aptly described by biographer Robert Caro as a "professional son."[45] "Mr. Sam" had no son, and LBJ skillfully maneuvered himself to fill that vacuum. His efforts paid handsome dividends, as Rayburn helped him to meet all the right people.

Johnson was able, following Franklin Roosevelt's victory in 1932, quickly to impress several New Deal insiders. Rayburn persuaded Texas senator Tom Connally to ask President Roosevelt to get Johnson, at the tender age of twenty-six, appointed as director of the National Youth Administration in Texas.[46] Johnson rapidly built a political network and secured loyal followers for the future statewide candidacy he was already planning.

When a death opened a seat in 1937, he left his NYA post to run for Congress. He was a long shot. One leading Texas politician expressed those odds by saying, "Who the hell is Lyndon Johnson?"[47] Tying himself tightly to President Roosevelt, Johnson ran ferociously. It was a forty-day campaign, and he covered the Tenth Congressional District relentlessly until entering a hospital to have his appendix removed two days before the election. He won in the multi-candidate field with 28 percent of the votes.[48]

After his election, even before he went back to Washington, young Lyndon got an opportunity to spend an entire day with his hero, President Roosevelt, in Texas.[49] "I've just met the most remarkable young man," Roosevelt told his aide Tommy Corcoran. "In the next generation," the president went on, "the balance of power would shift to the south and west and this boy could well be the first southern president."[50]

LBJ sought to take another big leap upward in a 1941 special election for a seat in the United States Senate but narrowly lost to sitting governor W. Lee "Pappy" O'Daniel after Johnson had initially appeared to have won. Convinced, probably correctly, that the election had been stolen from him, Johnson vowed to make sure it didn't happen again. In his second Senate race, in 1948, he wound up winning by eighty-seven votes in what is almost universally considered to have been another stolen election, but this time LBJ was the beneficiary. The sarcastic nickname that stuck to him after that eighty-seven-vote win, "Landslide Lyndon," pained him. By achieving a genuine landslide victory nationwide in 1964, he was able to ease the pain by removing the sarcasm.

Johnson was in his element in the United States Senate. As he had with Sam Rayburn in the House, he identified the man who could help him most in the Senate, Richard Russell of Georgia, and made himself into the powerful lifelong bachelor's substitute son. In a chamber in which seniority had been the rule, Johnson rose with astonishing speed and was his party's leader only four years after his election. Two years later, when the Democrats won back control of the body, Lyndon Johnson became the youngest majority leader in the Senate's history— and he transformed that position into one of far greater power than it had ever had before.

In his quest for power—which is to say in his quest for the presidency, which was always his ultimate objective—Lyndon Johnson showed himself to be enormously adaptable. He was able to transform himself into whatever his current environment required and was a relentless self-promoter.

LBJ was always a populist in the nineteenth-century, left-wing tradition, but when he reached the Senate, he put his views into a storage locker to which he could return when the time was right. Meanwhile, he posed as much more conservative than he was, supporting publicly, for example, the oil and gas interests that he privately opposed. But the move to the right had to be limited in order for Johnson to maintain his hopes of becoming a successful national candidate.

In 1956, when segregationists in Congress circulated a "Southern Manifesto" pledging resistance to the *Brown* school desegregation decision, Johnson joined with Tennessee's Estes Kefauver and Albert Gore (Sr.) as the only three senators from southern states who declined to sign. Johnson was maneuvering to establish viability as a national candidate—as, to be sure, were Kefauver and Gore.

During his years in Congress, Johnson and his wife accumulated a substantial amount of personal wealth. This was accomplished through a variety of means that we need not get into here, other than to say that it had not been by directing his feet to the sunny side of the street.

Maintaining support at home and being seen as acceptable nationwide was a difficult balancing act for a politician from a southern state during the civil rights era. Lyndon Johnson did it better than anyone else in the region, and he fixed his eyes firmly on the 1960 Democratic presidential nomination.

But as the appointed year for him to reach for the golden ring that had for so long been his objective drew close, Johnson vacillated. He was torn apart by an internal conflict between his desire for ultimate power, success, and love and his fear of failure. He kept moving to the edge of declaring his candidacy and then stepping back. He greatly underestimated how formidable John Kennedy would be as a rival for the nomination. Johnson saw Kennedy as "weak and pallid," "a scrawny man with a bad back, a weak and indecisive politician, a nice man, a gentle man, but not a man's man."[51] Even the apparent compliments in this description—*nice* and *gentle*—were seen by LBJ as feminine attributes, and attaching them to Kennedy was meant to reinforce the basic point of his inferiority: "not a man's man," with the unspoken but unmistakable implication, *like I am*. When Johnson did enter the race, it was all but over, after the primaries and with scarcely two months left before the Democratic National Convention.[52]

"If You Do This, You're Going to Fuck Everything Up": The Making of the Vice President, 1960

> My God, this wouldn't have happened except that
> we were all too tired last night.
> —Robert F. Kennedy
> (July 14, 1960)[53]

Because of what would happen in Dallas a little more than three years later, Kennedy's choice of a running mate, made in a hectic several hours on the day after he won the presidential nomination, turned out to be one of the most consequential decisions of the 1960 election. It determined who the president would be in 1964 and through the critical middle years of the decade, and, because absent Johnson's Vietnam policy, it is unlikely Richard Nixon could have been elected in 1968, it also greatly influenced who the president would be into the next decade.

The behind-the-scenes calculations and infighting that went on in the Biltmore Hotel in Los Angeles during that fateful Thursday have been recounted multiple times in various versions. Most notable was that Bobby Kennedy angrily opposed the choice of Johnson and did everything he could to sabotage it.[54] The already bad relationship between the younger Kennedy and Johnson reached a point of bitter hostility on this day (among the choice terms Johnson used to describe Bobby late that afternoon was "that little shitass"[55]) from which it would never recover, a circumstance that had large consequences in 1964 and beyond.[56]

There are two major questions about Johnson becoming Kennedy's running mate: Why did JFK choose LBJ? Why did LBJ accept? The answers to both are to be found in statistics: the first those of the Electoral College, and the second those of presidential mortality.

The straightforward answer to the first of those questions is that John F. Kennedy looked at the electoral map and concluded that it was unlikely he could win the election without Texas and a few other southern states that might be up for grabs.

During the back-and-forth over the second spot on the ticket, Johnson phoned John Nance Garner, who had been vice president in Franklin Roosevelt's first two terms. "The Vice-Presidency," Garner informed his fellow Texan, as he frequently did anyone who would listen, "isn't worth a pitcher of warm piss."[57]

So why would Johnson trade his place as the most powerful leader in the history of the Senate for a container of tepid urine? His explanation to Republican diplomat Clare Boothe Luce on the evening of the inauguration in 1961 says it all: "Clare, I looked it up: one out of every four Presidents has died in office. I'm a gamblin' man, darlin', and this is the only chance I got."[58]

For three years Johnson's experience in the office would largely confirm what "Cactus Jack" Garner had told him on that 1960 afternoon, but 1,228 days later, the vice presidency would prove to be worth a great deal more to Lyndon B. Johnson, as the contents of the pitcher he held were transformed from urine to fine wine—or his beloved Cutty Sark scotch.

"If you do this, you're going to fuck everything up," labor leader Jack Conway told Bobby Kennedy the morning of July 14, speaking of choosing Johnson as Jack Kennedy's running mate.[59] Conway and other opponents of Johnson were fearful of losing liberal support, but Kennedy probably would not have won the election without Johnson on the ticket. A different decision that day would have led to Johnson not being president in 1964 and the mid-sixties, and likely to Nixon not being president in the later sixties, though it might instead have led to Nixon holding the office in the early 1960s. It may have been the most fateful July 14 since 1789.

Gelded:
An Alpha Male in the Beta Position

Being vice president is like being a cut dog.
            —Lyndon Baines Johnson[60]

Lyndon Johnson was not someone to suffer gladly being a fool to someone else's king. Believing himself far superior to Jack Kennedy, Johnson set out after the election to carve for himself a position of power unprecedented in the history of the office he was about to assume. He sought, in essence, to continue to be the Democratic leader in the Senate by asking that he be named head of the Democratic Caucus. This would, he asserted, put him in a better position to get Kennedy's programs enacted. "All those Bostons and Harvards don't know any more about Capitol Hill than an old maid does about fucking," Johnson said to his aide Bobby Baker.[61] But the men who had followed his lead when he was a senator refused to have someone from the executive branch take power in their chamber.

The incoming vice president's other proposal was that he be given an office in the White House next to the Oval Office, a staff, "general supervision" over "a wide range of issues," and that "all the departments and agencies" that dealt with national security report to him. The only precedent for such an attempted power grab in the history of the American presidency was a letter Abraham Lincoln's choice for secretary of state, William H. Seward, sent to the new president shortly after his inauguration in 1861 asking that Lincoln give him extraordinary powers that would in effect make Seward the equivalent of a prime minister and reduce Lincoln to a figurehead. As Johnson did with Kennedy, Seward considered himself to be a clearly superior man to his president. Lincoln simply ignored Seward's proposal that he surrender his power to one of his subordinates, and Kennedy did the same. But ignoring is not the same as forgetting, and it is likely that Johnson's attempt to take power led Kennedy to exclude his vice president even more than he might otherwise have done.[62]

Having failed in his bold attempt to make the nothing office into a seat of power, Johnson settled into being a "yes man," someone who would defer to Kennedy in public but also most of the time in private. He sank into depression, drank more and more Scotch, and felt sorry for himself. "The Vice-Presidency is filled with trips around the world, chauffeurs, men saluting, people clapping, chairmanships of councils, but in the end, it is nothing," Johnson later remarked. "I detested every minute of it."[63]

He was in internal exile; he had nothing to do. Reporters described Johnson during his vice-presidential years with such words as *lonely* and *pathetic*. "This," Daniel Patrick Moynihan said of Vice President Johnson, "is a bull castrated very late in life." It was an image that could not but torment someone suffering from insecure masculinity as Lyndon

Johnson so obviously was, and he used it himself when he said that "being vice president is like being a cut [castrated] dog."[64]

As it turned out, though, that wasn't the right image. What happened to LBJ during his tenure—*sentence* might be a more appropriate word—as vice president proved to be more like a vasectomy: reversible.

4

DECLARING WAR ON RACISM AND POVERTY

LYNDON JOHNSON MOVES TO SPREAD "WHITE FREEDOM"

NOVEMBER 1963–JANUARY 1964

Lyndon B. Johnson delivering the State of the Union Address, January 1964.

He was coming back *to himself.* He was back where he belonged. He was back in command.
> —Horace Busby referring to LBJ on the night of November 22, 1963[1]

LYNDON JOHNSON TOOK CHARGE immediately when Kennedy aide Ken O'Donnell came to him with a two-word message: "He's gone."[2] What Johnson did in the first hours after he assumed the office was impressive by almost all measures, although his insistence that he be sworn in before leaving Dallas and that Attorney General Robert Kennedy must be called to find out the proper procedure was an unnecessarily cruel thing to do to the brother of the just-murdered president.[3]

"I knew that it was imperative that I grasp the reins of power and do so without delay," Johnson wrote in his memoir. "Any hesitation or wavering, any false step, any sign of self-doubt, could have been disastrous. The nation was in a state of shock and grief. The times cried out for leadership."[4] And leadership was what Lyndon Johnson gave the country in this highly uncertain time. Already on the night of the assassination when the new president returned to Washington, those around him saw a different man from the one they had been seeing for nearly three years.

As self-assured as Lyndon Johnson appeared in his first days as president, however, he remained a man tormented by insecurities. "I had to prove myself," he wrote of that period.[5] "I'm not sure whether I can lead this country and keep it together, with my background," Johnson said in a low voice, apparently speaking to himself, as journalist Hugh Sidey was leaving the Oval Office during the first days of Johnson's presidency.[6]

He often said that meetings with his advisers consisted of "Rhodes Scholars, men from Harvard, Phi Beta Kappas, and then there was one from Southwest Texas State Teachers College."[7] Johnson didn't trust most of them—in many cases for good reason. "Without them," Johnson later said, "I would have lost my link to John Kennedy, and without that I would have had no chance of gaining the support of the media or the Eastern intellectuals. And without that support I would have had absolutely no chance of governing the country."[8]

Central to all these worries was his nemesis, Robert F. Kennedy. An announcement from Bobby that he would run for president himself in 1964, Johnson later said, was "the thing I feared from the first day of my presidency." The despised younger brother announcing "his intention to reclaim the throne in memory of his brother"—*that* was Lyndon Johnson's great fear.[9]

◆ ◆ ◆

Having finally reached the presidency, Lyndon Johnson immediately reverted to his populist-liberal-New Deal past—to what he really believed. Already on the night of the assassination, he said to three aides who were in his bedroom, "By God, I'm going to pass Harry Truman's medical insurance bill."[10] On his first full day as president, Johnson told Walter Heller, chairman of the Council of Economic Advisers, to reassure his liberal friends. "If you look at my record, you would know that I'm a Roosevelt New Dealer," Johnson declared. "As a matter of fact, John F. Kennedy was a little too conservative for my taste." There was a lot more truth in that statement than there usually was when LBJ's lips moved.

Kennedy's death had made him a national hero. He was now a martyr, but a martyr for what? JFK's "'cause' was not really clear," Johnson later said. "That was my job. I had to take the dead man's program and turn it into a martyr's cause."[11] In reality, what Johnson was doing was dressing his own program in "the dead man's" clothes and selling it as what Kennedy had died for. It was brilliant marketing, but this strategy meant that the public would come to see much of what Johnson was able to accomplish as Kennedy's plan rather than his.

This circumstance caused Johnson much pain. Speaking after he left office of a day during his presidency when he had visited a poor family in Appalachia, Johnson recalled: "They had seven children, all skinny and sick. I promised the mother and father I would make things better for them. I told them all my hopes for their future." So far, so good. "They seemed real happy to talk with me and I felt good about that," Johnson continued. "But then as I walked toward the door, I noticed two pictures on the shabby wall. One was Jesus Christ on the cross; the other was John Kennedy. I felt as if I'd been slapped in the face."[12]

The Wake as Honeymoon

We have to do something to stop that hate, and the
way we have to do it is to meet the problem of injustice
that exists in this land, meet the problem of inequality
that exists in this land, meet the problem of poverty
that exists in this land. . . . Let's not just talk about it.
Let's get some action on it and *do something.*
                                        —Lyndon B. Johnson,
                                        Nov. 25, 1963

Honeymoons normally follow weddings, not funerals, but there was in
1964 a sort of honeymoon period for the American people following
the assassination of President Kennedy: a time in which a majority of
the nation's citizens wanted to "do good." It was, as historian Robert
Dallek has said, "as if the country wished to purge itself of feelings
that it was a sick society that fostered violence instead of healing and
education and uplift."[13]

   And Lyndon Johnson was just the man to preside over this national
honeymoon. He could give shape to the amorphous "do good" feelings of the nation, and he knew how to get Congress to move on
enacting them into law. "One must marvel at Johnson's total grasp of
the machinery of government" in these early weeks, for which there
was "no script," Hugh Sidey of *Time* later wrote, assessing his assumption of power as "flawless."[14]

   On the evening of the day that John Kennedy was interred in
Arlington National Cemetery, November 25, 1963, the new president
spoke extemporaneously to a hastily gathered group of about thirty of
the nation's governors who had come to Washington for the funeral.
Television was not Lyndon Johnson's friend, but he could be impressive when he spoke in person and off the cuff, as he did on this, only
his fourth night in office. It was obvious that he was speaking from the
heart, and what he said was, as one of the governors, California's Pat
Brown, put it, "astounding."[15]

   "Here is our president shot in the head and his wife holds his skull
in her lap as they drive down the street," Johnson said. "We have to do
something to stop that hate, and the way we have to do it is to meet

the problem of injustice that exists in this land, meet the problem of inequality that exists in this land, meet the problem of poverty that exists in this land, and the problem of unemployment that exists in this land."

He called for the passage of the civil rights bill "so that we can say to the Mexican in California or the Negro in Mississippi or the Oriental on the West Coast or the Johnsons in Johnson City that we are going to treat you all equally and fairly, and you are going to be judged on merit and not ancestry, not on how you spell your name."

Here was the real Lyndon Johnson. He had always had genuine compassion for the poor and downtrodden, but he had suppressed it whenever he calculated that it endangered his ambition to become president. Now he had reached his personal goal and was free at last to pursue his societal goals. When he included "the Johnsons of Johnson City," he was indicating that he saw himself as one of "them"—"one of the poor, one of the scorned, one of the dispossessed of the earth."[16] It was genuine populism, not the excluding, white nationalist hate that had often been used in the past by those in power to divide those below them and that has reared its ugly head again so menacingly in our own time. Johnson's brand of populism was not faux populism but the urge to reform coming from personal experience. He didn't *sympathize* with the oppressed; he *identified* with them. LBJ's motivation for helping the poor and discriminated against was not the noblesse oblige of the Kennedys or Roosevelts but rather the obligation that comes from having been in poverty.

The extemporaneous speech was truly remarkable. "Let's not just talk about it," the new president proclaimed. "Let's get some action on it and *do something*." He concluded by pledging to the assembled governors, "I am going to be at it from daylight to midnight, and with your help and God's help we are going to make ourselves proud that we are Americans, but we are [also] going to make the rest of the world proud that there is an America in it."[17]

Lyndon Johnson sought nothing less than "a vast, revolutionary, transformation of America,"[18] one that would outdo the accomplishments of Franklin Roosevelt and the New Deal, one that would eliminate poverty and injustice and bring the United States at last into line with the ideals stated at the beginning of the Declaration of Independence.

This was, as Johnson biographer Robert Caro has written, "a pivotal moment in the history of the United States,"[19] and Lyndon Johnson was directing the rotation in a masterful way. Here was the Lyndon Johnson who seemed destined to be rated among the greatest of American presidents.

"What the Hell's the Presidency For?"

The assassination of John F. Kennedy gave Lyndon B. Johnson what he had always wanted. He moved deftly and feverishly—"Lyndon acts as if there is never going to be a tomorrow," his wife said of him[20]— to secure his position and to begin staking his claim to the place he sought for himself: "the greatest presidential reformer in the country's history."[21]

The new president's first objective had to be to reassure the American people in a time of immense shock. To that end, he would, just five days after the assassination, deliver an address to a joint session of Congress that would stand as his introduction to millions of Americans who would be watching on television. Johnson used the speech to embrace his fallen predecessor but simultaneously to utilize JFK's martyrdom to set the stage for bold new proposals of his own. On the afternoon before his November 27 address, he met with a group of advisers who cautioned him not to push for the civil rights bill, which they said was a lost cause in the Senate and would antagonize southern senators whose support he would need on other issues. "The presidency," argued one of the "wise men" sitting around the table, "has only a certain amount of coinage to expend, and you oughtn't expend it on this." Johnson's response was direct and powerful:

"Well, what the hell's the presidency for?"[22]

Johnson began the speech with what was obviously a lie, but one that can be forgiven, since it was the sort of lie that was required under the circumstances: "All I have I would have given gladly not to be standing here today." But then he got into what he would do with the position in which he now found himself.

"Now the ideas and the ideals which he [Kennedy] so nobly represented must and will be translated into effective action," Johnson pledged to the nation on the eve of Thanksgiving. Turning the "let us begin" line of Kennedy's inaugural address into "let us continue," the new president identified his own program with that of his predecessor and called for the enactment of those proposals as a "memorial" to Kennedy. First and foremost, Johnson made clear, was civil rights. "We have talked long enough in this country about equal rights. We have talked for one hundred years or more. It is time now to write the next chapter, and to write it in the books of law."[23]

That chapter was one among many Lyndon Johnson would author during the coming year-plus in his quest to right wrongs, to fulfill the promise of America and, more than incidentally, to put himself on course to achieve his goal of becoming the greatest president in American history.

"Don't Stand in the Doorway, Don't Block Up the Hall": LBJ Launches a Revolution

Following his address to Congress on Thanksgiving Eve, Johnson set about laying the groundwork for his plan to transform America. When it came to civil rights legislation, as to all the social and economic initiatives he had in mind, his greatest obstacle would be southerners in Congress, particularly in the Senate. These politicians had been his friends and colleagues when he was in that body, but now his message to them would be essentially that contained in the Bob Dylan song that would debut just six days after Johnson's January 8, 1964, State of the Union address in which he would declare "unconditional war on poverty":

> *Come senators, congressmen*
> *Please heed the call*
> *Don't stand in the doorway*
> *Don't block up the hall*
> *For he that gets hurt*
> *Will be he who has stalled*[24]

One of the ways in which the southerners had most effectively blocked civil rights and other progressive legislation over the years was by refusing to pass other essential bills until the legislation they opposed was either withdrawn or had run out of time to be enacted. When Johnson took office, Kennedy's tax cut bill was bottled up in the Senate Finance Committee. Senator Russell Long summed up the committee's chairman, Virginia's Harry F. Byrd, in a way that suggests Mitch McConnell's leadership of the forces of reaction today by saying he "measured his success as a senator not by what he passed, but what he stopped from passing."[25]

Kennedy would never have been able to outmaneuver Byrd and the southern defensive line, but it was a different ballgame with Lyndon Johnson drawing the Xs and Os for the offense's game plan. The leader of the southern senators, Georgia's Richard Russell, fully understood what a game changer LBJ's ascension was. In a conversation with Agriculture Secretary Orville Freeman a few days after the assassination, Russell called Johnson "the most amazingly resourceful fellow," a "man who really understood power and how to use it. . . . That man will twist your arm off at the shoulder and beat your head with it," Russell said. "We could have beaten Kennedy on civil rights, but we can't [beat] Lyndon."[26]

A similar assessment of the change came from those Russell and his colleagues sought to keep in subjugation. During the second week of his presidency, Johnson met with the top civil rights leaders. "LBJ is a man of great ego and great power," Martin Luther King Jr., told two aides after his meeting with the new president. "He is a pragmatist and a man of pragmatic compassion. It may just be that he is going to go where John Kennedy couldn't."[27]

Johnson had to end Harry Byrd's blockage of the tax cut bill before he could get to the civil rights bill. Knowing that Byrd despised deficits, the president extracted from him an agreement that he would support the tax cut if Johnson could bring in his budget at under $100 billion. With the agreement secured, Johnson could go home to Texas for the holidays and see in the New Year of 1964 with the knowledge that he was truly in command.

While in Texas, Johnson set about developing his boldest goal of all: the transformation of America into a truly compassionate society through an all-out attack on poverty and its root causes. There had been some talk in the Kennedy administration of tackling intractable poverty, but nine days before the assassination, Census Bureau director Richard Scammon, whom Kennedy had charged with analyzing demographics for the 1964 election, had flatly told Kennedy, "You can't get a single vote more by doing anything for poor people. . . . Those who vote are already for you."[28] Kennedy indicated that he still wanted to do something, but there was no sense of urgency.

That changed overnight—literally—and the night was November 22, 1963. When Walter Heller mentioned a possible initiative on poverty to Lyndon Johnson on November 23, the new president immediately responded with great enthusiasm. "That's my kind of program," Johnson declared. "I'll find money for it one way or another. If I have to, I'll take money away from things to get money for people."[29]

He quickly decided that a bold new anti-poverty program would be the hallmark of his administration and that he would call for that program in his State of the Union address. The speech was crafted in Texas over the holidays by Johnson working with JFK's close associate and speechwriter Ted Sorensen and others. Johnson was especially enthusiastic about the idea of declaring *war* on poverty. The very terminology—*war* on poverty—suggests a desire to find a way out of his lifelong dilemma of pleasing both his parents—to do what would win his mother's approval in a way that would not make him seem a "sissy." Going to war against social injustice was a way for Lyndon Johnson to pursue ends that were likely to be seen as "feminine" through "masculine" means.

On January 8, President Johnson got the new year off to a remarkable and rousing start with his first State of the Union Address. After only four introductory sentences, he unveiled his bold proposals:

> Let this session of Congress be known as the session which did more for civil rights than the last hundred sessions combined; as the session which enacted the most far-reaching tax cut of our time; as the session which declared all-out war on human poverty and unemployment in these United States; as the session which finally recognized the health needs of all our older citizens.

A bit later, Johnson spoke the words that made the speech famous and those by which it would be remembered: "This administration today, here and now, declares unconditional war on poverty in America." "Our aim," he proclaimed, "is not only to relieve the symptom of poverty, but to cure it and, above all, to prevent it."

And Johnson left no room for doubt on his commitment to civil rights. "Let me make one principle of this administration abundantly clear," he said. "All of these increased opportunities—in employment, in education, in housing, and in every field—must be open to Americans of every color. As far as the writ of Federal law will run, we must abolish not some, but all racial discrimination. For this is not merely an economic issue, or a social, political, or international issue. It is a moral issue."[30]

"A moral issue," indeed. One Democrat called the speech "the Sermon on the Mount" and asked rhetorically how anyone could attack it.[31] Attack it some would, of course, but with his declaration of unconditional war on poverty, Lyndon Johnson had truly launched his presidency—and 1964.

But it was at the outset of that triumphant season that the new president made a decision that would eventually turn the honeymoon into another funeral—a couple of million funerals, in fact—including those of Johnson's reputation as a masterful leader for good and forever deferring the dream he mentioned in his January speech of creating a "Great Society." It would cause him to lose the love and support of the American people, for whom he believed he had done so much. "How is it possible that all these people could be so ungrateful to me after I had given them so much?" Johnson asked after he had left office. "Take the Negroes. I fought for them from the first day I came into office. I spilled my guts out in getting the Civil Rights Act of 1964 through Congress," he accurately said. "I tried to make it possible for every child of every color to grow up in a nice house, to eat a solid breakfast, to attend a decent school, and to get a good and lasting job." That sentence summarized what Lyndon Johnson had always sought to achieve. "I asked so little in return. Just a little thanks. Just a little appreciation. That's all. But look what I got instead. Riots in 175 cities. Looting. Burning. Shooting. It ruined everything."

"Then take the students," the former president went on. "I wanted to help them, too. I fought on their behalf for scholarships and loans and grants. I fought for better teachers and better schools. And look at what I got back. Young people by the thousands leaving their universities, marching in the streets. Chanting that horrible song about how many kids I had killed that day. And the poor, they, too, turned against me. When Congress cut the funds for the Great Society, they made me Mr. Villain."[32]

Surely the urban riots had a part, but there was another "it" that played the central role in ruining his Great Society. *It* was that other decision that he made at the outset of his presidency.

On Sunday, November 24, shortly after he learned of the killing of Oswald, Johnson met with Kennedy's national security team and the ambassador to South Vietnam, Henry Cabot Lodge. Lodge had returned to Washington for discussions following an early November coup overthrowing South Vietnamese President Ngo Dinh Diem, which President Kennedy had agreed to when it became clear that Diem would never be capable of gaining sufficient support to be an effective alternative to the communists. Late in that meeting, only about forty-eight hours into his presidency, Lyndon Johnson uttered the words that would eventually alter his trajectory from becoming "the greatest presidential reformer in the country's history" to the dustbin of history:

"I am not going to lose Vietnam."[33]

How important was Vietnam to be to Johnson's place in American history? The answer can be stated in the form of an equation:

$$LBJ - Vietnam = Mount\ Rushmore + LBJ$$

5

THE END OF THE OLD FRONTIER

DR. STRANGELOVE, OR:
HOW WE LEARNED TO START
LAUGHING AND HATE THE BOMB

JANUARY 1964

Peter Sellers as Dr. Strangelove.

Gentlemen! You can't fight in here;
this is the War Room!
—President Merkin Muffley
in *Dr. Strangelove* (1964)[1]

THE WEEKS BETWEEN THE horror of November 22 and the start of the new year seemed largely a time in which the nation had been put on "hold," pausing to reflect on what had happened. When the new year dawned on Wednesday, January 1, there was little to suggest that 1964 would be particularly different from 1963.

On the cultural front, "Dominique," sung in French by a Belgian Dominican nun, had been the number one song in America for the last four weeks of 1963. This soothing song with words that most American listeners could not understand seemed to meet people's needs. In the first week of the new year, the Singing Nun was knocked out of the top spot by Bobby Vinton's "There! I've Said It Again," which remained number one for the next four weeks until it was displaced by "I Want to Hold Your Hand." The Vinton song was a simple love song (what was being "said again" were variants of "I love you"). How different was that from the Beatles' desire to hold a girl's hand?

There was, though, at least one indicator in popular music of changing times during these weeks. Right behind "Dominique" on the charts was another song with words that were unintelligible to most listeners, but this one was ostensibly in English. "Louie, Louie," by the Kingsmen, had made its chart debut the same week in early November that "Dominique" did. The phenomenon of "Louie, Louie"—and its rise on the charts—was fueled almost entirely by the rumor that it contained "dirty" (i.e., sexual) lyrics that could be heard only by playing the record at a slower speed. The claim was false, but kids loved it and parents were horrified (which was, of course, the principal reason why kids loved it). Amazingly, the FBI investigated whether the song violated laws against the interstate transportation of obscene material. The FBI document on the investigation says it was launched because of complaints that the record contained "off-color lyrics which could be detected when the 45 RPM platter was played at 33⅓ RPM." The Federal Communications Commission, the Post Office, and the Justice Department all started investigations after several people, including Indiana Governor Matthew E. Welsh, made complaints. A February 1964 letter that was referred to the FBI's Criminal Division contained an enclosure stating that the song included these lyrics:

A fine little girl awaiting for me
She's just a girl across the way
Well I'll take her and park all alone
She's never the girl I lay at home . . .
At night at ten I lay her again
Fuck you girl, Oh, all the way
Oh, my bed and I lay her there
I meet a rose in her hair.

As they say, you can't make this stuff up—but the people construct-ing the complaints (or those trying to promote the record to kids) obviously *could* make up stuff. A three-month FBI investigation, from February to May of 1964, was undertaken. It found no obscenity. The official summary says: "All three agencies dropped their investi-gations because they were unable to determine what the lyrics of the song were, even after listening to the records at speeds ranging from 16 RPM to 78 RPM."[2]

Apart from the titillating false stories about what "Louie, Louie" had hidden within its noise, not much that was exciting was going on in popular culture when 1964 began. There was nothing remotely daring on television, where *The Beverly Hillbillies*, *Bonanza*, *The Dick Van Dyke Show*, *Petticoat Junction* (which may sound risqué but wasn't in the slightest), and *The Andy Griffith Show* garnered the top ratings.[3]

The top box-office movie when 1964 began was Walt Disney's *The Sword in the Stone*, an animated feature adaptation of the King Arthur legend, which had been released a week earlier, on Christmas Day. Perhaps benefiting to some extent from the identification Jacqueline Kennedy had made after her husband's death of his presidency with Camelot, the Disney movie would hold the top spot throughout 1964's first month.

In both music and film, though, a change was "gonna come" before 1964's first month was over. The meaningful coincidence of Dylan's "The Times They are a-Changin'" with Lyndon Johnson's War on Poverty speech discussed in the first chapter was just one such indicator.

Preserving Our "Precious Bodily Fluids":
Erectile Dysfunction & Earth Destruction

> I first became aware of it, Mandrake, during
> the physical act of love. . . . Loss of essence. . . .
> Women, er, women sense my power, and they
> seek the life essence. I do not avoid women,
> Mandrake . . . but I do deny them my essence.
> —Brig. Gen. Jack D. Ripper,
> *Dr. Strangelove* (1964)[4]

Among the things put on hold in the weeks following President Kennedy's assassination was the release of Stanley Kubrick's *Dr. Strangelove, or: How I Learned to Stop Worrying and Love the Bomb*. It had been filmed at the Shepperton Studios in England and was slated to hit theaters in the United States on December 12, 1963, with a first test screening scheduled for the evening of November 22. It turned out that viewers were otherwise occupied that evening. The release of the movie was delayed for seven weeks in the immediate wake of President Kennedy's death.

When it was released on January 29, 1964, the film was greeted with attacks from established critics caught up in the Cold War mentality. In a *New York Times* review, Bosley Crowther classified the movie as a "sick joke" and "dangerous." He said he was "troubled by the feeling, which runs all through the film, of discredit and even contempt for our whole defense establishment, up to and even including the hypothetical Commander in Chief."[5] "No Communist could dream of a more effective anti-American film to spread abroad than this," a *Washington Post* political writer warned. He called on top government officials to "take a look at this one to see its effects on the national interest."[6] *New Yorker* critic Dwight Macdonald said he was amazed that Columbia Pictures had allowed it to be made and predicted that theaters showing it would have picket lines protesting it.[7]

Instead, *Dr. Strangelove* was an immediate and huge hit, taking the top box-office rating for three weeks, another clear sign that, as Dylan's Columbia Records release sixteen days before had said, the times were a-changin'. Challenges to Cold War orthodoxy had suddenly become acceptable to significant numbers of Americans. *Dr. Strangelove* took the top movie position from Disney at precisely the same time that the Beatles took the top record position from Bobby Vinton. "Strangelovemania" gripped Americans simultaneously with Beatlemania.

Unlike the Beatles' music, there was nothing that could be properly classified as "feel good" about the film. It was a satirical comedy, but its subject was the destruction of the earth by nuclear weapons. Beyond what is often called "black comedy," *Dr. Strangelove* is, in the words of Kubrick, "a nightmare comedy." Perhaps the best way to describe the film is to say that it is insanely serious. While its main point is usually taken to be Kubrick's concern (particularly evident in his 1968 movie *2001: A Space Odyssey*[8]) that humans have turned over control of our destiny to machines and technology, the film's other major theme—that war is often about insecure men trying to affirm their masculinity—is of considerably more importance.

To see how that theme in the movie directly connects with the times, we need to take a brief look at the Cuban Missile Crisis, fifteen months before *Dr. Strangelove* premiered.

November 22, 1963, Minus 13 Months: The Cuban Missile Crisis

> If we have to start over again with another Adam
> and Eve, then I want them to be Americans and
> not Russians, and I want them on this continent
> and not in Europe.
> —Sen. Richard Russell (1968)[9]

In its early stages, the Cuban Missile Crisis was in part the sort of situation satirized by Kubrick in *Dr. Strangelove*: a means of comparatively measuring the male missiles of John Kennedy and Soviet Premier Nikita Khrushchev.

The Bay of Pigs and Berlin crises in 1961 had exacerbated the insecurities of both Kennedy and Khrushchev. "Both men soon behaved as if their personal manhood was at stake," historian James T. Patterson has rightly written. "A sort of *mano a mano* emotionality" infused relations between the superpowers in 1961 and '62.[10]

"We're going to take out these missiles," JFK flatly declared during the first meeting of the executive committee (ExComm) of the National Security Council that he set up to deal with the crisis.[11] As he contemplated the ramifications, though, Kennedy reconsidered. He backed away from the bomb-first-and-ask-questions-later position and brought his UN ambassador, Adlai Stevenson, into the deliberations. Stevenson counseled caution.

At the extreme on the other side was Air Force Chief Curtis LeMay (sometimes called "A-Bomb LeMay"), who told the president that a blockade rather than an attack was "a pretty weak response" and would be "almost as bad as the appeasement at Munich."[12]

The worst moment came on October 27, 1962, when an American U-2 plane was shot down over Cuba by a Soviet surface-to-air missile (SAM). The reaction of the ExComm members was virtually unanimous: the United States must launch air strikes against the SAM sites in Cuba by the next day. Vice President Johnson put it directly: "All I know is that when you were walking along a Texas road and a rattlesnake rose up ready to strike, there was only one thing to do— take a long stick and knock its head off."[13] It was the president who dissented. "It isn't the first step that concerns me," JFK said, "but both sides escalating to the fourth and fifth step—and we don't go to the sixth because there is no one around to do so. We must remind ourselves we are embarking on a very hazardous course."[14]

Understanding that the stakes were higher than they had ever before been in human history and that that fact made traditional, even natural, human responses inappropriate led John Kennedy to keep trying to avoid taking what he termed "one hell of a gamble" by initiating an attack.[15] He sent Khrushchev another diplomatic proposal, to which the Soviet leader agreed.

Once Khrushchev had "blinked," President Kennedy reverted immediately to the image of sexual contest, from which most of those around him had never moved away. "I cut off his balls," John Kennedy triumphantly boasted in private after Khrushchev accepted his proposal that the Soviets remove the missiles in Cuba in exchange for an American pledge not to invade the island and later to remove

American missiles from Turkey. An enraged Fidel Castro concluded that Khrushchev's backing down showed there the Soviet chairman was a man with "no *cojones*." Castro also called Khrushchev a *maricón* (a word similar to "faggot").[16]

"It's the greatest defeat in our history, Mr. President," a typically crazed LeMay screamed when Kennedy told the top brass of Khrushchev's agreement to his proposal. "*We should invade today.*"[17] LeMay saw Kennedy as Castro did Khrushchev: lacking balls.

LeMay's attitude was nicely captured in a line from Gen. Buck Turgidson, a character based loosely on him, in *Dr. Strangelove*. Suggesting that the United States launch a preemptive nuclear attack on the Soviet Union, Turgidson says, "Mr. President, I'm not saying we wouldn't get our hair mussed; but I do say no more than ten to twenty million killed, tops, uh, depending on the breaks."

Kubrick's seemingly outlandish depiction of the attitudes of some of the military leaders turns out not to be that far from the truth, even though he had no way of knowing at the time what was being discussed in ExComm in October 1962. During the missile crisis, the Joint Chiefs talked of an airborne invasion, which would "mop up Cuba in seventy-two hours with a loss of *only 10,000* Americans *more or less.*"[18]

◆ ◆ ◆

It is *Dr. Strangelove* that best captures the essential underlying sexual ingredient in the missile crisis—and in most military tests of will. "It looks like we're in a shooting war," Brig. Gen. Jack D. Ripper says in the movie, and it soon becomes obvious that he is starting a war because of his own difficulty with "shooting."

General Ripper is the embodiment of what can be termed Acute Masculine Insecurity Disorder. He starts a nuclear war because he is impotent (a problem he blames on the Communists and women—Reds and Pinks—and the fluoridation of water[19]). "I first became aware of it, Mandrake," Ripper tells the British exchange officer who works with him, "during the physical act of love. . . . Loss of essence . . . Women, er, women sense my power, and they seek the life essence. I do not avoid women, Mandrake . . . but I do deny them my essence."

He has decided that he won't let women sap him of his "precious bodily fluids."

Ripper's impotence is what leads him to use artificial omnipotence to destroy the world. He can't get *it* up, so he blows *everything* up. His erectile dysfunction leads to earth destruction.

In the final scene the former Nazi scientist Strangelove discusses, in the face of worldwide destruction, the prospects of going underground with "a ratio of, say, ten females to each male," the necessity of "the abandonment of the so-called monogamous sexual relationship . . . as far as men were concerned" and the fact that "the women will have to be selected for their sexual characteristics, which will have to be of a highly stimulating nature" because "each man will be required to do prodigious service along these lines." He himself is so stimulated by this prospect that his arm keeps rising to give a Nazi phallic salute and he is able to rise from his wheelchair and shout, "Mein Führer, I can walk!"

The most salient point that comes out of *Dr. Strangelove* is that men insecure in their masculinity are the source of many of the world's problems—and that this sort of manhood competition could destroy the world.

"I believe that a president who refrains from going to war may actually be showing more courage than one who follows the more politically popular course and launches military combat," Ted Sorensen later said, referring to Kennedy.[20]

Kubrick indicates that men who have the courage to act sensibly in such circumstances will be thought of as "pussies." One of the three roles Peter Sellers plays in *Dr. Strangelove* is the president, who takes the sort of reasonable positions to which Kennedy came as the threat of worldwide catastrophe grew more imminent. Sellers as the president is made to look much like Adlai Stevenson, one of the most dovish of the advisers JFK consulted during the missile crisis. But most telling is his name: Merkin Muffley. Both "Merkin" and "muff" are British slang terms used to refer to the area of the female genitalia, specifically a woman's pubic hair, or a pubic hair wig. It could not be clearer, then, that this fictional president is being called a "pussy." And when the president says he will give the Soviets the flight paths and targets of the American bombers so they can shoot them down, Gen. Turgidson plainly sees President Muffley in the same way that LeMay and others saw Kennedy: as a treasonous "pussy."

But, in a truly revolutionary stance, Kubrick does not portray being a pussy as something negative. The message is plain. Men need to have the courage to go against the stereotypical male behavior: The truly heroic man—a real man—may be one who is willing to act in ways that will get him called a "pussy."

Mohandas Gandhi and Martin Luther King Jr., and such other civil rights activists as Jim Lawson and John Lewis, were this sort of men. Most of the time, Jack Kennedy certainly was not. Yet when it counted the most, all his manhood hang-ups notwithstanding, John F. Kennedy was willing to expose himself to being called a pussy. He summoned the bravery to risk having that sexual imagery reversed at the most critical moment. Kennedy (and Khrushchev) averted a secular Armageddon through a willingness to *not* "act like a man."

Midnight for High Noon: The Waning of John Wayne's World

Eastward I go only by force. Westward I go free.
—John F. Kennedy (1960),
quoting Henry David Thoreau[21]

It has long been received wisdom that the self-image of America is rooted in the mythological Wild West, where men are men, guys good and bad shoot it out with each other, and the good guys always win. "And in a world we understood early to be characterized by venality and doubt and paralyzing ambiguities," Joan Didion wrote in 1965 of John Wayne, "he suggested another world, one which may or may not have existed ever, but in any case existed no more: a place where a man could move free, could make his own code and live by it."[22]

"A place where a man could move *free*": that was the American Dream—or the *male* American Dream. In its ultimate form, as championed by extremists of both the "conservative" and "hip" variety in the sixties, this might be termed the "Ultra-American Dream."

During the missile crisis, Kennedy had come, at least viscerally, to an understanding that in the time of the New Frontier the days of the Old Frontier were over. There could be no more *High Noon* duels when the guns in the holsters were thermonuclear.

A Texan in *Dr. Strangelove*, Major Kong (played by Slim Pickens), is symbolically the last American cowboy when, near the end of the movie, he rides a hydrogen bomb out of the bomb bay of his plane, gleefully waving his cowboy hat and shouting "YAHOO! YAHOO!" while triggering the destruction of the world. Between his legs, Kong has the dream of every sexually insecure man. No guy in a penis-measuring contest can top the ultimate firepower of this swollen thermonuclear erection. But, Kubrick is telling us, such extreme sexual prowess is self-destructive. The image is a wonderful representation of the impotent omnipotence of the nuclear age.

The idea that the frontier has run out, that cowboy America has reached the end of the trail, was reflected in the precipitous drop-off in the popularity of westerns as the sixties progressed. And this theme was to be presented again in two of the most important movies of the decade, both of which came out late in 1969. *Easy Rider*[23] and *Midnight Cowboy*[24] can be seen as "easterns," in which the protagonists, as Ken Kesey and the Merry Pranksters had in 1964, go back east from the West, where they had not found what they were looking for, to seek "IT"—what Jack Kerouac says, in *On the Road*, Dean Moriarty, his fictional Neal Cassady, was always looking for—in the East. "That great big, dumb cowboy crap of yours don't appeal to nobody," Ratso (Dustin Hoffman) tells Joe Buck (Jon Voight) in *Midnight Cowboy*.

The New Frontier's brush with nuclear war was the last gasp of the Old Frontier—or it might have been, had a new president haunted by the cowboy image of manhood not come into office.

◆◆◆

It is hard to imagine anything else that could have done as much as *Dr. Strangelove* did to show the absurdity of war and its ties to male sexual insecurities. With JFK's assassination, the commander in chief's decisions fell to Johnson, who had shown little sign during the missile crisis of having brought those insecurities under a degree of control.

It is truly remarkable that this film, set to debut at almost the moment that Lyndon Johnson unexpectedly became president, depicts a Texan in a cowboy hat with the ultimate "ol' Jumbo" between his legs leaping to his own and the world's destruction. (Recall that soon after he took office, LBJ told Pierre Salinger to portray him "as a tall tough Texan in the saddle."[25]) By some strange twist of fate, *Dr. Strangelove* turned out to be predictive of what was about to happen with Lyndon Johnson and Vietnam when he would metaphorically ride ol' Jumbo into the destruction of his goals, his accomplishments, his reputation, Vietnam itself, and to a substantial extent, his own country.

6

A Whiter Shade of Pink

The British Invasion, First Wave

February 1964–and Far Beyond

The Beatles' first appearance on the Ed Sullivan Show, *February 1964.*

Having been handed a historical moment . . . the
Beatles then ran with it—becoming inseparable
from the revolutions, not all of them for the better,
in culture, politics, sex and fashion soon to come.
                                    —Frank Rich (1995)[1]

Cultural historian Steven Stark said of February 9, 1964, when the Beatles first appeared on the *Ed Sullivan Show*: "The sixties as an era began that night."[2] It's a defensible claim. That Sunday evening was one of those moments that marked "the sixties," as defining in its own way as the decade's three assassination dates and the moon landing. Roughly 74 million people, almost half the population of the United States, watched as an estimated 75 percent of the nation's televisions that were on were tuned to the show. It was the largest audience for a television program up until that time. In introducing the Beatles, Sullivan said, "The city has never witnessed the excitement stirred by these youngsters from Liverpool who call themselves the Beatles."[3]

In a *New York Times* piece for the fortieth anniversary of the appearance, critic Allan Kozinn classified it as "one of those moments when everything changed, or at least, a point to which one can trace changes in everything from style in its broadest sense (in music, art and fashion, for example) to the way rock 'n' roll was marketed and perceived," and notes that "it was one of the few such moments in recent American history that did not involve an assassination or a surprise attack."[4]

Americans experienced together a nationwide television communion like that which they had shared in the days following the Kennedy assassination a little over eleven weeks before. In this common experience, though, reactions were more divided on the basis of age and sex. Older people were mostly unimpressed, and young females were generally more excited than young males.

The Beatles had arrived at New York's newly renamed John F. Kennedy Airport two days before, met by some four thousand screaming fans.[5] Their 45 single "I Want to Hold Your Hand" had already sold over 3 million copies, making it the fastest-selling single in pop music history. It was number one on the *Billboard* Hot 100 for nine weeks, finally displaced by another Beatles record, "She Loves You." By the end of March, the Beatles would have the top five records in America—a feat never remotely matched by any other artists before or since. The Beatles would hold the number one spot with a variety of songs until Louis Armstrong reclaimed the top spot for the United States with "Hello Dolly" in May. By mid-March, an estimated 60 percent of all singles being sold in the United States were by the Beatles.[6] They had six number one hits during 1964 and an amazing total of twenty-eight different songs on the *Billboard* Hot 100 during the year.[7] In August, their first movie, *A Hard Day's Night*, held the top spot in box office ratings for two weeks.

No other single entertainer or group has ever so completely dominated a year as the Beatles did in 1964. Why? Frank Rich was probably close to the mark when he said that kids had "an instinct that the Beatles were avatars of some change in our lives that we couldn't define but knew was on the way."[8]

The Beatles' February arrival was the beginning of the "British Invasion," one of the major developments of 1964. That phenomenon is usually described as the bringing back to America of African American blues. That's true, but somewhat misleading. Contrary to popular usage, the "invasion" was not a singular event. It came in two different waves. The second one was "black," as I will explain later, but perhaps the appropriate color to describe the first one is "pink." The first British Invasion, started by the Beatles early in the year, had almost nothing to do with the blues or the so-called "race music" that had become rock 'n' roll in the fifties. The Beatles, along with many of the other musicians in the first phase of the 1964 British Invasion, came from Liverpool, and, as one of John Lennon's friends in art school recalled, "There was no such thing, really, as the blues in Liverpool. I'm sure John had no idea who Muddy Waters was."[9]

These early Beatles sounded anything but blue. Their music in 1964 was just what the doctor ordered for America's youth in the post-assassination period. The basic message was the same as that of Bobby McFerrin's song a quarter century later: "Don't Worry, Be Happy."[10] The Beatles, their producer George Martin said, "had that quality that makes you feel good when you are with them."[11] And "with them" clearly extended to being with them through records or radio.

The happy sound continued through the first wave of the British Invasion with, among others, such artists as the Dave Clark Five (who were "Glad All Over")[12] in February, the Searchers (who sounded happy even though they were on "Needles and Pins" over losing their love)[13] in March, Billy J. Kramer and the Dakotas (who would never be "sad and blue," because he knew his love would never be bad to him)[14] in April, Peter and Gordon (who could not tolerate a "World Without

Love"),[15] Gerry and the Pacemakers (who advised never to "let the sun catch you crying"),[16] and the folksy Chad and Jeremy (who were "laughing all their cares away")[17] all in May, and toward the end of the year, the particularly cheerful and harmless-sounding Herman's Hermits. None of these musicians—almost all dressed in matching suits in their 1964 appearances—can reasonably be classified as carriers of the bacterium of what, as I explained in the Introduction, many young whites were fancying to be "black freedom" back to America, as the Invasion's second wave, which began in May, would.

A few other points about the significance of the Beatles on 1964 and the era that followed are in order.

Their music had something different about it. The first time Bob Dylan heard "I Want to Hold Your Hand" was in February while driving along the Pacific Coast Highway with a friend. "He practically jumped out of the car," the driver said of Dylan's reaction to the song. "Did you hear that? Fuck! Man, that was fuckin' great! Oh man—fuck!"[18]

It is significant that the Beatles were a group. They had no one leader; they were collaborative and nonhierarchical. They tried to make decisions by consensus. They usually spoke in the first-person plural. "We're all really the same person," Paul McCartney said. "We're just four parts of the one."[19] You can't get much more "sixties" than that. Important as the Beatles were in demonstrating it, though, it would be a serious mistake to think that the concept originated with them. The Student Nonviolent Coordinating Committee (SNCC) and Students for a Democratic Society (SDS) were pushing this idea before anyone in the United States had heard of the Beatles, and even in music there were girl groups and other Motown acts (including the male groups that were emerging in 1964, the Four Tops and the Temptations), not to mention such highly successful American white male groups as the Beach Boys and Four Seasons.

The Beatles represented youth empowerment. "The Beatles gave us something more than music," Joyce Maynard wrote in 1973, they made kids part of history. . . . Through the Beatles' existence we held some sort of control, we could act. Their appearance gave us our first sense of youth as power."[20] What the Beatles did in 1964 was spread youth empowerment far more widely, to a huge number of "kids" who had not been aware of what part young people had been playing in making history and might have missed what they would do on an even larger scale in the summer of 1964.

"I was tasting something," recalled one young female Beatles fan from New York. "I was totally going outside of myself—it was total freedom."[21] *Total freedom.* That's what was in the air in 1964. A large part of the Beatles' appeal and message was what would become perhaps the ultimate sixties directive: QUESTION AUTHORITY. The Beatles were, albeit in a jovial way, always questioning and ridiculing authority. Consider this scene from *A Hard Day's Night*: "Are you a Mod or a Rocker?" a reporter asks, referring to two conflicting youth groups in Britain. Ringo Starr answers, "Uh, no, I'm a mocker."[22] Indeed, they were mockers, and that was an important part of the band's impact.

The first wave of the British Invasion was revolutionary in a different way. To see what it was that the Beatles were mocking and challenging, we need to take a look at pre-1964 America and the two revolutionary threats Elvis Presley had represented a decade before. Each of the phases of the British Invasion brought back one of them.

Containment on the Home Front: Mid-Century American Civilization and Its Discontents

In the post–World War II years, Middle America had circled its wagons to defend the status quo against a variety of forces perceived as subversive, Communists, black people, women, and sex prominent among them. *Containment* was the name of the foreign and military policy used to keep Communist control from spreading geographically beyond the countries of Eastern Europe and, after 1949, China. Though it was never called by the name, there was also a containment policy on the home front. Internal containment meant keeping one sort of freedom (especially sexuality) contained, segregated. It would be tolerated, even encouraged, among African Americans, but must be kept isolated from white people. It also meant keeping women—middle-class white women, that is—in the container of the prescribed domestic role.

Ironies abounded. To fight communism's threat to individualism, Americans were pressed into a strict conformity that denied much individual freedom. That, in turn, combined with the new corporate culture to stifle the traditional ideal of manhood. Edith and Archie Bunker would later nostalgically sing, "You knew who you were then; girls were girls and men were men."[23] Yet many men in the postwar era were not, in fact, secure in the knowledge of who they were, so they had to reemphasize who they were *not*. If, as unmanly corporate yes-men, they really didn't know that men were men, it was all the more imperative that they know that "girls were girls." Lines had to be redrawn and made bold and unmistakable.

The line of division between the races was, of course, already well established. The line between Communists and "Americans" became a second absolute division. But, given that what was thought to be wrong was so wrapped up in threats to masculinity, another absolute line of separation, a thick, high wall, was constructed (or, more accurately, reconstructed and fortified) in post–World War II America: one between men and women. That wall had been breached in the Depression and World War II, when many men lost their status as providers, women became breadwinners, and women took jobs formerly reserved for men.

So, in the 1950s it was not only "Black and White Apart" and "Red and Red, White, and Blue Apart," but also "Pink and Blue Apart." Indeed, it was in the immediate postwar period that pink came to be associated with females and blue with males.[24] For all the racial segregation of the era, in the fifties the male/female line of division was more absolute and the one that it was more unthinkable to cross.

Radio Free Suburbia—
Black Freedom Penetrates the Plastic Curtain

I was only myself, . . . strolling in this violent,
dark, this unbearably sweet night, wishing I could
exchange worlds with the happy, true-hearted,
ecstatic Negroes of America.
                    —Jack Kerouac, *On the Road* (1957)[25]

As discontented Americans—particularly young, white, male Americans—increasingly felt themselves denied freedom by the constraints of mainstream American society and culture, it was the people living outside the fences of this Consumptionland—those who were denied most political, social, and economic freedoms—who came to be seen as on the cutting edge of freedom. This phenomenon had begun in the early part of the twentieth century and its growth accelerated in the fifties and extraordinarily in the sixties.

The white followers of black urban lifestyles included the relatively small number of Beats, such as Allen Ginsberg and Jack Kerouac, and a much larger number of young whites who were attracted to what was still called at the beginning of the fifties "race music" but was also classified as rhythm and blues and would become rock 'n' roll. It was all based on extremely racist assumptions about the "primitive" nature of African Americans, and those who imagined that they would like to trade places with black people were ignoring all the hardship that went along with their supposed freedom from middle-class morality.

As Norman Mailer said in his 1957 essay, "The White Negro," what was going on was "a wedding of the white and the black [in which] it was the Negro who brought the cultural dowry."[26] The most significant portion of that dowry was music, beginning in the 1940s with jazz, which Mailer called "the music of orgasm," and continuing in the fifties through rhythm and blues and into rock 'n' roll, the name of which was, like jazz before it, a euphemism for sexual intercourse. Here was the real music of orgasm, and radio was making it available to white kids in their own homes. "Living in a completely segregated world," as journalist and historian David Halberstam has written of the fifties, "the one thing that was not segregated was the radio dial."[27]

Much as the American government's Radio Free Europe penetrated the Iron Curtain with messages of freedom, black radio stations in the fifties constituted a sort of Radio Free Suburbia, beaming a message of freedom and liberation to the captive peoples behind the Plastic Curtain, the huddled masses of white kids yearning to breathe free. The wardens of the suburban gulag tried in a variety of ways to jam the messages coming across their borders, penetrating their defenses, but in the end the profits flowing from the spread of the music and the lifestyle it advertised were too great to be passed up.

In an era when the conventional message, indeed the imperative, of mainstream America was "Don't rock the boat," the daring musical imperative to "rock and roll all night," as Fats Domino put it in 1959,[28] hit many white kids like the song of a siren. They had been told that they were living in the center of the free world and living a better and freer life than any generation before them had ever experienced. Yet, it seemed that it was the Americans kept outside mainstream society who were free of the conventions that, in terminology that would become popular in the 1960s, were "cramping the style" of kids on the inside.

The have-nots appeared to have something that the haves did not. That something was *freedom*. Before this notion of black freedom could have a major impact inside white America, though, it needed a white messenger. "If I could find a white man who had the Negro sound and the Negro feel," Memphis record producer Sam Phillips had been saying, "I could make a billion dollars."[29]

Read His Hips:
Elvis and the Re-Coloring of America

> If there hadn't been an Elvis,
> there wouldn't have been the Beatles.
> —John Lennon (1965)[30]

"Loose lips sink ships," Americans were warned during World War II. But the fear in many quarters a decade after that conflict ended was that loose hips would shrink the gap between the races and the sexes. The loose hips that posed such a threat were, of course, those of a young man from Tupelo, Mississippi, by way of Memphis.

The emancipation that Elvis Presley was proclaiming was not only sexual but also racial. His music blurred the sharp line of separation between black and white. Even more menacingly, he began to smudge that other, much more ingrained, color line, the one between pink and blue, and it is that part of his revolutionary legacy that the Beatles carried forward in 1964.

Elvis removed the obstacle to white kids enthusiastically taking up "race music" by the simple expedient of changing the race of the performer. He quickly showed that he had something that appealed especially to young white females chafing at the repressive morality society had imposed upon them. Less than a month after his first song was played on the air, Elvis began to wiggle his legs beneath his loose pants while performing on stage. The crowd went wild, and Presley had a trademark.[31] Soon white southern girls in expanding concentric ripples emanating from the rock ('n' roll) Presley and Phillips had dropped into the culture pond in Memphis in May 1954 were screaming in delight as Elvis moved his hips, curled his lip, and sang in what had previously been a style confined to African Americans.

◆ ◆ ◆

White males in America who have felt a need to define themselves have long had two "Others" to use in identifying who they are not. The interplay between white males and those two Others was to become the leitmotif of the sixties. While most discontented young white males yearned to be like one of their primary "Others," blacks, they emphatically did *not* want to be like the other "Other," women. The sexual composition of fifties rockers was identical to that of the Catholic priesthood and their music was all about sexual bravado.

But Presley was different. Because of his provocative pelvic movements, he has often been characterized as "insistently masculine."[32] That's wrong. What most made him radically different from the others who were seeking to cross the racial line was that Elvis also identified at least in some respects with the other Other that so frightened most of the rebellious males as well as mainstream culture of the time. He seemed willing, at least to an extent, to be not only a "white Negro," but also a "male female."

Presley preferred to be around girls and women.[33] He liked to wear mascara and eye shadow, as well as pink clothing. While he was still driving a truck for a Memphis electrical contractor, he went to a women's hairdresser (although he would only go after hours, because he was embarrassed).[34] Presley was in this respect a prototype for the countercultural males of the second half of the sixties.

And for the Beatles, "The only person we wanted to meet in the United States of America was Elvis Presley. . . . Nothing really affected me until I heard Elvis," John Lennon said in 1965. "If there hadn't been an Elvis, there wouldn't have been the Beatles."[35]

The Girl Groups as a Bridge between Elvis and the Beatles

In a male-dominated world, girls had all sorts of frustrations and self-doubts. Early rock had, by and large, treated women as sex objects and given no consideration, much less voice, to their thoughts and feelings. Yet, shocking though it would have been to most people in the years leading up to 1964, girls had sexual desires, too.

Those feelings, along with almost all others girls had, were entirely unspoken in the music of the young before 1960. While it is certainly the case that many of the songs sung in female voices in the early 1960s were the opposite of liberating for girls who listened to them, other songs did give voice to girls and what was in their minds—and elsewhere in their bodies.

When the Shirelles' recording of Gerry Goffin and Carole King's "Will You Love Me Tomorrow" was released late in 1960, it was a startling change.[36] Here was a song about the question confronted by so many girls: *Should I believe my boyfriend's profession of eternal love and "go all the way" with him?*

Such songs were "girl talk" of the most important kind, and young female listeners heard it coming from a group of girls singing about *our* concerns; they were talking not only *to us*, but *with us*.[37] The girl group songs were *groups* of girls "talking about men, singing about men, trying to figure them out." They were leading girls to think that they needed to band together to deal with their common problems.[38] The coming together through such songs of girls and young women facing common problems was beginning to do what Betty Friedan's 1963 book, *The Feminine Mystique*, would do for somewhat older women: make them start to realize that they were not alone and that they needed to seek solutions to their common problems.

◆

Whiteout:
The British Invasion and American Music in 1964

I didn't know Negroes sang.
—John Lennon, upon first hearing
Little Richard (1956)[39]

That remarkable comment attributed to sixteen-year-old John Lennon accurately reflects the almost total absence of black people and culture in 1950s Liverpool. Lennon was, however, much taken by Little Richard when he did hear him. This was something he shared with Bob Dylan, who in his 1959 high school yearbook listed as his ambition "To join the band of Little Richard."[40] The Beatles were not influenced that much by the music of black men, but they were very much inspired by the music of black women.

"The Beatles loved all the girl groups," Ronnie Spector, the lead singer of one of them, the Ronettes, said of her first meeting with the group in London in January 1964, "and they knew every Motown song ever put out."[41] Before there was "Beatlemania," the objects of that affliction were themselves afflicted with "Girlgroupmania." The overwhelming majority of the girl groups the Beatles so admired were composed of African Americans (or, as in the Ronettes, women of mixed race). Black males were perceived by repressed white males to be "free" in a sexual sense, and there was a similar belief about black females. White females were even more sexually repressed than white males in the 1950s and early 1960s.[42] Black girl groups could give voice to the sexual longings of white girls. Because of the gender expectations of the time, black freedom for girls would be of a considerably milder sort than for guys, but the attraction was certainly there.

It was this tamer brand of black freedom—the female variety—that the Beatles joined in disseminating. Call it "pink freedom," which in the context of that era sounds even more oxymoronic than black freedom.

An easily overlooked result of the British Invasion in 1964 is that, in the same year that the Civil Rights Act was passed, American music was "whitened" to an extraordinary degree. The huge desire for anything English led not only to the domination of the pop charts by British performers but also to 1964 becoming the year with the lowest percentage of charting records by black artists since the rise of rock and roll a decade earlier.[43] During 75 percent of 1964's weeks, the *Billboard* number one song was by a white group or solo performer. The Beatles held the top position in eighteen of these thirty-nine weeks. Folk music manager Albert Grossman's comment that the Beatles greatest accomplishment was "making it cool for anyone to be white"[44] may be a bit harsh, but it is not inaccurate.

Then there's this: In all but one of the thirty-nine "white-topped" weeks the performers were male, and in all but one of the "black-topped" weeks the artists were female. The bottom line: the highest position in popular music in 1964 was dominated by white men (thirty-eight weeks) and black women (twelve weeks), with a white female and a black male each heading the chart in only one week.

Beyond these striking numbers, 1964 was musically dominated by whites—far and away most important, the Beatles—whose music and message at this time were greatly influenced by black girl groups.

Beatle(wo)mania

"Beatlemania was mainly a female affliction," as ethnomusicologist Laurel Sercombe has noted.[45] The point is significant. "If you told tough guys they [the Beatles] were better than Elvis, they beat you up," a male Beatles fan said. So, like many other male Beatles fans, he could talk about the Beatles "only to the girls."[46] One of the bases on which mainstream media dismissed the Beatles was that they were "for girls."[47]

The Beatles "sound like a male Shirelles," producer George Martin told readers of the Liverpool music newspaper *Mersey Beat* in 1963.[48] But they didn't only *sound* like the girl groups and *look* somewhat feminine. The Beatles were *saying* things about what was on girls' minds. Many of the early Beatles songs joined the "girl talk" conversations.

The Beatles recorded two Shirelles songs, "Boys" and "Baby It's You," both of which were included on their debut British album, *Please Please Me*. For Ringo Starr to sing that boys are "a bundle of joy" raised more than a few eyebrows in 1964 America. "It was a little embarrassing," Paul McCartney says, "because it went: 'I'm talking about boys, yeah, yeah . . . boys.' It was a Shirelles hit and they were girls singing it, but we never thought we should call it Girls just because Ringo was a boy. We just sang it the way they'd sung it and never considered any implications."[49]

Girls talked about boys, and the Beatles were directly entering girl talk conversation with this cover. And "Baby It's You" is a girl group song, about being in hopeless love with a cheating guy. The Beatles made no attempt to change the song from the way the Shirelles had done it.[50]

The four lads from Liverpool also took on the role of lasses in a cover of the Marvelettes' "Please Mr. Postman," which in 1961 had become the first number one hit for Motown (then called Tamla). John Lennon sings the lead speaking as a girl waiting patiently for her boyfriend to send her "a card or letter." (They did change "boyfriend" in the original to "girlfriend," but passively waiting for some communication from the one you love was clearly the sort of thing that would have been expected then of females, not males.)[51]

And when the early Beatles were not speaking *as* girls, they were often speaking *with* girls and *to* guys *for* girls in an "us" sort of way that was almost the antithesis of the messages in the blues-descended songs. Consider their second American single, "She Loves You." In it, they are speaking almost as the attorneys for the plaintiff girl who has been wronged, saying to the accused: "I think it's only fair . . . Apologize to her."[52] You wouldn't find an American bluesman—or his British imitator—apologizing to a girl. "Every girl wanted to be treated the way their songs indicated they would treat them," historian Elaine Tyler May has said of the Beatles. "There was a sweetness and gentleness in their view of women and romance."[53]

As Elvis Presley had done a decade earlier, in 1964 the Beatles refused to stay on one side of the absolute line drawn between the sexes. "What was both shocking and deeply appealing about the Beatles," a book by three feminist sociologists argues, "was that they were, while not exactly effeminate, at least not easily classifiable in the rigid gender distinctions of middle-class American life."[54] Beatlemania was "the first mass outburst of the sixties to feature women—in this case girls," these authors argue. It "was, in form if not in conscious intent, to protest the sexual repressiveness, the rigid double standard of female teen culture. It was the first and most dramatic uprising of *women's* sexual revolution."[55]

One of the main ways in which the Beatles helped to open the way for feminism was that they were showing that in order for women to break out of their severely circumscribed roles, it was necessary for men to change, too.

The arrival of the Beatles in the United States was another indication of the waning of John Wayne's World. Richard Starkey loved westerns as a child and, while his "Ringo" nickname is usually attributed to his wearing of multiple rings, he apparently initially took it from John Wayne's character, the Ringo Kid, in the classic 1939 film *Stagecoach*. But the androgynous Beatles were the antithesis of the Wayne persona.

In *A Hard Day's Night*, the Beatles are shown happily having women put makeup on them with powder puffs. "In my considered opinion," the character who is said to be Paul's grandfather says to them, "you're a bunch of sissies." Grabbing a powder puff from one of the women, John responds, "You know you're only jealous!" and dabs the old man with powder. The important thing here is that the Beatles didn't seem to mind being called "sissies." Apparently, they didn't particularly suffer from the masculinity fears that plagued Lyndon Johnson and so many other men. In 1964, that bordered on the revolutionary.

But before we get carried away with crediting four young males from England for helping to sow the seeds for women's liberation, we should look at what else was happening simultaneously. Some of these other developments were certainly more important than the first wave of the British Invasion in bringing about Second Wave Feminism.

7

"You Don't Own Me"

Asserting Women's Freedom through Song and Other Means

January–September 1964

Lesley Gore in 1964.

I'm young and I love to be young
I'm free and I love to be free
To live my life the way I want
To say and do whatever I please
　　　　—John Madara and Dave White,
　　　　"You Don't Own Me" (1963)[1]

1964's Mixed Musical Messages on Women's Place: Powerless or Empowered?

As 1964 was dawning, Jack Jones's recording of the Burt Bacharach/ Hal David song "Wives and Lovers," which had made its chart debut at the beginning of November, was climbing toward its eventual peak at number fourteen in the second week of January. In May, the recording would win the Grammy for Best Male Vocal Performance. It had a remarkably backward message for women. In order to understand how reactionary that message was, it should be put in the context of another 1964 song, the Dixie Cups' "Chapel of Love," which would top the charts for three weeks in June.

The lesson that the culture had been teaching young females was that the only happy ending for a girl was marriage. This point was made explicit in "Chapel of Love." The main hope offered in this classic is that getting married meant that they would never be lonely again.[2]

But, months earlier in "Wives and Lovers," Jack Jones had warned married women that they *still* needed to ask the Shirelles' question of their husbands: "Will you still love me tomorrow?" "Don't think because there's a ring on your finger / You needn't try anymore," Jones's voice cautioned married women, reminding them that, "day after day / there are girls at the office / and men will always be men."[3] So, if you thought goin' to the chapel would end your worries, girlie, have another think. The message couldn't be clearer: *Be nervous; be afraid; do whatever your husband wants; be subservient; buy things to make yourself more attractive. You must strive constantly to please your man, or you will lose him.*

The lesson of complete male dominance and control seemed to be: *Amuse him or lose him.* And if he does desert you, dearie, know that it's all your fault. Men, after all, "will always be men." That line sounds much like one from Tammy Wynette's 1968 song, "Stand By Your Man."[4] Wynette's song, though, indicated that the choice of whether to stay with a man was the woman's. According to "Wives and Lovers," the only choice women have is whether they will go to extraordinary lengths to please their man; whether to stay is entirely *his* decision. Nothing new there.

But 1964 witnessed two hit musical Declarations of Women's Independence, both of which were written the year before, the same year that *The Feminine Mystique* was published. In the week after "Wives and Lovers" topped out on the charts, a song with a radically different message, one that indicated that the times were decidedly a-changin' for women, soared past it in the *Billboard* rankings. Lesley Gore—who had risen to the top of the charts only eight months earlier with a musical pronouncement of female powerlessness in which she had cried helplessly at her party when Judy stole her boyfriend[5]—would reach number two at the end of 1964's first month, blocked from the top spot only by the Beatles attaining that position for the first time that same week. Gore's startling song would remain right behind the Beatles for three weeks.

This song's protagonist wasn't having any of that hand-holding stuff. The lyrics contained ideas that at least bordered on—no, let's revise that—that *were* revolutionary:

You don't own me
I'm not just one of your many toys
You don't own me
Don't say I can't go with other boys

And don't tell me what to do
And don't tell me what to say
And please, when I go out with you
Don't put me on display, 'cause

You don't own me
Don't try to change me in any way
You don't own me
Don't tie me down 'cause I'd never stay

So just let me be myself . . .

I'm young and I love to be young
I'm free and I love to be free
To live my life the way I want
To say and do whatever I please.[6]

The song was written by two men, John Madara and Dave White, but here was a woman—a *girl*, for god's sake; she was "just seventeen, you know what I mean"[7]—proclaiming her freedom from male domination, her independence, her refusal to be an object. This was something new—and, in the early weeks of 1964, second only to the just-arrived Fab Four in popularity.

"You Don't Own Me" burst forth as a supernova of freedom out of a genre (songs by young female vocalists) that had been populated over the preceding two years by such sentiments as "I wanna be Bobby's girl" and "I will follow him wherever he may go."

I'm a woman and "I'm *free* and I love to be *free*." Here was a bold, unmistakable proclamation that freedom is for females, too. This is the freedom that young white males had associated with blacks and demanded for themselves. Now women were insisting upon the same sort of freedom. *That* was revolutionary.

The title of a 1960 *Good Housekeeping* article by Betty Friedan that contained some of the argument she would publish in book form as *The Feminine Mystique* in 1963 put the issue directly: "I Say: Women are People Too!"[8]

Women are *people*? And *free*? The hell you say! These ideas attacked the belief that had, throughout history, provided the model for all other supposed relationships of inequality, that male is superior to female. Historical perspective provides context for this incipient revolution.

(She Can't Get No) Satisfaction: Naming a Nameless Problem

> Then you wake up one morning and
> There's nothing to look forward to.
> —"A "twenty-three-year-old
> mother in blue jeans" quoted in
> *The Feminine Mystique* (1963)[9]

As John F. Kennedy was telling voters in 1960 that the nation needed a New Frontier, there appeared to be little new activity along the oldest frontier in human existence, that between women and men. In 1959, the film *Some Like It Hot* had employed comedy to make a small crack in the wall between the sexes, but Barbie dolls were also introduced in 1959 and became all the rage among young girls. And in 1960, young women were jumping and shrieking at the sight of a handsome young presidential candidate who never even considered a woman for a prominent position in his campaign or, later, administration.

Yet, there were signs of a coming challenge even then. One was Friedan's short *Good Housekeeping* piece in September in which she lit a fuse by asking the question she said was on the minds of growing numbers of women: "Is this all?"

Writing of a "they" who told women what they needed and what they should want, Friedan noted that "they tell us . . . that all our frustrations were caused by education and emancipation, the striving for independence and equality with men, which made American women unfeminine." In interviews of women, she found a recurring theme that was expressed as, "I feel empty, somehow," or "useless," or "incomplete."

Friedan encouraged women to listen to their inner voices and "know that *it is not enough to be a wife and mother, because she is a human being herself.*" This call for women to be freed was ultimately even more threatening to the status quo than the rapidly growing movement for black people to be freed.

"Who knows what sons and daughters will become, when their mothers' fulfillment makes girls so sure they want to be feminine that they no longer have to look like Marilyn Monroe to prove it," Friedan asked, "and makes boys so unafraid of women they don't have to worry about their masculinity?"[10]

The issues and questions that Friedan raised in this little article were only a blip on the nation's radar screen at the time, but they opened a debate far more momentous than that held during the same month between John Kennedy and Richard Nixon. The large number of letters Friedan received in response to the article convinced her that the problem was widespread and led her to make her argument on a much broader scale in her book *The Feminine Mystique*, which was published in February 1963.

American women—middle-class, white, educated American women, that is—found themselves living in circumstances far better than those of similarly situated women at any previous time in history. They should have been happy, but millions of them were not. Friedan quoted a *Newsweek* article that contended that "from the beginning of time, the female cycle has defined and confined woman's role." "Though no group of women has ever pushed these natural restrictions as far as the American wife, it seems that she still cannot accept them with good grace."[11]

Don't bitch, be happy was the message that the media were sending to women who complained when they should know that women had never had it so good. That, though, was a big part of the problem. They assumed that others in their situation *were* happy, as women's magazines and television shows told them they were. *What's wrong with me?* The problem had no name. The complaints Friedan heard from many different women echoed one another: "I ask myself why I'm so dissatisfied." "I feel as if I don't exist." "I just don't feel alive." "But who am I?"[12]

In fact, this nonexistence/not alive status was the traditional view of marriage for women. It was always the end, not the means or the beginning. No one seems ever to have thought of using *commencement* as a synonym for *marriage* for a woman. And this premature death of the individual female was occurring at ever-earlier ages. In 1963, the average age at which a woman married was 19.8 years.[13] And we're not talking Arkansas here—that was the *national* average, meaning, of course, that many girls were getting married at ages considerably younger.

"Goin' to the Chapel" was the ending of fairy tales and many women's novels and stories. It was followed by: *And they lived happily ever after.* . . . But that "ever after" was rarely explored. It was sometimes referred to as "marriage blackout."[14] There was nothing new about marriage being "the end" for females. A century before, Harriet Jacobs wrote in her *Incidents in the Life of a Slave Girl* (1861): "Reader, my story ends with freedom; not in the usual way, with marriage."[15] For a woman, the tradition was that saying "I do" meant "*I don't*" exist anymore. Toni Morrison captured this view of marriage in her 1973 novel, *Sula*, when she described the thinking of a male character named Jude as he considered marriage: "The two of them together would make one Jude."[16]

In a paper titled, "They Did Own Me," Deirdre McGowan, an adult student in a 2004 course of mine, wrote about her personal experience that reflects the expectations for women that Friedan characterized as the "Feminine Mystique":

> When I entered the Sixties, I was seventeen, engaged to be married and a virgin. I was very much in love and eagerly anticipated a conjugal life of joyful monogamy, children and a perfect little house—which I would keep immaculately clean. I married and it wasn't long before my husband suggested that I really didn't need to finish college since I would be primarily a wife and mother. I was torn.
>
> My mother had taught and lectured me for years that my role in life was to catch a man and do everything in my power to give him pleasure and comfort. A marriage partnership included completing all of the chores associated with managing a household. A man should never be asked to clear the table, do a load of laundry or even pick up groceries. His life was to be made as easy as possible at home so that he could focus on maximizing his career. In retrospect, this attitude was especially strange since she had a bachelor's degree in physics from UC-Berkeley. But then she never worked. She was a mother.[17]

Who am I? The core of the "problem that has no name" seemed to be that these women, like their problem, had no "name"—no individual identity, no "self." Living in the "free world," they felt that they were without freedom. And the leading spokes*men* of American liberalism of the age told them that this was their role. A woman's job politically was "to inspire in her home a vision of the meaning of life and freedom," two-time Democratic presidential nominee Adlai Stevenson told Smith College's graduating class in 1955, "to help her husband find values that will give purpose to his specialized daily chores . . . to teach her children the uniqueness of each individual human being."[18]—except, it seemed, of herself and other women, who plainly were not seen as "individual human beings."

There were several reasons for the creation of what Friedan named "the Feminine Mystique." One, certainly, was the post–World War II "crisis in masculinity." Men felt a need to assert their manhood by having women under their domination. A man in need of seeing himself as a provider, protector, and penetrator has to have a woman to provide for, protect, and penetrate.

Another important factor in the equation—or, rather, the *inequality*: man > woman—was economic. The mass production economy had to have mass consumption, and women were seen in the fifties more as consumers than as people.[19] The most effective way of making women into society's designated buyers was to try to empty their heads of anything meaningful.

Women who suffered from the nameless problem turned to many potential solutions: having another baby, taking tranquillizers (Mick Jagger and Keith Richards would address this "remedy" in a song they wrote in 1965, "Mother's Little Helper"), excessive consumption of alcohol, extramarital sexual affairs, visits to psychiatrists,

Actress Ava Gardner holding a copy of The Feminine Mystique *at an airport in 1964.*

but none of them seemed to provide more than temporary relief. As long as these women thought the problem was only their own—*there's something wrong with me*—there was no solution. What Betty Friedan did was to awaken women to the fact that they were not at all alone in their suffering.

The hardcover edition spent six weeks on the *New York Times* Best Seller list in the late spring of 1963. But it was in 1964 that Friedan's arguments really struck a nerve with American women. The paperback edition published in that year was the top-selling nonfiction paperback for the year. More than 1.3 million copies of the first printing were sold.[20] A movement was aborning.

A Pill and a Prince:
Women in the Early Sixties

Women's rights are a lot of hooey.
—Harry S Truman (1945)[21]

When the calendar 1960s began, the above statement from fifteen years earlier by President Truman was still the order of the day.

There were signs warning of a curve in the road ahead in the first few years of the 1960s. The drug Enovid had been approved by the FDA in 1957 for the treatment of severe menstrual disorders. The agency also required that the drug be labeled with a warning that it would prevent ovulation. That "warning" was a selling point. Over the next few years, a large number of women claimed to have developed severe menstrual disorders and asked their physicians for prescriptions for Enovid.[22]

In May 1960, the FDA approved Enovid to be sold for the purpose of birth control. "The Pill" did not change the sexual behavior of women overnight, but it represented a wedge that would be pushed ever-deeper into the wall of containment over the ensuing years.

♦ ♦ ♦

For the most part, though, the early 1960s seemed to be steady as she goes for women. The new young president in 1961 may have been a symbol of change, but he emphatically did not qualify as a champion of change or progress for women. Congress passed and Kennedy signed into law on June 10, 1963, the Equal Pay Act, prohibiting paying women and men different salaries or wages for the same work. When JFK signed the bill, he said it would "call attention to the unconsciona-ble practice of paying female employees less wages than male employ-ees for the same job. This measure adds to our laws another structure basic to democracy."[23] It was an important step, but it accomplished far less than its name implied. Still, the Equal Pay Act became law less than four months after the publication of *The Feminine Mystique*, and it was among the straws that were "blowin' in the wind" on women's emancipation in the months leading up to 1964.

But the total number of women in the Cabinet and other positions of power in the Kennedy administration was a round one: zero. Kennedy himself never gave any hint of considering women as intellectually capable. At the beginning of the 1960s, Kennedy's attitudes about women and the all-male composition of his administration were entirely normal. The absence and subordination of women would raise few eyebrows, arched or otherwise, in the United States, circa 1961–1963. There was scarcely a suggestion in any prominent public forum that women were equal to men, and there seemed little reason to expect a dramatic change in the position of women. Yet this most fundamental of all revolutions was well underway by the decade's end and, as was the case in so many other areas of change, it was in 1964 that the change suddenly became apparent.

American Women: Report of the President's Commission on the Status of Women came out on October 11, 1963, six weeks before President Kennedy's death. It called for equal employment opportunity, the provision of affordable childcare, and paid maternity leave.[24] More than 83,000 copies went out within the next year, making the report a Government Printing Office bestseller.

The Smiths—Running for President and Adding "S-E-X" to the 1964 Civil Rights Bill

We are entitled to this little crumb of equality.
—Rep. Katharine St. George (R-NY)
February 1964[25]

During the same week that "You Don't Own Me" reached number two on the *Billboard* chart, there was another sign of hope for change in the status of American women. On January 27, United States Senator Margaret Chase Smith of Maine announced her candidacy for the 1964 Republican presidential nomination. Smith said that she had been told that "no woman should ever dare aspire to the White House—that this is a man's world and that it should be kept that way." Others, she said, contended that, as a woman, she "would not have the physical stamina and strength to run." She was going to try to prove them wrong.

It was a significant step, but where things still stood was reflected in the *New York Times* story on her announcement by the following two sentences: "Mrs. Smith, a trim woman with snow-white hair, wore a black suit and brown alligator heels. Her only accessories were two strands of pearls and a yellow rose pinned to her lapel."[26] It is doubtful that the outfit and "accessories" of a male candidate would have warranted mention.

The week after Senator Smith announced her candidacy for president—and the day before the Beatles' first appearance on *Ed Sullivan*—another politician named Smith, Representative Howard W. Smith of Virginia, got some laughs by offering an amendment to Title VII of the civil rights bill that was then before Congress. He proposed to add "sex" to race, color, religion, and national origin as categories that employers would be prohibited from using to deny employment. This addition was intended, Smith said in a jocular tone, "to prevent discrimination against another minority group, the women." "This bill is so imperfect, what harm will this little amendment do?" Smith asked.[27] The segregationist appeared to be playing it for laughs. A two-hour debate ensued in which many of Smith's male colleagues seized what they saw as an opportunity to display their humor by deriding the idea that women needed to be protected against discrimination. The debate was mockingly dubbed "ladies' day" in the House.

But it wasn't a laughing matter to most of the small number of women who were then members of Congress. As their male colleagues laughed, "every Congresswoman except one rose to argue for the proposed inclusion of women in the bill's protections."[28] "If there had been any necessity to have pointed out that women were a second-class sex," Representative Martha Griffiths (D-Michigan) noted, "the laughter would have proved it."[29]

The amendment was "simply correcting something that goes back, frankly, to the dark ages," Republican Representative Katharine St. George of New York said. "The addition of that little, terrifying word 's-e-x' will not hurt this legislation in any way." Speaking to the male members, she said: "We outlast you—we outlive you—we nag you to death. We are entitled to this little crumb of equality."[30]

In fact, there had for some time been talk of adding "sex" to the protected categories. "Would you support an amendment to include women in the civil rights bill?" Lyndon Johnson had been asked at a news conference a week before. "I realize there has been discrimination in the employment of women," the president responded, "and I am doing my best to do something about it. I am hopeful that in the next month we will have made substantial advances in that field."[31]

Martha Griffiths had been planning to offer a "sex amendment" herself but decided to wait when she learned that Smith was going to do it, because she calculated that he would bring about a hundred southern members with him to vote for it.[32] As much of a racial segregationist as he was, Howard Smith seems to have been a sincere advocate of women's rights. There is, though, no doubt that many of his male colleagues saw women's rights as a joke, and his frivolous tone in introducing the amendment seems to have been playing to them to assure the defeat of a law that would provide for equal treatment of the races.

Something New under the Sunshine:
A Travelin' *Woman*

Seven weeks after the Dixie Cups completed their three-week stay at number one goin' to the chapel and getting married, Gale Garnett reached the charts offering a drastically different view. In 1964's second musical declaration of women's independence, in its own way as radical as "You Don't Own Me," Garnett pierced the carefully constructed pink/blue wall between what was considered proper and acceptable behavior for the two sexes. She had written "We'll Sing in the Sunshine" in 1963 and recorded it herself in 1964. In a total reversal of the usual girl-needs-boy-but-boy-leaves-girl script, she tells her lover that she will never love him, because "the cost of love's too dear." She'll stay with him for a year, then move on. She tells her lover not to cling to her because "I'll soon be out of sight." Her daddy had told her, she relates, not to love any man, but instead to take what they may give and return what she can.[33]

In the traditional concept of "love 'em and leave 'em," the unstated antecedent to *'em* was, of course, *women*. Garnett's song switched *women* to the subject and made men the object. "We'll Sing in the Sunshine" made its chart debut during the first week in August. Garnett's song rose steadily, peaking at number four for three weeks in October.

Like "You Don't Own Me," Gale Garnett's musical announcement of female liberation reached a different and younger audience than did *The Feminine Mystique*, and their popularity was a clear indication that a fundamental change was beginning to bore into the foundations of society.

The beginnings of a push for dramatic change in the situation of women would arise out of the civil rights movement in the summer of 1964.

8

Emancipation Proclamations

Cassius Clay and Malcolm X

February 1964–February 1965

*Malcolm X and Cassius Clay / Muhammad Ali outside
the Trans-Lux Newsreel Theater, New York, 1964.*

I don't have to be what you want me to be.
I'm free to be what I want.
                    —Cassius Clay
                    (February 26, 1964)[1]

We are fighting for recognition as human beings.
We are fighting for the right to live as free
humans in this society.
                    —El-Hajj Malik El-Shabazz
                    (Malcolm X) (May 29. 1964)[2]

T WO WEEKS AFTER THE Beatles' first *Sullivan* appearance, before the short month of February was over, a brash, self-promoting young boxer with the melodious name Cassius Marcellus Clay Jr., shocked the sports world by defeating Sonny Liston to win the World Heavyweight Championship.

Younger sportswriters, as David Remnick has written, "really did see Clay as a fifth Beatle, parallel players in the great social and generational shift in American society." An "earthquake" was shaking America, "and this fighter from Louisville and this band from Liverpool were part of it, leading it, whether they knew it or not." Clay, whose name would be changed to Muhammad Ali in March 1964, and the Beatles were among the clearest indicators that the times they were a-changin' in 1964. Both would "become essential pieces of the sixties phantasmagoria."[3]

Declaring Personal Freedom by Ceding It

You just don't buck Mr. Muhammad and get away with it.
—Muhammad Ali, comment to
Alex Haley (1964)[4]

By the time of his title bout, Clay had become fast friends with another man of great importance to 1964 and American history, Malcolm X. Though Malcolm was almost seventeen years older than Clay, for a time in 1963 and 1964 they were, as the boxer's physician, Ferdie Pacheco, later said, "like very close brothers."[5] What had brought the two men together was their attraction to the teachings of a movement called the Nation of Islam (NOI).

By the beginning of the 1960s, Malcolm had emerged as the best-known spokesman of the NOI. His charisma, intellect, and speaking ability far exceeded those of the group's nominal leader, a man named at birth Elijah Robert Poole who insisted on being called "The Honorable Elijah Muhammad." "While black nationalist and separatist ideas coming from Elijah Muhammad seemed cranky, cultlike, backwaterish, and marginal," essayist Gerald Early has noted, "the same ideas coming from Malcolm seemed revolutionary, hip and vibrant."[6]

THEM, as Malcolm significantly referred to The Honorable Elijah Muhammad by 1964 when writing notes about the leader of the Nation of Islam,[7] had been born in 1897 into a family headed by a Georgia sharecropper and Baptist preacher. He joined the Great Migration of southern blacks to the north around the time of World War I, moving to Detroit, where he became a follower of Marcus Garvey's Universal Negro Improvement Association. In 1931, Poole converted to an ardent support of W. D. Fard, later known as Wallace Fard Muhammad, who in 1930 founded the Nation of Islam. Fard developed a set of teachings that combined an emphasis on clean living and self-improvement for African Americans with a cosmology that contended that originally all people had been black, created from the darkness of outer space, until an evil scientist named Yakub developed a race of white devils. When Fard disappeared in 1934, Poole, who had taken the name of Elijah Muhammad, raised Fard to the level of deity and declared himself to be the new Messenger.[8]

Under Elijah Muhammad's leadership, the Nation of Islam grew slowly in some urban areas. Its blend of a strict regimen of self-improvement with a preaching that matched the experiences many black people had with whites made it possible for the NOI to recruit some of the most desperate African Americans, including those who were imprisoned.

Among the prisoners who were attracted to the message of Elijah Muhammad in the late 1940s was a young man named Malcolm Little. Little was born in Omaha in 1925. His father, like Poole's, was from Georgia and a follower of Marcus Garvey. Malcolm's first experience with white hate and violence came even before he was born, when hooded Klansmen on horseback surrounded the Little family home, broke all its windows, and told the pregnant Mrs. Little that they better leave town because "the good Christian white people" wouldn't stand for her husband "spreading trouble" among the "good" Negroes.[9] The family moved to Lansing, Michigan, where Malcolm's father lost his life and his mother was said to have lost her mind. Louise Little was institutionalized when the doctor who examined her concluded that she had paranoia because "she claims to have been discriminated against."[10]

Malcolm was an excellent student, but when he told his white English teacher in Michigan that he wanted to be a lawyer, the teacher's response was: "That's no realistic goal for a nigger."[11] Malcolm dropped out of school and entered a life of crime, eventually being sent to prison. "In the society to which I was exposed as a black youth here in America," Malcolm X would say in 1964, "for me to wind up in a prison was really just about inevitable. It happens to so many thousands of black youth."[12] While incarcerated, Malcolm learned of the teachings of the Nation of Islam, began a correspondence with Elijah Muhammad, and soon after his release, became a leading figure in the group, noting "When I heard 'The white man is the devil,' when I played back what had been my own experiences, it was inevitable that I would respond positively."[13]

Representative of the transformation—the rebirth—of joining NOI and rejecting definition and control by whites was the elimination of a person's slave name, which was replaced by an "X," "erasing the past, the legacy of slavery, and the life of self-loathing."[14] Malcolm Little became Malcolm X.

The Nation of Islam first came to widespread (white) public attention in July 1959, when a five-part television documentary narrated and coproduced by Mike Wallace, *The Hate That Hate Produced*,[15] was aired. It was Malcolm X who emerged from the expanded interest as the face and voice of the NOI. For a time, Elijah Muhammad pushed Malcolm to become more visible, thinking, he said, "it will make *me* better known."[16] By the beginning of 1964, though, those days were over. The NOI leader had determined to get rid of his young follower.

In declaring their own freedom, both Malcolm and, especially, Clay ceded that freedom to a man who demanded absolute obedience to what he said. Elijah Muhammad was a con man running a money-making racket. He attracted followers by telling them things that were incontestably true about what white people had done to black people, adding good moral teachings, and only later, like other rackets disguised as religions, offering absurd stories that the gullible would believe. By the time that Clay was publicly expressing his allegiance to the NOI in 1964, Malcolm had reluctantly come to realize that THEM was what could more accurately be called TDEM—The Dishonorable Elijah Muhammad, a charlatan, grifter, and abuser of women.

"I did many things as a [Black] Muslim that I'm sorry for now," Malcolm told Alex Haley. "I was a zombie then—like all [Black]

Muslims—I was hypnotized, pointed in a certain direction, and told to march. Well, I guess a man's entitled to make a fool of himself if he's ready to pay the cost. It cost me twelve years."[17]

"Who Made Me Is Me"—
Something New: A Self-Made Black Man

In an age of celebrity, when fame was conferred
on the loudest self-promoters, Cassius Clay was
reaching for the moon.
—Randy Roberts and
Johnny Smith[18]

But listen here. When you want to talk about who
made me, you talk to me. Who made me is *me*.
—Cassius Clay (1961)[19]

For his part, Cassius Clay remained oblivious to the harsh truths about the NOI leader, the realization of which was shaking Malcolm X's world to its foundations in the early months of 1964.

Clay grew up in what qualified as a middle-class black family in Louisville. Certainly, his family's living standards were not middle class by contemporary white criteria, but the Clays were above the poverty line. "In those days," one of his schoolmates remembered, "there was no other way to think of his circumstances as anything other than black middle class."[20] There was, though, something the two men shared that transcended the differences in their earlier lives: the experience of being black in white America. From the time he was about ten years old, Clay later said, there were many nights when he lay crying in bed wondering why black people had to suffer so much.[21]

Frustrated with living in a situation that he could not change, young Clay was open to believing the sort of nonsense that Elijah Muhammad peddled. As one of Cassius's teachers said, "You can bear being miserable if you accept a prediction that tomorrow will be better."[22]

By the time Clay was exposed to them, the prophecies of Elijah Muhammad had crystallized into the promise that the long rule of the white man would come to an end in 1970, when a half-mile-wide, wheel-shaped spacecraft, the "Mother Ship," containing 1,500 bombers, would descend from the skies and destroy the white people.[23]

Clay had gotten into boxing in 1954, at age twelve, less than ten years before he would become World Heavyweight Champion. His talent was obvious, but Clay was very unlike most others who went into boxing. He was never a bully or a street fighter. Nor was he involved with the vices into which so many young athletes, especially in boxing, are drawn. When he turned professional, Clay said, "Here I am, just nineteen, surrounded by showgirls, whisky, and sissies, and nobody watching me. All this temptation and me trying to train to be a boxer."[24]

After winning a gold medal at the 1960 Olympics in Rome, Cassius Clay spent the next few years enhancing his fame and fashioning for himself a persona that was at once as traditionally American as apple pie, strikingly "sixties," revolutionary, and defiantly *black*. "The self-made man" is at the heart of American mythology, and Clay was consciously working to make himself through self-promotion. But the concept of the American self-made man had always been white. "Black Pride" and "Black is Beautiful" were terms that would be commonplace in the later sixties, but Cassius Clay was already epitomizing them in the first years of the decade. "I'm beautiful," he often proclaimed. Apart from the small Nation of Islam, such pride in blackness was rarely heard in the years prior to 1964.

"I had to prove you could be a new kind of black man," Ali told David Remnick in the 1990s. "I had to show that to the world." During his time of self-creation in the early 1960s, Clay "declared himself free of every mold and expectation."[25] While the general (that is, white) public was oblivious to the fact, early in 1963 *Ebony* magazine pointed out that Cassius Clay was "a blast furnace of racial pride," "His is a pride that would never mask itself with skin lighteners and processed hair, a pride scorched with memories of a million little burns."[26]

Everything Cassius Clay did in these years was calculated. Remnick has made a point that is easily overlooked—and one that reflects how well Clay/Ali fit with other cultural aspects of the emerging sixties: "Clay may have been the most self-aware twenty-one-year-old in the country. Like the most intelligent of comedians or politicians or actors, he was in complete command of even the most outrageous performances."[27]

Clay promoted his early 1963 Madison Square Garden fight with Doug Jones by reciting an ode to himself at a poetry night at Greenwich Village's Bitter End, perhaps the hippest place in the country, where young folk singers and comedians performed.

During the years when Clay was developing both as an athlete and as an unforgettable personality, heavyweight boxing was dominated by two other black men—Floyd Patterson and Sonny Liston. The contrast between the two men could hardly have been starker. Floyd Patterson was "the Good Negro." A practicing Catholic, he worked with the NAACP and supported integration. "Floyd Patterson sounded like a Freedom Rider," wrote Murray Kempton in the *New York Post*. Sonny Liston represented, poet LeRoi Jones (later Amiri Baraka) said, "the big black Negro in every white man's hallway, waiting to do him in."[28] Liston was the "Threatening Nigger," the "Big Black Buck," the "Black Beast" who, some whites feared, would rape "their" women.

As a child, Liston had been subjected to severe physical abuse from his father. "The only thing my old man ever gave me was a beating," he recalled.[29] Illiterate and virtually unemployable at any but the most menial jobs, Liston turned to crime and wound up in the Missouri State Penitentiary in 1950. Malcolm Little was in prison in Massachusetts at the time, but their experiences behind bars led the two men in different directions. Malcolm took up Elijah Muhammad's perverted version of Islam; Liston took up boxing.

When Sonny Liston turned professional in 1953, he signed on with an organized crime–affiliated management, which was hardly unusual in boxing, as was dramatized the following year in the Best Picture Academy Award–winning film, *On the Waterfront*. The Nation of Islam provided young black men in prison with another choice.

While Patterson was avoiding a fight with Liston, Cassius Clay was fashioning himself into something distinct from either of them.

His boxing record was perfect, but he was much more known for his mouth than his fists. Before a second Liston-Patterson title bout was staged in Las Vegas in July 1963, Clay flew there to taunt Liston and get him to agree to a title fight with him.

Everything Clay said and did before the second Liston-Patterson fight was calculated to infuriate Liston. "Sonny Liston is nothing. The man can't talk. The man can't fight," Clay declared. "The man needs talking lessons. . . . And, since he's gonna fight me, he needs falling lessons."[30] A few nights before Liston's rematch with Patterson, Clay found the champion shooting dice at a Las Vegas casino. "Look at that big ugly bear," Clay shouted from across the room, "he can't even shoot craps. Look at that big ugly bear. He can't do nothing right." Fuming, Liston walked over to Clay. "Listen, you nigger faggot," Liston said. "If you don't get out of here in ten seconds, I'm gonna pull that big tongue out of your mouth and stick it up your ass."[31] "I ain't going to lie," Ali told Alex Haley in a 1964 *Playboy* interview. "This was the only time since I have known Sonny Liston that he really scared me."[32] Clay's fear was genuine. All the braggadocio act notwithstanding, he was frightened whenever he fought.

Brothers in Black:
Clay, the NOI, and Malcolm

> Some contagious quality about him made him one
> of the very few people I ever invited to my home.
> —Malcolm X, on Cassius
> Clay (1964)[33]

The principal way in which Cassius Clay was dealing with his pervasive private fears was through something else he was hiding from the public: his newfound faith in Elijah Muhammad's twisted version of Islam.

Clay had first become acquainted with the Nation of Islam in 1959 when he was in Chicago for a Golden Gloves tournament. He brought home a record album of sermons by Elijah Muhammad. Then he read an issue of the organization's publication, *Muhammad Speaks*. He was taken, even in 1959, with the message of self-respect and racial pride, and the rejection of alcohol, smoking, and promiscuity.

Clay visited NOI mosques whenever he was in a city that had one. It was at a Nation gathering in Detroit in 1962 that he first met Malcolm X. Malcolm had never heard of him, but he pretended he had. "Ours were two entirely different worlds. In fact, Elijah Muhammad instructed us Muslims against all forms of sports."[34] Over the ensuing months, the two men became fast friends. "It was almost as if they were in love with each other," Ferdie Pacheco, said.[35] "More than anyone else, Malcolm molded Cassius Clay into Muhammed Ali."[36]

"Ali thought Malcolm was the smartest black man on the face of the earth, because everything he said made sense," Pacheco remembered. "Malcolm X was bright as hell, convincing, charismatic in the way that great leaders and martyrs are. It certainly rubbed off on Ali." The fighter never bought the idea that all white people were evil. He had many white associates that he liked and trusted. "There were no white devils that he could see," but "the Muslims filled a deep need in him, especially Malcolm X."[37]

As 1963 progressed, Elijah Muhammad was becoming more fearful that Malcolm was overshadowing him, and Malcolm was learning more about Elijah's hypocrisy and immorality. The NOI leader determined that he must rid himself of his more intelligent, articulate, and charismatic follower.

In August 1963, Malcolm defied Elijah Muhammad's order to all members of the NOI by attending the mainstream civil rights organization's massive March on Washington.[38] Malcolm's remarks in Harlem a few days after President Kennedy's assassination gave Elijah Muhammad the ammunition he needed to try to rein in his putative subordinate. Malcolm said that the assassination was an instance of "the chickens coming home to roost." "Being an old farm boy myself," he added, "chickens coming home to roost never did make me sad; they've always made me glad."[39] Malcolm said he meant "that the hate in white men had not stopped with the killing of defenseless black people, but that hate, allowed to spread unchecked, finally had struck down this country's Chief of State."[40] There is no question that Malcolm meant what he said. When news of the assassination reached him on the afternoon of November 22, he was with a group of NOI associates at a restaurant. Malcolm's immediate response was, "That devil is dead."[41]

Elijah decreed that Malcolm must be silenced for ninety days. On February 10, 1964, one of his former assistants at his Mosque No. 7 told him that he had been asked to wire Malcolm's car with a bomb. "And then I knew . . . any death-talk for me could have been approved of—if not actually initiated—by only one man." He was left in "a state of emotional shock. I was like someone who for twelve years had had an inseparable, beautiful marriage—and then suddenly one morning at breakfast the marriage partner had thrust across the table divorce papers." Realizing that the man to whom he had given total allegiance now wanted him dead, Malcolm "became able finally to muster the nerve, and the strength, to start facing the facts, to think for myself."[42]

It was during the ninety-day period of silencing that Cassius Clay's title fight with Liston would take place. The row with Elijah notwithstanding, Clay invited Malcolm and his family to stay with him in Miami while he prepared for the fight. Word of Clay's attraction to the Nation of Islam had been trickling out. In February, it escalated. A *Miami Herald* reporter interviewed Clay's father, who confirmed that his son had joined the Black Muslims and said that they were ruining him.[43]

Malcolm's affection for Clay was genuine, but more than friendship was now involved in his efforts to get as close to the boxer as possible. Once he had seen the light—or the darkness—about Elijah Muhammad, Malcolm began to plan a new black nationalist organization. Though he plainly had no difficulty in drawing notice himself, he saw Clay as "a one-man publicity machine, capable of attracting Malcolm's desired audience: young, idealistic, angry black men."[44]

"This fight is the truth," Malcolm told Clay. "It's the Cross and the Crescent fighting in the prize ring—for the first time. It's a modern Crusades—a Christian and a Muslim facing each other with television to beam it off Telstar for the whole world to see what happens!" Malcolm gave the challenger greater confidence in the outcome by asking him rhetorically, "Do you think Allah has brought about all this intending for you to leave the ring as anything but the champion?"[45]

But Malcolm's rival wasn't about to cede Clay and the potential publicity he could bring to a movement. A few days before the fight, the

NOI leader called Clay and warned him that "all good Muslims should stay away from Malcolm" while he was suspended.[46] At this point, Clay stuck with his friend and mentor.

"Float Like a Butterfly; Sting Like a Bee": The Fight

> *Yes, the crowd did not dream*
> *When they laid down their money*
> *That they would see*
> *A total eclipse of the Sonny!*
> *I am the Greatest!*
> —Cassius Clay, "A Song of
> Myself" (1964)[47]

After he goaded Liston into giving him a title bout, Clay had begun working on a psychological warfare campaign. "The big thing for me was observing how Liston acted *out* of the ring," Ali told Alex Haley in a *Playboy* interview published in October 1964. Clay had "set out to make [Liston] think what I wanted him thinking; that all I was was some clown. . . . The more out of shape and overconfident I could get him to be, the better."[48]

When Liston arrived at the Miami airport, Clay was there to escalate his psychological campaign. "Liston came down off the plane, all cool, and the press was ganged around waiting for an interview. That was when I rushed in the scene, hollering, 'Chump! Big ugly bear! I'm going to whip you right now!' Stuff like that." Clay kept up his madman act. When Liston was taken inside a locked airport lounge, Clay stood outside, shouting at the top of his lungs. "You think I'm jiving, chump? I'll fight you free, right here!" It was all an act, Ali later told Haley. "I didn't want nobody in Miami, except at my camp, thinking I wasn't crazy. I didn't want nobody never thinking nothing about I had any fighting ability."[49]

Plainly, Liston was overconfident. "He's a fag," the champion said of Clay. "I'm a man."[50] When his assistants warned that Clay was the real thing, Sonny said, "I'll put the evil eye on this faggot at the weigh-in and psych him right out of the fight."[51] But Clay turned the weigh-in on the morning of the fight, February 25, into a circus in which he was the ringmaster. He arrived early, wearing a blue denim jacket with the words "Bear Huntin'" embroidered on it. He and his assistant trainer, Bundini Brown, both began shouting: "Float like a butterfly! Sting like a bee!" Clay's "eyes were bugging out" and he jumped "around like a mental patient." His pulse and his blood pressure were both sky high. His outbursts were described in the press as "hysterical." Yet when his personal physician took his vital signs an hour later the doctor said, "it was the most amazing thing ... the pulse was at fifty-four, normal for him, and his blood pressure was one-twenty over eighty. It was all an act."[52]

Hardly anyone gave Clay a chance of winning the bout, but he had a plan for the fight, and his crazy antics leading up to it were part of that design. "I knew that Liston, overconfident as he was, and helped by reading what all of the newspapers were saying, he never was going to train to fight more than two rounds."[53]

Clay "floated like a butterfly," dancing away from Liston's blows. The champ tired after two rounds, and Clay pummeled his opponent in the sixth. After the round, Liston returned to his corner. Ali recalled, "I happened to be looking right at Liston when that warning buzzer sounded, and I didn't believe it when he spat out his mouthpiece. . . . And then something just told me he wasn't coming out! I give a whoop and come off that stool like it was red hot." Clay "went dancing around the ring, hollering down at them reporters, 'Eat your words! Eat! Eat!'" He "hollered at the people, 'I am the *king*!'"[54]

Robert Lipsyte, a twenty-six-year-old features writer whom the *New York Times* sent to cover a fight that the paper hadn't expected to be significant enough to dispatch its main boxing writer, was sufficiently young and hip to "get" Clay. He summed up the night nicely—and generationally: "Poetry and youth and joy had triumphed over the 8–1 odds."[55]

After his victory, Clay went to a small black hotel with Malcolm, star running back Jim Brown of the Cleveland Browns, and a few others to rest and discuss serious issues beyond the world of sports.[56] Though not a member of the Nation, Brown agreed with many of the organization's stated goals and admired Malcolm X. "Well, Brown," Malcolm said to him, "don't you think it's time for this young man to stop spouting off and get serious?" The football player concurred. Later, when Clay and Brown were alone, the former talked about the rift between the NOI's leader and Malcolm. Clay indicated that he was not going to be able to continue to follow Malcolm. He told Jim Brown "how Elijah Muhammad was such a little man physically, but such a great man, and he was going to have to reject Malcolm and choose Elijah."[57]

"The World Is All Shook up about What I Believe"— Cassius Clay Becomes Muhammad Ali and Breaks with Malcolm

Nobody asks other people about their religion. But now I am the champion, I am the king, so it seems the world is all shook up about what I believe.
—Cassius Clay
(February 27, 1964)[58]

The sixties had arrived in the world of sport with a huge shockwave on the night of February 25, 1964. At his press conference the next morning, the new world champion seemed a different man, in keeping with what he had privately discussed with Brown and Malcolm in the wee hours that morning. He was subdued. "I'm through talking," he declared. "All I have to do is be a nice, clean gentleman." When a reporter asked him if he was a "card-carrying member of the Black Muslims," Clay responded with a touch of anger. "Card-carrying, what does that mean?" He went on to say, "I believe in Allah and peace. I don't try to move into white neighborhoods. I don't want to marry a white woman." In a very "sixties" statement, Clay declared: "I know where I'm going and I know the truth and I don't have to be what you want me to be. I'm free to be what I want."[59]

Elijah Muhammad had not had much interest in Clay until he won the heavyweight championship, which the Messenger had not thought possible. Now that Clay had won, Elijah saw him as an asset for his operation and a potential replacement for Malcolm X.[60] He promptly announced to a Nation meeting in Chicago that the new champion was one of his disciples. A group of reporters found Clay and Malcolm eating breakfast the next morning and asked the former about Elijah Muhammad's statement. "That is true, and I am proud of it," Clay said, adding that he didn't know why there was so much commotion about it.

Clay insisted that "followers of Allah are the sweetest people in the world" and credited his new religion with bringing him the "inner peace" that made it possible for him to defeat Liston. "I like white people. I like my own people," he said sincerely. "They can live together without infringing on each other." Noting that Islam means "peace," he said, "You can't condemn a man for wanting peace. If you do, you condemn peace itself."[61]

The way Clay saw the Nation of Islam was vastly different from the reality of Elijah Muhammad's racket. Mainstream white commentators were aghast. The World Boxing Association threatened to remove the new champion's title for behavior "detrimental to boxing."[62] Civil rights leaders were angry with Clay's embracing of an organization that opposed integration. Floyd Patterson offered to fight him for free, "to get the championship away from the Black Muslims."[63]

The new champion was inseparable from Malcolm X in the early days after the Liston fight, but Elijah Muhammad was intent on splitting them apart. The assignment of the new name was part of that effort and was soon followed by emissaries from Chicago visiting Ali in Harlem, calling for his loyalty to the true "Messenger" and the rejection of the "pretender."

The decision to accept the new name bestowed on him by the leader of the Nation was a critical turning point in the life of the man who would be known as Muhammad Ali. Elijah Muhammad's offer of a new Muslim name was not without strings—chains—attached. "Muhammad Ali is what I will give to him *as long as he* believes in Allah and *follows me* [emphasis added]."[64] The new champion had just proclaimed himself to "free to be what I want." Now he was being called upon to surrender that freedom—his very name—to the dictatorial leader of a cult. He had always loved his birth name. The day after the self-appointed Messenger had changed the fighter's name, the new champion told a press conference in Louisville, "I plan to fight under the name Cassius Clay, unless I'm ordered not to."[65]

Obviously, those are not the words of a free person. In effect, he was saying to white society, "I don't have to be what you want me to be," *but I do have to be what Mr. Muhammad wants me to be.* It was a far cry from the independence that he had asserted as recently as the fall of 1963: "But I'm the boss, I'm the onliest boss."[66]

"Elijah Muhammad had given me my name," Ali recalled in his 2004 autobiography, *The Soul of a Butterfly.* "I felt that he had set me free! I was proud of my name and dedicated to the Nation of Islam as Elijah presented it. At that point in my journey, I just wasn't ready to question his teaching."[67]

Clay's affection for Malcolm was genuine, and accepting the new name meant breaking decisively with him. Rejecting the new name, on the other hand, might have cost him his life.[68] Ali chose to go with the "Messenger." When Alex Haley visited him after he had received his new name, Muhammad Ali told him: "You don't just buck Mr. Muhammad and get away with it. I don't want to talk about him [Malcolm] no more."[69]

The loss of his close friendship with the former Cassius Clay was devastating to Malcolm. Both men undertook overseas trips during the ensuing months. Their paths crossed in Accra, Ghana. Seeing his recently close friend, Malcolm called out to him, "Brother Muhammad! Brother Muhammad!" Ali's response was cruel: "You left the Honorable Elijah Muhammad. That was the wrong thing to do, Brother Malcolm."[70] It was not Muhammad Ali's finest hour. Nor were there many subsequent fine hours in this respect in 1964, as he attacked Malcolm and other former friends on whom Elijah Muhammad had turned.

"The fact is that my being a Muslim moved me from the sports pages to the front pages," Ali declared. "And because I'm a Muslim, I was welcomed like a king on my tour of Africa and the Middle East. I'm the first world champion that ever toured the world that he is champion of."[71] As he recognized, it was his conversion to Islam that raised Muhammad Ali to the position of world historical figure.

To assure that his new propagandist would toe the NOI line and not be free to be what he wanted, Elijah Muhammad dispatched his son to accompany Ali on the Africa trip. Everywhere the champ went, he was mobbed by cheering crowds. He sampled local food, kissed babies, shook hands, smiled and waved. In Ghana, he shouted, "Who's the king?" "You!" the crowd yelled back. "They never turned out like this for Queen Elizabeth," said a man in the crowd at Accra.[72] "At that moment in young Cassius's career, Malcolm said, "he had captured the imagination and support of the entire dark world."[73]

Ali met with the leaders of Ghana and Egypt, Kwame Nkrumah and Gamal Abdel Nasser. Both men were autocratic rulers, but Ali had great praise for them. Though he had been given his new name several weeks earlier, it was on his trip to Africa, basking in the adulation of Muslim crowds, that Cassius Clay became Muhammad Ali.[74]

Malcolm's Emancipation—Mecca and Beyond

> In the past, yes, I have made sweeping
> indictments of *all* white people. I never
> will be guilty of that again.
> —Al-Hajj Malik El-Shabazz
> (Malcolm X) after his spring
> 1964 Mecca pilgrimage[75]

Realizing that the man he had followed for twelve years was a con man might have been the best thing that ever happened to Malcolm X—apart, of course, from the fact that it led to his murder less than a year later.

"For twelve long years," he wrote, "I lived in the narrow-minded confines of the strait-jacket world created by a strong belief that Elijah Muhammad was a messenger direct from God and my faith in what I now see to be a pseudo-religious philosophy that he preaches."[76] His rupture with the man he had seen as holy, quickly followed by the loss of his friend Cassius, left Malcolm adrift and seeking new answers—indeed, asking new questions.

Malcolm spoke in early April at a gathering in Cleveland organized by the Congress of Racial Equality. His address, "The Ballot or the Bullet," is among the most important statements from 1964. He pushed for unity among African Americans (a term he used and argued for in the speech) to achieve their common purposes. "All of us have suffered here, in this country, political oppression at the hands of the white man, economic exploitation at the hands of the white man, and social degradation at the hands of the white man," he pointed out. "Now in speaking like this, it doesn't mean that we're anti-white, but it does mean we're anti-exploitation, we're anti-degradation, we're anti-oppression. And if the white man doesn't want us to be anti-him, let him stop oppressing and exploiting and degrading us."

"Nineteen sixty-four threatens to be the most explosive year America has ever witnessed," Malcolm said. "It isn't that time is running out—time has run out!" Saying that he viewed "America through the eyes of the victim," he declared, "I don't see any American dream; I see an American nightmare. . . . You let that white man know, if this is a country of freedom, let it be a country of freedom; and if it's not a country of freedom, change it."[77]

◆ ◆ ◆

In mid-April, Malcolm flew to Cairo before proceeding to Jedda and, he hoped, Mecca.[78] In Cairo he saw throngs of Muslims of all complexions headed for Mecca being warm and friendly, and recalled, "The feeling hit me that there really wasn't a color problem here. The effect was as though I had just stepped out of a prison."[79]

While he was in Jedda awaiting approval to go on to Mecca, Malcolm began a "radical alteration" in his "whole outlook about 'white' men." There he started to conclude that "white man," as the term was commonly used, "described attitudes and actions toward the black man, and toward all other non-white men," much more than skin color. He said he had seen in the Muslim world "men with white complexions [who] were more genuinely brotherly than anyone else had ever been."[80]

Malcolm's hajj led him finally to understand that Elijah Muhammad's teachings were incompatible with the Qur'an.[81] As his time in Mecca went on, Malcolm's understanding of the degree to which he had been misled by Elijah Muhammad crystallized. "There on a Holy World hilltop," he said, "I realized how very dangerous it is for people to hold any human being in such esteem, especially to consider anyone some sort of 'divinely guided' and 'protected' person."[82] On the trip, he changed his name to El-Hajj Malik El-Shabazz, though to most people he would always remain known as Malcolm X.

At the end of June, he announced the creation of the Organization of Afro-American Unity, with the aim of promoting joint international action among people of African ancestry across the Western Hemisphere. Elijah Muhammad had taken Muhammad Ali from him, but Malcolm was still far more a focus of public attention than was the "Messenger"—and now it was even worse for the latter, because Malcolm was a powerful rival, not within, but outside the Nation.

"The die is set and Malcolm shall not escape," Louis X (later known as Louis Farrakhan) wrote in late 1964. "Such a man is worthy of death."[83] "Hypocrites like Malcolm should have their heads cut off," Elijah Muhammad said to Louis X in March 1964.[84] A cartoon appeared in the NOI paper, *Muhammad Speaks*, showing Malcolm's severed head bouncing along as it grew devil's ears.[85] Attacks on Malcolm's family escalated, including a firebombing of their home on February 14, 1965. A week later, Malcolm was shot and killed at Harlem's Audubon Ballroom. A member of the Nation from Newark confessed to the murder. The convictions of two other NOI members who were long imprisoned were finally overturned in 2021.[86]

Muhammad Ali, Malcolm X, 1964, the Sixties, and Beyond

> You can't separate peace from freedom, because
> no one can be at peace unless he has his freedom.
> —El-Hajj Malik el-Shabazz
> (Malcolm X) (January 7, 1965)[87]

Muhammad Ali and Malcolm X each began 1964 with one name and ended the year with another. Both name changes were related to their intertwined quests for what practically everyone seemed to be seeking in 1964: *freedom*—and both were stimulated by Elijah Muhammad. The difference was that Malcolm X chose to take a new name; Cassius Clay was told to take a name given to him by the Nation of Islam leader. Malcolm's taking a new name was part of his declaration of independence; Clay's was part of his acceptance of a new dependence.

Both men were major figures on the American—and, as the year progressed, world—scene in 1964, but the import and influence of both grew much greater after that year, despite the fact that Malcolm outlived calendar 1964 by less than two months.

"Even his sharpest critics recognized his brilliance—often wild, unpredictable and eccentric," the *New York Post* said following Malcolm's murder, "but nevertheless possessing promise that must now remain unrealized."[88] That assessment was right about his brilliance but proved to be wrong in concluding that, because of his death, Malcolm's promise would remain unrealized. While Muhammad Ali became larger than life during his own lifetime, Malcolm X would become larger than life in his death.

◆ ◆ ◆

The cultural and historical impact of Cassius Clay/Muhammad Ali was both enormous and spread across several different sectors of society. It is important to realize that reactions to Cassius Clay (and even more to Muhammad Ali) were generational. Here was something new in the world: a "hip" boxer. "Here was this funny, beautiful, skilled young man. . . . He combined Little Richard and Gorgeous George," young *New York Times* sportswriter Robert Lipsyte said. "He was not the sort of sweet dumb pet that [older] writers were accustomed to. . . . They didn't see the fun in it. And, above all, it was fun."[89]

Though Clay's experiences as a young black man were very different from those of white middle-class baby boomers, the latter could relate to him. It was in 1964 that the ascending youth culture began decisively to throw off the acceptance of gerontocracy—hierarchal authority based on age. The audacious but playful challenges that the young boxer made against the established order very much fit with that new dynamic.[90]

His impact on black youth was even more direct and powerful. More than a year before Clay won the title, Eric Springer wrote in the *Pittsburgh Courier* that he was a new type of cultural hero: a symbol "of change that is occurring in our youth." The writer linked Clay with the courageous young activists in the South, such as the students who had integrated Central High School in Little Rock in 1957 and James Meredith entering the University of Mississippi in 1962.[91]

Clearly, Clay/Ali was a major force in promoting the "black is beautiful" concept and black pride. Following Ali's ill-advised 1980 fight with Larry Holmes, an elderly African American attendant in a men's room in Caesars Palace, the bout's venue, was asked by sportswriter Jerry Izenberg for whom he had bet. The reply encapsulated a major part of Ali's impact on black Americans: "Come on, mister, you gotta know I bet on the man who gave me my dignity, Muhammad Ali." "It wasn't an epitaph," Izenberg said. "It was a eulogy."[92]

In sports, Clay/Ali began the revolt of the black athlete, which would become widely noticed in 1967 and '68 with Harry Edwards's proposal for a boycott by black American athletes of the 1968 Olympics and the "Black Power" salutes on the medal stand by sprinters Tommie Smith and John Carlos at those games. As Eldridge Cleaver said, "What white America demands in her black champions is a brilliant, powerful body, and a dull bestial mind—a tiger in the ring and a pussycat outside the ring."[93] Muhammad Ali shattered that expectation.

"Meet the Beatles"

In popular culture viewed through a wide-angle lens, Clay/Ali was a major force.

The Beatles' second appearance on *Ed Sullivan* was from Miami, nine days before the Liston-Clay title bout there. Two days later, "hip" publicist Harold Conrad arranged for the Beatles to stop by the Fifth Street Gym, where Clay was training, for a photo op. Clay was said never to have heard of the Fab Four and they knew almost nothing about "The Greatest," but it was a publicity opportunity not to be passed up. It turned out to be one of those 1964 moments from which the sixties were emerging: "a meeting of the New, two acts that would mark the sixties."[94]

When the Beatles arrived and found that Clay was late, they were annoyed, but their mood changed as soon as the fighter burst through the door, laughing. "Hello there, Beatles!" Clay yelled. "We ought to do some road shows together; we'll get rich!" Photographer Harry

Benson said that Clay "mesmerized" the Beatles. Young, fresh, innocent, handsome, playful, Cassius seemed to be a darker-skinned version
of them. Clay said the Beatles had come to be seen with him because
they needed publicity. The gym "shook with laughter and screaming
and poetry," Lipsyte wrote. "The five young men danced and laughed
and cavorted like co-conspirators in a gigantic hoax."

The photo op was silly but memorable. For one series of shots, with
the band members standing in a row, Clay pretended to punch George
Harrison and the rest fell down. The Domino Theory in action.[95]

Cassius Clay and the Beatles, Miami, February 1964.

The highjinks with the Beatles were far from Cassius Clay's only cross-
over into music. He had recorded a passing good rendition of Ben
E. King's "Stand by Me" the previous September. Columbia released
the record the day after he defeated Liston, and it sold more than
100,000 copies in just over a week. Early in March, he recorded a song
written for him by Sam Cooke.[96] Clay said of his singing that he was
"better and prettier than Chubby Checker."[97]

But the new champion's connections with music go much farther.
Elvis Presley had brought "race music" to white American youth in
the fifties. In the sixties, Cassius Clay/Muhammad Ali was conveying
to white people another African American cultural creation, one of
which almost all of them had previously been ignorant. Though his
art as a boxer was more noted than his verbal skills, much of Clay's

impact on American culture was the result of his being a verbal artist. His rhyming boasts and put-downs of opponents were straight out of the African American formalized street corner game known as "the dozens," in which males compete in exchanging insults as a crowd looks on.[98]

In this way, Ali was a bridge between the slave origins of this form of verbal art and the emergence of hip-hop music in the late 1970s and 1980s. Some have gone as far as arguing that he was the first rapper. His use of the insulting rhyming couplets of the dozens to taunt and show disdain for opponents is similar to what later artists in the genre would do.[99] He is mentioned in what is often classified as the first hip-hop record, the Sugarhill Gang's 1977 "Rapper's Delight" ("I got more clothes than Muhammad Ali"). One critic has contended that Clay's 1964 victory over Liston, following all his rhyming boasts and predictions of victory and greatness constituted the birth of hip-hop.[100] Public Enemy's Chuck D has said that Ali was a boyhood hero of his as "one of the first black men to come along and speak his mind."[101] That assessment, of course, points to Ali's influence far beyond the world of music.

"No Vietcong Ever Called Me Nigger"

Muhammad Ali's influence on American society grew exponentially when he refused to be drafted into the military in February 1966. That stance put him in the forefront of African American opposition to the American war in Vietnam. SNCC had become the first important black organization officially to come out against the war only six weeks earlier, stating: "We recoil with horror at the inconsistency of a supposedly 'free' society where responsibility to freedom is equated with the responsibility to lend oneself to military aggression."[102] Ali's often-quoted statement, "Man, I ain't got no quarrel with them Vietcong" was ridiculed by many at the time. Yet he courageously added, "How can I shoot those poor people? Just take me to jail."[103] Or, as he is said to have put it directly, "No Vietcong ever called me nigger."[104]

His boxing championship was taken from him when he refused to join the military. But he had become another kind of champion. As

1967 progressed and the war in Vietnam further regressed, Ali became a huge hero—"The Greatest" in a new way—to the largely white anti-war movement. Massive crowds turned out for his appearances on college campuses.

Jerry Izenberg captured some of what Muhammad Ali was to the sixties when he wrote in 2016 that his "nonstop staccato banter" became "the background music to drastic changes in America itself, during the 1960s and 70s."[105] The reality, though, is that he provided the era that began in 1964 with much more than its backbeat.

♦♦♦

> Malcolm was our manhood, our living black
> manhood! . . . our own black shining Prince!
> —Ossie Davis
> (February 27, 1965)[106]

Following the outbreak of riots in Harlem and Rochester in July 1964, a meeting of several African American writers, artists, and intellectuals concluded that "Malcolm X alone could secure the allegiance of Negroes at the bottom." "Malcolm cannot be corrupted," said Clarence Jones, Martin Luther King's legal counsel, "and the Negroes know this and therefore respect him. They also know he comes from the lower depths, as they do, and regard him as one of their own." Though none of the black intellectuals present was a follower of Malcolm, all were reported to have "expressed an almost reverent respect for him and predicted that he would play a front role in the racial struggle."

"The people in Harlem," novelist John Oliver Killens said at this 1964 meeting, "must be made to feel that their lives are worth something. No white man has ever been executed for killing a Negro in this country." Clarence Jones added that "Harlem's teen-agers and young adults had seen too much police corruption to have any respect for the law."[107]

Though his murder six months later prevented Malcolm from playing his "front role in the racial struggle" in the flesh, that role would continue to grow in subsequent years. In 1964, he had reached a new insight that "the white man is not inherently evil, but America's racist society influences him to act evilly. The society has produced and nourishes a psychology which brings out the lowest, most base part of human beings."[108]

Malcolm pulled no punches in stating the extent of the problem: "Indeed, how *can* white society atone for enslaving, for raping, for unmanning, for otherwise brutalizing *millions* of human beings, for centuries?"[109] It is a question that continues today to be central to the issue of "Which Way, America?"

Malcolm's legacy was greatly enhanced by the publication of his autobiography, as told to Alex Haley, in October 1965. *Time* magazine would name it one of the ten most influential books of the twentieth century.[110] "Sometimes," Malcolm said to Haley in the interviews for that book, "I have dared to dream to myself that one day, history may even say that my voice—which disturbed the white man's smugness, and his arrogance, and his complacency—that my voice helped to save America from a grave, possibly even a fatal catastrophe."[111] The bottom line is that he *did* help to move America in that direction, even if the jury is still out on the "fatal catastrophe" part.

Malcolm, comedian and activist Dick Gregory said, "spoke like a poor man and walked like a king."[112] He has continued to walk that way ever since.

◆ ◆ ◆

Years later, after Ali had seen Elijah Muhammad for what he was, he came to realize that Malcolm had been "a visionary, ahead of us all." Ali said that the NOI leader had helped blacks not to look down on themselves but that "Malcolm was the first to discover the truth, that color doesn't make a man a devil. It is the heart, soul and mind that define a person."

"Malcolm X was a great thinker and an even greater friend," wrote Ali. "I might never have become a Muslim if it hadn't been for Malcolm. If I could go back and do it all over again, I would never have turned my back on him."[113]

9

"This Damned Vietnam Thing"

"We've Got to Conduct Ourselves Like Men"

Lyndon Johnson with some of his Vietnam advisers, March 1964.

You know, everybody is ignorant, only on different subjects.
　　　　　　　　　　　　　　　　　　—Will Rogers[1]

W HEN LYNDON JOHNSON SAID "I do" at his marriage ceremony to the presidency on Air Force One in Dallas on November 22, 1963, he found his bride already pregnant with a war conceived before he married her—a war with several fathers, both French and American. Some believed that John F. Kennedy had planned to abort this embryonic war. Be that as it may, Johnson brought it to term and became its stepfather; he adopted the war, sired by others, and made it his own, bringing it up rapidly.

◆ ◆ ◆

"We're doing just fine, except for this damned Vietnam thing," Johnson remarked to Senator Richard Russell in June. "The businessmen are doing wonderful. They're up 12, 14 percent investment over last year. The tax bill has just worked out wonderfully. They're only 2.6 percent of the married people unemployed. . . . And 16 percent of these youngsters, and I'll have them all employed."[2]

That "damned Vietnam thing" was the biggest cloud on the generally sunny American horizon in 1964. It was in this year that Johnson took the fateful steps that would lead the nation into the morass of the Vietnam War and thereby undermine his great accomplishments. Nothing played a larger role in transforming the early, hopeful, coming together that was evident in 1964 into the largely hopeless, coming apart that occurred later in the sixties than America's expanding misadventure in Vietnam. The Lyndon Johnson and Richard Nixon administrations literally tore apart the Vietnamese nation; in doing so through a war that was seemingly without purpose or end, those political leaders also tore apart the American nation. We are still living with the consequences.

The massive tragedy that the American war in Vietnam became was a tragedy precisely because it need never have happened. Decisions that were made in 1964 set the course to disaster.

Lyndon Johnson took those steps in full awareness both that success would be almost impossible and that the bad foreign war would destroy his good domestic war on poverty. After Johnson left the White House, he told historian Doris Kearns that he "knew from the start" that "if I left the woman I really loved—the Great Society—in order to get involved with that bitch of a war on the other side of the world, then I would lose everything at home. All my programs. All my hopes to feed the hungry and shelter the homeless. All my dreams to provide education and medical care to the browns and the blacks and the lame and the poor. . . . Oh, I could see it all coming all right."[3]

Why, then did he go ahead and do what he believed would destroy all his hopes and dreams and accomplishments? Few questions about 1964 and American history are as important.

What We Don't Know Can Hurt Us— A Few Points about Vietnamese History

I prefer to sniff French shit for five years
than eat Chinese shit for the rest of my life.
—Ho Chi Minh (1946)[4]

The American War in Vietnam was about *freedom* and different, conflicting meanings of that word.

By the time the United States began a significant involvement in Vietnam, providing financial support for France's military struggle to retain its colony in Indochina in 1950, the American definition of *freedom* in any international context had come to be colored by the concept of *the free world*, a term that appears to have been first used in October 1941, when Franklin Roosevelt adviser Mordecai Ezekiel started a publication of that name to promote the struggle against the Nazis.[5]

As long as the free world was understood in opposition to Hitler, the Soviet Union was, incongruously, part of it. After V-E Day, however, a chill came over relations between the recent anti-fascist Allies to Germany's east and west. The operative worldview from the later 1940s onward juxtaposed "the free world" to those portions of the planet controlled by communists. *Freedom* became simply an antonym for *communist*.

These Cold War concepts held little meaning for people in Vietnam—or, for that matter, most other areas of the Third World. To many, probably most, Vietnamese, *freedom* meant independence from foreign domination, with which they and their ancestors were all-too-familiar through much of their history. Vietnamese history, though, was a subject on which the ignorance of almost all Americans was nearly complete when the 1960s began. What little those Americans familiar with the region thought they knew centered on the French experience in Indochina. The deeper, very long history of Southeast Asia was unknown to all but a few academic specialists who studied the region. And most of those in the State Department who did have such knowledge were hounded out of the government on the basis of allegedly being insufficiently anti-Communist during the McCarthy hysteria of the early fifties.[6] Beginning a decade later, the United States was to pay an enormous price for this ignorance.

The first and most salient point that emerges from Vietnam's past is that extraordinarily long periods of Chinese domination both greatly influenced Vietnamese culture and left the Vietnamese people with a deep and abiding dislike and distrust of China.

It has long been the Vietnamese way to borrow whatever they found useful from the practices of those who invaded them, while simultaneously rejecting and struggling against domination by those outsiders. They did this with the Chinese over many centuries and with the French in the nineteenth and twentieth centuries, when Vietnamese nationalists took up European ideas, adapted them to Vietnamese circumstances, and used them against the Europeans. Nor have the Vietnamese, either during their struggle against the United States or in the decades since their victory, hesitated to adopt those American ideas and ways that appeared likely to be beneficial to them, including, wholeheartedly in recent years, capitalism. The Vietnamese have never seen any reason to reject a good idea just because it came from an enemy.

Ho Chi Minh expressed the feelings of his countrymen toward the Chinese when he told colleagues in 1946 why, after years of leading a struggle to free Vietnam from French colonialism, he was inviting the French back in temporarily to replace the Chinese (then under the nationalist Chaing Kai-shek): "You fools! Don't you realize what it means if the Chinese remain? Don't you remember your history? The last time the Chinese came, they stayed for a thousand years. The French are foreigners. They are weak. Colonialism is dying. The white man is finished in Asia. But if the Chinese stay now, they will never go." Ho concluded with a metaphor that nicely captures Vietnamese feelings about China: "As for me, I prefer to sniff French shit for five years than eat Chinese shit for the rest of my life."[7]

But what about when the Chinese and Vietnamese became communist—wouldn't that make them natural allies? In a word: No. At the 1954 Geneva Conference that ended the First Indochina War, Pham Van Dong, the head of the Vietnamese Communist delegation, said Communist China's Zhou Enlai "has double-crossed us." In 1963–1964 and later, Mao Zedong maneuvered to have the war continue in Vietnam to weaken the Vietnamese as well as to tie up American power. Mao, Pham Van Dong later said bitterly, "was always ready to fight to the last Vietnamese."[8]

In 1979, less than four years after the Vietnamese Communists had reunified the whole country under their rule, Communist China invaded northern Vietnam and the "comrades" fought a brief but bloody border war that killed tens of thousands in less than a month.

History and geography eclipse ideology.

What has this to do with the United States in 1964? One of the principal American rationales for fighting in Vietnam was to block Chinese expansion. In fact, given the fundamental hostility of the Vietnamese toward China—a strong, unified Vietnam under a popular national leader, Ho, would provide the best bulwark against China, irrespective of communism.

In 1967, Cambodia's Prince Norodom Sihanouk noted that the communism that Washington was trying to destroy in Vietnam was, "in no sense inspired by China, but is hostile to Chinese expansionism." Sihanouk stated that Vietnamese communism actually constituted "a nationalist barrier between China and the rest of South-East Asia. The truth is that America, by waging war against Vietnam, is playing China's game."[9]

That line is worth repeating, with emphasis, because it summarizes the horrible truth about the misadventure in Southeast Asia upon which President Johnson launched the United States in 1964: *"America, by waging war against Vietnam, is playing China's game."*

"Foresight Is 20/20":
The Book That Could Have Averted a Disaster,
The Quiet American

> Why don't you just go away, Pyle, without causing
> trouble? I never knew a man who had better
> motives for all the trouble he caused.
> —Fowler to Pyle in *The Quiet*
> *American* (1955)[10]

On rare occasions, an author foresees future events with such clarity that it is stunning to read his or her book after those events have transpired and realize how different things might have been had the work's prophecies been heeded at the time. Such surely was the case with Graham Greene's novel *The Quiet American.*

Written while Greene was living in Saigon in the last years of French Indochina in the early 1950s and published in 1955, this novel foresaw the deepening involvement of the United States in Vietnam, the wrongheaded reasons why it would happen, and the inevitability of the ultimate failure of the misadventure. Lyndon Johnson began in 1964 to act out the script of the tragedy Greene had written:

The failure by the United States to understand the people in Vietnam and their history and culture:

When undercover CIA agent Alden Pyle (who represents the United States in the novel) says of the Vietnamese, "They don't want communism," journalist Thomas Fowler responds, "They want enough rice . . . They don't want to be shot at. They want one day to be much the same as another. They don't want our white skins around telling them what they want."[11]

The belief that the Vietnamese could be placed in Western Cold War categories and won for "Democracy":

Pyle "didn't even hear what I said; he was absorbed already in the dilemmas of Democracy and the responsibilities of the West; he was determined—I learnt that very soon—to do good, not to any individual person but to a country, a continent, a world."[12] Here was the essence of the sort of American thinking that led to the tragedy in Vietnam. "In a way you could say they died for democracy," says the CIA's Pyle later. "I wouldn't know how to translate that into Vietnamese," responds Fowler.[13]

The prejudice against the French that would keep Americans from learning anything from their failure:

"These people are so friendly when you treat them right," says Pyle. "The French don't seem to know how to handle them."[14] Later, Pyle confidently and foolishly proclaims, "At least they won't hate us like they hate the French."[15]

The disastrous results of well-meaning but misinformed intervention:

"I never knew a man who had better motives for all the trouble he caused."[16]

And the end that would turn out to be what could have been had in the beginning without all the bloodshed:

"You know better than I do that we can't win. . . . But we are professionals: we have to go on fighting till the politicians tell us to stop. Probably they will get together and agree to the same peace that we could have had at the beginning, making nonsense of all these years."[17]

The Quiet American seemed to say it all—so much so that during the American war in Vietnam, American journalists who had been "in-country" for a while gave copies of the book to their newly arriving colleagues.[18]

If only American policymakers had read the novel and understood its accuracy before, as Greene put it, "he comes blundering in and people have to die for his mistakes."[19]

"We've Got to Conduct Ourselves Like Men":
LBJ Chooses to Pursue the Impossible Nightmare

It's damned easy to get in a war, but it's gonna be
awfully hard to ever extricate yourself if you get in.
                                    —Lyndon B. Johnson (May 1964)[20]

What would JFK have done? That has long been among the most perplex-
ing questions about the American misadventure in Vietnam. There is
no easy or conclusive answer.

Kennedy had seen the folly of the French war in Vietnam in the
early 1950s. He had no desire to deepen the United States involvement that he inherited from the Eisenhower administration. In
September 1963, he said of the South Vietnamese: "In the final analysis, it is their war. They are the ones who have to win it or lose it."
In October, he said, "It would be our hope to lessen the number of
Americans" in Vietnam by the end of the year. Another piece of the
plan was to make clear that the United States would leave. "That is
our object, to bring Americans home," Kennedy declared at a press
conference eight days before his death.[21] We shall, of course, never
know whether Kennedy would have carried out a complete American withdrawal.

Like his predecessor, Lyndon Johnson was ambivalent about Vietnam. When the French sought direct American intervention in 1954,
LBJ had made clear that he no desire to get involved in a faraway
war, declaring: "I am against sending American GIs into the mud and
muck of Indochina on a blood-letting spree to perpetuate colonialism
and white man's exploitation in Asia."[22] He understood from the start
that victory would be nearly impossible. But a combination of political
considerations and his own fear that he would not seem "manly" led
him to ride off in a cowboy hat on a trail that he knew would be highly
likely to lead to disaster. Disinterested in war though he was, Johnson
felt a need to take bellicose stands.

In the early days of his presidency, Vietnam was not a major item on
Johnson's agenda, though it was plainly a potential source of difficulty.
Or worse. He had "a terrible feeling that something has grabbed me
around the ankles and won't let go," Johnson told his aide Bill Moyers

one evening during his first weeks in office.[23] The problem, though, proved to be more that he wouldn't let go of it than that it wouldn't let go of him.

Looking back on the information he was receiving about Vietnam in the early days of his presidency when he wrote his memoir, Johnson concluded that he was getting "an excess of wishful thinking" that had "misled" him "into over-optimism."[24] Among his difficulties in dealing with the Vietnam situation was his feeling of intellectual and educational inferiority to all those "Harvards" who had been Kennedy's chief advisers on foreign and military policy and now were his. Surely, they knew more than Johnson did—an opinion shared by the president and the advisers.

And, among the intellectual advisers, some of the most vociferous advocates of war were as intent on proving their manhood as Johnson was about his. Walt W. Rostow is a prime example. During World War II, Rostow had worked in the OSS, helping to select targets for Allied bombers. Never directly involved in combat himself and looking the opposite of a "tough guy"—short, thick glasses, every bit the intellectual—Rostow was always playing the part of one and advocating military action. His influence on Johnson and the war was substantial.

Kennedy's background gave him confidence that he—and his team of brilliant intellectuals—knew at least as much about the way to handle military situations as did the Joint Chiefs of Staff. LBJ had no such self-assurance and was, moreover, worried about looking weak and cowardly and feared the political damage looking weak could cause him.

To keep them from turning against him in the election year of 1964, Johnson gave the top military people reassurances. Most infamously, the president said to the Joint Chiefs at a White House reception before Christmas 1963: "Just get me elected, and then you can have your war."[25] Presumably, this statement was no more sincere or reliable than most of what he said, but it later gave those prone to see conspiracies a juicy bone on which to chew.

At the end of January 1964, another coup was staged in Saigon. Changes in the government of South Vietnam would continue with bewildering frequency through 1964 and well into 1965. Americans had little influence on the changes, and none of them provided a stable government likely either to gain the support of the people or provide a workable partner for the United States.

In a telephone conversation in early February with John Knight of the Knight Ridder newspaper chain, Johnson summarized the unpalatable alternatives he faced in Vietnam. "One is to run and let the dominoes start falling over. And God almighty, what they [right-wing Republicans] said about us leaving China would be just warming up compared to what they'd say now. . . . And so it really boils down to one of two decisions—getting out or getting in. . . . But we can't abandon it to them, as I see it."[26]

Early in March, Johnson sent Defense Secretary Robert McNamara to Saigon. When he returned, McNamara made the usual rosy statements in public, but he privately told the president that the situation had "unquestionably grown worse" since his last trip there in December. Johnson approved McNamara's calls for an open-ended commitment to South Vietnam, and a National Security Council Action Memorandum expanded the importance of Vietnam by classifying it as a "test case" of American foreign policy and will to stand by the nation's commitments. This was a shift in policy that would have enormous consequences.[27]

In private telephone conversations in the spring of 1964, Johnson made clear that he understood that a war against guerrilla fighters in Southeast Asia would be "damned easy to get in" but "awfully hard to ever extricate yourself if you get in."[28] In a remarkable phone discussion with his longtime mentor, Sen. Richard Russell of Georgia, on June 11, Johnson said that he didn't know what to do about Vietnam and was "in a hell of a shape." "If I lose it, I think [the American people will] say I've lost. I've pulled in. At the same time, I don't want to commit us to a war."

In a strikingly accurate prediction, Russell estimated that it would "take a half million men. They'd be bogged down in there for ten years." Johnson seemed to agree. But, he told Russell, when he had raised in a discussion with a friend in Texas the night before the possibility of withdrawing before the United States got more deeply involved, the friend had responded, "Goddamn, there's not anything that'll destroy you as quick as *pulling out*, pulling up stakes and running. America wants, by God, prestige and power." Johnson told Russell that he had responded, "Yeah, but I don't want to kill these folks." "I don't give a damn," the friend, A. W. Moursund, shot back. "I didn't want to kill 'em in Korea, but if you don't *stand up* for America . . . They'll forgive you anything except *being weak*."[29]

It was a rare outbreak of truth-telling on Johnson's part when he said, "but I don't want to kill these folks." Recall the story about Johnson as a boy not wanting to kill animals but killing a rabbit so his father wouldn't classify him as a "coward" or a "sissy. The sexual associations implicit in the words I italicized in Moursund's warnings to Johnson were presumably not made intentionally or consciously; that's just the way many men talk and think. But Johnson, with his acute masculine insecurity, understood the stakes. Before he ended his call with Russell, the president said to him: "We've got to conduct ourselves like men."[30]

That comment obviously reflects Johnson's masculinity doubts, but that motive blends with his fear of losing support from voters—he had from the moment he succeeded John Kennedy, been concerned about the possibility of losing in 1964—who were likely to turn on a leader who did not conduct himself "like a man."

Johnson wanted to pull out; he didn't want to kill anyone. But that would not be "manly," and his political opponents—and his friends . . . and his inner demons and doubts—would classify him as weak, as his father would have. He later gave exactly this as his reason for doing what he didn't want to do in Vietnam. They would say "that I was a coward. An unmanly man," LBJ told Doris Kearns in 1970. He said he had a recurring dream in which thousands of people were running toward him and shouting at him: "Coward! Traitor! Weakling!"[31]

Lyndon B. Johnson wasn't going to be seen—couldn't put himself in a position where he would see himself—that way. Tim O'Brien's words are worthy of repeating, because they so perfectly capture what we see happening with Johnson in 1964:

"It's not a happy ending. I was a coward. I went to war."[32]

Paint It Black with a Union Jack

"Black Freedom" Returns to America: The British Invasion, Second Wave

May–December 1964

James Brown and Mick Jagger at the TAMI Show,
Santa Monica, California, October 1964

We turned American people back to their own
music. And that's probably our greatest contribution
to music. We turned white America's brain and
ears around.

—Keith Richards, *Life* (2010)[1]

T HEY'RE A BLUES COVER band, that's sort of what the Stones are," Paul McCartney remarked in 2021.[2] The comment caused a minor stir, but he was right about what the band that launched the second wave of the British Invasion intended to be and still were in 1964. Since they had been brought together in 1962 by Brian Jones, they saw their mission as, in the words of Mick Jagger biographer Philip Norman, "to bring the blues to Britain the way Saint Augustine had once brought Christianity."[3] They sang songs written by American R&B artists.

In September 1963, Jagger and Keith Richards were worried. They did not yet see themselves as songwriters, and they needed a hit song. Their manager, Andrew Loog Oldham, left the band in the studio and went for a walk, on which he ran into John Lennon and Paul McCartney. (Oldham had previously worked with the Beatles.) When he told them about the Stones' predicament, they returned to the studio with him and said, "Hey Mick, we've got this great song." It was one they were writing for a forthcoming Beatles album but that they weren't planning to release as a single. "So they played it and we thought it sounded pretty commercial, which is what we were looking for," Jagger recalled.[4]

Jagger, Richards, and Jones took the Lennon-McCartney song and turned it into a something that was clearly a Rolling Stones song. Bill Wyman described the process as "dirty it up a bit and bash it out . . . we kind of completely turned the song around and made it much more tough."[5] "I Wanna Be Your Man" was released in Britain at the beginning of November 1963 and became the Rolling Stones' first big hit in the United Kingdom. It came out in the United States as the B-side of the band's first American single, a cover of Buddy Holly's "Not Fade Away," in March 1964, a month after the Beatles' first *Ed Sullivan* appearance.

Beyond the musical divergences in the two bands' renderings of "I Wanna Be Your Man," there are other striking differences. With Ringo Starr in the lead on the Beatles' version, the voice sounds quite feminine. On the Stones' adaptation, Mick Jagger sounds . . . well, like Mick Jagger. The greatest difference, though—the difference that sums up that between the two phases of the British Invasion—is the meaning a listener gets from the lines "I wanna be your lover, baby / I wanna be your man." Being a girl's *lover* in the Beatles' version sounds like a guy who wants—shall we say, "to hold your hand." The song is like a Valentine's Day card. But there is no mistaking what wanting to be the girl's *lover* means in the Stones' rendering. Jagger isn't talking about sitting on the settee and perhaps sharing a kiss along with a nice, chilled glass of lemonade. The Beatles sound like they want to "make nice," the Stones like they want to "make nasty." The Stones "didn't want to hold your hand," as Joyce Maynard has said in her book *Looking Back: A Chronicle of Growing Up Old in the Sixties*, "they wanted [what they would call the next year] 'satisfaction,' 'girly action.'"[6]

And the way in which the Rolling Stones transformed this Beatles' composition from a "silly little love song" into a provocative sex song— by "dirtying it up" and making it "much more tough"—provides us with a microcosm of what they and the other second-wave bands did to the British Invasion that the Beatles had begun. The early Beatles were romantic; the Stones were sexual. Playing with the Rolling Stones was, in the words of one of their 1965 songs, "playing with fire."

The first wave of the 1964 British Invasion was seduction; the second wave was consummation.

Breaking Through the Rebuilt Walls of Containment

The first major breaching of the defenses of Middle America by the subversive forces of "race music," which had begun in Memphis and surrounding areas in 1954 and spread nationally in 1956, had been blunted in the late 1950s and early 1960s. Mainstream culture was injected with temporarily effective antibiotics to destroy this "black freedom" plague. As early as 1956, Pat Boone took deadly aim at rock with his cover of Little Richard's "Tutti Frutti." Then Elvis went into the army, and Buddy Holly died in a plane crash. What passed for rock 'n' roll during JFK's time as president was, with a few notable exceptions, bland stuff.

While commercial forces in the United States were whitening and taming the music at home in these years, the spores of the Mississippi Delta blues found a more hospitable cultural climate in the British Isles and Europe in which to bloom among white people. Beginning at the end of May 1964, in the double disguise of white face and British accents, the music of black freedom made its second attack on the conventional ways of white America. This one would not so easily be turned back, though much of it was eventually co-opted by the forces of consumerism and commerce.

The timing of the British Invasion was, for several important reasons, ideal. Baby Boomers were on the scene in force, with their leading edge just reaching college age, and the percentage of young white Americans attending college was exploding, yielding a critical mass of young people in self-contained and self-referential communities in which a youth-centered culture could blossom rapidly. The civil rights movement had made African Americans and the culture associated with them more attractive, and the Motown Sound had over the preceding few years opened white America to black performers in a nonthreatening way. Widespread and growing prosperity provided millions of white kids with the luxury of being able to consume while denouncing consumption and luxury.

As we have already seen, the way for the shock troops of black freedom to invade the United States in 1964 was opened by the not-particularly-shocking first wave of the British Invasion. "Without the Beatles probably nobody could have broken the door down," Richards acknowledges. "And they certainly weren't bluesmen."[7]

Significantly, the Stones came to the black performers and their music via the same route that led many white Americans into the music: Elvis Presley. Perhaps even more than Presley, though, it was another white American performer who stirred aspiring young British musicians. When Buddy Holly toured England early in 1958, Jagger attended one of the shows. So, independently, did Eric Clapton, Dave Clark, Jeff Beck, and several other future big names of British rock.[8] It was the music of these white American performers that led the young Englishmen to its roots in the blues.

Once they got back to the blues, many of the British fans became obsessed with the music. As a student, Eric Burdon, later the front man for the Animals, the first group in the second wave of the British Invasion to reach number one in the United States with "House of the Rising Sun" in September 1964, used his own blood as the ink to write the word *Blues* on the cover of one of his books.[9] When Keith Richards became an aficionado of the blues, he didn't do anything that extreme, but he, too, went all in and soon found similarly blues-infatuated mates in Mick Jagger and Brian Jones.

Playing at Being Black to Play the Blues . . . Without Getting Beaten Black-and-Blue

"Everybody wants to be Black until it's time to be Black."
—Keenan Scott II, *Thoughts of a Colored Man* (2021)

The connection between black music and the fear of a break in the walls of containment of sexuality and women and the segregation of the races was apparent to some of those patrolling those border barriers. Segregationists were aware that black music was a leading carrier of the dreaded infection I refer to as black freedom. The White Citizens' Council of Greater New Orleans stated the threat clearly in a circular:

STOP

Help Save the Youth of America
DON'T BUY NEGRO RECORDS

(If you don't want to serve negroes in your place of business, then do not have negro records on your juke box or listen to negro records on the radio.)

The screaming, idiotic words, and savage music of these records are undermining the morals of our white youth in *America.*

Call the advertisers of the radio stations that play this type of music and complain to them!

Don't Let Your Children Buy, Or Listen To These Negro Records.[10]

Both the staunch opponents of black people obtaining white freedom and the transmitters to white people of black freedom saw African Americans and the nature of their "freedom" in a similar way.

"Why are Negroes so immoral?" a white student at the University of Mississippi asked visiting white civil rights workers during the summer of 1964, as the second wave of the British Invasion was crashing onto American shores.[11] Such views were not confined to the South. Three-quarters of those polled nationwide in a late 1963 survey said, "Negroes have lower morals." A respondent in Nevada declared: "Negroes are oversexed. They're wild."[12] That was the same view that the Beats, hipsters, and white R&B fans had of black people: they were primitive and immoral—the difference being that most white people saw "immorality" as negative and inferior, while the "white Negroes" saw it as positive and desirable—freedom from middle-class mores, in a word, *cool*. "Undermining the morals of our white youth in *America*" is what the white shock troops championing black freedom sought to do. "Oversexed"? "Wild"? You can almost hear Kerouac's Dean Moriarty shouting, "Wheeoo! let's go!"[13]

Kerouac had perfectly summarized the view of black freedom that he and other Beats took when he wrote in *On the Road*, "I walked . . . in the Denver colored section, wishing I were a Negro, feeling that the best the white world had to offer was not enough ecstasy for me, not enough life, joy, kicks, darkness, music, not enough night. . . . I wished I were . . . anything but what I was so drearily, a 'white man' disillusioned."[14]

In truth, Kerouac and Neal Cassady (Dean Moriarty in the book) didn't seem to want to have that much to do with black people. They desired to adopt their speech, drugs, sex lives, and music but not have more contact than necessary. Put simply, they wanted to *play* at being black.

Jagger, Richards, Burdon, and other British blues wannabes felt the same way about what the white world of England had to offer as Kerouac's narrator, Sal Paradise, did about the white world of America. They, too, couldn't "get no satisfaction"—enough ecstasy. They, too, yearned to "exchange worlds with the happy, true-hearted, ecstatic Negroes of America." They wanted more *freedom*: black freedom. They wanted to be *men* in the way that such songs as Muddy Waters's

"Mannish Boy" defined manhood: being a lover man who could make love to many women—a "hoochie coochie man."[15]

On the early songs through 1964, Jagger sang in an affected southern black accent. The Rolling Stones were painting themselves black, but they certainly weren't doing it in a blackface way. Minstrel show, vaudeville, and other white performers in America from the late nineteenth and well into the twentieth century painted their faces black for laughs. They were ridiculing black people. The Stones and other British bluesmen were doing the opposite; they were in awe of African American musicians and sought to make themselves like them, not to make fun of them. And, far more than appears to have been the case with Kerouac and his friends and characters, they liked to be with black people.

At some point in their manic attempt to learn and copy the bluesmen, the band that would come to be known as the Rolling Stones realized "that blues are not learned in a monastery. You've got to go out there and get your heart broke and then come back and then you can sing the blues," Richards recalls. "At that time we were taking it on a purely musical level, forgetting that these guys were singing *about* shit. First you've got to get in the shit. And then maybe you can come back and sing it."[16]

But the experiences thought to be the source of the music were seen as those involving sex and broken hearts, not the *real* "shit" that African Americans faced. The Stones and other whites saw living the life that produced the blues as sex and broken hearts, not poverty, oppression, and hopelessness. They didn't appreciate that a major source of the blues was having been beaten black-and-blue. They sought to experience the "hardship" that produced the blues by having promiscuous sex and losing lovers (for whom there was an endless line of eager replacements). It was not far removed from Kerouac's description of Dean: "To him sex was the one and only holy and important thing in life."[17] It's all the romanticism of oppression—without the reality.[18] There was little acknowledgment of the enormous burdens that were part and parcel of the lives of the "happy, true-hearted, ecstatic Negroes of America" with whom they thought they wanted to "exchange worlds."[19] They loved the music—and the sex—while largely ignoring the weight of oppression that produced it.[20] As Norman Mailer had put it in 1959, "We want the heats of the orgy and not its murder, the warmth of pleasure without the grip of pain."[21]

The Role-ing Stones?:
How Much of Rock's Greatest Act Was an Act?

The answer to the question about whether the Stones were the polar opposites of the Beatles is best stated in a line from another singer-songwriter, Kris Kristofferson: "partly truth and partly fiction."[22] Those same words describe what the Stones themselves were at the outset.

A large portion of the difference between the major groups that dominated the two waves of the British Invasion was real. Jagger and Richards not only knew that "Negroes can sing," they worshipped American bluesmen. The Beatles were far more attracted to other genres of American music—particularly, as we've seen, the girl groups. But this difference was significantly exaggerated by the opposing images that were created for the two bands.

Richards says the Rolling Stones liked all the "chick songs [i.e., girl groups], doo-wop, uptown soul: the Marvelettes, the Crystals, the Chiffons, the Channels." Both groups liked that kind of music, but only the Beatles could perform it, because it fit their image and ran counter to that of the Stones. If the Stones had tried "to play anything like that," Richards says, "It would have been 'What? They've gone mad.' Because they wanted to hear hard-duty Chicago blues that no other band could play as well as we could. The Beatles certainly could never have played it like that."[23]

The Beatles and Rolling Stones were different but not nearly as different as their images. The Stones took their name from a 1950 song by Muddy Waters, "Rollin' Stone." The story is that Brian Jones was asked in a telephone conversation with *Jazz News* what the band's name was. He saw a copy of *The Best of Muddy Waters* album on the floor and gave the song title as their new name.[24] Accidental or not, the association of the group with Waters was appropriate.

One indicator of the real difference between the early Beatles and the Rolling Stones is in the choice of which covers of African American songs would be included in their first American albums. *Meet the Beatles*, usually considered to be their first American album, contained only songs written by John Lennon and Paul McCartney and one by another white composer, Meredith Willson. The group's first African American song released in the United States was Chuck Berry's "Roll Over Beethoven," the opening track on *The Beatles' Second Album* (April 10, 1964). The song calls for a revolution, but only in music. In contrast, the Stones' *England's Newest Hitmakers*, released fifty days later, is chock full of covers of African American R&B songs: Willie Dixon's "I Just Want to Make Love to You," Jimmy Reed's "Honest I Do," Slim Harpo's "I'm a King Bee," and Rufus Thomas's "Walking the Dog"—along with Chuck Berry's "Carol" and Marvin Gaye's Motown "Can I Get a Witness."

Harpo's highly sexual "I'm a King Bee" was the stuff young males' dreams—and their parents' nightmares—are made of:

> *Well I'm a king bee, baby*
> *Buzzing around your hive*
> *Yeah I can make honey baby*
> *Let me come inside*[25]

There's a message of black freedom that's easy to understand—and one that the Stones obviously supported. But there was also a "partly fiction" side to "England's Newest Hitmakers."

When he became their manager, Andrew Loog Oldham saw an opening for an "anti-Beatles." "It registered subconsciously," he thought after the Beatles had made it in England, that "another section of the public was going to want the opposite."[26] Oldham set out to take the already somewhat uncouth band and dirty them up much more. "You will find them so different from the Beatles in every respect," the Stones' comanager Eric Easton wrote of the band to an American radio executive shortly before their first American tour.[27] Members of the group realized, Richards recalls, "the role that we were being cast in, and there was no fighting it anyway, nobody had really played it before, and this would be kind of fun."[28]

The blending of truth and fiction that was the Rolling Stones by the time they first arrived in the United States in June 1964 worked well.

Bringing It All Back Home

Their love of African American music led the British performers to love America and gave them a hunger to learn more about it. They idealized the nation across the ocean as they idolized the blues musicians. The Rolling Stones in America during 1964 were like kids living out their wildest dream.

While they were in New York in early June, Jagger and Richards eagerly made a pilgrimage to one of the shrines of the music they worshipped, Harlem's Apollo Theater. James Brown was performing there that week. They had no money, and in New York they slept on the living room floor at the Spanish Harlem home of the mother of the Ronettes' Ronnie Bennett (who would marry Phil Spector in 1968). Mick was in awe of "the Godfather of Soul" and watched his dance moves as an attentive pupil, learning what would come to be known as "Moves Like Jagger."[29] Ronnie took them backstage at the Apollo, where they were starstruck fans rather than stars themselves.[30]

The Stones' love for America faced some challenges as they made their first tour of the nation in June 1964. Even in New York, the band members' long hair prompted such sneers as "Ya fuckin' faggot!" and "Look at that goddamn faggot!"[31] Elsewhere, though, it was far worse. The band members were finding out that there are at least two Americas, and they are vastly different places.

The other performers on their first American tour—the Chiffons,

Poster for the Rolling Stones' first American tour, June 1964

an African American "girl group" that had had a number one hit in 1963, "He's So Fine," and three white male pop song Bobbys—Vee, Goldsboro, and Comstock—were poorly chosen for what Oldham and the Stones were marketing, as were most of the sites. When the band stopped at a diner or truck stop in the American heartland, they would be greeted by "How you doing, girls? Dance with me?" Richards says that they were seen as "definitely a threat. And all you'd done was ask, 'Can I use your bathroom?' 'Are you a boy or a girl?' What are you gonna do? Pull your cock out?"[32]

It seems significant that the most important way in which these white British purveyors of black freedom were perceived as a threat, particularly by white men in the South, was the same as that which most worried many white men about blacks: that these different, alien males might take "their" women away. "WOULD YOU LET YOUR DAUGHTER MARRY A ROLLING STONE?"[33] That British headline, which was pushed by Oldham as part of his bad-boy-image-creating campaign, posed exactly the question that racists in the United States were asking about their daughters and African Americans. This parallel reflects how successful Oldham and the band were at painting what they represented as black.

The reaction these British bluesmen got from Americans of African ancestry was radically different from what they received from many of those whose forebears had come to America from the band's homeland. Here's how Richards describes being in a southern juke joint: "The only thing that makes me stand out is that I'm *white*! Wonderfully, no one notices this aberration. I am accepted, I'm made to feel *so* warm. I am in heaven!"[34]

The pattern of rejection by whites—particularly older, male, and southern or rural whites—and acceptance by blacks (and a greater degree of acceptance by whites who were young and/or female and/or from urban America) reflects the divisions in sixties America that were coming into focus in 1964. And while the Rolling Stones and other second-wave British Invasion bands were not especially interested in bringing white freedom to blacks, they were being rejected or accepted by many of the same demographic groups that rejected or accepted the civil rights movement.

It is worth emphasizing that the reception black people in southern juke joints and elsewhere offered the white British musicians, as described by Richards, seems almost identical to how black people in Mississippi welcomed into their homes white summer project volunteers who came to join the struggle against racism during the summer of 1964.

Similarly, the reception many whites in the South gave the Stones later in the Long 1964 was much like that accorded the white volunteers in what white Mississippians saw as a Northern Invasion in 1964. In the Mississippi Delta, birthplace of the music that inspired the second wave of the British Invasion, a volunteer described the sort of greeting they got from local whites and being amazed "to walk along the street and have some little old lady who looks for everything like your mother give you the finger."[35]

Here was a major crossroads of the different freedom roads of 1964. The Stones were whites from across the ocean who had adopted the music and *some* of the lifestyle of the African Americans and came into the South to partake of black freedom. Simultaneously, whites from other parts of the United States who were outraged at the ways in which portions of that "free" lifestyle were imposed on African Americans came into the South to join in the struggle to bring "white freedom" to the region's black people. Both groups were generally accepted by the region's black people and strongly rejected by most of its white people.

"Go East, Young Men and Women": The Road Trip That Invented the Sixties Counterculture

"In 1964 . . . Ken Kesey lit the fuse for
the explosion that started the sixties."
—*Magic Trip* (2011)[36]

During the time that the Rolling Stones were making their way eastward from California across the less-than-welcoming midsection of America toward New York, a different type of band set out from the Golden State to cross the nation in "the reverse order of the pioneers." The link between the imagined black freedom for which Kerouac had longed and the emergence of the "If it feels good, do it!" ethos of the sixties could not have been clearer than it was in the journey of Ken Kesey and his band of Merry Pranksters in their wildly painted, drug-laden bus. The trip began on June 17, while the Stones were in Detroit, four days before the murders of three freedom workers in Mississippi riveted the nation's attention. "Everybody I knew had read *On the Road*," Kesey later said of the genesis of the trip, "and it opened up the doors to us the same way drugs did." Neal Cassady himself—the prototype of the self-indulgent, fuck-anybody-if-it-gives-*me*-a-moment-of-pleasure lifestyle that came to define the counterculture—showed up for the trip and drove the bus. People kept "egging [Cassady] on to greater heights of self-indulgence, and he always did it, he always tried to be *more* of this hero that was this self-indulgent *On the Road* legend."

The Merry Pranksters' real-world destination was the New York World's Fair, which had opened eight weeks before, though they also sought out Kerouac, Allen Ginsberg, and LSD advocate Timothy Leary (who wouldn't see them) in New York. The Pranksters' hoped-for destination, which was beyond the real world, was indicated by the name they gave to the bus, "Further"—a realm they would enter through mind-altering drugs. "The whole notion of the trip—take an acid trip—came out of that summer."[37]

"Further" was crazily painted in the colors and psychedelic fashion that would soon become iconic of the sixties. In retrospect, its appearance across America in the summer of 1964 can be seen as symbolic of the shift from the repressive, grayscale fifties to the vibrant, explosively colorful "free" sixties.

The Stones Begin to Roll

"By the end of that first American tour, we thought we'd blown it in America," Richards recalls. "We'd been consigned to the status of medicine shows and circus freaks with long hair."[38] When the band had appeared on *The Hollywood Palace* TV show in mid-June, host Dean Martin introduced them as a sick joke. After they finished, Martin rolled his eyes and said, "The Rolling Stones . . . aren't they great?"

But their appearance on this show marked June 13, 1964, as a watershed—a breakthrough in the spread of black freedom to a wide audience in the United States. The song they performed, Willie Dixon's "I Just Want to Make Love to You," was overtly sexual. There was Mick Jagger on a prime-time American network television show, singing with a sexy leer[39]:

> I don't want you to be no slave
> I don't want you to work all day
> I don't want you to be true
> I just want to make love to you, baby[40]

That was a message that had never before been vocalized on national television. Eight years earlier, Elvis Presley had made provocative movements on television; now the Rolling Stones were giving voice to that message.

Elvis had his hips; Mick had his lips.

After that television appearance, the band was back to touring the American interior, where they didn't seem to fit. At one stop, the audience was fewer than fifty, the majority of whom looked to be "homophobic rednecked cowboys."[41] Such low points were put in the shade, though, by Oldham having arranged for them to do a recording session in Chicago between their gigs in San Antonio and Minneapolis. The Mississippi Delta was the original holy land, the Bethlehem, of the music they worshipped, but 2120 South Michigan Avenue, Chicago, was the address of their heaven: Chess Records, the label of Jagger's and Richards's African American blues idols. As a fanatical follower of the blues, teenager Mick Jagger had corresponded with Marshall Chess, the son of one of the Chess brothers. It was their practice not to allow outsiders to record in their studios, but Marshall talked his father and uncle into making an exception for the Stones. On June 10 and 11, in the inner sanctum of blues, these young, white Englishmen were treated the same way as the older black men they worshipped. The band recorded twelve songs in two all-day sessions, as one after another of the men they venerated—Willie Dixon, Buddy Guy, Chuck Berry, and the man himself, Muddy Waters—came through, listened, and encouraged them.[42]

Then it was back to the tour, including stops in Omaha and Harris-
burg, before returning to New York and performing at Carnegie Hall.
As Richards remembers it, "We were suddenly back in England with
screaming teenyboppers. America was just coming around. We realized
that it was just starting."[43]

The Carnegie Hall shows, apart from the magical two days at Chess
Studios, were the bright light at the end of the tunnel that the band's
first American tour had been.

♦♦♦

During the summer between the first and second American tours of
the Rolling Stones, the band's reputation as "bad boys" was enhanced
by riots that occurred at several of their appearances in the UK and
on the Continent. A riot at Blackpool, England, in late July started
when a man in front of the stage spat on Keith Richards and the
guitarist rammed his pointed boot into the man's face. The band had
to flee for their lives.[44] For their second American tour, the Stones
arrived in New York on October 23, two days after rioting fans had
fought with police after their show in Paris. Now, Oldham could
present England's Newest Hitmakers as what amounted to Europe's
Newest Shitmakers—an opportunity he wasn't going to pass up.[45]
Two days after their arrival, the Stones made their first appearance
on the *Ed Sullivan Show*. At the beginning of the Beatles' third time
on his show on February 23, Sullivan had referred to them as "a
group of fine youngsters."[46] He had a different reaction to Mick Jagger and company. Although the band looked more mainstream than
it usually did (all but Jagger were in jackets and ties, and the front
man had on a neat white sweatshirt), and there was nothing particularly raunchy about the two songs they performed—Chuck Berry's
"Around & Around" and their hit "Time Is on My Side"[47]—what
was described as a "riot" broke out among the fans, who were said
to have trashed the studio. That characterization was almost entirely
hype, but Sullivan called the Stones "lewd," apologized for allowing
them on the air, and declared: "I promise you they'll never be back
on our show again. It took me seventeen years to build this show,
and I'm not going to have it destroyed in a matter of weeks." *Newsday*

pontificated that even these toned-down Stones were "obsessed with pornographic lyrics." [48]

As had been the case with Elvis, commercial and ratings considerations moved Sullivan to retract his ban on sexualized "white Negro" performers, but not before he wrote to Oldham: "We were deluged with mail protesting the untidy appearance—clothes and hair of your Rolling Stones. Before even discussing the possibility of a contract [for another appearance], I would like to learn from you, whether your young men have reformed in the matter of dress and shampoo."[49] The Stones were back on *Sullivan* in May 1965, looking remarkably neat in sports jackets, albeit perhaps in need of a bit of shampoo.

As late as 1967, Sullivan demanded that the group change the words of "Let's Spend the Night Together" to "Let's Spend Some Time Together."[50] He was trying to do with this song the opposite of what the Stones had done with "I Wanna Be Your Man" in 1963: clean it up and make it much tamer, to turn it away from an unmistakably Stones song. When Jagger sang the emasculated words, he rolled his eyes.[51]

You Always Say That You Want to Be Free

It might seem a stretch to see the Rolling Stones as already such a major influence in the United States in calendar 1964. When they arrived on their second American trip in October, "Time Is on My Side," had just entered the Billboard Hot 100. It was only their fourth single to chart, with the highest peak among its predecessors, "Tell Me," having only reached #24 in August. Even their first American album, *England's Newest Hitmakers*, had not broken into the Top 10, topping out at #11 in August. Recall that the Beatles had twenty-eight charting songs, six of them #1, in 1964.[52]

But the impact that the leading musical transmitters of "black freedom" were already having was evident three days after their first Sullivan appearance. On October 28 and 29, 1964, a show called TAMI (Teen Age Music International[53]) was filmed in Santa Monica for the purpose of making a film. The organizers chose the upstart Stones over numerous leading American performers—many of them the

African American artists they adulated, including Chuck Berry, Bo Diddley, Ray Charles, Marvin Gaye, Smokey Robinson, and James Brown himself, along with the Beach Boys, the Supremes, Lesley Gore, and others—to headline as the last act and lead into the grand finale with all the artists joining them on stage.[54] Jagger had by this time carefully copied Brown's dance moves, and he put them on display. The audience, composed mostly of young white females, can be seen bursting with unleashed sexual energy.[55] Posters for the British release of the film further emphasized the primacy of the Stones by calling it "Gather No Moss."

Movie poster for the British release of the TAMI Show *under the title* Gather No Moss.

The degree to which Oldham's image making succeeded can be seen in British critic Geoffrey Cannon's commentary calling the Stones "perverted, outrageous, violent, repulsive, ugly, tasteless, incoherent, a travesty. That's what's good about them."[56] Or, as Tom Wolfe put it, "The Beatles want to hold your hand but the Stones want to burn your town."[57] That was an interesting way to put what these proselytizers of black freedom were advocating in a year that would see the beginning of the urban black uprisings of the sixties.

Few white American kids in 1964 were likely to be attracted by the idea of burning their towns. What *did* excite young Americans was the actual message the Stones were carrying, which can be specified by altering Wolfe's statement to: *The Beatles wanted to hold your daughter's hand; the Stones wanted to fuck her.*

That, of course, was precisely the aura that the band and its manager were trying to put forth. The Stones were the most effective vendors selling black freedom to white American youth. Their words and actions carried the message much more clearly, explicitly, and defiantly than Presley's pelvic motions and appearance had, and they brought that message to an audience vastly larger than that which read Kerouac.

The Rolling Stones had been successfully sold as "forbidden fruit"—a food for which there was a hungry and rapidly growing market in 1964 America. And they cleared the way for legions of reinforcements, both coming across the Atlantic from their homeland and arising from white imitators in the original homeland of the music.

Policemen holding back excited Rolling Stones fans in New York where the band are on tour, June 1964.

As he did in so many songs, Keith Richards provides a memorable riff on what black freedom meant and rock music's role in spreading it: "But I think the Beatles and the Stones particularly did release chicks from the fact of 'I'm just a little chick.' . . . When you've got three thousand chicks in front of you that are ripping off their panties and throwing them at you, you realize what an awesome power you have unleashed. Everything they'd been brought up not to do, they could do that at a rock-and-roll show."[58]

Everything they'd been brought up not to do, they could do.

That's what "black freedom" was all about to white kids, and the revolution those words reflected was well underway by the time 1964 came to its end.

11

A MIDSUMMER NIGHT'S NIGHTMARE

THREE DEAD IN MISSISSIPPI

JUNE 1964

FBI Poster for three civil rights workers missing in Mississippi, summer 1964.

I belong right here in Mississippi. . . . Nowhere in the world is the idea of white supremacy more firmly entrenched, or more cancerous than in Mississippi. . . . So this is the decisive battleground for America: and every young American who wants to have a part in the decision should be here."

—Mickey Schwerner, May 1964 (a month before he was killed by Klansmen)[1]

MISSISSIPPI IN 1964 WAS the site of some of the most important battles in the struggle over freedom and its meaning. It was like a foreign country or another world . . . or maybe hell. Here's a story that some in the Freedom Movement liked to tell during that year:

> A black student in Chicago who was seeking to find his mission in life was awakened in the middle of the night by a voice firmly instructing: "Go to Mississippi! Go to Mississippi!"

> Shaking and sweating, the student replied, "All by myself?"

> "Have no fear," the voice of God answered. "I'll be with you—as far as Memphis."[2]

♦ ♦ ♦

The Mississippi Summer Project—"Freedom Summer"—a major effort to bring "white freedom" to the black residents of the state with the highest percentage of African Americans, was the crossroads of 1964 and the era. It became the font from which many of the extraordinary changes of the sixties flowed.

The primary goals of the Summer Project were, first, voter registration and the organization of the Mississippi Freedom Democratic Party to challenge the seating of the lily-white state party at the Democratic National Convention in August; and, second, to establish Freedom Schools and community centers in towns around the state.

SNCC: Transforming the Civil Rights Movement into a Freedom Movement

They say that freedom is a constant struggle,
They say that freedom is a constant struggle,
They say that freedom is a constant struggle,
Oh, Lord, we've struggled so long,
We must be free, we must be free.
                    —traditional spiritual

The Student Nonviolent Coordinating Committee (SNCC, pronounced "Snick") had arisen in the spring of 1960 out of the
sit-in movement. Although that phenomenon began in February in
Greensboro, North Carolina, a larger group of young black people
in Nashville had been training for several months in nonviolent resistance and preparing to stage sit-ins there. The major influence on the
Nashville students was Rev. James Lawson, a pacifist black Methodist
minister who had studied Gandhi's concept of nonviolent resistance,
satyagraha ("soul force"), and then worked with Martin Luther King
Jr., during the Montgomery Bus Boycott in the mid-fifties. Among
his disciples in Nashville were Diane Nash and John Lewis. "Jim
came south, almost like a missionary," Lewis said of him. "A nonviolent teacher, a warrior, to spread the good news."[3] Lawson was one
of the most important and inspirational people in the movement.
"In his own right, he was a great moral force," Lewis affirmed. "We
regarded him as our real teacher in nonviolence. I think he could
have been the most important man in the civil rights movement, if
he wanted."[4]

But Jim Lawson *didn't* want. He is much less well-known than
others, largely because that's the way he wanted it. Philosophically
opposed to the concept of leadership, Lawson advocated decision by
consensus. Such distrust of leaders and hierarchy became a hallmark
of the freedom movements of the sixties. Lawson kept himself so
much out of the limelight that it was startling when he reemerged at
age ninety-two to give an extraordinary, inspirational eulogy and call
for renewed action at the funeral of John Lewis in 2020.[5]

On April 15, 1960—Good Friday—Lawson, Nash, Lewis, and some
three hundred other sit-in participants from around the South that Ella
Baker, then sixty years old and a longtime civil rights activist, con-

vened at Shaw University in Raleigh, North
Carolina. "My theory," Baker often stated,
"is strong people don't need strong leaders."[6]
The Student Nonviolent Coordinating Committee was organized that Easter weekend
on the basis of that approach, with leaders
having little power, and decisions made by
consensus. SNCC was the first organization

of young people committed to change and freedom to be formed in the 1960s, and it had a large influence on 1964 and the entire decade.

The young activists in the field in the South came to believe that integration was not the primary need of poor, rural black people in the region. They increasingly saw that breaking down segregation laws, while desirable, would have little effect on the lives of this constituency they had chosen to organize.

The people on whom SNCC focused lacked in that most precious commodity, freedom. What was needed to attain that freedom and make real differences in the lives of people living in entrenched poverty and powerlessness was political and economic power. SNCC fieldworkers were concluding that power must be taken away from the white oppressors, and the way to do that appeared to be getting black people registered to vote.

If black political power were to be gained, the place to do it was in the most racist-controlled parts of the Deep South, where black people were concentrated in large numbers. The fact that these were also the most dangerous areas (precisely because the large black populations held the potential to take power if they were not kept in subjugation) also appealed to the audacity of the young SNCC activists. *Where is it most dangerous? Well,* that's *where we want to go.* They judged the three most dangerous racist enclaves in the nation to be Greenwood and McComb, Mississippi, and Albany, Georgia, and chose them as their targets.

♦ ♦ ♦

Robert Parris Moses had grown up in Harlem, earned an MA in philosophy at Harvard, and been a high school mathematics teacher in New York. Long politically active, he was inspired and energized by the 1960 sit-ins and went south to join the movement, quickly winding up in SNCC. He was sent to Mississippi to try to identify potential leaders among the state's black populace.

Moses was to become legendary in the movement. Intellectual in appearance and demeanor, he was the sort of person to whom others, from sharecroppers devoid of formal education to distinguished professors, would listen. When Bob Moses spoke, it was often necessary to listen intently in order to follow what his soft voice was saying, but

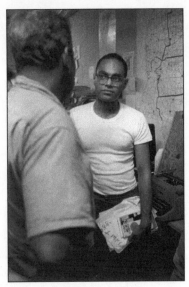

Bob Moses, 1964.

it was worth the effort. People *heard* Moses, and when they did, many were ready to act.

His personal magnetism made him a natural leader, but, like Jim Lawson's, his nature and philosophy led him to oppose the whole concept of leaders. "The people on the bottom don't need leaders at all," he asserted. "What they need is to have confidence in their own lives."[7] Moses perhaps more than anyone else promoted—and lived—the ideal that soon came to be called "participatory democracy."

After a fall 1960 visit to Mississippi during which local activist Amzie Moore convinced him that "in hard-core areas of the Deep South voter registration *was* 'direct action,'"[8] Moses returned to Mississippi in July 1961 and went to McComb to encourage black people to register. Those attempting to do so were savagely attacked, beaten, and in a couple of cases, shot. In response to calls about the brutal incidents in McComb, the Justice Department said there was nothing it could do. This response fed a growing disillusionment with the federal government and the "liberal establishment" on the part of young activists in the sixties. The disillusionment led to a bitter split, greatly exacerbated in 1964, particularly in the battle over seating the largely SNCC-created Mississippi Freedom Democratic Party (MFDP) at the Democratic National Convention in August. It was to have a profound impact on the course of the decade—and the course of American history down to the present.

The shift from desegregation to seeking political power transformed the movement's objective from civil rights to *freedom*. Instead of the "Civil Rights Movement," SNCC organizers on the ground in the Deep South spoke of the "Freedom Movement."

The Freedom Vote

> Quite a turnout for people who Senator Eastland
> said were too lazy to even register.
> —Aaron Henry (November 1963)[9]

The 1964 Mississippi Summer Project arose after COFO (the Council of Federated Organizations, a coalition of the major civil rights groups operating in Mississippi that had been formed in 1962) conducted a parallel "Freedom Vote" at the time of Mississippi's statewide elections in 1963. In this mock election, unregistered black people would be encouraged to vote at designated polling places set up in churches and black businesses around the state for a Freedom ticket of black state NAACP leader Aaron Henry for governor and white Tougaloo College chaplain Edwin King for lieutenant governor. The Freedom Vote was intended to demonstrate "that the Negro people of Mississippi would vote if they were allowed to register free from intimidation and discrimination."[10]

Allard Lowenstein, a prominent white liberal in his mid-thirties who was newly arrived in Mississippi, suggested that he could, through his connections at Yale and Stanford, recruit students to come to Mississippi to assist during the week or so leading up to the election. Approximately a hundred students answered the call.[11] They experienced harassment, arrests, and in at least one instance being shot at. The bullets did not hit anyone, but, as Ed King pointed out, "In Mississippi it is an error to confuse good intentions with poor aim."[12] Approximately 83,000 black Mississippians cast ballots from November 2 to 4. It "did much more for the movement, toward uniting Mississippi, than anything else we have done," concluded Dave Dennis of the Congress of Racial Equality (CORE, an organization dedicated to nonviolence and racial equality that had been founded by an interracial group of students at the University of Chicago in 1942 and become one of the leading forces in the civil rights movement).[13]

During the week following the Freedom Vote, COFO began a series of meetings to consider the pros and cons of bringing in a large number of volunteers the following summer and what it might mean for the nature of the Freedom Movement.

Some of the students who came in for the mock election had rubbed SNCC veterans the wrong way. Differences in class as well as race had led some of the newly arrived students to try to take over, displacing local black residents from whom they were unwilling to take instructions. An influx of privileged white students might do some temporary good, but many in SNCC feared it would undermine their longer-term goal of developing an indigenous black leadership and bottom-up power structure. If white people went around the state telling black people to register and vote, little would have changed. "When the one who looks like the oppressor comes and tells them to do something," SNCC field secretary Willie (later Wazir) Peacock recalled in 1979, "it's not commitment. It's done out of that same slave mentality."[14]

Two considerations weighing on the other side of the argument ultimately prevailed. Bob Moses insisted on going forward with the use of white students. Fannie Lou Hamer agreed: "If we're trying to break down this barrier of segregation, we can't segregate ourselves."[15] Esteem for Moses among the movement veterans was such that his strong endorsement of bringing in the white recruits was dispositive, and Mrs. Hamer's was among the most respected local voices in the movement. "She was SNCC itself," declared James Forman, COFO's executive secretary, and she was a perfect example of the kind of indigenous leadership that SNCC had been trying to find and develop in Mississippi.[16]

There was also another major consideration that favored proceeding with the large-scale Summer Project. It had become painfully clear that the national media would pay little or no attention to the brutal treatment of African Americans in Mississippi, but they did show interest in the white "Yalies" when they came to the state. "These students bring the rest of the country with them," Moses noted. "They're from good schools and their parents are influential. The interest of the country is awakened and when that happens, the government responds."[17] Federal protection might finally be forthcoming if the children of powerful whites were in the line of fire. And there would definitely be a response "to the death of a white college student."[18]

Freedom Fighters:
Insurgency and Counterinsurgency in the
Southern United States

> Guerrillas must move among the people
> as fish swim in the sea.
> —Mao Zedong[19]

"Black folks had a life, and I began learning how to enter into it," Bob Moses said.[20] He and other SNCC field secretaries lived with local people. They wore blue denim overalls and white T-shirts, as did the people they lived and worked with. They shared the danger and the beatings with their hosts. "It was like guerrilla war," Willie Peacock said of Greenwood, Mississippi. "We could stop anywhere and duck out of sight, go into somebody's house," he said, precisely expressing the fish-in-the-sea relationship. "They would see us at night and the cops would think it was an opportunity to get us, speed up and try to turn around. When they turned around we'd be watching out a window somewhere, see them come back to try to find us."[21]

The black shacks in Mississippi where the SNCC freedom fighters took up residence were in a different world from the White House in Washington, and the situation looked vastly different from the two perspectives.

If the SNCC people in the field saw themselves as insurgents—and they did—the whites in control in the region saw them that way even more. Eisenhower and Kennedy differed over the wisdom of building a counterinsurgency force against guerrillas in the Third World overseas. The authorities in the domestic Third World that was the Deep South, however, did not hesitate to build counterinsurgency forces to defeat the nonviolent brushfire war that the SNCC militants were fomenting. Irregular forces—Klansmen and other violent night riders—supplemented the state and local counterinsurgency force and used violence to support the status quo.

As it focused more on fighting against the violent guerrillas in southern Vietnam, the Johnson administration offered little assistance to the nonviolent SNCC guerrillas in the southern United States. "The guerilla war in Mississippi is not much different from that in Vietnam," Moses said. "But when we tried to see President Johnson, his secretary said that Vietnam was popping up all over his calendar and he hadn't had time to talk with us."[22]

The SNCC and other freedom fighters shared some similarities to the Peace Corps and even the Green Berets. Like both those organizations, they were there to help the local people help themselves. And, like the Green Berets, they were undertaking these efforts in hostile and dangerous territory. They had their own badge-of-honor attire, which they adopted from the mode of dress of the people they sought to free: they could be called the "Blue Overalls."

"White Negroes" or "White Niggers"?: Distinguishing among White Black Wannabes

As the Rolling Stones were nearing the end of their first American tour during the middle of June 1964, several hundred young Americans, most of them white, were being exposed to another type of African American music and to people seeking a different type of freedom from that represented by "England's Newest Hitmakers."

On Sunday, June 14, while the Stones played in Olympia Stadium in Detroit, 250 miles to the south, on the campus of Western College for Women in Oxford, Ohio, volunteers were beginning a weeklong training session to prepare them to spend the summer in Mississippi. Many were carrying guitars (unlike those of the Stones, theirs were acoustic), and they were greeted by freedom songs and spirituals.[23] Fannie Lou Hamer, at this point still unknown to the nation, was there from her home in the Delta town of Ruleville. She led choruses of "Oh, Freedom," "This Little Light of Mine," and many other songs that shared an ancestry in slave spirituals with the blues songs the Stones were covering but had evolved in a different direction and contained a different vision of the meaning of *freedom*.

The army that went to fight nonviolently in a war for freedom in the American South was stocked with volunteers only, not draftees, as was the military sent to fight in Vietnam. They were told they would be struggling not only for the freedom of black people in Mississippi but also for their own. "Don't come down to Mississippi this summer to save the Mississippi Negro," Bob Moses told the just-arrived volunteers on June 14. "Only come if you understand, really understand, that his freedom and yours are one."[24]

♦♦♦

One thing that local police and officials in Mississippi had in common with much of the rest of the nation is that they failed to distinguish between the two main strands of the decade's freedom-seekers. They saw the white people invading their state as, in the words of Governor Paul Johnson Jr., "your beatnik-type people. Nonconformists, hair down to their shoulder blades, some that you'd call weirdos."[25] "Many had on hippie uniforms and conducted themselves in hippie ways," White Citizens' Council leader William J. Simmons recalled in 1985, using an anachronistic word that he considered a negative to classify the freedom workers.[26]

Such equations are mistaken. The white students who had applied to participate in the Summer Project were being trained to bear the sort of treatment black people in Mississippi endured as part of their daily lives. When they went to Mississippi to join the struggle to bring white freedom to black people, they would be classified by many Mississippians of their own race as "nigger lovers" and so become, for the duration of their time in the state, "white Negroes" (some of the local white people did categorize them as "white Niggers."[27])—but decidedly not of the Neal Cassady–Jack Kerouac species or the hipsters about whom Norman Mailer had written in "The White Negro." Early white SNCC field workers in the South such as Bob Zellner, Sandra Cason, and Tom Hayden, along with native Mississippians Ed and Jeannette King and a small number of others, had already chosen to become "white Negroes" of this very different sort. They were associating themselves with the black experience not because they *thought* black people had freedoms that were denied to white people but because they *knew* black people were denied freedoms white people had.

As the attention of the world fell on Philadelphia, Mississippi, after three civil rights workers disappeared there in June, one local white resident wrote to *New York Times* editor Turner Catledge, who had grown up in Neshoba's county seat. The letter writer quoted a local black man as saying, "If you wuz ever a nigger on Sadday night, you'd always wanna be a nigger."[28] A clearer statement of the notion of "black freedom" sought by the Sal Paradise "white Negro" types would be difficult to imagine. That, though, was not the sort of black freedom sought by that the hundreds of young white people who went to Mississippi in 1964, most of them from privileged, educated backgrounds similar to those of many of the Beats. They were temporarily joining the ranks of "white niggers" to assist African Americans in obtaining the rights and freedoms that would make them *black people*, equal in every way to white people.

These two groups of white people did, however, have one important similarity. Both could simply leave the black worlds they had chosen, for their different reasons, to join and return to their safe, secure white worlds.

Murder of White People?—*That's* News!

The national impact of what happened as the Mississippi Freedom Summer began was well described decades later by Walter Cronkite of CBS News: "The time capsule that had been the Old South and had been left alone for so long was being pried open like a rusty tomb. During that week in June, the country would be shocked by the skeletons it began to find."[29]

Mt. Zion Church in the Longdale community in rural Neshoba County, Mississippi, had agreed to host a Freedom School. During the first week that the volunteer orientation was taking place in Ohio, on Tuesday night, June 16, Klansmen attacked members of the church and burned the building. The purpose of the church attack was to lure

Michael "Mickey" Schwerner, a white CORE field secretary from New York who had been working in Meridian for several months, to come to Neshoba County to investigate.[30] The Klan referred to the bearded Schwerner as "Goatee" and had targeted the New York Mets baseball cap-wearing "Yankee Jew" for "elimination."[31] The Mississippi State Sovereignty Commission, a state agency established in 1956 that had devolved into a secret police unit, had circulated to local sheriffs and Klansmen (in many cases one and the same) a description of Schwerner and his vehicle.[32]

Three days after the Neshoba County church burning, on Friday evening, June 19, the Senate passed the civil rights bill. It was frightening news for diehard white racists. Two days later, on Sunday, June 21—Midsummer Day, the date of the summer solstice—Schwerner, his friend James Chaney (a local black CORE activist), and a just-arrived white summer volunteer, Andrew Goodman, drove up to Neshoba to investigate the incident. A deputy sheriff arrested them for alleged speeding and took them to the county jail in Philadelphia, where they were held incommunicado until well after dark and then released and told to "get out of town." They were never heard from again.

The next morning, Bob Moses was in Ohio speaking to the second group of volunteers when he was informed of the disappearance of the three young men. As he relayed the news, in an instant the prospect that their summer in Mississippi might end in their deaths became far more real to the mostly young people in the room.[33]

♦♦♦

The night before, while the trio was held in the jail, they were denied their right to make a telephone call, and the jail receptionist told a caller from the COFO office that they were not in custody.[34] They were held until a group of Klansmen could be assembled to kill them. Times had changed, though. It was, one supposes, an example of the decline of traditional values that a public lynching as a form of family entertainment would no longer be accepted by polite society, even in Mississippi. Another aspect of this murder was a break with lynching tradition. "The murder of the boys is the first interracial lynching in the history of the United States," an attorney for the Goodman family noted.[35] When the lynch mob was in place along the road back to Meridian, the deputy "freed" the three freedom workers, only to overtake them on the road and turn them over to his Klan brothers, who took them to an isolated location, where they shot and killed all three. The Klansmen took the bodies to bury in an earthen dam on the land of a wealthy white man in the county and then drove the CORE car into the Bogue Chitto swamp, where they burned it.

With white people missing and probably dead, much of what the movement had been seeking from the federal government since 1961 and had been repeatedly told was impossible happened almost instantly. By Tuesday morning, the disappearance was front-page news in the *New York Times*.[36] Later that day the burned-out station wagon was found. President Johnson sent former CIA director Allen Dulles to Mississippi as his personal representative "to evaluate law observance,"[37] and ordered two hundred sailors from the Meridian Naval Air Station to conduct a search for the missing young men. The number of FBI agents in Mississippi was soon increased tenfold, from fifteen to 150, and the Jackson office became the agency's largest.

Martin Luther King Jr., holding photos
of Schwerner, Chaney, and Goodman,
December 4, 1964.

Governor Johnson and other Mississippi officials claimed the disappearance was a hoax and a Communist plot to besmirch the good name of Mississippi. The missing men, they said, were actually "vacationing on a beach in Cuba."[38] In July, when J. Edgar Hoover visited the state, Governor Johnson told him that "as long as he sat in the governor's chair, ignorance, hatred, and prejudice would not take over in [Mississippi]."[39] As a candidate for the state's highest office the year before, Johnson had entertained audiences at his stump speeches by telling them that NAACP stands for "niggers, alligators, apes, coons and possums."[40]

The movement was now, in some places and at some times, under "the protective glow of the national media."[41] But the national media's attention was focused on the three men who had disappeared in Philadelphia, leaving most of what else was going on in the state almost as much in the shadows as it had been. As the search for Schwerner, Chaney, and Goodman went on, other bodies of murder victims were found. The lower halves of two bodies were discovered in a bayou near the Mississippi River. A body of an unidentified teenager wearing a CORE T-shirt was come across in another river. "Mississippi is the only state where you can drag a river any time and find bodies you were not expecting," one of the Summer Project volunteers wrote in a July letter. "Things are really much better for rabbits—there's a closed season on rabbits."[42] But the national media showed little interest in these unexpected bodies. They were *black* bodies. The distinction was not lost on the black freedom fighters in Mississippi.

12

REENACTING
RECONSTRUCTION(S)

THE CIVIL RIGHTS ACT AND
THE GREAT SOCIETY

FEBRUARY–JULY 1964

*President Johnson handing pen to Martin Luther King Jr,
while signing the Civil Rights Act, July 2, 1964.*

No administration in this country is going to commit
political suicide over the rights of Negroes.
                         —Bob Moses (June 14, 1964)[1]

A T THE TIME MISSISSIPPI Summer Project director Bob Moses was addressing the above words to volunteers on the first night of their orientation in Oxford, Ohio, a president was taking the risk of doing exactly that.

More than six months earlier, shortly after he became president, Lyndon Johnson asked staunch segregationist Sen. Richard Russell of Georgia to come and talk with him about the civil rights bill. "Dick, you've got to get out of my way. I'm going to run you over," Johnson told his erstwhile mentor. "I don't intend to cave or compromise."

"You may do that," Russell responded, "but by God, it's going to cost you the South and cost you the election."

"If that's the price I've got to pay," LBJ declared, "I'll pay it gladly."[2]

We can readily dismiss the "gladly" part. Lyndon Johnson was terrified of defeat. But he did proceed to run over former colleagues in the Senate's southern bloc to enact the most significant legislation protecting "the rights of Negroes" since Reconstruction. While there were times when Johnson thought pushing civil rights might be politically helpful, he greatly feared Russell's prediction.

On the night after he signed the historic bill into law, Johnson looked dejected. Special Assistant to the President Bill Moyers asked him why. "Because, Bill," the president answered, "I think we just delivered the South to the Republican party for a long time to come."[3] More than a half century later, that "long time" is still with us, though Virginia has become a usually Democratic state and the narrow Democratic victories in the 2020–2021 presidential and Senate races in Georgia offer some indication that the "long time" won't be forever.

Despite his fears, Lyndon Johnson pushed on. The big question, of course, is: *Why?* Why did Lyndon Johnson work so hard to bring "white freedom" to black and other minority people? Like almost all questions concerning Johnson, there is no single answer.

♦

"I'm Going to Be the President Who Finishes What Lincoln Began"

Free at last, free at last. Thank God Almighty, I'm free at last.
—Lyndon Johnson, spring 1964, on
why he was pushing civil rights[4]

One simple explanation for Johnson's remarkably strong stand for civil rights would be his overriding quest to become the greatest president in history. "He said over and over and over again in those days," Johnson aide Roger Wilkins recalls, "'I'm going to be the president who finishes what Lincoln began.'"[5]

An additional reason for his powerful commitment to civil rights was that he believed it was right, moral, and necessary. Johnson asserted that he "wanted power to give things to people—all sorts of things to all sorts of people, especially the poor and the blacks."[6] He identified with the downtrodden. Johnson absolutely wanted to get the credit for helping people, but he genuinely did want to help them. Lyndon Johnson, so skilled as an "insider" in Washington, continued even as president to identify himself with the outsiders.

When Mississippi Senator John Stennis told LBJ that the people of his state would never accept the provisions in the civil rights bill, citing the segregationists' view of the meaning of *freedom* ("It's just impossible. I mean I believe that a man ought to have the right—if he owns a store or runs a café, he ought to have the right to serve who he wants to serve"), Johnson responded:

Well, you know, John, the other day a sad thing happened. My cook, Zephyr Wright, who had been working for me for many years—she's a college graduate—and her husband drove my official car from Washington down to Texas. . . . They drove through your state and when they got hungry, they stopped at grocery stores on the edge of town in colored areas and bought Vienna sausage and beans and ate them with a plastic spoon. And when they had to go to the bathroom, they would stop, pull off on a side road,

and Zephyr Wright, the cook of the Vice President of the
United States, would squat in the road to pee. And, you
know, John, that's just bad. That's wrong. And there ought
to be something to change that. And it seems to me that if
the people of Mississippi don't change it voluntarily, that it
is just going to be necessary to change it by law.[7]

That's just bad. That's wrong. That brief, simple, *moral* statement sums up
Lyndon Johnson's view on racial discrimination and the imperative to
remedy it.

◆ ◆ ◆

There were four hurdles the civil rights bill would have to clear to become
law: the House Rules Committee, the full House, the Senate Judiciary
Committee, and, finally, the inevitable filibuster by southern senators.

The Senate was accurately described by Minnesota's Hubert Humphrey as the graveyard of civil rights bills (a circumstance echoed when
Republican Mitch McConnell proclaimed himself "the Grim Reaper" as
Senate majority leader in the 2010s). Getting a bill with real teeth through
the House posed a major challenge in itself. As chairman of the House
Rules Committee, Howard Smith of Virginia, an unyielding defender of
segregation, could block such a bill from reaching the House floor.

Lyndon Johnson knew how to get things done in Congress. If
Smith wouldn't agree to send the bill to the full House, the new president and his allies in that chamber would force his hand by circulating
a discharge petition. If they could get the signatures of a majority of
House members, the bill would go straight to the full House. That
move led Smith to allow the bill out of his committee.[8]

Johnson skillfully combined public appeals with private pressure on
members of Congress, working the phones incessantly. After ten days
of debate, the House of Representatives voted overwhelmingly (290
to 130) for the bill on February 10.[9]

Without taking even a brief pause to catch his breath, Johnson
turned his attention to the Senate. At a news conference, the president declared that the segregationists could "filibuster until hell freezes
over; I'm not going to put anything on that floor until this is done."[10]

George Wallace's Bid for the
Democratic Presidential Nomination

If it hadn't been for the nigger bloc vote, we'd have won it all.
—George C. Wallace after the
1964 Maryland primary[11]

By the time the civil rights bill reached the full Senate, a new challenge to its passage had materialized. Less than a year after he had temporarily "stood in the schoolhouse door" to block the desegregation of the University of Alabama, Governor George Wallace was attempting to stand at the door of the United States Senate to block the desegregation of the United States.

In January 1964, Wallace announced that he was looking to enter several primaries in northern states as a candidate for the Democratic nomination for the presidency.[12] He told audiences at his appearances that his candidacy constituted a referendum on the civil rights bill. Those who opposed the bill should, he said, vote for him.

White Party of America supporters of George Wallace demonstrating to kill the civil rights bill.

The conventional wisdom is that Wallace did surprisingly well in two non-southern primaries, winning, respectively, 34 and 29 percent of the Democratic votes cast in Wisconsin and Indiana.[13] However, considering the percentage of Americans outside the South who let their racism show during the presidency of Barack Obama—and, even more, how many millions of Americans cheered and endorsed the at best thinly veiled racism of Donald Trump in 2016 and ensuing years—perhaps Wallace's numbers should not have been surprising. Be that as it may, Johnson saw a clear effect of the Wallace campaign on the filibuster. In the president's view, the Wallace candidacy "stiffened the southerners' will to keep on fighting the civil rights measure until the liberal ranks [in the Senate] began to crumble."[14]

Johnson feared that a Wallace primary victory in a state outside the old Confederacy might doom the civil rights bill. Political analysts started to speculate that Wallace might be able to win in Maryland's Democratic presidential primary on May 19. In hopes of preventing such an outcome, the president ordered all the help he could—political advisers, speechwriters, money, and prominent Democratic senators— to be sent to bolster his Maryland stand-in, Senator Daniel Brewster. Johnson's pressure worked. Brewster defeated Wallace handily, getting 59 percent of the vote. It was an important step toward defeating the filibuster.[15]

Wooing Ev Dirksen and Enlarging the Meaning of Freedom

> You get in there to see Dirksen; you drink with Dirksen,
> you talk with Dirksen, you listen to Dirksen.
> —LBJ to Hubert Humphrey
> (spring 1964)[16]

Unless the segregationists in the Senate gave up, the only way to break the filibuster was to get two-thirds of all senators to vote cloture—that is, to end the debate and bring the bill to a vote. Cloture votes had often been taken on civil rights bills in the past; all had failed. Lyndon Johnson and his allies had to find a way to make it different this time. Republican senators from the Midwest and West would be essential to obtaining the requisite two-thirds vote. The key man in getting their votes was Everett

McKinley Dirksen of Illinois, the Senate Republican leader. Johnson tried to diminish his own centrality in the Senate struggle, "so that a hero's niche could be carved out for Senator Dirksen, not me."[17]

Johnson assigned the task of winning over Dirksen to Minnesota Senator Hubert Humphrey. The president was concerned that liberal Democrats would not want to work with Dirksen. "Now don't let those bomb throwers talk you out of seeing Dirksen," the president instructed Humphrey."[18] Humphrey later remarked that he "would have kissed Dirksen's ass on the Capitol steps" to get the minority leader's support for cloture.[19]

Senator Dirksen proved to have no objection to becoming a "hero in history." The Illinois Republican met with Humphrey several times in May in the minority leader's office, where LBJ's instructions to "drink with Dirksen" were not difficult to follow—a section of the office was named the "Twilight Lodge" and every number on the clock there was "5."[20] The result was an amended bill that both Dirksen and the Leadership Conference on Civil Rights endorsed.[21]

While Humphrey was working the inside game with Dirksen, Lyndon Johnson was handling public opinion. Like an evangelical preacher, he exhorted his fellow citizens to do the moral thing. "Now I knew that as president I couldn't make people want to integrate their schools or open their doors to blacks," LBJ later said, "but I could make them feel guilty for not doing it and I believed that it was my moral responsibility to do precisely that—to use the moral persuasion of my office to make people feel that segregation was a curse they'd carry with them to their graves."[22]

Johnson also believed that civil rights reform was a practical matter for the white South. As biographer Robert Dallek has nicely put it, Johnson "was determined to administer the unpleasant medicine that would cure the region's social disease." Racial integration in the South would, Johnson was convinced, lead to economic and political integration of the South with the nation.[23]

Johnson shrewdly allowed Dirksen to rewrite the bill, without altering its substance but putting it in his words, so that he could claim to be its coauthor. "You're worthy of the Land of Lincoln," the president told Dirksen in a phone call. "And the Man from Illinois is going to pass the bill, and I'll see that you get proper attention and credit."[24]

The combination of Johnson's outside and inside games and the courting of Dirksen worked. A cloture vote was taken on June 10, and Senator Dirksen was given center stage. Quoting Victor Hugo, the minority leader proclaimed: "'Stronger than all the armies is an idea whose time has come.' The time has come for equality of opportunity. . . . It will not be stayed or denied. It is here!"[25]

Less than sure of the outcome, the pro–civil rights forces took no chances. In a dramatic moment, Senator Clair Engle arrived in a wheelchair. The California senator was dying from a brain tumor and unable to speak. When he was called upon to vote, he pointed to his eye to indicate an "aye" vote. Cloture wound up passing with four votes above the required two-thirds, 71 to 29.[26] Only one Democrat from a state that had been part of the Confederacy, Ralph Yarborough of Texas, voted to end debate, while all but two of the other Democrats voted that way. On the Republican side, twenty-seven senators, all from outside the old Confederacy, voted to end debate, while six, including the only Republican senator from a former Confederate state, John Tower of Texas, and soon-to-be Republican presidential nominee Barry Goldwater of Arizona, voted against.

Dick Russell's reaction to being beaten by his longtime pupil—his substitute son—on this issue so dear to his heart was magnanimous. "Now you tell Lyndon," Russell had said to Bill Moyers after the filibuster began, "that I've been expecting the rod for a long time, and I'm sorry that it's from his hand the rod must be wielded, but I'd rather it be his hand than anybody else's. Tell him to cry a little when he uses it."[27] Russell's attitude reflects the importance of it being a southern president who pushed through civil rights legislation. It was what would later be termed Nixon-to-China—the idea that the only president who could get away with doing something very controversial was one who came out of a background that gave him cover for doing so.[28]

With the filibuster broken, the Senate approved the bill on June 19, two days before Schwerner, Chaney, and Goodman were murdered in Mississippi. The president asked his legislative aide, Lee White, whether he thought they should have a major signing ceremony. "It's so monumental," White responded. "It's the equivalent of the signing of the Emancipation Proclamation and ought to have all the national attention you can focus on it."[29] Johnson agreed and signed the Civil Rights Act in a nationally televised ceremony on the evening of July 2.

In his speech, Johnson stressed the concept of *freedom* that was at the heart of almost everything going on in 1964. Noting that it was the week of July Fourth, the president referred to the "small band of valiant men" who "began a long struggle for freedom. . . . Those who founded our country knew that freedom would only be secure if each generation thought to renew and enlarge its meaning."

As to the deprivation of rights and liberties to some Americans because of the color of their skin, the president proclaimed: "Our Constitution, the foundation of our Republic, forbids it. The principles of our freedom forbid it. Morality forbids it. And the law I will sign tonight forbids it." Directly addressing another of the competing conceptions of *freedom* that was so central to the national dialogue in 1964, that of a business owner to deny entrance to anyone he wanted to exclude, Johnson stated that the bill "does not restrict the freedom of any American, so long as he respects the rights of others."

"Let us close the springs of racial poison," Lyndon Johnson preached in conclusion. "Let us pray for wise and understanding hearts. Let us lay aside irrelevant differences and make our nation whole."[30]

◆ ◆ ◆

On the evening of July 2, when President Johnson signed the act, Summer Project volunteers and local African Americans crowded into the Freedom House in Vicksburg, Mississippi. When someone shouted, "He's signing!" they gathered around a television set. A cheer went up and people started singing "We Shall Overcome," then changed the words to "We *Have* Overcome."[31]

That assessment was far from true at the time—even in 2020s America it isn't true—but it reflects the genuine import of the legislation. It was the dawning of a new day in America, albeit one on which large numbers of white Americans in the third decade of the twenty-first century are trying to bring sunset.

For his part, Lyndon Johnson was worried. "The thing we are more afraid of than anything else," he had told Hubert Humphrey in May, "is that we will have real revolution in this country when this bill goes into effect." "It doesn't do any good to have a law like the Volstead Act [the law enacted in 1919 to carry out the Eighteenth Amendment, prohibiting the manufacture and sale of intoxicating beverages] if you can't enforce it."[32]

Apart from the violence in Mississippi that was in reaction to the Summer Project, violence and calls for massive resistance did not follow the signing of the 1964 Civil Rights Act. Senator Russell believed that this was due to the fact that it was an act of Congress, not "judge or court made law."[33]

♦ ♦ ♦

Lyndon Johnson knew that the Civil Rights Act would not be sufficient to achieve the transformation he wanted to bring to his native region. He told Humphrey, "The right to vote with no ifs, ands, or buts, that's the key. When Negroes get that, they'll have every politician, north and south, east and west, kissing their ass, begging for their support." This was a point on which Johnson and people in the Southern Freedom Movement agreed. James Bevel of the Southern Christian Leadership Conference had put it dramatically when he told young African Americans in Birmingham in 1963 that when blacks vote, "'Niggers' become 'colored constituents.'"[34]

Reenacting Another Reconstruction: Finishing What FDR Had Begun

> Our first objective is to free 30 million Americans from the prison of poverty. Can you help us free these Americans? And if you can let me hear your voices!
>
> —Lyndon Johnson,
> campaigning in 1964[35]

By the summer of 1964, Lyndon Johnson was well on his way to his objective of becoming "the president who finishes what Lincoln began." But the role he envisioned for himself went far beyond even that lofty goal. He wanted not only to complete the Lincoln revolution but also to finish the Roosevelt revolution. "I'm going to be president for nine years and so many days," Johnson told Bill Moyers, "almost as long as FDR," and he made clear that he saw it as his "chance to finish what Roosevelt had begun."[36]

"I'm sick of all these people who talk about what we can't do," Johnson said in late March to Richard Goodwin, the Kennedy aide LBJ had made his speechwriter. "Hell, we're the richest country in the world, the most powerful. We can do it all, if we're not too greedy. . . . We can do it if we believe it."[37]

Johnson was a true believer in what Franklin Roosevelt had tried to do. Economist Eliot Janeway remembered a late-night gathering in 1943 or 1944 at the home of Abe Fortas (whom Johnson would appoint to the Supreme Court in 1965). Lyndon Johnson, then a young congressman, came up into Janeway's face and said: "The difference between you and me, El'yit, is, you're *for* Roosevelt, but Ah *believe* in Roosevelt."[38] In the Long 1964, LBJ saw himself as the second coming of FDR.

Lyndon B. Johnson's aspiration, in short, was to complete and outdo the achievements of the two men many regarded as the nation's two greatest presidents, Abraham Lincoln and Franklin D. Roosevelt. Modesty was never Johnson's strong suit.

He set out to achieve these objectives simultaneously. As he was working feverishly on the civil rights bill, Johnson was pushing forward vigorously with his War on Poverty and enlarging the objective. A key to making the program palatable to Americans who were better-off economically was to argue that it would not be based on redistribution—taking from the haves to give to the have-nots—but on growing the whole economy. The idea was to make the pie bigger, enabling the slice going to the poor to grow without reducing the size of the slices going to the rich or middle class.

The persistence of widespread poverty had been brought to the public's attention by Michael Harrington's 1962 book, *The Other America*.[39] Lyndon B. Johnson did not need a book to acquaint him with poverty, though, and the need to do something about it. He sought to get the War on Poverty launched as quickly as possible and told Walter Heller to get him a plan by January 1964. The most significant person in drafting the plan was David Hackett, a close friend of Robert Kennedy since prep school and the model for Phineas, the heroic athlete in John Knowles's 1959 novel *A Separate Peace*.[40]

Shortly before Christmas 1963, Heller submitted a plan that had been drafted in only three weeks. The proposal was for a series of demonstration programs in various neighborhoods around the country to try out ideas and see which ones worked. The "War on Poverty" would then be launched on the basis of what was learned from the limited trials. Key to the demonstration programs—which received the name "Community Action Program" (CAP)—was Hackett's belief that the poor themselves must be directly involved in developing and running them.

But Lyndon Johnson was not one to wait or go small-scale. He wanted something that would "be big and bold and hit the whole nation with real impact."[41] He insisted that the Community Action Programs be available immediately to any community that wanted one, with the federal government covering most of the cost. "In one stroke," as historian Allen Matusow has written, "Johnson escalated community action from an experimental program to precede the War on Poverty into the very war itself."[42]

Johnson's demand for, as his role model Franklin Roosevelt had put it, "action—and action now" in the War on Poverty meant finding a commanding officer. The president soon decided that the ideal choice to lead the effort against poverty was Sargent Shriver, a Kennedy brother-in-law who had successfully overseen the launching of the Peace Corps. Shriver provided the positives of a Kennedy association without what were, from Johnson's perspective, the enormous negatives of the Kennedy who appeared to want to lead the war on poverty, Robert Kennedy.[43]

As soon as he looked at the proposal that had been drawn up, Shriver concluded that the CAP plan would never fly. Although the fact had escaped Johnson's notice (presumably because of his haste in trying to get a program going), involving the poor themselves would mean confronting entrenched local power. Those in power in cities across America were unlikely to take kindly to having that power challenged by poor citizens backed by a federal program.

The new "poverty czar" would have ditched CAP if he could have, but it had too much momentum to discard. What Shriver did instead was to reduce it to one of several approaches included in the bill, which contained a Jobs Corps, Volunteers in Service to America (VISTA, a sort of domestic Peace Corps), incentives to hire the unemployed, adult education, work study, and other programs in addition to the Community Action Program.

The fact was that the bill had been created far too hastily, without any trials of ideas to see what might work and what wouldn't. Lyndon Johnson had no better grasp on how to fight the war he wanted to than the one he didn't, in Vietnam. But he sought to make a statement; the details could be worked out later. Democrats outside the South in both houses were virtually unanimous in their support for the legislation, while southern Democrats were divided, and Republicans were heavily against it.

When President Johnson signed the Economic Opportunity Act into law on August 20, right before the start of the Democratic National Convention, he proclaimed: "Today for the first time in all the history of the human race, a great nation is able to make and is willing to make a commitment to eradicate poverty among its people."[44]

Our Guy:
Building a Great Society

Lyndon Johnson was a big man determined to accomplish big things. He felt a need for a "big theme" to bring together all he sought to do. FDR had his New Deal and JFK his New Frontier; LBJ needed a catchy name for his program. In early April, he called on Bill Moyers and Dick Goodwin to come to the White House pool for one of the new president's skinny-dipping sessions. There, the massive, naked chief executive told his bare-bottomed aides that he would have a program that would go beyond Kennedy's—a "Johnson program, different in tone, fighting and aggressive," than JFK's. He wanted to present to the American people proposals that would move the nation "toward some distant vision—vaguely defined, inchoate, but rooted in an ideal as old as the country."[45]

Princeton historian Eric Goldman, who had come to Johnson's White House as an adviser a few weeks after the assassination, suggested as a name for the new president's program the title of Walter Lippmann's 1937 book, *The Good Society*. Goodwin altered it to "Great Society" and drafted a speech on that theme. Johnson loved the draft speech and decided to have it expanded into the vision statement of his presidency. He delivered it as the commencement address at the University of Michigan on May 22. Johnson's speech would combine the objectives contained in the civil rights and economic opportunity initiatives and place them within a grand vision for America's future.

"For a century," Johnson said, "we labored to settle and to subdue a continent. For half a century we called upon unbounded invention and untiring industry to create an order of plenty for all of our people. The challenge of the next half century is whether we have the wisdom to use that wealth to enrich and elevate our national life, and to advance the quality of our American civilization."

Johnson asked whether Americans would "build a society where progress is the servant of our needs, or a society where old values and new visions are buried under unbridled growth. For in your time," he said to the graduates, "we have the opportunity to move not only toward the rich society and the powerful society, but upward to the Great Society."

"The Great Society," the president proclaimed, "rests on abundance and liberty for all. It demands an end to poverty and racial injustice, to which we are totally committed in our time. But that is just the beginning." He spoke of beauty, nature, expanding knowledge, protecting the environment, and community.

The Great Society, the president said, "is a place where men are more concerned with the quality of their goals than the quantity of their goods." It was "not a safe harbor, a resting place, a final objective, a finished work. It is a challenge constantly renewed, beckoning us toward a destiny where the meaning of our lives matches the marvelous products of our labor."

"So," he concluded, "let us from this moment begin our work so that in the future men will look back and say, 'It was then, after a long and weary way, that man turned the exploits of his genius to the full enrichment of his life.'"[46]

The crowd of eighty thousand received the speech with great enthusiasm, and a substantial majority of the wider public appeared to feel the same way. Johnson was euphoric.[47] He was the man for the times in 1964. It wasn't that most people believed, as Johnson himself apparently did, that poverty could be conquered. In a 1964 Gallup Poll that asked respondents whether they thought that poverty would ever be eliminated, "no" topped "yes" by a huge margin, 83 percent to 9 percent.

But, particularly in the wake of the Kennedy assassination, people loved Johnson's confidence and enthusiasm, his clear belief that the United States could become much better. Americans were yearning for a call to idealism and betterment; many were tired of the materialism associated with the fifties. They might not—indeed, *did* not—believe that the "Great Society" could be achieved, but they liked the vision and optimism.

When the president delivered his speech in Ann Arbor, Mary Wells's "My Guy" was in its second straight week at number one on the *Billboard* chart. Lyndon Johnson was increasingly becoming "Our Guy" to the American people. He was polling at a 75 percent approval rating, with only about 10 percent indicating doubts about his policies and performance.

The vision to which Johnson gave voice in Ann Arbor in May captured many of the hopes of those involved in the freedom quests of the 1964. And much in the speech is recognizable as what large numbers of Americans are still struggling for in the 2020s.

The Fire *This* Time—Urban Rioting

All minorities recognizable by the color of their skin
have experienced the irrational quality of the police
force evident in the slaying of the 15-year-old boy.
                                    —Barbara Benson (July 1964)[48]

Less than three weeks after the Great Society speech, the Senate voted cloture on the civil rights bill. It was at this point that President Johnson made his comment to Dick Russell that "we're doing just fine, except for this damned Vietnam thing. We're doing just wonderful."[49]

As it happened, though, Vietnam was not the only "damned thing" about to cloud the blue skies that Johnson was seeing.

On July 16, exactly two weeks after Johnson signed the Civil Rights Act into law, and on the same night that Barry Goldwater accepted the Republican presidential nomination, a fifteen-year-old African American was shot and killed in Harlem by a New York City policeman. The incident began after the white superintendent of a group of apartments turned a hose on black kids who often sat on the steps to the buildings. According to them, the superintendent shouted at them, "Dirty niggers, I'll wash you clean."[50] They responded by throwing bottles and garbage-can lids at the superintendent, who retreated inside one of the buildings. A boy not involved in the original incident, James Powell, pursued him, and when Powell exited the building an off-duty policeman shot and killed him. There was an almost immediate confrontation between neighborhood youths and police. Over the following days, these clashes escalated into the first major ghetto riot or uprising* of the 1960s.

By the night of June 18, thousands of black people were in the streets of Harlem, breaking windows, looting stores, and shouting at the police, "Killers! Killers!"[51] When a police officer tried to disperse one of the crowds by yelling, "Go home, go home," people in the crowd responded, "We *are* home, baby."[52]

The causes of the 1964 rioting were brilliantly explained by a black woman in Brooklyn who wrote a letter to the editor of the *New York Times* after the outbreak. Barbara Benson said that she wept "at the damage done to this city and the world by the Harlem riots" and was especially concerned that "this rioting may have made a Goldwater victory more likely." But she felt the need to try to explain what leads to rioting. Her words sound all too contemporary more than a half century later:

"All minorities recognizable by the color of their skin have experienced the irrational quality of the police force evident in the slaying of the 15-year-old boy. Many of us have been stopped by police and,

---

* The words "riot" and "uprising" were used by different sides to describe the same phenomena, the former by most whites, the latter by blacks and, as the decade went on, a growing number of whites on the left. I'll use the two words interchangeably.

yes, many frisked for no other reason than that a Negro in a certain neighborhood 'seems suspicious.'

"Let no one be deceived," Benson wrote. "Many Harlem police are sadistic in their administration of the law, insatiable in their beatings, unable to discern men from children, and irrational in their fear of the black man, as well as incapable of telling one black man from another."[53]

There was no need for the various commissions set up from 1964 through the end of the decade to find the causes of urban uprisings. This letter said it all.

◆ ◆ ◆

President Johnson feared the riots would make Goldwater a viable threat to win the November election. "If we aren't careful, we're gonna be presiding over a country that's so badly split up that they'll vote for anybody who isn't us," Press Secretary George Reedy said to Johnson after the Harlem riot had been going on for a couple of days.[54]

Johnson felt the need to condemn the riots while simultaneously emphasizing the centrality of the pursuit of racial equality and justice. On July 20, he issued a statement on the situation in Harlem in which he declared: "In the preservation of law and order there can be no compromise—just as there can be no compromise in securing equal and exact justice for all Americans."[55]

Over the next few weeks, as the Mississippi Freedom Summer was facing violence almost daily, northern urban uprisings spread to the Bedford-Stuyvesant area of Brooklyn;[56] Rochester, New York; three New Jersey cities (Jersey City, Paterson, and Elizabeth); and then to the Chicago area. At the end of August, immediately following the Democratic convention in Atlantic City, a serious riot erupted less than sixty miles to the west, in Philadelphia.[57] Like the others, the underlying cause was a series of charges of police brutality against African Americans.

White policemen beating and killing black people with impunity was, to be sure, nothing new in 1964. Nor was the phenomenon of such actions sparking rebellions by black residents without precedent.

Two terrified African American girls flee police officers during a race riot in the Bedford-Stuyvesant neighborhood of Brooklyn. July 21, 1964.

But the incidents of resistance by black residents became much more common in 1964 and ensuing years of the sixties. As historian Elizabeth Hinton demonstrates in her 2021 book *America on Fire*, the vicious policing that remains one of the principal battle lines of today has continued since 1964 to be the cause of many outbursts of rebellion by African Americans.[58] When it comes to white policemen being convicted of murdering a black person, it still almost never happens more than a half century later. The 2021 murder conviction of the Minneapolis cop who killed George Floyd provides some hope for change on this front, but the police killings of black people continued during and after that trial.

♦♦♦

The prospect that white "backlash" might turn the nation against Johnson and to Goldwater was, as election chronicler Theodore White wrote, "a midsummer political thunderhead—frightfully black and dangerous as it approached, but then over very quickly."[59] The urban riots in summer of 1964 did not shake the hopeful liberal consensus of the year, and Johnson was elected by an overwhelming vote. However, the riots and Vietnam represented two thunderheads on his horizon that portended great trouble. It was to be the much larger uprising in the Watts district of Los Angeles in August 1965—an uprising that came five days after Johnson signed the Voting Rights Act into law—that would wind up producing the sort of dramatic political backlash that Johnson had feared but avoided in 1964.[60]

13

THE CROSSROADS OF FREEDOM

THE MISSISSIPPI FREEDOM SUMMER

JUNE–AUGUST 1964

Ku Klux Klan wanted poster for Bob Moses, 1964

"Mississippi can't be exaggerated.
—Bob Moses (1964)[1]

LEGEND HAS IT THAT it was at a crossroads in the Mississippi Delta in the 1930s that bluesman Robert Johnson, the forefather of the music that the second wave of 1964's British Invasion brought back to white America, met Satan at midnight and traded his soul for the ability to play guitar like no one else.[2] If we consider that the source of the blues that Johnson and so many other African American Mississippians created was the horrible life they experienced at the hands of the devilish system under which they lived, perhaps there is some metaphorical truth to the legend.

Mississippi was clearly the crossroads of the major freedom quests of 1964. It was the birthplace of the music that spread the notion of "black freedom" to growing numbers of white youth. And it was where the African American quest for "white freedom" faced its biggest challenges and fought its key battles in the summer of 1964.

At the 1964 Mississippi crossroads there was to be no deal with the devil to sell a soul; rather the devil, in the form of racism and oppression, was to be fought nonviolently in order to try to redeem the soul of America.

For many people on the COFO/SNCC staff, it was the debate during the winter of 1963–1964 over whether to conduct the Summer Project, not the project itself in the summer of 1964, that constituted the crossroads experience. From their perspective, bringing in white volunteers did amount to making a deal with the devil in which the soul of the movement was exchanged for the temporary gains that a group of outsiders might bring.

"Young Americans . . . Charged with New Energy and Determination"

But I just can't comprehend why people must die to achieve something so basic and simple as Freedom...
—Sylvie, Summer Project volunteer, June 24, 1964[3]

After Schwerner, Cheney, and Goodman vanished on June 21, Summer Project volunteers were scared. Who in their right mind wouldn't be? Parents frantically called their sons and daughters, begging them to come home. Psychiatrist Robert Coles met with anxious volunteers in the days after the three young men disappeared. He classified a few of the volunteers as being "near psychosis," and he sent eight of them home. The effect of the news from Neshoba on the rest of them, however, was different. "Suddenly hundreds of young Americans became charged with new energy and determination," Coles said. "Suddenly I saw fear turn into toughness, vacillation into quiet conviction."[4] The Mississippi Freedom Summer thus began to change the country's outlook in a way that marked the arrival of the sixties.

Bob Moses told the second group of volunteers what they already knew but were trying not to believe. "The kids are dead." He went on to explain what, as he saw it, was at stake in going forward with the Mississippi Summer Project: "In our country we have some real evil, and the attempt to do something about it involves enormous effort . . . and therefore tremendous risks." He told the volunteers that if any of them were hesitant about what they were getting into, they should leave.[5] With only a few exceptions, they didn't leave for home; they left for Mississippi. The Summer Project would go on.

The volunteers were chosen principally from the most prestigious private and public universities. "We were, in fact, trying to consciously recruit a counter power-elite," James Forman recalled two decades later.[6] Roughly 1,200 people applied and 900 participated.[7] Approximately 90 percent were white. Remarkably, over 40 percent were women, a fact that would have major consequences for the project, for the decade, and for the future.

Mississippi officials and the local media referred to the Summer Project as an "invasion," and it was. Freedom Summer was a case of selective service—this nonviolent army was assembled through selective recruiting that weeded out people with doubts about facing the risks. In the days after the Neshoba disappearance, the *Washington Post* praised the volunteers going to Mississippi as a "breathtakingly admirable group of youngsters."[8]

◆ ◆ ◆

White Mississippi girded for an invasion. In Jackson, Mayor Allen Thompson assembled "Allen's Army," an all-white police force that the mayor boasted was "twice as big as any city our size." It included "Thompson's Tank," a specially ordered new "13,000-pound armored battlewagon" that *Newsweek* described as a "twelve-man tank, abristle with shotguns, tear-gas guns, and a sub-machine gun." "It's a wonderful thing," the mayor declared.[9]

A week before the first wave of volunteers arrived, rumors spread in Mississippi that the number of "invaders" on their way was thirty thousand and Negro gangs were "forming to rape white women"! Such terrifying stories led to a run on gun shops by local white residents.[10]

When the Freedom Summer volunteers completed their basic training and packed up for the trip to Mississippi, the feeling was, as one of the students wrote, "a strange [combination] of children headed for summer camp and soldiers going off to war."[11] They embarked with "a mixed air of anxiety and buoyant bravado" similar to the mood of armed forces facing a traditional war.[12] SNCC Chairman James Forman called them "Moses and His Boys, the Nonviolent Guerrillas."[13]

Links to Vietnam were made even at the outset of the Summer Project. "The guerilla war in Mississippi is not much different from that in Vietnam," Moses said at the June orientation in Ohio.[14] "How is it," a volunteer at Western College for Women asked Justice Department representative John Doar, "that the government can protect the Vietnamese from the Viet Cong and the same government will not accept the moral responsibility of protecting the people in Mississippi?"[15]

In one sense, the experience of the Summer Project volunteers was more like that of World War II vets than that of their contemporaries who fought in Vietnam. The War in Mississippi was another "Good War," a contest between what could clearly be seen as good and evil. Since the sit-ins of 1960, as historian Sara Evans has written, "the romance and daring of black youth" had provided "an unassailable cause. The good guys seemed so good . . . and the bad guys seemed so bad."[16] The veterans of the freedom struggle in the southern United States firmly believed, as did most of the veterans of World War II, that their service was for a noble cause. Vietnam veterans were often less sure about the nobility of their war. In two other respects, though, the experiences of the unarmed forces in the southern United States differed sharply from those of the armed forces of both World War II and Vietnam. For all the fear, danger, and violence the volunteers in

Mississippi experienced, it was not remotely on the level that combat veterans had faced in World War II or Vietnam—or in the American South a century before. And none of the vets of the unarmed forces had engaged in the sorts of brutal actions that left some vets of the armed forces with PTSD—though what those in the Freedom Movement went through also left many of them with serious psychological scars.

While the Movement was committed to nonviolence in principle, there were many involved in it who firmly believed in self-defense. The Neshoba murders led Dave Dennis of CORE to conclude that nonviolence "is a waste of good lives. You have to put some injury on your enemy to get respect."[17] When the bodies of the slain Freedom workers were found in early August, Stokely Carmichael told a rally in Greenwood, "Another thing. We're not goin' to stick with this non-violence forever." He and others wanted to bring guns into the Greenwood office, but Bob Moses talked them out of it. In the week after the bodies were found, Bob Zellner, a white SNCC veteran, tried to interest others in his plan to kill Neshoba Sheriff Lawrence Rainey and Deputy Cecil Price, who clearly were principals in the murders, but could find no one who would join with him.[18] "They start anything, I have a gun," said Hartman Turnbow of the Delta town of Tchula, "and my wife—she got one, too." "Sweets" Turnbow carried a revolver in a paper bag that she kept on her lap.[19] Local Klan members and police generally knew which black residents were armed, and having such armed African Americans nearby often provided some protection to unarmed, nonviolent Movement workers.

The Purpose of an "Agitator": To Get the Dirt Out

> Before you all came, Mississippi was a white man's land. Now it will become a human land.
> —Freedom School pupil,
> Greenwood, Mississippi (1964)[20]

The purpose of the volunteers was explained to African Americans in Mississippi in a variety of ways. "Y'all gonna hear a lot of different stories from white folks about what these people are and why they're down here," Deacon Robert Miles told his congregation at the West Camp Baptist Church in Panola County in the Delta. "White folks are gonna tell you they're agitators. You know what an agitator is? An agitator is the piece in the center of a washing machine that spins around to get the dirt out. Well that's what these people are here for. They're here to get the dirt out."[21]

Both the Freedom Democratic Party and the Freedom Schools were intended to create "parallel institutions" in the black community. "If we are concerned about breaking the power structure," wrote Charles Cobb, the SNCC field secretary who pushed the idea of Freedom Schools, "then we have to be concerned about building our own institutions to replace the old, unjust decadent ones which make up the existing power structure. Education in Mississippi is an institution which must be reconstructed from the bottom up."[22]

The prospectus that was sent to volunteers who would teach in the Freedom Schools, "Notes on Teaching in Mississippi," explained that the black students "have been denied free expression and free thought. Most of all . . . they have been denied the right to question. The purpose of the Freedom Schools is to help them begin to question."[23]

The Freedom Schools were revolutionary not only in the sense that they challenged the Mississippi power structure but also in the educational method they employed. The ideals of breaking down hierarchy, encouraging participation, and developing local people to achieve their full potential were all woven into the pedagogy. It was their role, Cobb said, "to fill an intellectual and creative vacuum in the lives of young Negro Mississippians, and to get them to articulate their own desires, demands, and questions." Historian and activist Staughton Lynd developed a program intended to turn the traditional role of a teacher upside down and maximize student participation. "The Freedom School teacher is," said Florence Howe, who taught in the Jackson Freedom Schools, "to *learn with* the students." Students were encouraged to bring their own experiences with the institutions and practices of Mississippi into the discussion.[24]

Among the innovations of the Freedom Schools was the teaching of African American history. It was a revelation to many of the students that people like them *had* a history. The rise of black history, as well as that of other ethnic histories and women's history, as the sixties blossomed was in part the result of what began in the Mississippi Freedom Schools in the summer of 1964.

Turning Mississippi—and America—Right Side Up

If Negroes mobilize the power of their souls,
[they can] turn this nation upside down in order
to turn it right side up.
                    —Martin Luther King Jr.
                    Greenwood, Mississippi
                    (July 21, 1964)[25]

Along with the local African Americans, the SNCC fieldworkers, and the Project volunteers, Mississippi saw a stream of nationally known figures during the Freedom Summer. Among them were such "usual suspects" as Pete Seeger, who also persuaded other folk singers, including Judy Collins and Phil Ochs, to go to Mississippi to support the Freedom Movement.[26]

At the invitation of Bob Moses, Martin Luther King Jr., visited the state in July for the first time since the funeral of Mississippi NAACP leader Medgar Evers, who had been murdered by a white supremacist more than a year before. Attorney General Robert Kennedy called President Johnson on the morning of July 21 to inform him that King was on a plane bound for Mississippi. "If he gets killed," Kennedy said, "it creates all sorts of problems." Johnson immediately telephoned FBI Director J. Edgar Hoover, who loathed King and, to put it mildly, didn't like Bobby Kennedy. "There are threats that they are going to kill him [King]," Hoover informed LBJ. Johnson told Hoover to have FBI agents in front of and behind King everywhere he went in Mississippi.[27]

The relationship between King and the young activists in SNCC was uneasy. Many of those who worked in near anonymity on the frontlines in Mississippi and elsewhere in the Deep South resented King's fame and his penchant for flying into a trouble spot, getting all the media attention, and then leaving. Some in SNCC referred to King derisively as "de Lawd." Still, King said he thought SNCC's Mississippi Summer Project was "the most creative thing happening today in civil rights."[28] Well aware that it might be a suicide mission, King accepted the invitation from Moses. Not only would he go, but he would make Greenwood his first stop and later go to Neshoba County. No one could question his courage. On the other hand, a small phalanx of FBI agents accompanied him. The contrast between the treatment accorded King and the FBI's insistence that it could offer fieldworkers and volunteers no protection was unmistakable.

In Greenwood, King said to residents at an impromptu talk outside a pool hall and a café, "You must not allow anybody to make you feel you are not significant. Every Negro has worth and dignity. Mississippi has treated the Negro as if he is a thing instead of a person." That last sentence succinctly captured the essence of Mississippi's closed society. That evening an overflow crowd at the Elks Hall in Greenwood chanted, "We Want Free-dom! We Want Free-dom!" as they awaited King's arrival. When he spoke, King told his audience, "If Negroes mobilize the power of their souls," they could "turn this nation upside down in order to turn it right side up."[29]

In a marvelous juxtaposition, Martin Luther King Jr.'s visit to Vicksburg two days later coincided with what was to the small city's white population its most important annual event, the Miss Mississippi pageant. White Mississippi was almost as wrapped up in beauty pageants as it was in football.

And, on July 23, 1964, even with the man some of them called "Martin Luther Coon" in the state, white Mississippians could keep the old ways going. As white Vicksburg was enthralled by the swimsuit competition that evening, King spoke before an overwhelmingly black audience at a local church.[30] The woman chosen as the winner of the beauty pageant and the men and women chosen as delegates by the Mississippi Freedom Democratic Party would head to the same destination: the decaying boardwalk empire in New Jersey that would host both the Democratic National Convention from August 24 to 27 and the Miss America pageant two weeks later. Because of the Freedom Movement and its national publicity, the mostly black Mississippi Freedom Democrats would have a better chance of success in Atlantic City than would the white Miss Mississippi. Even the voters in a beauty pageant could not ignore what was going on in the Magnolia State. Miss Mississippi, a position that had produced two Miss Americas in the past few years, didn't even make the list of ten semifinalists.[31]

A few weeks later two of the nation's most noted black performing artists, singer Harry Belafonte and actor Sidney Poitier (who the previous year had become the first African American ever to win the Best Actor Oscar, horrifying much of white America when presenter Anne Bancroft embraced him and kissed him on the cheek[32]), arrived in Greenwood. There wasn't enough money to send the Freedom Democratic delegation to Atlantic City, and Belafonte had answered the call to raise the needed funds. He decided to take $60,000 in cash to Greenwood himself, and asked Poitier to go with him, joking "They might think twice about killing *two* big niggers."[33] After their small plane landed in Greenwood on the night of August 10, Belafonte and Poitier were placed in the middle car of a three-car caravan to go into town. Belafonte had a satchel stuffed with cash on his lap.[34] Klansmen in other cars rushed after them; a truck with a two-by-four strapped to the front bumper repeatedly rammed the back of the rear car as the drivers of all the SNCC vehicles swerved to avoid their pursuers. The chase was the basis for one that Poitier would reprise in a fictional Mississippi town called Sparta in *In the Heat of the Night*, which won the Academy Award for Best Picture of 1967. The pair made it to the Elks Hall, where Belafonte led the singing of freedom songs. "I am thirty-seven years old. I have always been a lonely man," Poitier said in a wavering voice after he rose to speak. "I have been lonely because I have not found love, but this room is *overflowing* with it."[35]

◆ ◆ ◆

In the '64 Mississippi Summer, the movement held "Freedom Days" in various towns around the state. During one in Gulfport in August, a white man punched one of the volunteers. The assailant ran up to a policeman standing on a nearby street corner. "I got me one," he proudly proclaimed as he rubbed his sore knuckles, then asked whether the policeman was "the law." The cop's response neatly captured the state of the state that summer: "We don't have any law in Mississippi."[36]

Terrorism in the name of religion was widespread that year in a state that liked to call itself the most religious in America. The mixing of hatred, racism, and violence with what passed for Christianity in much of white Mississippi was all too ordinary. "This summer, within a very few days, the enemy will launch his final push for victory here in Mississippi," the Imperial Wizard of the Klan announced just before the Summer Project began. "And a solemn, determined spirit of Christian reverence must be stimulated by all members."[37]

Klansmen burned churches—lots of them. At least thirty-five were burned or bombed in Mississippi that summer.[38] The place that was called "the bombing capital of the world" in 1964 was not in the Middle East but in the "good Christian" town of McComb, Mississippi.[39]

Among the reasons given for raiding black churches was that they were said to be housing stockpiles of weapons to be used in a Communist takeover.[40] An early August caller to the Vicksburg Freedom House explained to the white woman who answered the phone: "Listen, I said I'm gonna bomb y'all. And there ain't gonna be no Freedom School and no freedom there or anyplace else, and no *nothin'*!"[41]

At the Freedom School in Canton, a town north of Jackson, an incident occurred at the beginning of July that was as symbolic of the warped views and purposes of the opponents of the Mississippi Freedom Movement as the burning of churches. Local whites broke into the building housing the school and its small library collection and urinated on the books.[42]

Police are for arresting the victims of hate crimes. Churches are for burning. Books are for pissing on. As Bob Moses had told the recruits in Ohio before they departed for the state, "Mississippi can't be exaggerated."

◆

"Freedom High"—
Mississippi's Freedom Summer as the
Fulcrum of the Sixties

This was history in the making. This was going to be
written down, talked about. This was a sea change in
the United States.

—Chris Williams, Summer
Project volunteer[43]

At the final meeting in Ohio of the second group before its departure
for Mississippi, a young woman's voice rose singing, "They say that
Freedom is a long, long struggle." Other voices joined in, and soon
everyone was standing with arms around those next to them, "singing
in one voice." In a letter she wrote that night, volunteer Pam Parker
said that it was at this moment that she "knew better than ever before
why I was going to Mississippi and what I am fighting for. It is for freedom—the freedom to love. It is something that no one can have until
everybody has it."[44] It was at moments like this that the volunteers and
veterans experienced what the movement termed a "Freedom High."

Songs—*freedom* songs—were the salve that healed wounds and the
thread that stitched and held together movement people of differing
views and strong opinions. After heated debate, someone would get
out a guitar or begin singing a cappella, and others would join in. Tem-
pers that had flared only minutes before were cooled and a degree of
harmony was reinstated through harmonizing. Singing together both
symbolized and reminded people in the movement that they were in it
together and working for the same goals, even if they disagreed over
tactics or other lesser matters.[45]

By the time of the Democratic National Convention at the end of
August, the Mississippi Summer Project was coming to an end, but
its repercussions, which would continue throughout the rest of the
decade and well beyond, were beginning to be felt in other parts of
the nation.

Mississippi's Freedom Summer was the central event of the forma-
tive long year that marked the arrival of the sixties. It played a crucial
role in spawning many of the most important developments in the rest

of the decade, beginning with the primacy of young people. The civil rights movement was, starting with the sit-ins in 1960, largely youth-led, but it was with the Mississippi Summer Project that the young guerrillas firmly took over from the old guard. Student activism in the civil rights movement led directly to the Free Speech Movement at Berkeley, which was started by veterans of the Mississippi Summer. Antiwar teach-ins were inspired in part by the Mississippi Freedom Schools set up in 1964. Radical feminism had one of its most significant origins in the reaction of women in the Summer Project to their treatment by men in the Freedom Movement, which will be covered later. The move toward Black Power arose among SNCC participants in the Mississippi Summer Project. The approximately one hundred medical doctors, nurses, and psychologists who volunteered in Mississippi that summer provided the basis for the Medical Committee for Human Rights, which was instrumental in the development of Medicaid.[46] Head Start was inspired in part by the Freedom Schools, and the Child Development Group of Mississippi became one of the first and largest of the nation's Head Start programs the following spring.[47] Black history was taught in the Freedom Schools and that experience led to the spread of the teaching of the histories of previously omitted categories of people. The split between traditional liberals and young activists that surfaced then would become apparent in the struggle over the seating of the Mississippi Freedom Democratic Party at the Democratic National Convention in Atlantic City in August and would combine with the divisive impact of the American war in Vietnam to destroy the Democratic coalition that had been built during the New Deal, opening the way for the turn to the right in later years. The democratization of the nominating process of the Democratic party was an outgrowth of the challenge the MFDP made at the party's national convention.

Although, as will be discussed in Chapter 16, Bob Moses and his nonviolent guerrillas emerged from the summer with the feeling of defeat after having registered few new voters and not getting the Freedom Democrats seated in Atlantic City, they had taken a major step toward victory and, in many ways, turning "the nation upside down in order to turn it right side up."

14

"Extremism in Defense of Liberty"

Goldwater and the Republicans

July 1964

Supporters of Barry Goldwater's presidential campaign, Chicago, February 1964.

And this party, with every breath and every heartbeat, has but a single resolve, and that is: *Freedom!*
—Sen. Barry Goldwater
(July 16, 1964)[1]

THE Mississippi Freedom Democratic Party was not the only insurgent, antiestablishment political group that saw itself as the "Freedom Party" in 1964. The right-wingers who took control of the Republican Party that year defined themselves with the same word, though a different definition. While black and white activists were struggling to bring "white freedom" to black people in Mississippi, white activists gathered at the Republican National Convention in San Francisco to talk about a competing conception of freedom and secure that party's 1964 presidential nomination for Arizona senator Barry M. Goldwater. In his acceptance speech, Goldwater would utter the word *freedom* twenty-three times (and *free* an additional dozen times) and underline it repeatedly in the text from which he read.[2]

Freedom Extremists, Freedom Parties, and Young Americans for Freedom

The market economy, allocating resources by the free play of supply and demand, is the single economic system compatible with the requirements of personal freedom.

—"Sharon Statement"
(September 1960)[3]

While what we think of as the sixties that were emerging in 1964 principally involved the two conceptions of *freedom* on which I mainly focus in this book, a very different understanding of the word was being promoted by some Americans who saw themselves as oppressed in ways distinct both from African Americans seeking entry into the white freedom of mainstream society and young whites seeking to escape from the constraints of that society by gaining what they imagined to be black freedom. At a time when many in the world of business had come to accept the consensus view that had emerged from the New Deal and World War II that government has an important role to play in counteracting the excesses of a market-based economy, more conservative businessmen sought to regain an economic freedom that they believed had been taken from them by Franklin D. Roosevelt. In

1964, this minority faction took control of the national Republican Party apparatus and nominated Barry Goldwater for the presidency. Before we get into Goldwater's campaign for the nomination and the July convention, some background on the movement dedicated to this other definition of freedom—which would be soundly defeated in 1964, but would have enormous success in the longer run, becoming by the 1980s and the Reagan presidency one of the year's major legacies, and be central to the battle lines of the 2020s—is in order.

Reactionary businessmen who, in the words of historian Heather Cox Richardson, "hated regulations and the taxes that leveled the playing field between employers and workers," yearned to return to the sort of freedom to accumulate wealth without government interference that men like them had enjoyed in the 1920s or, even better for their interests, the Gilded Age of the late nineteenth century.[4] As Goldwater put it in 1964, "This cancerous growth of the federal government must and shall be stopped."[5] But how could such freedom for a few at the expense of the many be achieved after most people had come to see government intervention as beneficial? There were two possible routes: Subvert democracy or find a way to get people to vote against their own interests. During the 1950s, as historian Nancy MacLean details in her 2017 book *Democracy in Chains*, some on the radical right—most notably then-obscure Virginia economist James McGill Buchanan—were beginning to explore how to limit democracy. Over time, they would conclude that there was "no way to reconcile robust individual property rights with universal voting rights." After all, "what poor man in his right mind would ever consent to rules that would keep him poor?"[6] Though their heirs in the 2020s would launch a full-blown effort to limit democracy, in 1964 that possibility seemed too far-fetched to be taken seriously by most conservatives. They would have to try to find a way to win over a majority of voters.

The people conservatives would target for conversion were the sort of discontented Americans, largely in the South, Midwest, and West, who had been the backbone of the populist movement in the late nineteenth century. During that period, those who felt left out of the gains the American economy was registering saw the source of their troubles as powerful forces in the East, which they identified as bankers and financiers—generically referred to as "Wall Street" or "the

Interests." It is certainly true that, after some notable early attempts to unite the exploited across the racial divide in the South, populism became racist. There was also a clear streak of anti-Semitism in the populist attacks on bankers. Still, the main thrust of populism earlier in the nation's history was against rich Wall Street exploiters. And these earlier American populists had seen government as much more a part of the solution than the problem. After the collapse of the Populist Party following the Democratic-Populist fusion in support of the presidential candidacy of William Jennings Bryan in 1896, lowercase-"p" populists largely identified with the Democratic Party. Most people in this segment of the populace were enthusiastic backers of Franklin Roosevelt's New Deal. In 1936, FDR carried every state in the West, South, Plains, and Midwest—most of them by substantial margins.

The key to a conservative resurgence in the mid-twentieth century and beyond would be to stand populism on its head by identifying the Republican Party with "the people" and persuading them to see Democrats as the enemy.[7] This goal could be accomplished by changing the perception of who the troublemakers and evildoers were from Wall Street to Washington—from bankers to bureaucrats, from greed to government, from the Interests to the intellectuals, from established wealth to a vaguely defined Eastern Establishment, from the plutocrats to the poor, from those on Wall Street to those on welfare.

If such a redirection, or *mis*direction, could be accomplished, the consensus that had emerged from the New Deal that positive governmental action is necessary for the good of the people could be undermined and the rich freed to accumulate more and more of the national wealth and income. The bringing of the exploited into the party of the exploiters could be accomplished only by selling to the masses of Americans what Roosevelt had termed "fear itself."

In a famous essay that appeared in the November 1964 issue of *Harper's*, historian Richard Hofstadter, who had won the Pulitzer Prize for General Nonfiction earlier in the year for his 1963 book, *Anti-Intellectualism in American Life*,[8] called what the radical right was seizing upon "The Paranoid Style in American Politics." There was always an audience for conspiracy "theories"[9] and directing hatred and blame toward some group—some Other, some *them*—that could be said to be responsible for the troubles facing people who were part of that audience. In the past *they* had been, among others, Masons, international bankers, Catholics, munitions manufacturers, and Communists.[10]

For the Republican Party to gain the allegiance of discontented people who had long and accurately identified *them* as the party of Wall Street and who were helped by the very government policies right-wing businessmen loathed, would be no mean feat. A gaggle of young Republicans began the process in the years immediately after World War II by exploiting patriotism to charge that Democrats in the Roosevelt and Truman administrations were in league with foreign Communists. Senator Joseph McCarthy of Wisconsin was the practitioner most identified with this deception. But the essential person in the redirection of populist anger from Wall Street to Washington was Richard M. Nixon, a man who was himself tormented by resentments against the "Eastern Establishment" and primed to give voice to the similar antipathies harbored by others. The symbolic turning point came in 1952 when Nixon, whose place as Dwight Eisenhower's running mate was endangered by a scandal, saved his career through a speech he gave on national television and radio. During what came to be known as the "Checkers Speech" because of his reference to his children's dog of that name, Nixon said that his wife, Pat, "doesn't have a mink coat." Pausing a moment for effect, he continued: "But she does have a respectable Republican cloth coat, and I always tell her she'd look good in anything."[11]

The twin notions that Republicans don't have mink coats and that "Republican" and "cloth coat" fit together naturally were revolutionary to the politics of a nation that had for decades taken it as axiomatic that the Republican Party is the party of the rich. The assertion that Democrats were traitors was a start, but more ammunition was needed. Just as racism had been used to divide left-wing populists in the 1890s, it was one of the important fears that the radicals of the right exploited in the 1950s and since to bring white people who were benefiting from the New Deal state into a movement that sought to destroy it.[12] The intellectuals of the right who developed in the 1950s what would come to be known beginning in the early 1960s as "Movement Conservatism"[13] did not hesitate to add racism to the pro-business, anti-communist, anti-tax, anti-labor ingredients in their recipe for winning over working- and middle-class whites. Opposition to the Supreme Court's unanimous 1954 *Brown* decision banning school segregation was prominent in starting the long stealth campaign launched by James McGill Buchanan.[14] William F. Buckley Jr., who became conservatism's most familiar front man, fully endorsed racial segregation. In 1957, Buckley wrote an editorial titled "Why the South Must Prevail" in his magazine, *National Review*. In it, he argued against full democracy, saying that in areas where whites are a minority, they are "entitled to take such measures as are necessary to prevail, politically and culturally," because they are "the advanced race."[15] Buckley had also characterized Africans as "semi-savages" who would only be capable of self-government "when they stopped eating each other."[16]

In September 1960, about 90 young "conservatives"[17] met at Buckley's estate in Sharon, Connecticut, to establish an organization called Young Americans for Freedom and develop the organization's declaration of principles. To YAF, a completely free market—by which they meant little to no taxation, no regulation of business, no labor unions, no social safety net—was the sine qua non of *freedom*. "Political freedom cannot long exist without economic freedom," the Sharon Statement proclaimed.[18] This group and like-minded self-identified conservatives set about to organize and take control of state Republican parties for the purpose of securing the 1964 Republican presidential nomination for their chosen candidate, Barry Goldwater.

Freedom Is His Flight Plan

Goldwater has been a rather casual student
of his own works.
                              —Richard Rovere (July 1964)[19]

Freedom Is His Flight Plan is the subtitle of an admiring biography of Barry Goldwater that was published in 1962.[20] Goldwater was an experienced pilot who liked nothing better than to be in the cockpit of a plane. But *freedom* in the meaning he would give the word by the later 1950s does not appear to have been his flight plan earlier in life. In 1952, he had supported moderate Dwight Eisenhower over "Mr. Conservative," Robert Taft, but his position changed dramatically over the years of the Eisenhower administration. Goldwater started calling the Eisenhower administration a "dime-store New Deal," meaning that the first post-FDR Republican president was doing nothing to overturn the social and economic programs established in the Roosevelt years.[21]

The right wing loved the rhetoric, and the more love they gave him, the more Goldwater gave them to love. In his 1960 book, *The Conscience of a Conservative*, which bears his name as author but of which he seems to have written little, Goldwater unequivocally said, "I do not undertake to promote welfare, for I propose to extend freedom. My aim is not to pass laws, but to repeal them."[22] "The conservative and his conscience," as political journalist Richard Rovere has neatly written, "must have met sometime between 1952 and 1956."[23] William F. Buckley and his followers facilitated that meeting. Buckley's *National Review* began to champion Goldwater as a central part of their effort to take control of the Republican Party, which they did in 1964.

◆ ◆ ◆

The Barry Goldwater who became the presidential nominee of the Republican Party in 1964 was a largely fictional character. Right-wingers had written a script about him, ghostwritten books, newspaper columns, and speeches of which Goldwater was, as Rovere nicely put it, "the author of record,"[24] and sent him out to sell their ideology to the masses so that they could gain the power to implement their radical pro-business program of "turning the economy over to private interests" and overturning the New Deal State.[25] In this sense, Goldwater was the experimental version of a product that the right-wing political engineers would roll out in an improved version at the end of the 1964 general election campaign in the form of Ronald Reagan. Reagan, as a trained actor, was far better able to internalize the script and present and sell it to the public.

"I've often said that if I hadn't known Barry Goldwater in 1964 and I had to depend on the press and the cartoons, I'd have voted against the son of a bitch," Goldwater liked to joke in later years, underscoring how that "son of a bitch" was mostly a product created by the radical right to be marketed to the public.[26] It must have been dismaying to those believers in the infallibility of the marketplace that the product they placed on the shelves in 1964 was overwhelmingly rejected by consumers.

"Mr. Conservative" or "Mr. Inconsistency"?

I'm going to do all I can to see that women can
go out in the streets of this country without being
scared stiff."
—Barry Goldwater (July 17, 1964)[27]

There were glaring inconsistencies at the heart of Goldwater's outlook:

Barry Goldwater was for a weak federal government—except when he wasn't.
Barry Goldwater was for states' rights—except when he wasn't.
Barry Goldwater was for strict construction of the Constitution—except when he wasn't.
Barry Goldwater was for protecting civil liberties—except when he wasn't.

There was a flagrant discrepancy between Goldwater's view of the proper powers of the national government at home and abroad. Put simply, he and his supporters believed that the powers of the American federal government should be extremely limited at home but virtually limitless abroad. They believed in "states' rights"—a term that was almost always a euphemism for segregation—at home but not in the rights of nation states abroad. The United States government should not be able to force states or American citizens to do much of anything but should be able to force nations and citizens of foreign countries to do whatever the American government decided was best for them.

Communism, Goldwater accurately stated, "has interfered and intervened times without number in the domestic affairs of free nations."[28]

But the response he proposed was for the United States to interfere and intervene in the affairs of other nations as well. "Our objective must be the destruction of the enemy as an ideological force and the removal of communists from power wherever they hold it."[29] Goldwater's view of the power and proper role for the United States government would, as Rovere said, have the nation "perpetually at war, perpetually crusading, perpetually subjugating."[30]

Perhaps even more striking in its inconsistency was Goldwater's view of the powers of the federal government to intervene to fight street crime in American cities compared with his steadfastly held position that the federal government has no power to intervene in southern states to protect black citizens.

In a news conference after his acceptance speech, the nominee declared that during the campaign he would raise the issue of the "abuse of law and order in this country, the total disregard for it, the mounting crime rate." The responsibility of dealing with this problem, he said, "should start at the Federal level." He cited a story about "a young girl in New York who used a knife to attack a rapist." She, he asserted, "is now getting the worst of the deal and the rapist is probably going to get the Congressional Medal of Honor and sent off scot-free." (In fact, the woman to whom he referred had already been cleared of charges and the alleged rapist had been indicted.) "That kind of business has to stop in this country and, as the President, I'm going to do all I can to see that women can go out in the streets of this country without being scared stiff."[31]

Yet, Goldwater stated repeatedly that the federal government is powerless to protect civil rights workers or black citizens in southern states. Law enforcement in those cases was, he maintained, a matter for state and local authorities.

Winning without a Majority

In 1964, the right-wingers promoting Goldwater and the goal of "freeing" large corporations and the very wealthy from taxation and regulation were a minority even within the Republican Party. They were seen as extremists in a party that still contained many moderates and more than a few liberals. What those who were beginning to call themselves movement conservatives had succeeded in accomplishing over the previous few years was seizing control of the party's organizations in a large number of states. At a time when presidential primaries were relatively few, the nomination was largely in the hands of delegates chosen by these state party groups.

Even with the work his supporters did in gaining control of state parties, Goldwater would have been unlikely to get the 1964 nomination were it not for developments that seriously wounded the prospects of the two men who had seemed the most likely to fight it out for the nomination.

Always ready to enter the arena again, Richard Nixon had sought to reestablish his presidential credentials after his narrow 1960 loss to John Kennedy by returning to his native California and running for governor in 1962. His defeat by Pat Brown in that contest—a defeat after which he told reporters, whom he despised as members of an elite from which he felt excluded, "You won't have Nixon to kick around anymore, because, gentlemen, this is my last press conference"—effectively removed him from the 1964 presidential field.[32]

Nixon's removal left New York governor Nelson Rockefeller as Goldwater's principal competition. But the generally liberal Rockefeller had been divorced by his wife in 1962. While divorce was in the early stages of what would become a rapid increase in the American population as the 1960s went on, it remained a major hurdle for a presidential candidate to clear. Nor was it likely to be politically helpful that Rockefeller's first wife had been granted the divorce on the grounds of "extreme mental cruelty."[33] And "Rocky," as the governor was usually called, added to the height of the hurdle in May 1963 by marrying another woman, Margaretta Large Fitler Murphy, known as "Happy," who had herself divorced only a month before her marriage to Rockefeller. A Michigan Republican summarized the difficulty the second marriage presented for the presidential hopeful: "The rapidity of it all—he gets a divorce, she gets a divorce—and the indication of the break-up of two homes. Our country doesn't like broken homes."[34]

The apparent elimination of Nixon and Rockefeller's self-inflicted problem improved Goldwater's prospects of winning the nomination. The campaign's strategy was to avoid all but a few primaries and depend on the right-wingers who had gained control of the Republican organizations in many states to provide him with the delegates needed for the nomination. It eventually worked, though opposition to his candidacy almost derailed it in New Hampshire and California.

Extremism in a Candidate's Statements *Is* a Political Vice

He was all voice and very little mind.
—Norman Mailer on Barry
Goldwater (July 1964)[35]

The assassination of President Kennedy had not been a positive development for Goldwater's candidacy. It gave extremism a bad name and, for reasons I'll get to in a moment, he had developed a reputation as an extremist. In the wake of the Kennedy assassination, but also of the images of dogs and fire hoses being used on children in Birmingham in the spring of 1963 and the killing of four little girls in the bombing of the Sixteenth Street Baptist Church in the same city in September 1963, a large majority of Americans was not receptive to an argument on the virtues of extremism.

Goldwater's identity as an extremist had developed from numerous impolitic positions and statements prior to the time the Republicans named him as their 1964 presidential nominee. During his Senate career, he called for repealing the graduated income tax and voted against federal aid to education, farm subsidies, federal grants to states, and a vast array of social welfare programs.[36] He had supported the anti-Communist rants of Senator Joseph McCarthy. In that, Goldwater did not differ from most Republicans in the early 1950s, but he seems to have been more of a believer than were many members of the party, who saw McCarthy as a dangerous but politically useful demagogue. When many other Republicans turned on McCarthy after he had attacked Eisenhower and been seen by the public to be a bully and a fool in the televised Army-McCarthy hearings in 1954, Goldwater stood by his Wisconsin colleague. He was among the twenty-two senators who voted against censuring McCarthy at the end of that year.[37]

Three years after the unanimous *Brown* desegregation decision—at about the same time that William Buckley was coming out in full support of segregation—Goldwater said he opposed the decision.[38] In 1964, Goldwater was one of only six Republicans in the Senate who voted against cloture on the Civil Rights bill, and he went on to vote against its enactment as well. His opposition to the *Brown* decision and his vote against the Civil Rights bill brought him the support of the Ku Klux Klan.

Goldwater was considerably friendlier to the use of nuclear weapons than were most Americans. He liked to call them "nukes" and speak of "tactical nuclear weapons," terminology that many would label as oxymoronic as well as politically moronic. He raised the prospect that "low-yield atomic weapons" could be used in Vietnam.[39] He voted against the Limited Nuclear Test Ban Treaty. In an October 1963 interview, Goldwater indicated that NATO commanders should have "the power to use nuclear weapons on their own initiative in an emergency."[40] Coming exactly a year after the Cuban Missile Crisis, this statement was alarming. When *Dr. Strangelove* reached movie screens in the weeks before the New Hampshire primary, it seemed that Goldwater's apparent desire to allow weapons of mass destruction to be used without a presidential decision to do so could open the door for a real-life General Jack D. Ripper to bring about nuclear annihilation.

Goldwater's solidarity with McCarthy made him popular with such extremists as the John Birch Society, a conspiracist group that saw communists everywhere. The organization's founder, Robert Welch, declared that President Eisenhower was a "dedicated, conscious agent of the Communist conspiracy." Bob Dylan mocked the group in a 1963 song, "Talkin' John Birch Paranoid Blues."[41] Goldwater wanted to distance himself from these conspiracy kooks, but much of his base was aligned with them, so he accepted their support. "Every other person in Phoenix is a member of the John Birch Society," Goldwater told Buckley and Russell Kirk, another leading conservative, in 1962. "I'm not talking about commie-haunted apple pickers or cactus drunks. I'm talking about the highest caste of men of affairs." In April 1964,

Goldwater said, "I don't consider the John Birch Society as a group to be extremist."[42]

The 1964 Goldwater campaign worked with such "patriotic organizations" as the Birch Society to distribute upward of six million copies of a book published on June 1, *None Dare Call It Treason*, by John A. Stormer,[43] which contended that elite Eastern liberals were treasonously working to bring Communist domination to the United States and the world and that major American institutions were controlled by Communists.

◆ ◆ ◆

Announcing his candidacy in Arizona on January 3, 1964, Goldwater declared, "I will not change my beliefs to win." He pledged: "I will offer a choice, not an echo." He said that he would not have entered the race if he thought he would get less than 45 percent of the vote in the general election, because he would not want to embarrass the conservative movement.[44] In the end, he would fall far short of that percentage.

In truth, while Goldwater was certainly offering a choice—that of rejecting the government acting as the balance wheel in the economy that it had become and of taking it considerably farther as Lyndon Johnson was doing—he was also offering an echo of a bygone era, of a time before Franklin Roosevelt's New Deal: the days of Calvin Coolidge and even William McKinley.

The Goldwater base in 1964 and those who repeated their arguments later represented a shrinking portion of the American population that considered its way of life threatened. Norman Mailer, who did some of his best writing in his quadrennial pieces on political party conventions, noticed possibly significant characteristics about the people in the Goldwater movement who assembled in San Francisco in mid-July for their hero's nomination. "An astonishing number" of the Goldwater girls and boys "had blue eyes," Mailer said. The Goldwater girls "had the faces of young ladies who listened to their parents, particularly to their fathers, they were full of character, but it was the character of tidiness, industry, subservience."[45]

The people in the Goldwater movement were, in short, representative of a significant segment of Middle America. They were *very* white.

Overwhelmingly, they were Protestant. They tended to be distrustful of people from urban areas. It was apparent that they believed that women and minorities should know their places and be content in them. They had no liking for immigrants whose complexions were darker than theirs, whether their migration had been voluntary or in chains. Catholics and Jews were suspicious characters. They were likely to applaud a comment Goldwater made about sawing off the Eastern Seaboard and letting it float out to sea.*

Freedom Extremists Come Together in San Francisco

> ". . . a frustrated posse, a convention of hangmen
> who subscribe to the principle that the executioner
> has his rights as well.
> —Norman Mailer (July 1964)

The 1964 Republican convention enshrined Nixonian hatred of the news media in the party. In his address on the second day of the gathering, former President Eisenhower (by no means a fan of Goldwater) called on Republicans to "particularly scorn the divisive efforts . . . [of] sensation-seeking columnists and commentators."[46] The delegates did just that; a wild demonstration ensued on the floor. Goldwater supporters shook their fists angrily in the direction of the media booths in the arena. NBC reporter John Chancellor was shoved off the convention floor by guards while television cameras transmitted the action to the nation's viewers; he signed off with, "This is John Chancellor, somewhere in custody."[47] Among the big-selling buttons at the convention was one reading "STAMP OUT HUNTLEY-BRINKLEY"—a reference to Chet Huntley and David Brinkley, the coanchors of NBC's nightly national news program.[48]

When Nelson Rockefeller was allotted ten minutes to speak in favor of a proposed platform amendment that would condemn

---

* Readers of a book published after the period of 2016 to 2020 will surely notice the correspondence of this list of the composition, beliefs, and motivations of the Goldwaterites to those of the followers of Donald Trump. The latter would, however, presumably add the cutting off of the Western Seaboard.

Civil rights activists dressed up as KKK members to protest racists supporting Barry Goldwater, San Francisco, July 1964.

extremist organizations, he noted that during the California primary he had suffered "at first-hand" from the tactics of "extremist elements." He mentioned bomb warnings, "threats of personal violence," "unsigned threatening letters," "smear and hate literature," and "strong-arm and goon tactics." The gallery, filled with Goldwater followers, exploded into boos and jeers, preventing the New York governor from continuing his speech. At one point, Rockefeller sought the right to be heard by telling those assembled in the hall, "It's still a free country, ladies and gentlemen."[49] The delegates shouted down the proposed amendment to condemn extremist groups with a thunderous "No," indicating that it was their view that freedom of speech applies to such groups as the Birch Society and the Klan, but not to a sitting governor of their own party.

Rockefeller was the embodiment of what the extreme right most hated. The pent-up frustrations and fears of the people who were attracted to this movement centered on an elite who, it was claimed, were selling out America. While the details of this generalized belief vary, the broad outline is that there is an international Communist-banker-Jewish conspiracy that works through such institutions as the Council on Foreign Relations. It was largely the same argument that Nixon, McCarthy, and others had been using about the "treason" of members of the Eastern Establishment. To many of the adherents to this worldview, the internationalist conspiracy was headed by the Rockefeller family. Nelson Rockefeller's brother David, president of the Chase Manhattan Bank, was often seen as the Lucifer of the imagined internationalist plot.[50] So, to many of the Goldwater supporters, Nelson Rockefeller was not simply a competing candidate; he was a demon in their midst.[51] They made their views of him known to all.[52]

When the roll of the states was called on Wednesday evening, July 15, Goldwater won the nomination in a landslide, with the backing of more than two-thirds of the delegates. He and his supporters had, as journalist Tom Wicker accurately put it, "crush[ed] the moderate forces that had controlled his party for a quarter-century."[53]

♦ ♦ ♦

For his acceptance speech, Goldwater would have the biggest audience of his life, as television carried his image and words into the living rooms of tens of millions of Americans. It was his opportunity to define himself for voters. He would be unfiltered by the "liberal media." Here was his chance to show the American people that he was not that "son of a bitch" they portrayed.

Freedom was, of course, the theme of the speech. "We can be freedom's missionaries in a doubting world," the nominee proclaimed. "Now my fellow Americans, the tide has been running against freedom," the newly anointed Republican standard bearer asserted. "Our people have followed false prophets. . . . We must, and we shall, set the tide running again in the cause of freedom. . . . Every breath and every heartbeat has but a single resolve, and that is freedom." And on it went: "The land of the free," "human freedom," "freedom's mission," "the words of freedom," "the author of freedom," "free nations," "only the strong can remain free," "defense of freedom," "to be free," "forces of freedom," "a free society," "unified and free," "all free men," "freedom's light." "The road to freedom is a long and a challenging road," Goldwater said. "This is a party, this Republican Party, a party for free men, not for blind followers, and not for conformists."

But, in the most famous words of his address, he made it clear that he had no problem with extremism: "I would remind you that extremism in the defense of liberty is no vice. And let me remind you also that moderation in the pursuit of justice is no virtue."[54] Goldwater underlined these lines in the copy of the speech from which he read. He intended these sentences to be the ones that would be remembered, the words that would define him. They were, and they did.

Two nights earlier, the Goldwater forces had seemingly made unmistakable what the candidate meant when they rejected the proposed platform plank Nelson Rockefeller had supported, which would have denounced extremist organizations and specifically named the John Birch Society.[55] Goldwater backers considered such right-wing extremists to be champions of "liberty" and welcome members of the new Republican coalition.

Lyndon Johnson saw immediately what a politically senseless thing Goldwater's extremism declaration was. "What'd he [Goldwater] say yesterday about extremists?" Johnson asked Bill Moyers the next day.

"He said, 'Extremism in the defense of liberty is not a vice,'" Moyers replied.

"Well, I'd just say extremism to destroy liberty *is*."[56] And Johnson's campaign would continue to say it all the way to Election Day.

Why would Goldwater make such a statement? There was a degree of revealing consistency in Goldwater's address between all his talk of freedom and his acceptance of extremism: Total freedom inevitably begets extremism, which had been an evident danger in the American ideal since Merry Mount in the 1600s. While Goldwater spoke in his acceptance speech and at other times of "freedom . . . balanced so that liberty lacking order will not become the license of the mob and of the jungle," his tolerance of extremism—tolerance, that is, of intolerance—pointed in the direction of freedom without restraints. A similar extreme concept of freedom was already being pushed by the Beats and would soon become widespread in the counterculture.

♦

Another Shade of Freedom—
The Bleaching of the Republican Party

> I now believe I know how it felt to be a Jew in
> Hitler's Germany.
> —Jackie Robinson, on the treatment
> of black people at the GOP
> convention (July 1964)[57]

Nineteen sixty-four was the year that the Party of Lincoln made a decisive turn toward becoming the white man's party, though the completion of that turn would take decades. That year, the Republicans adopted the Southern Strategy developed by F. Clifton White, who was the planner behind the right-wing takeover of the Grand Old Party and the nomination of Goldwater.

Just as there was in the early 1960s a "Movement," often written by its supporters with a capital *M*, for *freedom* in the civil rights sense, there was also developing in those same years a "Movement," often capitalized by its adherents, on the other side, for *freedom* in the "conservative," free market, property-supremacy sense. These two freedom movements were very much at odds. Indeed, it was in part the goals of the former—beginning with the *Brown* decision[58]—that called the latter into existence. In a deeper sense, though, it was opposition to the New Deal that set the right-wing movement in motion. It sought to reverse the status quo and was a revolt against the modern world in most of its manifestations. It is still that, more than a half century later. Its adherents had no tolerance for modern morality, for internationalism, for government social programs or government regulation of the market, for racial or religious diversity, or for an understanding of the world based on modern science. They were staunchly opposed to pluralism. They were, in a word, *singularists*—people who took the "this is a white man's country" stance.

In the simplest terms, both freedom movements sought to move America—but in opposite directions. The civil rights freedom movement sought to move America forward toward its conception of freedom as well as to the fulfillment of the traditional American values stated in the opening words of the Declaration of Independence. The "conservative" freedom movement sought to move America backward toward its conception of freedom: freedom for certain categories of people and for the rich and corporations to be without government "interference."

One of the favorite, most meaningful songs of the civil rights Freedom Movement was "Ain't Gonna Let Nobody Turn Me Around." The movement conservatives were determined to be the ones who *did* turn them and the whole nation and modern world around. The truth was that they were not conservatives at all. The word *conservativism* should be "despised," one of the property-freedom movement's later leading intellectuals, Murray Rothbard, declared in 1977. The radical right was, he proudly proclaimed, "the party of revolution."[59]

To this movement, John F. Kennedy was anathema as an immoral Irish Catholic internationalist who came to support civil rights. Lyndon Johnson, the apostate southerner-westerner who was the champion of big government and racial equality, was even worse.

This "conservative" freedom movement was opposed in equal measure to both of the other major definitions of *freedom* in the decade. They were white people who were opposed both to "black freedom" of the "sex, drugs, and rock 'n' roll" variety and to black people obtaining "white freedom."

Less than two weeks after President Johnson had said, as he signed the Civil Rights Act, "Let us close the springs of racial poison,"[60] the Goldwater Republicans uncapped those springs at their national convention.

At their party's convention in August, the Democrats would wrestle with the Freedom Party's challenge to the seating of Mississippi's all-white delegation. The month before, every southern state's delegation to the Republican National Convention in July was entirely white. Nor were all-white delegations a feature only of the South. Of the 1,308 delegates in San Francisco's Cow Palace, a mere fourteen (1.1 percent) were black. And those few were harassed by white people. One of the fourteen reported that black delegates were "shoved, pushed, spat upon, and cursed with a liberal sprinkling of racial epithets."[61]

How bad was it? Jackie Robinson said being on the floor of his party's national convention let him know "how it felt to be a Jew in Hitler's Germany."[62] Robinson had integrated the national pastime; now he was witnessing the dis-integration of his national party, whose support for members of his race had suddenly become something from a past time. "For those of us who revere the memory of Abraham Lincoln," a Republican National Committeewoman said, "this is a difficult pill to swallow."[63]

Four years earlier in his campaign against Jack Kennedy, Richard Nixon had wavered between seeking what was then called the Negro vote and going for the white South. And, a few weeks before the party convened in San Francisco, Republicans in Congress had voted overwhelmingly (136–35 in the House and 27–6 in the Senate) in favor of the Kennedy-Johnson Civil Rights bill. The Goldwater faction had seized the party's national convention and many of its state party organizations, but it did not reflect the position on race of Republican officeholders or the rank and file of the party around the nation. Not yet. But the die was cast.

The parties in 1964 and thereafter were profoundly affected by two major demographic upheavals that have reshaped the United States since the 1960s. The Republicans would be the beneficiaries from 1968 onward of the accelerating shift of population and of political power from the Northeast to the West and South. By turning from Nelson Rockefeller and the Eastern Establishment to Barry Goldwater and the western-southern insurgents in 1964, the Grand Old Party hitched its wagon to opposition to the other major demographic change that was building in the United States: the growth in population and, potentially, power of people of color.

◆ ◆ ◆

There was a sort of symmetry, based on reactions to differing understandings of *freedom*, in entrances and exits from the two parties' 1964 conventions. The Young Americans for Freedom and their ideological allies had taken over the San Francisco convention, and as candidate Goldwater came out in favor of extremism in his acceptance speech, forty members of the New York delegation walked out of the Cow Palace, presumably to back the Democratic nominee.[64] Six weeks later, the Freedom Democratic Party and its supporters held their "walk-in" at the Democrats' Atlantic City convention and took the vacant seats reserved for the Mississippi delegation, after which almost all the regular Mississippi delegates declined to sign a pledge to support President Johnson and left the convention hall to back the Republican nominee.

The issue that had been present since the first Reconstruction was drawn again in 1964: Would the South be remade in the image of the nation, or would the nation be remade in the image of the South? From that year onward, the Democratic Party would be associated with the former effort and the Republican Party was moving toward association with the latter.

Freedom's Just Another Word for . . . What?

Though he was all about freedom, Barry Goldwater understood that what the word means is in the perceptions of the person who says it and those who hear it. "Say we included [in a declaration of principles] a statement like 'We believe in the freedom of the individual,'" Goldwater said in a 1962 interview. "All right, Senator Javits [a liberal Republican from New York] can take that in New York and apply it to civil rights, the Negro question, everything else. I can take it and apply it to 'right to work.' I can apply it to states' rights."[65]

Freedom, Goldwater appeared to be saying, is just another word: it can be given almost opposite meanings by different people.

What does *freedom* mean? That was the question in 1964—and throughout American history. Were the activists in Mississippi or the Goldwaterites at the GOP convention in San Francisco the true "freedom party"? Were the young conservatives who backed Goldwater or the young SNCC field workers the true "young Americans for freedom"?

Both party conventions in 1964 featured conflicts in which grassroots insurgents opposed the normal, "reasonable" politics of the party's insiders. A major difference was that the right-wing insurgents had taken control of the Republican convention away from the party's establishment, while the insurgents from Mississippi faced a convention controlled by Lyndon Johnson, who, his disdain for the establishment notwithstanding, had now become its head. Although they of course disagreed almost entirely with Goldwater's positions, the SNCC freedom fighters would have heartily endorsed his statement—had it come from other lips—"moderation in pursuit of justice is no virtue."

Nineteen sixty-four was not a year for either sort of outsider, but both made major gains for the future. The time of those on the Democrats' left would come over the next few years. That of the actual extremists on the Republicans' right would take longer to germinate but would have devastating effects beginning in the late 1970s and continuing into the 2020s. The Goldwater movement can be seen, as Kurt Andersen puts it, as "an unsuccessful beta test" seeking a way "to exploit popular unease with the culturally new as a way to get a green light for" what Andersen terms "the unmaking of America": the eventually successful quest to persuade enough of the American public that policies that would "free" large corporations and the very wealthy from taxation and regulation are beneficial to everyone.[66]

Historian Rick Perlstein has summarized the result: "A right-wing fringe took over the party from the ground up . . . while a helpless Eastern establishment-that-was-now-a-fringe looked on in bafflement. Experts . . . began talking about a party committing suicide. The Goldwaterites didn't see suicide. They saw redemption."[67]

15

LBJ PROPOSES TO
"THAT BITCH OF A WAR"

THE TONKIN GULF

AUGUST 1964

US Navy jets taking off from the USS Constellation *in a raid
on North Vietnam, August 1964.*

There was nothing there but black water and
American fire power.
> —James Stockdale, on what he saw
> below him on August 4, 1964.[1]

The only freedom we really have is the freedom
to say no.
> —Joseph Heller, *Catch-22* (1961)[2]

I N AUGUST 1964, TWO decisive turns were taken that would unravel the liberal Democratic coalition at the height of its power and triumph. Lyndon Johnson, who would receive a huge mandate for liberalism in November, was the person most responsible for both. In early August, his misleading statements about a putative incident in the Gulf of Tonkin off North Vietnam set the administration on a course toward full-scale war. Later in August, it was Johnson's treatment of the Mississippi Freedom Democratic Party at the national convention in Atlantic City that completed the disillusionment with liberalism and distrust of the national Democratic Party among many young people associated with the Freedom Movement. Johnson, though, saw himself as trying to avert both of these outcomes.

In one of the remarkable coincidences of 1964, those two issues that would tear apart the liberal coalition intersected on August 4.

♦♦♦

One of the consequences of the nomination of Barry Goldwater came less than three weeks after his acceptance speech. Lyndon Johnson's mid-June assessment that "we're doing just fine, except for this damned Vietnam thing"[3] seemed to be very much the case with respect to his election prospects as the calendar flipped from July to August. He had gotten the Civil Rights bill enacted. There was widespread support for his Great Society and War on Poverty goals and proposals. And he was leading Goldwater in opinion polls by unprecedented, almost incredible, margins. In a July Gallup Poll, Johnson led 77 percent to 20 percent.[4]

Johnson believed that the only thing the Republican nominee had as a potentially effective argument against him was that he was "soft" on communism and the fight in Vietnam. Goldwater had hit hard on Vietnam in his acceptance speech, charging that "failures infest the jungles of Vietnam." "And I needn't remind you, but I will; it has been during Democratic years that a billion persons were cast into Communist captivity and their fate cynically sealed."[5] This specter of the charges Republicans made against Harry Truman for "losing China" haunted Johnson.

The president was looking for an event in Vietnam that would enable him to counter the argument that he was "soft" by providing a rationale for the passage of a Congressional resolution giving him unrestricted power to conduct war in that country. A draft of such a resolution had been in the works since May and then placed "on the shelf" awaiting an auspicious moment to ask Congress to pass it.

In December 1963, within three weeks of his assumption of the presidency, Lyndon Johnson had asked for new proposals for "covert operations by South Vietnamese forces, utilizing such support of US forces as is necessary, against North Vietnam." Johnson didn't want the United States involved on any major level, but he wanted North Vietnam to back down. It was an approach with almost no chance of success, inasmuch as his insistence on keeping the actions covert clearly indicated to North Vietnamese leaders that the United States was *not* prepared to "pay any price" to stop them.

Not knowing what to do, Johnson wanted to have a free hand to do whatever he decided he must do, whenever he might so decide. He and his top advisers wanted a Congressional resolution giving the president a blank check to conduct whatever military operations in Vietnam he deemed necessary to pass "quickly, overwhelmingly, and without too much discussion of its implications."[6] That would be difficult to achieve in the absence of some sudden change in the situation in Vietnam, so he decided to wait. At a White House meeting on June 10, Defense Secretary Robert McNamara suggested "that in the event of a dramatic event in Southeast Asia we would go promptly for a Congressional resolution."[7]

As it happened, they had to wait less than eight weeks for the requisite "dramatic event."

The Real Gulf of Tonkin Incident—August 2

We knocked hell out of 'em . . . and we haven't pulled out. We've pulled *up*.
—Lyndon B. Johnson
(August 3, 1964)[8]

At the end of July, an American destroyer, the USS *Maddox*, was sent on a patrol along the North Vietnamese coast as part of an operation codenamed DESOTO. One of its principal objectives was to gather information about coastal defenses that could be useful for the raids being conducted by South Vietnamese forces. The *Maddox* was not supposed to be directly involved in raids, but forays were stepped up at the time of the destroyer's mission. In the few days leading up to August 2, two coastal locations were shelled, a total of eight agents who were airdropped into North Vietnam were captured, and American planes on bombing missions in Laos hit targets inside North Vietnam. It looked to the North Vietnamese like the United States was coordinating actions to escalate the war.[9]

On the night of August 2, North Vietnamese torpedo boats rushed toward the *Maddox* as the American ship approached Hon Me Island, which had been the target of a South Vietnamese attack two nights earlier.[10] American reports at the time indicated that the North Vietnamese had fired first, but a 2000 National Security Agency study determined that "the *Maddox* fired three rounds to warn off the communist boats" as they approached. "This initial action was never reported by the Johnson administration, which insisted that the Vietnamese boats fired first," the NSA study noted.[11]

President Johnson's initial reaction to the August 2 skirmish was cautious. He considered it likely that the North Vietnamese action was in response to the ongoing covert actions by South Vietnamese and American forces. He also thought the engagement might have been on the initiative of a local commander, not a matter of policy by the North Vietnamese government or military. (In fact, it had been the initiative of a local commander, the head the Vietnamese Institute of Military History said in 1997.[12]) "There have been some covert operations in that area that we have been carrying on," the president told Robert Anderson, treasury secretary under Eisenhower and former secretary of the Navy and deputy secretary of defense, the morning after the event, "blowing up bridges and things of that kind, roads and so forth. So I imagine they wanted to put a stop to it. So they . . . fired and we respond immediately . . . knock one of 'em out and cripple the other two." Johnson was trying to convince moderate Republicans such as Anderson that his reaction had been "tough."

Anderson's response was less than fully encouraging on that score. "You're going to be running against a man who's a wild man on this subject. Any lack of firmness he'll make up. . . . You've got to . . . [show] we're not soft." That last word was, of course, one likely to make Johnson cringe. "We knocked hell out of 'em," he asserted. "and we haven't pulled out. We've pulled *up*." But Anderson still saw trouble coming from "wild man" Goldwater: "I just know that fellow's going to play all of the angles."[13]

Scarcely more than a half hour after the conversation with Anderson, the worried president was on the phone with McNamara, saying, "Now I wish that you'd give me some guidance on what to say. I want to leave an impression . . . that we're gonna be firm as hell without saying something that's dangerous." Johnson told the defense secretary that people calling him (apparently referring to his conversation with Anderson) "all feel that the Navy responded wonderfully. And that's good. But they want to be damned sure I don't pull 'em out and run. . . . That's what the country wants because Goldwater is raising so much hell about how he's gonna blow 'em off the moon."[14]

By the late morning of August 3, Johnson was convinced that he needed to respond more forcefully if there was another incident—and that he *needed* another incident to give him the opportunity to demonstrate that he wasn't "soft." The charge was primed for what happened the next day.

A Wild Flying Fish Chase:
August 4 in the Gulf of Tonkin and Washington

Tim O'Brien gives us an example of "a true story that never happened" in *The Things They Carried*.[15] August 4, 1964, provides an example of a false story that never happened yet had an immense impact.

On the morning of August 4, McNamara interrupted Johnson's regular Tuesday breakfast with Democratic leaders of Congress to inform the president that the *Maddox*, which had been joined in the Tonkin Gulf by another American destroyer, the *C. Turner Joy*, was reporting radar indications of hostile ships nearby and suspected an attack was imminent. The main reason for this belief was that intercepted signal intelligence of North Vietnamese communications purportedly indicated they were planning an attack. This was probably the most important error in the intelligence and would lead to American reprisal bombing raids the next day. In fact, North Vietnamese communications referring to the August 2 incident were mistakenly read as indicating that Hanoi was ordering a new attack. The misreading left Americans at all levels, from the president down to the officers on the ships in the Tonkin Gulf, expecting a new incident.[16]

According to National Security Adviser McGeorge Bundy, at some point early in the morning (Washington time) of August 4, Johnson decided to use the expected incident finally to get Congress to give him full authority to do whatever he might decide was necessary in Vietnam.[17]

Johnson and McNamara prepared their response. About an hour after telling the president that the Pentagon would be prepared to recommend a response, McNamara was back on the line with the president to inform him that "we just had word by telephone from Admiral Sharp [Admiral Ulysses S. Grant Sharp Jr., who had just become the new commander of the United States Pacific Command in Honolulu] that the destroyer is under torpedo attack." An almost inaudible sound was LBJ's response to this confirmation of what he expected and had come to believe he needed politically but that he also feared, because he didn't want to get more deeply involved in the war. He then asked where the torpedoes were coming from.

"We don't know," was McNamara's significant reply. "Presumably from these unidentified craft that I mentioned to you a moment ago."[18] Johnson and McNamara required little evidence to convince them that what they expected was happening. At a lunch in the early afternoon, Johnson told McNamara, Secretary of State Dean Rusk, and others that he agreed "a firm, swift retaliatory strike must be carried out."[19]

Meanwhile, a new message had arrived from the scene of the supposed attack. Now Captain John Herrick on the *Maddox* indicated that there was considerable doubt that any attack had, in fact, occurred. The State Department summary of what he communicated said that "a review of the action makes many reported contacts and torpedoes fired 'appear doubtful.' 'Freak weather effects' on radar, and 'over-eager' sonarmen may have accounted for many reports. 'No visual sightings' have been reported by the *Maddox*, and the Commander suggests that a 'complete evaluation' be undertaken before any further action."[20]

This information was not what those at work finalizing their plans for "a firm, swift retaliatory strike" were expecting. They had set their course, and they didn't want to hear anything that might alter it. McNamara did not call President Johnson to tell him that there was now serious doubt that a North Vietnamese attack had occurred, and it appears that McNamara kept Johnson in the dark throughout the rest of the critical day of August 4 about the report from Herrick and Sharp and the sensible suggestion by the latter to pull back and undertake a "complete evaluation."[21] There is no evidence to indicate that McNamara ever told the president about this most significant information before Johnson ordered the airstrikes that were "retaliating" for acts that McNamara knew may not have occurred.

Instead, McNamara, Deputy Secretary of Defense Cyrus Vance, and the Joint Chiefs of Staff met in the Pentagon just before 5 p.m. to, as the summary of the meeting put it, "marshal the evidence to overcome lack of a clear and convincing showing that an attack on the destroyers had in fact occurred."[22] McGeorge Bundy said that the goal throughout most of the day was "catching up" with the fact that the president had already set his course. McNamara, Bundy said, was "asking on behalf of a president who had already committed himself to having a resolution and a speech and had the air time."[23] But McNamara was also asking on behalf of a president from whom he had apparently withheld critical evidence that might have led that president to wait.

McNamara and others around Johnson had for months been advocating bombing the North. "At that time there's no question that many ... people ... were looking for any excuse to initiate bombing," Undersecretary of State George Ball later said.[24] McNamara wasn't about to let this excuse get away from them.

While the group in the Pentagon was engaged in the dubious project of sorting evidence to find some that would support the belief that the North Vietnamese had attacked, McNamara received word that it had leaked to the press that a second attack had occurred.[25] He telephoned the president about twenty minutes after the meeting began to tell him the story was out. Johnson had already seen it.[26]

Whatever prospect there may have been that the group might have come to its senses and decided to wait to see where the evidence pointed rather than "marshal evidence" to reach the predetermined conclusion evaporated when the report of the alleged second attack went public. After Robert Anderson had cautioned him against caution—warned him about the political danger of appearing soft—Johnson was not going to risk following an ask-questions-first-and-shoot-later approach. Goldwater and others would skewer him if he did not take immediate, forceful action. If, on the other hand, he went ahead with the attack on North Vietnam that he had approved earlier in the day, the president could probably neutralize the issue of weakness and leave Goldwater with nothing on which he could mount a plausible political assault on the administration. Proceeding with the contention that the North Vietnamese had attacked American ships in international waters would also provide Johnson with the rationale for obtaining congressional authority to do whatever he deemed necessary in Vietnam.

Johnson met with the leadership of both parties in Congress at 6:46 p.m. to inform them of the supposed North Vietnamese attack and the response he was making to it. "Some of our boys are floating around in the water," Johnson lied to the leadership. The statement that McNamara had read to the president little more than an hour earlier said that there had been no American casualties or damage. "I think I know what the reaction would be if we tucked our tails," President Johnson said, probably thinking as much of the reactions of his political opponents at home as those of foreign nations.

Montana senator Mike Mansfield, the majority leader and an East Asian historian, saw what few others did that evening: where the decisions and actions of this date could—and, as it turned out, would—lead. We "may be getting all involved with a minor third-rate state. Then what is to come in response? The Communists won't be faced down. A lot of lives to mow them down."[27]

And Vermont Republican Senator George Aiken, who would gain fame in 1966 for suggesting that the United States could just declare victory in Vietnam and leave,[28] saw clearly where the president's actions had put Congress with regard to the resolution Johnson would seek: "By the time you send it up, there won't be anything for us to do but support you."[29]

♦ ♦ ♦

Between the strike order and Johnson's meeting with congressional leaders, Secretary of State Dean Rusk told the National Security Council, "The unprovoked attack on the high seas is an act of war for all practical purposes."[30] The flaw in the powerful argument that McNamara and Rusk were making was that no second North Vietnamese attack had occurred. There had been no "act of war," for purposes practical or otherwise, by North Vietnam against the United States, though there was about to be one by the United States against North Vietnam.

The commander of the naval air squadron flying above the area where the attack was thought to have occurred was James Stockdale.[31] I "had the best seat in the house to watch that event," he later wrote, "and our destroyers were just shooting at phantom targets—there were no PT boats there. . . . There was nothing there but black water and American fire power." He said that he was ordered by his superiors to keep quiet about what he saw—and *didn't* see.[32]

The 2000 National Security Council historical study's conclusion on the events of August 4, 1964, is unambiguous: "It is not simply that there is a different story as to what happened; it is that *no attack* happened that night. . . . In truth, Hanoi's navy was engaged in nothing that night but the salvage of two of the boats damaged on August 2.[33]

In a 1995 meeting in Hanoi with McNamara, General Vo Nguyen Giap finally convinced the former defense secretary that there had been no North Vietnamese attack on August 4. McNamara said Giap's flat statement that no attack occurred settled the question as far as he was concerned. "It's a pretty damned good source," McNamara said.[34]

Rather than an act of war, what had happened in the Tonkin Gulf in the dark of night on August 4, 1964, was "The Keystone Kops Go to Sea." The officers on neither American destroyer knew where the other destroyer was. At one point, the *Maddox* had its guns trained on the *Turner Joy* and was about to fire. Sonar reports of the sound of torpedoes rushing past one of the American ships reached a ridiculous number before it was realized that the sounds were those of the ship's own propellers. American pilots overhead were within a split second of bombing the destroyers, thinking that they were the nonexistent enemy PT boats.[35]

"Hell, those dumb, stupid sailors were just shooting at flying fish!" Lyndon Johnson himself said to George Ball only a few days after the event.[36] "For all I know, our Navy was shooting at whales out there," Johnson told Bill Moyers about a year later.[37]

Have You Heard the News Today, from Mississippi and Vietnam? Real Bodies and an Unreal Attack

Throughout the day on August 4, as the president and his advisers in Washington were preparing to retaliate for the presumed attack in the Gulf of Tonkin, a crew with a bulldozer was secretly searching for bodies in rural Neshoba County, Mississippi. After weeks of the FBI turning up bodies and partial bodies of African Americans in Mississippi, information from paid informants had led to the discovery of the *important* bodies of the three missing civil rights activists, which had been buried in an earthen dam.

As Johnson was awaiting word that the retaliatory attacks on North Vietnam had been carried out, he received a phone call concerning this other major problem of the summer. Cartha "Deke" DeLoach, the FBI's White House liaison, called just after 8 p.m. "Mr. Hoover," he said, "wanted me to call you, sir, immediately." A search party of FBI agents had found three bodies southwest of Philadelphia, Mississippi. There was, DeLoach told the president, "every reason to believe" that they were the remains of Michael Schwerner, James Chaney, and Andrew Goodman.[38]

At 9:35 p.m., President Johnson was able to speak by phone with Mississippi Governor Paul Johnson Jr., who had been on a boat offshore. It was a cordial conversation in which Mississippi's Johnson assured America's Johnson of his full cooperation.[39]

The president had also been trying to get Senator Goldwater on the phone. He would inform him of what was about to happen in Vietnam and, Johnson expected, get his opponent's support. At 9 p.m. LBJ received word that Goldwater, who had been on a boat off the California coast, would be back and would talk with him on a regular phone in about twenty-five minutes.[40] A few minutes later, LBJ spoke again with McNamara and told him that he would mention in his public announcement of retaliation against North Vietnam that Goldwater had assured him of his full support. "I think it makes us sound like we're very much together and buddies and agreein' on bombing everybody," Johnson said to McNamara, strongly suggesting the main reason for his action.[41]

When Goldwater called just after 10 p.m., Johnson read to him the statement he would make to the American people that night. "That's a good statement, Mr. President. I don't know what else you could do. I think you've taken all the right steps," Goldwater told his political opponent, "and I'm sure you'll find that everybody will be behind you." A moment later, Goldwater added, "Like always, Americans will stick together." Listening to the recording of the conversation, as Johnson closes with, "Thank you, Barry. Bye, fella!"[42] one imagines Johnson smiling as he says the last two words, understanding them to mean that this was the final goodbye to Goldwater's candidacy.

When the president went on the air to inform the public about what was happening off the coast of North Vietnam, it was approaching midnight Eastern time. He said: "Renewed hostile actions against United States ships on the high seas in the Gulf of Tonkin have today required me to order the military forces of the United States to take action in reply." "We still seek no wider war," Johnson declared. He said that he would immediately ask Congress to "pass a resolution making it clear that our Government is united in its determination to take all necessary measures in support of freedom and in defense of peace in Southeast Asia." For good measure, LBJ added that "just a few minutes ago I was able to reach Senator Goldwater and I am glad to say that he has expressed his support of the statement that I am making to you tonight."[43]

◆

The Real Consequences of an Unreal Event:
Writing a Blank Check for War

I believe that history will record that we have made
a great mistake.
                                —Sen. Wayne Morse
                                (August 7, 1964)

The bombing raids ordered to retaliate for a nonexistent attack had
very real consequences. On August 5, there were sixty-four American
air strike sorties against four North Vietnamese torpedo boat bases
and the oil storage facility in Vinh, which was largely destroyed. Two
American planes were shot down, resulting in the death of one pilot
and the capture of the other, Everett Alvarez Jr., who became the first
American prisoner of war in Vietnam. Alvarez would remain a POW
for eight years.

To Hanoi, the raids on their territory were unprovoked, since they
had not attacked the American ships. The American bombing convinced them that the United States would use any fabricated excuse to
carry out war in their territory.

In the United States, the most important real consequence of the
unreal event was Congress's ceding of its power to decide on war to the
president. The resolution that Johnson formally requested on August
5 said that "Congress approves and supports the determination of
the President, as Commander in Chief, to take all necessary measures
to repel any armed attack against the forces of the United States and
to prevent further aggression." It also stated that the United States
was "prepared, *as the President determines*, to take all necessary steps,
including the use of armed force, to assist any member or protocol
state of the Southeast Asia Treaty Organization requesting assistance
in defense of its *freedom* [emphasis added]."[44] The resolution was introduced in Congress the next day, debated for only nine hours in committee and on the floor, and passed by both the House (416–0) and
Senate (88–2) on August 7. It was just the sort of "quick, overwhelming, without-too-much-discussion-of-its-implications" endorsement
that Lyndon Johnson wanted.

Despite that outcome, there was some discussion of the declaration's implications. The two senators who distinguished themselves by voting against the Gulf of Tonkin Resolution, Democrats Ernest Gruening of Alaska and Wayne Morse of Oregon, contended that the resolution amounted to a "predated declaration of war power" to the executive branch and was therefore unconstitutional as well as unwise. Their colleagues weren't buying that argument, though several expressed serious concerns.

"We now are about to authorize the president if he sees fit to move our Armed Forces" into both Vietnams, Laos, Cambodia, Thailand and any other SEATO nation, Gruening accurately pointed out. "That means sending our American boys into combat in a war in which we have no business, which is not our war, into which we have been misguidedly drawn, which is steadily being escalated. This resolution is a further authorization for escalation unlimited. I am opposed to sacrificing a single American boy in this venture. We have lost far too many already."

For his part, Morse said: "I believe that history will record that we have made a great mistake in subverting and circumventing the Constitution of the United States." Morse predicted that "future generations will look with dismay and great disappointment upon a Congress which is now about to make such a historic mistake."[45]

History would vindicate Morse's position and confirm his prediction, but he was severely attacked for it at the time. The *Washington Post* referred to his comments as "the reckless and querulous dissent of Senator Wayne Morse."[46] The truth is that it was the senators and representatives who voted for the resolution who were reckless, and even more so Robert McNamara and the many other hawks among the "best and brightest" advising Lyndon Johnson on Vietnam.

McNamara was delighted with the overpowering passage of the resolution, telling Johnson that there was "near-unanimous support for everything you may do in the future, and generally a blank-check authorization for further action."[47] By the time the resolution passed, Johnson was aware that there may have been no action to prompt his reaction, but he was delighted, describing the Gulf of Tonkin Resolution as "like grandma's nightshirt—it covered everything."[48]

1964's Most Critical Day?

Fine—I couldn't be better. I just feel wonderful!
—Lyndon Johnson (ca. 9:40 p.m.
on August 4, 1964)[49]

During his telephone conversation with Mississippi Governor Paul Johnson Jr. after 9:30 on the night of August 4, 1964, the president mentioned that he had been so busy with Vietnam and Mississippi that he hadn't "even been to dinner." But when the governor asked, "How are you gettin' along?" Johnson enthusiastically responded, "Fine—I couldn't be better. I just feel wonderful!"[50] It certainly seemed to have been a day to make him feel wonderful. He had accomplished so much. He had proven his "manhood" by ordering the bombing of North Vietnam. He had maneuvered his opponent in the presidential election into endorsing what he was doing. He had assured himself of getting the resolution for a free hand in Vietnam. And, as a cherry on top, he had put himself and his Democratic leaders in Congress in a position to use patriotism to assure easy passage of his signature anti-poverty bill.

August 4 was one of the most eventful days of 1964. The great irony is that the biggest event on that eventful day never happened.

Having signed the Civil Rights Act a month before, Lyndon Johnson added the Economic Opportunity Act—signed on August 20—and, in mid-1965, would sign the Voting Rights Act and a host of social legislation, including Medicare and Medicaid to his legacy. Conservative commentator George F. Will captured his place in history in 2013, writing "Lyndon Johnson was second only to Franklin Roosevelt as a maker of the modern welfare state and second to none in using law to ameliorate America's racial dilemma."[51]

In seizing the opportunity presented by a putative North Vietnamese attack on American ships, though, Johnson got much he had not bargained for. The key words of the Gulf of Tonkin Resolution, giving the president the authority, "as Commander in Chief, to take all necessary measures to repel any armed attack against the forces of the United States and to prevent any further aggression" served as the concept sketch for the script of a major tragedy. Johnson had made his proposal of marriage to "that bitch of a war." The Gulf of Tonkin Resolution was the engagement ring.

But, having indulged in a bit of premarital intercourse with the war, Johnson was in no hurry to set a wedding date. He still had hopes of being able to break off the engagement. While Robert McNamara and most of Johnson's top advisers continued to push for escalating the war, Johnson remained torn about increasing military actions in Vietnam. When McNamara came to him on September 18 with a report of another attack on American ships, Johnson was not amused. "You just came in a few weeks ago and said they're launching an attack on us—they're firing on us," the president said, "and we . . . concluded maybe they hadn't fired at all."[52] When McNamara preached to him during the fall on the merits of a program of systematic aerial assaults on North Vietnam, Johnson called it "your bombing bullshit."[53]

Having demonstrated that he was "manly," the president could present himself as the tough-but-sensible peace candidate in the November election. Winning the election was one thing, but avoiding being seen as "the first president to lose a war" was another, and the war in Vietnam wouldn't go away after November 3.[54]

16

MRS. HAMER GOES TO ATLANTIC CITY

THE FREEDOM PARTY VS. THE ANTI-FREEDOM PARTY

AUGUST 1964

Fannie Lou Hamer testifying before Credentials Committee for Democratic National Convention, Atlantic City, August 22, 1964.

If the Freedom Democratic Party is not seated now, I question America.

—Fannie Lou Hamer
(August 22, 1964)[1]

[Atlantic City] was the turning point of the civil rights movement. . . . We . . . had arrived at the doorstep and found the door slammed in our face.

—John Lewis (1998)[2]

"C OULDN'T HAVE BEEN BETTER," President Johnson said in response to House Majority Whip Hale Boggs's question following the passage of the anti-poverty bill on August 8, a few days after LBJ had snatched the Vietnam issue out of Barry Goldwater's hands. Boggs's question was: "I think we've had a great week. Don't you?"[3] LBJ could look forward to August being a great month for him, capped by the Democratic National Convention, which he was scripting as his coronation party. The convention—and *he*—would be crowned by his acceptance of the Democratic presidential nomination on his fifty-sixth birthday, August 27.

But Johnson could not savor his seemingly triumphant week for long. On the same day that he voiced the "couldn't have been better" assessment from his Texas home, some five hundred miles to the northeast, 2,500 people convened in an African American part of Jackson, Mississippi. It was certainly not a typical political convention. Most of the delegates were dirt-poor rural black people. The Mississippi Freedom Democratic Party convened to choose delegates to go to Atlantic City and challenge the seating of the all-white regular Democrats. That intention gave Lyndon Johnson cause to worry, centered on two matters: his nemesis, Robert F. Kennedy, and the Mississippi challenge. He had, moreover, convinced himself that they were connected.

The party was referred to by interchangeable names: the Mississippi Freedom Democratic Party (MFDP), the Freedom Democratic Party (FDP), or simply the "Freedom Party." The last of these designations neatly contrasted the party with the white regulars from Mississippi, implying that the latter constituted the "Anti-Freedom Party," which it did.

Washington attorney Joseph Rauh, among the most prominent Democratic liberals in the nation, had agreed to serve as legal counsel to the Freedom Party. At the state convention, Rauh explained how the challenge would work. The chances for success, he told the assembled freedom workers, were excellent.[4] That prospect was precisely what was keeping Lyndon Johnson awake at night.

The Freedom Party organizers worked at the state convention to get "as radical a delegation" as they could, Bob Moses recalled, "people who would stand up when they got to Atlantic City."[5] The demographics of the delegation were sixty-four black people and four white people. It included some of the old guard Mississippi NAACP leaders, but it was mostly made up of "grass-roots" people, "men and women who," in the words of historian John Dittmer, "had little formal education or social status but who spoke—with authority and from experience—in the name of the dispossessed."[6]

LBJ . . . FDP . . . RFK . . . FBI

Lyndon is way out of line.
—J. Edgar Hoover (July 1964)[7]

Since becoming president, Lyndon Johnson had decisively taken the side of freedom, but that did not mean he would want to support seating the Freedom Party at *his* convention. The day after the state FDP convention, the president called United Auto Workers president Walter Reuther, asking him to pressure Joe Rauh to stop the Freedom Party from taking their challenge to the convention floor. "The only thing that can really screw us good," Johnson said, "is to seat that group of challengers from Mississippi." It wasn't that he was against their goals; he feared the effect of a floor fight on his reelection prospects. "If they give us four years," the president of the USA said to the president of the UAW, "I'll guarantee the Freedom delegation somebody representing views like that will be seated four years from now. But we can't do it all before breakfast."[8]

Johnson was very much on the side of bringing "white freedom" to black Americans and correctly saw himself as moving much more rapidly along the road toward that goal than had any president before him. But, while Johnson loved to speed his car around Texas back roads, he believed that there was a speed limit on the road to full "white freedom" and equality.

Johnson worried over white backlash, particularly after George Wallace's showings in Democratic presidential primaries. The anti-freedom party in Mississippi had already turned against the president when he pushed through the Civil Rights Act. When the official, all-white, party met in Jackson in late July, "virtually every delegate" at this ostensibly Democratic convention was planning to vote for Republican nominee

Barry Goldwater.[9] Less than a month before setting out for Lyndon
Johnson's coronation party along the Jersey shore, these white Mississippi Democrats passed resolutions denouncing the recently signed
Civil Rights Act and calling for "separation of races in all phases of
our society."[10]

LBJ couldn't believe that African Americans and the Freedom Party
in Mississippi did not appreciate what he was doing. He was preparing
to name Hubert Humphrey, the major politician in the country most
closely identified with the cause of civil rights, as his running mate.
But he was holding back the naming of Humphrey until the latter
showed he could solve the Mississippi challenge. "If I mess with a
group of Negroes that were elected to nothing, that met in a hotel
room," he told Humphrey on August 14, "and throw out the governor
and elected officials of the state—if we mess with them, we will lose
fifteen states without even campaigning." LBJ told Humphrey to get
"the Negroes to realize that they've got the president, they'll have the
vice president, they've got the law [the Civil Rights Act], they'll have
the government for four years . . . Why in the living hell do they want
to hand—*shovel*—Goldwater fifteen states?"

Humphrey's response was significant: "We're just not dealing with
. . . emotionally stable people on this, Mr. President."[11] What he presumably meant was that the MFDP people were political neophytes
and believers in the idea that what is right should prevail, without
compromise.

The next day, Johnson spoke with NAACP president Roy Wilkins,
mistakenly thinking that he could have major influence on the Freedom Party. If he were a Negro, LBJ said, he would let the Mississippi
regulars sit wherever they wanted to and concentrate on the election.
"And the next four years, I'd see the promised land."[12]

On July 29, Johnson had informed the brother of the late president
that he would not be his running mate. After waiting more than a day
for Bobby Kennedy to issue a public statement that he was taking himself out of the running, Johnson decided to make an announcement
that he had concluded that it would be "inadvisable" for him to choose
as his running mate "any member of the Cabinet or any of those who
meet regularly with the Cabinet."[13] He specifically mentioned Attorney
General Robert Kennedy in a list that included several other names.

That move, though, did not end Johnson's fear of a Bobby plot. In August, the president became increasingly fearful that a scheme was afoot to stampede the convention to nominate Kennedy. The president told Richard Russell after the national convention had begun that he thought the Mississippi challenge was "Bobby's *trap*."[14] Even after Robert Kennedy had announced on August 25 that he was running for the United States Senate from New York, LBJ remained suspicious that "this Freedom Party was born in the Justice Department" as part of a devious plan to damage Johnson and steal the nomination.[15]

His obsessive fears had led Johnson in late July to order the launching of a major, illegal political espionage program. At LBJ's request, the FBI sent a "special squad" of twenty-seven agents and support staff to his own party's convention to collect intelligence for him and to take clandestine actions to ensure that nothing happened "to embarrass the president." This activity was so over the top that even J. Edgar Hoover was reluctant to do it, saying, "Lyndon is way out of line." Hoover nonetheless instructed his assistant, Deke DeLoach, to "give him [the president] whatever help he wants."[16] Thus, only six weeks after Johnson had demanded that the FBI intervene on the side of the Mississippi freedom fighters to solve the Neshoba murders, he turned the same agency against those Mississippi freedom fighters—and against the FBI's nominal superior, the attorney general. According to the later testimony of the FBI's William Sullivan, the special squad was intended to collect useful information, "particularly in bottling up Robert Kennedy—that is, in reporting on the activities of Bobby Kennedy."[17] FBI agents used bugs and wiretaps and posed as reporters (NBC cooperated by giving them press credentials) and members of the convention security staff to gather information on the plans of the Freedom Party and to block those plans.

In 1976, a Senate select committee chaired by Idaho Democrat Frank Church detailed the operation at the 1964 convention. The agents were, the Church Committee found, "able to keep the White House fully apprised of all major developments during the convention's course" through the use of undercover agents infiltrating groups, wiretaps, and bugging the headquarters of SNCC and CORE.

The electronic surveillance was not approved by the attorney general, as the law seemed to require, for the obvious reason that the attorney general was among the targets of the clandestine program. The White House was able, the Church report said, "to obtain the most intimate details of the plans of individuals supporting the MFDP's challenge."[18]

Johnson's clandestine FBI operation at the 1964 Democratic Convention was, as Dittmer has said, "a Watergate that worked."[19]

◆ ◆ ◆

> If you seat those black buggers, the whole
> South will walk out.
>
> —Gov. John Connally (D, Texas)
> to LBJ (August 1964)[20]

Ironically, Johnson's insistence on complete control over his party's national convention brought increased national media attention to the MFDP challenge, because the Mississippians were the only story in town. Interest in the challenge had been primed by the Neshoba murders and further increased by the discovery of the bodies three weeks before the convention. MFDP supporters with large posters of the Neshoba victims maintained a vigil on the boardwalk throughout the convention.

Johnson's fears of losing the entire South seemed to be grounded in more than paranoia. Almost all the southern leaders in the Senate and about a third of the governors from the region sent word that they had other commitments and would be unable to attend the Democratic National Convention. There was, moreover, the possibility that Republicans would claim—with or without evidence—that Communists were involved with the Freedom Party, a charge that could be explosive if the president supported seating their delegates.

Johnson was scrambling to find a compromise that would not only avoid a floor fight and walkout by southern state delegations, but also avoid the appearance that he was siding with segregationists. That task became considerably more difficult before the formal opening of the convention.

Mississippi, America, and the World, According to Mrs. Hamer

There's got to be a change—not only for Mississippi, not only for the people in the United States, but people all over the world.

—Fannie Lou Hamer
(August 23, 1964)[21]

On Saturday, August 23, the credentials committee met to hear arguments from the contesting Mississippi delegations. Joe Rauh, representing the Freedom Party, presented witnesses at the televised hearings. When Fannie Lou Hamer of Ruleville, Mississippi, began to provide a riveting account of her life of poverty, evictions, and beatings, President Johnson suddenly commandeered the networks for "an important announcement." In fact, Johnson said nothing of importance; he wanted to get Mrs. Hamer and her powerful testimony off the nation's TV screens. But cameras in the hearing room continued to record, and Mrs. Hamer's moving words went out to a much larger audience on the evening news telecasts.

After she had recounted the horrors she had endured in Mississippi, Mrs. Hamer reached the climax of her speech: "All of this is on account of we want to register, to become first-class citizens. And if the Freedom Democratic Party is not seated now, I question America. Is this America, the land of the free and the home of the brave, where we have to sleep with our telephones off the hooks because our lives be threatened daily, because we want to live as decent human beings, in America?"[22]

Women on the credentials committee were said to have been especially moved by Mrs. Hamer's account of a beating she had endured in the jail in Winona, Mississippi, and the other horrors she recounted.[23] The decision on what to do about the Mississippi dispute was postponed.

Suddenly a national celebrity, Mrs. Hamer was sought out by the media for interviews, in which she expanded upon her thinking. Asked why she stayed in her home state, she responded, "Why should I leave Ruleville and why should I leave Mississippi? I go to the big city and with the kind of education they give us in Mississippi I got problems. I'd wind up in a soup line there. That's why I want to change things in Mississippi. You don't run away from problems—you just face them."

On whether she hated white segregationists, the sharecropper said: "Maybe plenty people could hate them. I feel sorry for anybody that could let hate wrap them up. Hate will not only destroy us. It will destroy them." And, in words that must have caused Lyndon Johnson's anxiety to soar, Mrs. Hamer proclaimed: "Do you think I came here to compromise and sit in a back seat at this convention?"

"I'm proud of being black because of my heritage," she explained. "The Negroes are the only race in America that had babies stole from their breasts and mothers sold from their families." But she remained an optimist. "One day I know the struggle will change," Hamer said. "There's got to be a change—not only for Mississippi, not only for the people in the United States, but people all over the world."[24] As she would later put it, "I tell people I don't want no equal rights anymore. I'm fightin' for human rights."[25]

♦♦♦

President Johnson, whose theme for the convention was "harmony," was increasingly agitated by what the "agitators" from Mississippi were doing. By the morning of August 24, he was terrified that African Americans were "getting ready to take charge of the convention." He thought the reaction on the part of millions of white people in all regions to what was going on would be, "they'd say that, hell, the Negroes have got more power in the Democratic party than the president has, and the damned nigras are taking it over—and to hell with the Democratic party."[26]

Johnson thought black people should appreciate what he had accomplished for them. Among the more remarkable achievements was that a plank in the Democratic platform stating that the Civil Rights Act of 1964 "deserves and requires full observance by every American and fair, effective enforcement if there is any default"[27] had been, Johnson said, "agreed to unanimously." When he informed Senator Russell of this development, the Georgian exclaimed, "My God, that's a miracle of major proportions!"[28]

The president dialed up the pressure to prevent a floor fight over the seating of the Freedom Party, using all the levers at his disposal. The FBI surveillance provided him and his operatives with critical information. At a Freedom Party meeting on Sunday afternoon, a black congressman asked Bob Moses for a list of the people on the credentials committee who were supporting the challenge. He told Moses that he would use it to show the committee chair how much support the FDP had. The real reason for wanting the list soon became apparent. Almost everyone on it got a call and was pressured with threats to deny them or their family members federal appointments and using other tactics of the sort that had long enabled LBJ to bring legislators to his side when he needed their votes.[29]

The credentials committee met and a motion was made that the FDP be awarded two seats. Later that night, a caucus of African American delegates met and several black Freedom Party delegates attended. They listened as several of the nation's most prominent African American leaders said that they must support their president, but that was not the top priority of many of the Freedom Party delegates. "We have been treated like beasts in Mississippi," Annie Devine of Canton said, tears welling in her eyes. "They shot us down like animals. We risk our lives coming up here. . . . Politics must be corrupt if it don't care none about the people down here."[30] It was one of the many illustrations of how far apart the black Mississippians and the liberals in Washington were.

The president was seeking to find a solution sufficiently acceptable to both sides that the less extreme white southerners would stick with him at the same time that it satisfied the aspirations of African Americans and liberals in the rest of the country. Johnson believed that what he was doing through the Civil Rights Act and the social programs was much more important to the future of African Americans than was the seating of the MFDP.[31] The compromise he finally offered would deny seating to the "anti-freedom party" except for the few that would pledge to support the Democratic ticket in the fall; would seat two Freedom Party members as "at-large" delegates and welcome the rest of the MFDP people at the convention as "honored guests"; and, most important by far, would provide that the composition of delegations to future Democratic National Conventions would be reflective of the population of the state. There would be no more all-white delegations. A case could be made that this provision was even more important than the Civil Rights Act in losing the white South for the Democrats.

Johnson assigned Hubert Humphrey the task of getting the compromise accepted by the Freedom Party and their supporters. Word was passed to Humphrey that he would not get the vice-presidential nomination if he failed to get the compromise approved. He and his Minnesota protégé, Walter Mondale, pleaded with the FDP delegates to accept the offer. Humphrey told them that his nomination depended on their acceptance of the deal, and that he would work "for old people, senior citizens, healthcare, education, jobs, and integration, and schools, and all of this."[32] According to one of the Freedom delegates, Humphrey told them that it was essential that he become vice president, because if he wasn't there to restrain Johnson, the president would escalate the war in Vietnam.[33] (Humphrey, of course, did not prove to be as effective a restrainer as he thought he would be.) "I'm the best person to be vice president," he pleaded.

"Well, Mr. Humphrey," Mrs. Hamer responded, "do you mean to tell me that your position is more important than four hundred thousand black people's lives?" She told him that if he got the vice presidency "this way, you'll never be able to do all those things for good. . . . You'll never be able to do it. . . . Senator Humphrey, I'm gonna pray to Jesus for you."[34]

Pushing forward with his compromise plan, Johnson insisted on naming the two delegates, apparently to prevent Mrs. Hamer's selection. When Ed King, one of those Johnson had named, said during negotiations on Tuesday that he would step aside and let someone else be selected by the Freedom Party delegation take the spot, Humphrey said of Mrs. Hamer, who was not present, that Johnson had told him that "illiterate woman must never be allowed to speak again at a Democratic convention." Humphrey added, "And look at her, the way she dresses, her grammar; this is not the kind of person white America needs to see representing black people."[35] It was not a comment likely to win over Bob Moses and the delegates. During this meeting on Tuesday afternoon, August 26, the first time the MFDP had been given the details of the proposed compromise, the credentials committee was, unbeknownst to the Mississippians, meeting and voting in favor of Johnson's compromise. When word of this fait accompli reached them, the Freedom Party representatives were irate about having been sold out.

Johnson Contemplates Withdrawal

By God, I'm going to go up there and quit! Fuck 'em all!
—Lyndon Johnson
(August 25, 1964)[36]

At the moment of his triumph, Lyndon Johnson was sinking into one of his periods of despair and self-pity. By Tuesday morning, with the Mississippi matter still unsettled and his Bobby anxiety reaching new heights, Johnson drafted a message saying he would not run. Among the reasons he cited in several private conversations was that it would remove suspicion that he had ordered the bombing after the Tonkin incident for self-serving political reasons—which he in fact had.[37] Was he serious? It is impossible to know. In his despondent periods, Johnson was capable of going through with such a withdrawal. But he also must have been aware that the reactions to his message would be likely to include an immediate acceptance of the compromise on Mississippi and a return to the harmony within the party that he so desired.

His mood improved greatly on Tuesday afternoon when he was told the compromise had been agreed to. His despondency vanished and he waxed philosophical. "I think it's a good solution," the president said of the compromise. "Our party's always been a group that you can come to with any bellyache and injustice . . . . That's what the Democratic party's for. That's why it was born. And that's why it survives." "Long as the poor and the downtrodden and the bended know that they can come to us and be heard," Johnson proclaimed. "And that's what we're doing. We're hearing 'em."[38]

But "the poor and the downtrodden and the bended" members of the Mississippi Freedom Democratic Party thought otherwise. In their view, the National Democratic Party wasn't hearing them at all.

Morality versus Politics

> We're not here to bring politics to our morality,
> but to bring morality to our politics.
> —Bob Moses (August 25, 1964)[39]

By the time the convention voted overwhelmingly to approve the compromise, both Mississippi factions had rejected it. The regular party bolted the convention. "The Mississippi Democratic delegation did not leave the National Democratic party," the statement by the Mississippi regular delegates explaining why they were bolting the convention said. "It left us."[40] That argument has remained in vogue among many white southerners ever since.

Mississippi Freedom Democrats Annie Devine, Fannie Lou Hamer and Edwin King on the convention floor, Atlantic City, August 25, 1964.

Using credentials provided to them by supporters from other state delegations, Freedom Party delegates entered the Convention Hall and occupied the seats designated for Mississippi's delegation. This "walk-in" leading to a "sit-in" on the floor of Lyndon Johnson's convention was a further embarrassment to the president and breach in his "harmony" script.

One final attempt was made to persuade the MFDP to accept the compromise the following morning. A host of national civil rights leaders, including Martin Luther King, urged them to accept what they had gained. Veteran civil rights activist Bayard Rustin tried to get the delegates to see that there is a difference between protest and politics. "The former," he said, "is based on morality and the latter is based on reality and compromise. If you are going to engage in politics, then you must give up protest. . . . You must be willing to compromise, to win victories and go home and come back and win some more."[41] Several members of the Freedom Party were inclined to accept such arguments, but the tide was turned by a few of the impassioned black women in the delegation. Fannie Lou Hamer summed up the argument by famously saying, "We didn't come all this way for no two seats when ALL of us is tired."[42]

The problem was that the two sides were coming from vastly different backgrounds and understandings. To the insiders, even those who saw themselves as champions of the downtrodden and representatives of the poor, politics was a game to be played to get the best outcome possible, and compromise was essential for that purpose. What Johnson was offering represented significant progress. The Freedom Party delegates, though, were unlike any delegation that had ever been seen at a major party national political convention. They were not *representatives* of the poor; they *were* the poor—largely composed of sharecroppers and genuinely poor people. They believed in the Bible, that is, the Sermon on the Mount, and in American ideals, not in compromise.

"We're not here to bring politics to our morality," Bob Moses declared, "but to bring morality to our politics."[43] Almost any Goldwaterite at the Republican convention six weeks earlier could have said the same thing. Both the Freedom Democrats and the "Freedom Republicans" spoke of freedom and morality; both were more interested in what they believed was right than in making political compromises that would help produce victory at the polls.

Rather than accept politics as the art of the possible, the Freedom Democrats sought to create a politics that made the impossible possible.

◆ ◆ ◆

With the Mississippi challenge more or less settled for the national party, albeit with one side not having agreed to the compromise, Lyndon Johnson was able to return his eyes to his coronation and the November election. First, he formalized the selection of Hubert Humphrey as his running mate. Johnson had emphasized repeatedly, in person and through intermediaries, that he expected absolute loyalty from his vice president. Humphrey assured Johnson that he would have it. That pledge would be a growing problem for Humphrey as the Vietnam War worsened and his own presidential ambitions became ensnared in Johnson's war policies.

Johnson had pushed back a planned tribute to President Kennedy until Thursday, after his nomination was official, so that there would be no chance of an emotional moment causing a stampede to give the nomination to Bobby Kennedy. There may have been some cause for LBJ's concern. When Robert Kennedy appeared before the delegates on Thursday evening, there was a spontaneous outburst of applause and weeping that went on for nearly twenty minutes. After the crowd finally quieted and he was able to speak, Kennedy included in his remarks as a remembrance of his brother lines from *Romeo and Juliet* that had been suggested to him by Jacqueline Kennedy:

> *When he shall die,*
> *Take him and cut him out in little stars,*
> *And he will make the face of heaven so fine*
> *That all the world will be in love with night,*
> *And pay no worship to the garish sun.*

There can be little doubt that the last line was intended to be a reference to Lyndon Baines Johnson.[44]

Johnson's acceptance speech was something of an anticlimax, but that didn't matter. He had apparent harmony in his party and Barry Goldwater for an opponent. The Democratic platform took deadly aim at Goldwater's acceptance of extremism, stating: "We condemn extremism, whether from the right or left, including the extreme tactics of such organizations as the Communist party, the Ku Klux Klan and the John Birch Society." The first word in the first heading of the domestic section of the Democratic platform was "FREEDOM," and the word was sprinkled liberally throughout the document.[45]

Democrats were not about to let the American electorate forget Goldwater's embrace of extremism. The Republican campaign had bought a billboard on the Atlantic City boardwalk, where it would be difficult for anyone attending the Democratic convention to miss, showing a picture of their candidate with the campaign's slogan, IN YOUR HEART, YOU KNOW HE'S RIGHT. Democrats countered by putting a small sign below, which read: YES - - - EXTREME RIGHT.

Goldwater billboard and Democratic response, Atlantic City boardwalk, August 1964.

Democrats had more fun with the Goldwater slogan, coming up with such versions as "In your guts you know he's nuts,"[46] and "In your heart, you know he might," a reference to the possibility that Goldwater might "push the button" to start a nuclear war.

But, for the longer run, it was the clash over the seating of the Freedom Party that had the greatest significance.

The National Liberal View:
A Series of Victories by the Freedom Democrats

> The Freedom Democrats won a series of victories
> that not even the most hopeful of their number
> expected to win five days ago.
> —Richard Rovere
> (August 28, 1964)[47]

"They're completely irrational," Walter Reuther said to President Johnson on the first evening of the convention, speaking of the Freedom Party people. "They don't know the victory they got is the proposition that next time no one can discriminate against Negroes."[48]

"The action of the Credentials Committee in respecting the 'moral,' as distinct from the legal, claims of the Freedom Democrats was unexpectedly bold," Richard Rovere said in a *New Yorker* article on August 28. "The President may not have welcomed it, but he endorsed it, and in so doing he authorized the introduction of an entirely new element in American party politics." The convention's action through the Mississippi compromise, Rovere contended, had "struck as heavy a blow at 'states' rights' as has been struck by any recent legislation or court decision."

Rovere was largely correct in seeing the compromise as a victory of enormous significance. "It is a remarkable and perhaps a historically unprecedented thing," he wrote, "that a great national party, firmly in command of government power, is making an effort to absorb and give voice to a protest movement that spends much of its energy trying to undermine the party's authority in exactly those places where the authority is most firmly entrenched."[49]

The understanding by people in the Freedom Movement of what had happened in Atlantic City was different. "We had played by the rules, done everything we were supposed to do," John Lewis of SNCC said, "had played the game exactly as required, had arrived at the doorstep and found the door slammed in our face."[50] "For many people," Joyce Ladner of SNCC said, "Atlantic City was the end of innocence."[51]

When the credentials committee voted to accept the compromise, its chairman, former Pennsylvania governor David L. Lawrence, called it a "turning point" in the history of the Democratic Party.[52] He was right—in more ways than he realized.

Another Strand of Freedom:
On the Outside, Questioning the Inside

> Are you going as 'In' members of society to pull
> the 'Outs' in with you? Or are we all 'Outs'?
>   —Vincent Harding (June 1964)[53]

It was certainly the case, as journalist Milton Viorst has said, that "blacks and liberal whites had never worked more productively, or more harmoniously, than in the first months of the Johnson presidency."[54] That cooperation was among politicians, liberal insiders, and the leaders of mainstream civil rights organizations. Beneath that congenial surface, however, there were serious fault lines that became apparent in the weeks following passage of the Civil Rights Act. At least two other segments of the nation's African American population wanted things that went well beyond the act's provisions.

The voices of one such segment—urban black people outside the South—were heard in the uprisings that began scarcely more than two weeks after the July 2 signing of the Civil Rights Act. "We knew that the victories at lunch counters and ballot boxes meant little to blacks locked in northern ghettoes," recalled Julian Bond of SNCC. "They demanded results, concrete results, as the urban riots in the North would later make very clear."[55]

Another portion of the black population, the desperately impoverished residents of the rural Deep South, was beginning to be heard from during those same weeks as the Mississippi Summer Project proceeded. Their disillusionment with what they started calling "the white liberal establishment," which became manifest at the Democratic National Convention, was already simmering earlier in the summer.

The enormous importance of the "white freedom" that Johnson and the Civil Rights Act were beginning to make available to African Americans is beyond question. It would start to let black Americans "inside" by banning racial discrimination. But, even before the Summer

Project began, some people involved in the Freedom Movement in the South and other young radicals were starting to question how much they wanted to be inside what they more and more saw as a corrupt, money- and consumption-driven political and economic system. They were moving toward a goal and a definition of *freedom* that broke out of and transcended the double helix of white "Ins" trying to get out and black "Outs" trying to get in. "Are you going as 'In' members of society to pull the 'Outs' in with you?" historian and SNCC member Vincent Harding asked the volunteers at Oxford, Ohio, describing what had been the essential objective of the civil rights movement. "Or are we all 'Outs'? Are you going to bring the Negroes of Mississippi into the doubtful pleasures of middle-class existence, or to seek to build new kinds of existence in which words like 'middle-class' may no longer be relevant? Are we trying to make liberal readjustments or basic change?"[56] By the time the Summer Project ended, many of its veterans were seeing themselves neither as outsiders trying to get in nor as insiders trying to get out, but as outsiders no longer wanting to get in until they changed "in."

In a letter written home at the end of the Mississippi Summer Project, one of the volunteers spoke to this developing feeling that getting black Americans inside to obtain "white freedom" wasn't what the Movement's objective should be: "I sometimes fear that I am only helping to integrate some beautiful people into modern white society with all of its depersonalization." The white volunteer expressed "a genuine respect and admiration for a culture which, for all the trouble, still isn't commercialized and depersonalized as is our Northern mass culture."[57]

"After Atlantic City," Cleveland Sellers of SNCC later said, "our struggle was not for civil rights, but for liberation."[58] Although Martin Luther King Jr. was still trying to gain white freedom for black people by getting on the inside, he had eloquently captured the spirit of the new ideal of freedom and democracy when he said of the FDP delegates, "For it is in these saints in ordinary walks of life that the true spirit of democracy finds its most profound and abiding expression."[59]

What was emerging was a desire not for another New Deal, but for a New Ideal.

17

Speaking Freely

Berkeley

September 1964—Spring 1965

Mario Savio speaking to Free Speech Movement crowd at the University of California at Berkeley, December 2, 1964.

I wanted to be like Bob Moses. I wanted
to *be* Bob Moses if I could do it.
— Mario Savio (June 1964)[1]

MISSISSIPPI'S FREEDOM SUMMER WAS followed by a Freedom Fall in California, and the two were directly connected. In late September in Berkeley, on the campus of the flagship of the University of California system, the student protest movement that was to be such a major part of the sixties was born.

The Free Speech Movement (FSM) at Berkeley arose from issues largely generated in the recent events in Mississippi. The student with whom the FSM is most identified, Mario Savio, had just returned to the campus from the Mississippi struggle. There, his idealism and belief in the possibility of change for the better had grown stronger. "It's wonderful . . . to be part of such a change for good that's sweeping across our country," Savio wrote while he was in jail in Mississippi in early July. "The history of the world is pivoting on the internal changes that are going on today in America—and we are in part the agent of that change. A breath of freedom."[2]

While black Americans were victims of segregation, white students in the sixties were beneficiaries of another form of segregation—that of college-age youth on campuses. Students in large residential universities became a "continuing Community."[3] Huge universities were to potential youth power what heavily black areas in the Deep South were to potential black power.

There had been a smattering of protests by white students in the first years of the calendar 1960s, but they had seemed isolated and didn't spread to other campuses or student groups. But what happened in Berkeley in the fall of 1964 *was* contagious. It was for good reason that one Berkeley administrator called Savio "Typhoid Mario."[4]

As was the case in music, in social protest young white people took their inspiration from African Americans, who led the way. In the spring of 1960, young white people observing the sit-ins began to perceive the profound gap between American principles and American practices. "There was a feeling that they were us and we were them, and a recognition that they were expressing something we were feeling as well, and they'd won the attention of the country," noted Rennie Davis, who was nineteen when the sit-in movement began in 1960 and was to become one of the key players in Students for a Democratic Society.[5]

The Sixties Arrive on Campus

The most exciting things going on in America
today are movements to change America.
                    —Mario Savio (December 1964)[6]

Prior to the rise of the Free Speech Movement in the fall of 1964, American colleges were largely still in the fifties. "Students are permitted to talk all they want so long as their speech has no consequences," wrote Savio about "contemporary campus life." "The University is well structured, well tooled, to turn out people with all the sharp edges worn off, the well-rounded person," he said. "The 'futures' and 'careers' for which American students now prepare are for the most part intellectual and moral wastelands. This chrome-plated consumers' paradise would have us grow up to be well-behaved children."[7]

What happened was accurately summarized by Hal Draper, a socialist thinker at Berkeley who played an important role in the events that fall: "From the middle of September 1964 until the end of the year . . . the University of California campus at Berkeley was the scene of the largest-scale war between students and administration ever seen in the United States."[8]

The University of California as a whole, and Berkeley in particular, were the crown jewels in American public higher education in the 1950s and early 1960s. Clark Kerr, who had been the chancellor at Berkeley from 1952 to 1958, when he became president of the University of California as a whole, was the quintessence of what was seen as the best in higher education in this period. Kerr devised a hierarchical system of community colleges, four-year Cal State colleges, and top-tier campuses of the University of California. He was hailed around the world as an educational genius and appeared on the cover of *Time* magazine in 1960.[9]

Kerr was, moreover, a prime example of what younger radicals would call "corporate liberals." In this regard, he corresponded to the establishment liberals in Washington and New York who saw themselves as champions of reform and social justice. Kerr had distinguished himself in the early 1950s by fighting against the firing of Berkeley professors who declined to sign a "loyalty oath" stating that they were not members of the Communist Party. Such positions made him anathema to the far right, which labeled him the "red chancellor."[10]

A small but growing number of students were not pleased with the educational system over which Kerr presided. In 1962 David Horowitz, a teaching assistant at Berkeley who would in the 1970s flip to being a champion of the conservative side, wrote a book called *Student*. In it, he argued that the university had come to be set up like a factory. The professors were the assembly-line workers and the students were the raw material those workers fashioned into products. But "a man is not a product," Horowitz proclaimed, "nor is he an IBM record card."[11]* "There are just too many nonsense hours spent by American students," one of those deeply involved in the FSM said, "hours to 'do' much as one 'does' time in prison."[12]

In a lecture at Harvard in the spring of 1963, Clark Kerr recognized many of the issues that Horowitz had addressed the previous year: "The undergraduate students are coming to look upon themselves as a 'class.'" Kerr coined the term "multiversity" for the huge new universities such as those over which he presided. These institutions served multiple purposes, including the needs of government, business, and the military and the advancement of science, but in this new "knowledge industry," undergraduate "students find themselves under a blanket of impersonal rules."[13] Kerr warned that there was a spirit of revolt developing among students. He understood the issues, but he proved incapable of dealing effectively with them, in part because his approach was always to play the role of mediator and try to balance different interest groups in order to keep the support of all.[14] This was exemplary of the concept of "countervailing power" postulated as the liberal ideal by economist John Kenneth Galbraith in the early 1950s.[15] In the fall of 1964, his balancing act stopped working.

Socially concerned Berkeley students came together to support civil rights. In May 1960, inspired by the sit-ins conducted by black students over the preceding months, a group of white students from Berkeley traveled across the bay to San Francisco and joined with others to protest hearings scheduled by the House Committee on Un-American

---

* Early computers, most of which were manufactured by IBM (International Business Machines), used cards with holes punched in various locations as their means of storing and accessing data.

Activities (HUAC) in what became the first major clash of the 1960s between police and white students. In the fall of 1963, a few Berkeley students joined with the contingent of Stanford students who went to Mississippi before the state election to help with the Freedom Vote— and then took part in the 1964 Mississippi Summer Project. They also sought ways to participate directly closer to home, targeting racial discrimination by businesses operating in the Bay Area.

The Ghosts of Communist Scares Past

> Provisions of the policy of The Regents concerning
> 'Use of University Facilities' will be strictly enforced
> . . . including the 26-foot strip of brick walkway.
> —Dean of Students Katherine
> Towle (September 14, 1964)[16]

The policies that led to the confrontation between students and the UC administration in 1964 stemmed from other restrictions that were legacies of past Communist scares. After two events in 1934, the San Francisco General Strike and Upton Sinclair's socialist campaign for governor, stirred a Red Scare in California, the university responded by banning political advocacy on campus. This ban was still in effect in 1964, but for years there had been a sort of safety valve to release the growing pressure of student advocacy. The Bancroft Strip, a small area of brick sidewalk just outside the main gate to the Berkeley campus where Telegraph Avenue dead ends into Bancroft, was thought to be city property and so not under the university's political speech regulations. There, student advocacy groups of all persuasions could preach, recruit, and raise funds. "Noisy, colorful, forever animated," as Milton Viorst put it, "the Strip, more than anything else, gave Berkeley its reputation as America's most uninhibited campus."[17] As the head of the Berkeley chapter of Friends of SNCC, Savio intended to continue to utilize the Strip for activities supporting the Freedom Movement in the South. But the university announced in mid-September that it would start applying the campus speech regulations to this safety valve.

What led to the change in policy was pressure from California's powerful right wing, headed by former United States Senator William Knowland, the publisher of the *Oakland Tribune* and the state manager of Barry Goldwater's presidential campaign. Knowland's fuse reached its end in early September, when Berkeley civil rights activists began picketing the *Tribune* itself, in large part because the paper was pushing Proposition 14, a referendum to annul California's fair housing law. The publisher demanded that the administration enforce its regulations on the Bancroft Strip.[18]

On September 14, a week before fall semester classes began, all student organizations received a letter from Dean of Students Katherine Towle informing them of an expanded enforcement zone including the campus entrance on Bancroft Way and Telegraph Avenue.[19] The cause of the "war" that ensued in the fall of 1964 in Berkeley was akin to what had ignited the American War for Independence: the revocation of privileges that had long been held. In response, the full spectrum of campus organizations joined together to create the United Front. "For the first time ever, all the political groups on campus united in opposition to what the administration was doing," Michael Rossman wrote, "Not only the various socialist splinter groups, and CORE and SNCC, and the Young Democrats, who have never been very radical. Also the Young Republicans, Students for Goldwater, and even the Intercollegiate Society for Individualists, whom my political friends think of as young fascists."[20]

On the day classes began, September 21, a few hundred students picketed Sproul Hall, the main administration building, carrying such signs as UC MANUFACTURES SAFE MINDS and BOMB THE BAN.[21] Within a few days, some student groups were challenging the new rules by setting up tables on the Strip. On September 30, representatives of the administration took the names of some of those at the tables and summoned five of them to the dean's office. Five hundred other students accompanied them, saying they violated the rules, too, and wanted equal discipline. From the outset, the students were following the exhortation attributed to Benjamin Franklin: "We must, indeed, all hang together, or most assuredly we shall all hang separately."

The dean refused to drop the charges and five hundred students began a sit-in inside Sproul Hall.

Birthing a Student Movement:
The Police Car Blockade

Catch-22 says they have a right to do anything
we can't stop them from doing.
                              —Joseph Heller (1961)[22]

The Berkeley protest began with students who had been trying to bring
white freedom to black Americans in Mississippi and brought their
activism home. Then the administration took away long-established
rights the students had held—Constitutional rights, they believed. The
white students were now being denied portions of white freedom.
Beyond the issue of free speech, there was, as the students saw it,
a denial of democracy. They were being subjected to regulations on
which they had not been consulted. The upper-middle-class, wealthy,
educated youth began to see *themselves* as the oppressed. This perception was a subspecies of the growing feeling within this demographic
that having white freedom amounted to being trapped, while at the
same time portions of that freedom were being denied.

On the morning of October 1, in response to the summary suspen-
sions of eight students the night before, student groups moved tables
in front of Sproul Hall, directly violating the long-standing regulations
against such activities on campus property. Jack Weinberg, a former
graduate student and a veteran of the civil rights movement, was sitting at the largest table, that of Student CORE. When approached by
a dean and asked to remove himself and the table, Weinberg refused.
Campus police were summoned to arrest him. When a police car
arrived, Weinberg went limp, and policemen carried him into the car.
Then, without any prompting, students began to sit down around the
car so it could not take Weinberg away. It was, said Jackie Goldberg,
who would be one of the key people in FSM, "the only spontaneous act
I've ever seen in my political career."[23] The car would remain trapped
there, with Weinberg inside it, for the next thirty-two hours.

Over the preceding days, Mario Savio had emerged as the leading
figure in the movement. Like his model, Bob Moses, Savio came to his
position of prominence because he embodied moral authority, integ-
rity, and experience with the movement in the South. He had taken

from his summer involvement with SNCC in Mississippi the concept that "the leader was on the same level as the people."[24] As Berkeley history professor Lawrence Levine later said, this was not a case of "leader and led, preacher and convert, manipulator and manipulated." Rather, "Mario was carrying on a *dialogue* with students who came to listen to him because many of them were *already* aroused."[25] Mario Savio had a gift for putting people's "visceral reactions into words . . . To express the way a large number of people were feeling but no one had yet said they were feeling."[26]

Affected by a serious speech impediment in his youth, Savio literally found his voice in speaking for others. As recently as the spring of 1964, before he joined SNCC in Mississippi, "he stuttered so badly that even his private conversation was difficult to listen to. 'Every time he raised his hand to speak, people in the class sort of shuddered and felt sorry for him,' recalled a student in Savio's philosophy section."[27] When he spoke as and for himself—"I"—he stammered and was inarticulate. When he spoke for the movement—"We"—his speech problems vanished and he became a powerful orator.[28] Now, when he spoke in the first person, it was implicitly in the plural. He was embodying the emerging spirit of the sixties, which in its early period was along the lines of what John Steinbeck wrote of developing among the Dust Bowl refugees as they made the journey west in *The Grapes of Wrath*: "This is the thing to bomb. This is the beginning—from 'I' to 'we.'"[29] That was also what SNCC was striving to achieve.

Savio saw an opportunity to use the paralyzed police car—"the symbol of the other side"—as a speakers' platform. The police made no objection. Speakers for freedom standing on top of an immobilized police car provided a perfect image for the emerging sixties ideal of freedom over authority.[30]

It was now past noon, and masses of students coming out of classes quickly swelled the crowd around the car to about seven thousand people who listened to speakers for hours. In midafternoon, Savio led a group of about two hundred students into Sproul Hall to try to get the administration to negotiate. When they got no response, they began a sit-in. The protest, inside the building and outside around the car, continued into the night.[31]

All was peaceful until around 11 p.m., when a group of a few hundred fraternity members arrived and began throwing lighted cigarettes and eggs at the demonstrators and called them communists and Jews. They said the protesters should go home and take a bath, and shouted for "law and order."[32] The confrontation was finally defused when a Catholic priest, Father James Fisher, climbed up on the car around 1:30 a.m. and said, "Hatred will beget bloodshed: the kind of cat-calling going on today will get worse as the night goes on." Then he concluded by telling them that what was going on was not going to promote the rationality that he presumed the students were at the university to develop. "I have nothing more to say," he concluded, and got off the car. There was complete silence for some time, and then the attacking students began to depart.[33]

At a three-hour session the next morning, administrators and law enforcement officials hammered out a master plan for a "massive police effort" armed with pistols, billy clubs, and tear gas. The mini army numbered nearly one thousand.[34] UC President Kerr was fearful that Sheriff Frank Madigan, known for utilizing brutal tactics in black neighborhoods in Oakland and eager to introduce the students to "law and order," might precipitate a bloodbath.[35]

Berkeley Chancellor Edward Strong was ready to send in this massive force, but Kerr received a call from Governor Edmund "Pat" Brown, who told him that he "feared there would be bloodshed," he "didn't want another Alabama or Mississippi," and instructed him "to step in and prevent it."[36] Late that afternoon Kerr negotiated. The result by the evening was an agreement based on a proposal from an ad hoc group of faculty. Among its provisions was that the university would begin a process for deeding the Bancroft Strip to the city, which would presumably reinstate open political advocacy there.[37] It didn't satisfy Savio, but he acceded to the moderate majority of the student negotiating committee and accepted the compromise. He went to sell it to the students outside Sproul Hall.[38] Savio scaled the car again, read the agreement, moved that it be accepted, and said everyone should go home. The demonstration ended just in time for many of the participants to walk over to the Greek Theater for a concert by Joan Baez. "It's a fine night," the folk singer said when she took the stage. "The students have won, and I'm glad."[39]

But had the students won? The agreement, which was overblown as the "Pact of October 2," was an armistice that was a worthwhile achievement in the short run, but it was not a treaty for lasting peace. "We had avoided a Kent State, or a Jackson State, or a Tiananmen Square," Clark Kerr wrote nearly four decades later.[40]

Question Authority

We have a saying in the movement that
we don't trust anyone over thirty.
—Jack Weinberg
(November 1964)[41]

We don't respond as children toward
their parents; we respond as equals.
—Mario Savio
(October 12, 1964)[42]

The "Free Speech Movement" was organized and named only after the events of October 1–2. Through the second half of October, the FSM's steering committee negotiated with the Campus Committee on Political Activity (CCPA) on campus political regulations and free speech.

"Question authority" became perhaps the most basic refrain of the sixties. Though the statement is often attributed to Timothy Leary,[43] the ideal was evident in both the civil rights movement and its off-spring born in Berkeley in the fall of 1964. Deference to authority was, obviously, a major impediment to overthrowing white supremacy in the South.[44] Among the most fundamental forms of expected deference was that of the young being expected to accept the authority of their elders.

"Don't trust anyone over thirty" was a saying in the FSM, Jack Weinberg told a *San Francisco Chronicle* reporter in November.[45] It would join its sibling, "Question authority," among the leading mantras of the era. Weinberg was talking about not trusting the "Old Left." He and others in the FSM were angered by published stories indicating that Communists were behind the scenes directing the students.[46]

The press, university administrators, and politicians oscillated between two opposite takes on the student action: They belittled and ridiculed it as a lark, "a civil rights panty raid."[47] Simultaneously, they portrayed it as a "sinister Communist plot."[48] President Kerr and others charged that some of the students had adopted the tactics of Mao Zedong and Fidel Castro. "There is an extreme left wing element" in the "hard core leadership" of the protests, Kerr told a reporter during the police car blockade. "Forty-nine percent of the hard core group are followers of the Castro-Mao line."[49] By late November, a writer in the *San Francisco Chronicle* was matter-of-factly calling it "the Marxist dominated Free Speech Movement."[50] There is no record of either Mao—who famously preached "political power grows out of the barrel of a gun"[51]—or Castro, who took power through guerrilla warfare, having been disciples of *satyagraha*. In fact, the FSM tactics came not from China and Cuba but from Alabama and Mississippi—and India and the Holy Land.

A particularly noteworthy aspect of the negotiations between the CCPA and the entire Free Speech Movement was that the students acted as equals with their elders from the faculty and administration. Students, Savio and his colleagues insisted, "had to be seen as citizens with rights rather than as children in need of guidance."[52]

The very recent history of the Mississippi Summer Project and the Freedom Democratic Party challenge in Atlantic City less than six weeks before the FSM began shadowed the Berkeley standoff. Kerr tried to deal with the FSM challenge much as Lyndon Johnson had sought to deal with the FDP challenge: find a compromise that would give a little to each side. For his part, Savio had in mind what SNCC and the MFDP considered to have been a betrayal by Establishment liberals in the form of the compromise Johnson had pushed through at the Democratic convention. Convinced they held the moral high ground, neither the Freedom Movement nor the Free Speech Movement was willing to accept the sort of small concessions that the Establishment liberals offered them. On the other side, Governor Brown, like President Johnson with Vietnam, was trying to preserve his liberal image but not appear "soft."

Placing Bodies on the Gears

On the first university campus outside Mississippi
to be taken over by the cops . . . this generation has
stood up and continued to speak plainly of truth.
—Ralph J. Gleason
(December 9, 1964)[53]

When the seventh session of the CCPA on November 7 failed to resolve the issue of the university's authority to discipline the students charged more than a month earlier, the FSM decided to set up tables again in violation of the ban on on-campus advocacy.[54] In arguing for the reactivation of the tables, Mario Savio had made the case that the defiant action would strengthen the FSM. He was right. The argument that the students were simply trying to exercise and protect their Constitutional rights was persuasive to faculty and mainstream students. As early as mid-October, a petition supporting the FSM's quest for constitutional rights on campus was signed by 650 fraternity and sorority members from thirty-seven Greek organizations on campus. One of the objectives of the petition was to counter "the egg throwing image of the fraternities."[55]

As part of the implementation of the "Pact of October 2," Kerr had tasked an ad hoc committee of the Academic Senate, chaired by law professor Ira M. Heyman, with resolving the "disciplinary cases of the suspended FSM students." The committee's final report, issued on November 13, found against the administration actions.

The FSM turned its focus to the meeting, on the Berkeley campus, of the UC Board of Regents on November 20. The crowd for the rally on that day would have been large because of the importance of free speech to so many students, but it was further swelled by the presence of Joan Baez. She sang Dylan's "The Times They Are a-Changin'" and freedom songs from the civil rights movement. A crowd estimated at four to five thousand showed up.

Mario Savio and Joan Baez at FSM rally, Fall 1964.

It was the day before the football game with Stanford, long known in the Bay Area simply as the "Big Game" and, surrealistically, the FSM rally was coordinated with the "Beat Stanford" rally. Jack Weinberg and Art Goldberg of FSM led "Beat Stanford!" cheers and Cal cheerleader Jamie Sutton led "Three cheers for FSM!" ovations. FSM speakers paused while the Cal band and the pom-pom girls paraded.[56]

A delegation of FSM people, including Savio, attended the meeting as observers, but the Regents would not allow them to speak. The Regents unanimously and "with *no discussion*" sided with Kerr and rejected the Heyman Report. FSM called for a sit-in, which turned out to be small and short. The Free Speech Movement was at a low point. Perhaps seeing the failure as an opportunity to finish off the FSM, the administration sent out new disciplinary letters to Savio and three other students over the Thanksgiving break. It was a miscalculation of epic proportions. Rather than destroying the FSM, the action reinvigorated it. It seemed to confirm what Art Goldberg, who was among the four who received the letters, called the "atrocity theory." He believed there was no reason for the movement to worry about its "down periods," because the administration could be counted on to arouse the students with a new "atrocity" against student rights.[57]

The new and seemingly vindictive administration actions outraged mainstream students. Graduate student teaching assistants joined the cause, announcing that they would go on strike if the administration did not meet FSM demands by the end of the week. Masses of students would now support a sit-in. A rally, to be followed by a sit-in in Sproul Hall was called for December 2. Joan Baez was again recruited to assure a large crowd.

The crowd for the noon rally on December 2 numbered an estimated six thousand. They heard Savio give his most memorable speech. Fully utilizing the images that Kerr had raised of the university as a factory, Savio defiantly proclaimed:

> [We] don't mean to be made into any product, don't mean to end up being bought by some clients of the University. . . . We're human beings! . . .
>
> There's a time when the operation of the machine becomes so odious, makes you sick at your heart, that you can't take part. . . . And you've got to put your bodies upon the gears and upon the wheels, upon the levers, upon all the apparatus, and you've got to make it stop. And you've got to indicate to the people who run it, to the people who own it, that unless you're free the machine will be prevented from working at all.[58]

Savio's speech was a powerful, lyrical enunciation of what the sixties at their best were all about: justice, nonviolent resistance, antiauthoritarianism, humanism and, above all, *freedom*. It was, as Savio biographer Robert Cohen says, "a passionate moral summons to stop evil."[59] In it were the images of a human swallowed up and run through machines that Charlie Chaplin had so compellingly presented in his 1936 masterpiece, *Modern Times*.

Savio called upon the students to enter Sproul Hall and join in a sit-in. During this nonviolent direct action, he said, "We'll do something which hasn't occurred at this university in a good long time!" They would, he said, conduct "Freedom Schools." It was, of course, another idea he was trying to transfer from the Mississippi Freedom Summer. "We're gonna spend our time learning about the things this University is afraid that we know! We're going to learn about freedom up there, and we're going to learn by doing!"[60] They called it the "Free University of California."[61]

Kerr wanted to negotiate with the students,[62] but Chancellor Strong and Vice Chancellor Alex Sherriffs contacted Governor Brown's office, falsely reporting that the protestors were becoming violent and pressing the governor to overrule Kerr and send in the police. Alameda County Assistant District Attorney Edwin Meese III (who would later be attorney general of the United States in the Reagan Administration) also urged the governor to send in the cops to put an end to the "anarchy." Brown agreed, and a massive force of more than four hundred police from four different organizations mobilized at 3 a.m. to clear the building.[63]

The largest mass arrest in California history ensued. The students went limp when seized and it took twelve hours to complete the taking of nearly eight hundred protestors into custody. When they were out of the sight of cameras, some of the police treated the students with brutality. Savio reported that some of the police called the students "pigs and Communists."[64] Ralph J. Gleason, who would become the cofounder of *Rolling Stone* magazine three years later, noted in an insightful *San Francisco Chronicle* column that Berkeley had become "the first university campus outside Mississippi to be taken over by the cops."[65] The police invasion brought the Free Speech Movement much more national—and international—attention. The next day it was on the front page of the *New York Times.*[66]

As Savio had anticipated, the police invasion of their campus, invited by their university's administration, outraged large numbers of Berkeley students and substantially strengthened the FSM. The arrested students spent the night at the Santa Rita Prison Farm, singing freedom songs and, in Savio's case, writing a letter inspired by the example of Martin Luther King Jr.'s "Letter from Birmingham Jail" the previous year.[67]

The Greek Theater Debacle

It was an accident that looked like fascism.
—Clark Kerr (2003)[68]

When the students made bail and returned to campus, it was largely to a heroes' welcome. A meeting of more than a thousand faculty members denounced the arrests and called for the ouster of Chancellor Strong. Some twelve thousand students attended a noon rally, at which Savio called upon them to march through the campus to urge a strike by students and faculty. More than ten thousand students and teaching assistants heeded the call and boycotted classes.[69]

Now facing a faculty revolt along with a reinvigorated and much larger student revolt, Kerr huddled secretly for more than three hours with Governor Brown on what to do next. Kerr suspended classes for Monday, December 7, and called a university-wide meeting to take place in the Greek Theater. Some fifteen thousand students and faculty attended what became the climax of the free speech struggle.

Kerr had planned the meeting not as a discussion, but as a presentation of a "compromise" that he and the department chairs had reached. No freedom to speak would be permitted at this Free Speech meeting. Savio decided that he must speak. As the meeting was declared adjourned after Kerr finished his presentation, Savio slowly walked onto the stage and to the podium. Before he could say a word, as the *New York Times* described it, "two campus policemen grabbed him. One put his arm around Mr. Savio's throat, forcing his head back, the other grabbed him in an arm lock." One of the cops grasped Savio's necktie (he was, uncharacteristically, dressed for the occasion in a jacket and tie), and pulled him by it. Police dragged the most visible advocate of free speech away from the microphone so that he could not speak. Savio was hauled off to a dressing room, and pandemonium broke out as students rushed the stage and police tackled them. The photo of the police seizing Savio appeared on front pages around the country the next day and became one of the iconic images of the sixties. "It was an accident that looked like fascism," Kerr maintained decades later.[70]

As things calmed down, Savio was released and allowed to go to the podium, where he said, "This is a disastrous situation here" and asked the crowd to "clear this disastrous scene and get down to discussing the issues" at Sproul Plaza. The rally there was the largest of the entire Free Speech Movement, with about ten thousand people in attendance.[71]

Seeing victory within its grasp, the FSM called off the strike so the Faculty Senate could meet in a calm atmosphere and come up with a solution. The next day, December 8, a Faculty Senate meeting at which a record number of faculty members was present, endorsed the main objective of the FSM—"the content of speech or advocacy should not be restricted by the University"—by nearly 9 to 1. The Free Speech Movement had won.

The Free Speech Movement, 1964, and the Sixties

> Mario . . . took the cork out of the bottle.
> —Sheila, message in Mario Savio
> memorial book (1996)[72]

"Our action has electrified the entire state—as well as many thousands in other states," Savio had written from the Santa Rita Prison.[73] He was right. Students across America and around the world were inspired by what they saw as a principled protest utilizing the tactics of nonviolent civil disobedience adopted from the civil rights movement. The Berkeley students had launched what would become one of the major features of the sixties: student protest. Students on hundreds of campuses would use FSM-like tactics to protest the Vietnam War and other issues.

But the Free Speech Movement also represented the dividing line between the pre-1964 fifties and the sixties in other important ways. The split between the "question authority" young, whose numbers would grow exponentially as the American war in Vietnam escalated, and a traditional, respect authority older generation was strikingly evident in reactions to the Free Speech Movement.

Ralph Gleason saw the FSM clash as the basis of the generational conflict that would be emblematic of the sixties.: "a struggle between a C. Wright Mills–Paul Goodman–*Catch 22* generation for whom the bomb dropped before they were born and a generation where cleanliness is next to godliness and you don't make waves, just ride on them."[74] Gleason's inclusion of *Catch-22* in defining the younger generation was on the mark. Joseph Heller's 1961 masterwork was difficult for older readers to appreciate, but it strongly resonated with the young, and one of the author's definitions of Catch-22 seemed to fit perfectly with the Berkeley situation. "Joseph Heller's authoritative work on constitutional law offers the following definition of Catch-22," Marvin Garson wrote in an FSM leaflet. "'Catch-22 says they have a right to do anything we can't stop them from doing.' This fundamental section has been construed by American law enforcement authorities to override any conflicting provisions in our Constitution." "On October 2," Garson continued, "we first realized that Catch-22 is the fundamental law in California and the world, so we began to act accordingly to protect ourselves."[75]

Beyond the campus(es), though, the FSM actions were unpopular. A poll of Californians found that 74 percent disapproved of the FSM.[76] This was at a time when Lyndon Johnson had just won the largest landslide victory in the history of American presidential elections. The broader middle-class white population was opposed to "disorder" and disrespect for authority, which they perceived in both the FSM and the civil rights movement. The "coming apart"[77] of both America and the liberal coalition that would take place at a rapidly accelerating speed in the years following 1964, along with the bitterness of the divisions, was evident in the reactions of some Californians to the Berkeley protests. "When you act in defiance of the law and resort to mobs taking over—they ought to crack some skulls a-plenty. . . . As for police brutality, give them plenty of it."[78] These words in a letter from an Oakland resident in the last month of calendar 1964 foreshadow the rancorous tearing apart of American society that would come to characterize the sixties, peaking in 1968.[79]

◆◆◆

On March 3, 1965, a nonstudent from New York walked onto the Berkeley campus with a sign emblazoned with what Clark Kerr later described as "an old-fashioned four-letter Anglo-Saxon word that was just then entering theatrical productions on Broadway but was not yet recognized by standard dictionaries." The young man sat down with his FUCK sign on the steps of Sproul Hall, where he was arrested.[80] Some students in the Free Speech Movement supported the idea that free speech includes obscenities, while others saw it as trivializing their crusade. Over the next ten or so days, some students used loudspeakers and signs to exercise what they claimed to be their right publicly to, as the *New York Times* delicately put it, "utter four-letter words not ordinarily used in polite conversation."[81]

Most of the faculty "considered ludicrous the whole hostile public reaction to the word," Kerr recalled. "Who cared?" But public reaction beyond the campus to what was quickly dubbed the "Filthy Speech Movement" was indignation. Governor Pat Brown and some of the Regents who had not been overly upset at the Free Speech Movement in the fall were much more outraged at the public use of a vulgar sexual term. Kerr said they seemed far more threatened by Freud than Marx.[82]

Beyond the immediate reactions, those advocating for full freedom of speech, including "four-letter words not ordinarily used in polite conversation," were in the vanguard of a larger and soon-to-be-victorious movement to end virtually all censorship.

◆ ◆ ◆

The rupture between the young activists and the Democratic establishment was among the most important developments in the sixties and was well underway by the end of 1964. In the later years of the decade, the rift between liberal Democrats and freedom activists would be of great benefit to the Right, beginning with Ronald Reagan's startling victory over Pat Brown in the 1966 California governor's race. Reagan ran on people's fear of "disorder," specifically against the Berkeley student revolt and Brown's putative weakness (his sending in of the police notwithstanding) in dealing with it, which he conflated with the Watts uprising of the following summer. Reagan promised to "clean up the mess" in Berkeley.[83]

It wouldn't seem proper, though, to end our examination of the Free Speech Movement on a negative note. The FSM was one of the reasons for hope as calendar 1964 drew to a close. "We can take great pride in having, for once, reversed the world-wide drift from freedom," wrote Berkeley history student Barbara Garson, who would become widely known two years later for her antiwar play *MacBird!* She looked forward to the spread of the sort of consensus-based, participatory democracy that the FSM had used. "I look past government by the grunted consent of the governed. Someday we will participate actively in running our own lives in all spheres of work and leisure."[84]

Garson's optimistic—even utopian—outlook represents the dawning of the sixties. And her reference to "the world-wide drift from freedom" is another reminder of how much the events and issues of 1964 shape the central concerns of the 2020s.

18

"To Be President of ALL the People"

The 1964 Election

July–November 1964

Lyndon Johnson campaigning in Austin on election eve, November 2, 1964.

If you want me to continue, then I pledge you that I will continue to be President of all the people.
—Lyndon B. Johnson
(November 2, 1964)[1]

T HE AMERICAN PEOPLE HAVE given emphatic notice that they want to move forward constructively along the road of international understanding and domestic progress," a *New York Times* editorial stated the day after the election. "The overwhelming vote for the Johnson-Humphrey ticket reflects popular attachment to the policies of moderate liberalism that have prevailed through more than three decades of Democratic and Republican rule and that have contributed so notably to national prosperity and security."[2]

So it seemed at the time, but those who saw Lyndon Johnson's record landslide victory—61.1 percent to Goldwater's 38.8 percent and 486 to 52 in the electoral vote—as predictive of the coming direction of American politics were very mistaken.

The Goldwater Campaign

In a 1963 conversation with journalist Ben Bradlee, President Kennedy had predicted the course of a Goldwater presidential candidacy. "People will start asking him questions, and he's so damn quick on the trigger that he'll answer them," Kennedy said. "And when he does it will be all over."[3]

The conservative's proclivity for saying things that turned people against him was evident throughout his campaign. After he had surgery to remove bone spurs from the heel of his right foot in December 1963, one of his supporters remarked. "I'm glad he has one foot in a cast, or he'd have that one in his mouth, too."[4] JFK's assassination assured the Arizona senator's rejection, for it totally discredited "extremism," which Goldwater openly embraced.[5] Much of the public saw Kennedy's murder as the fruit of "the hatreds polluting American life," and they were determined to reject those hatreds.[6]

Barry Goldwater had the certitude of an ideologue. His ideology was, it seemed to many observers, a curious combination of contradictory elements. Goldwater's incongruous aims have been succinctly stated by historian William O'Neill: "He hoped to replace the limited welfare state with an unlimited warfare state."[7] In all this, Goldwater in 1964 was the precursor of the brand of right-wing Republicanism that would dominate the party a half century and more later.

By all accounts, Goldwater lacked a burning desire to be president. He was also afflicted by a greater political handicap: He was not a liar. A wonderful example of how he would say what he thought without considering the consequences had come on a stop in Georgia during the primary campaign in the spring. One of his supporters was selling a concoction he called "Gold Water: The Right Drink for the Conservative Taste." When the man for whom the drink had been named sipped it, he immediately spat it out and said, "This tastes like piss! I wouldn't drink it with gin!"[8]

To say that Goldwater was not a liar is not to say that he told the objective truth, but that he told the truth as he saw it. Goldwater stated that people who were unemployed were so because they lacked intelligence or ambition.[9] He was against Social Security and openly said so. One of the most effective Johnson television commercials in the fall showed the fingers of two hands tearing up a Social Security card.[10] His comment three years before about the country being better off "if we could just saw off the Eastern seaboard and let it float out to sea"[11] opened the way for another LBJ ad, which consisted of a saw cutting through a map of the United States then a voice-over reading his quote.[12]

In Dixie Land, He Took His Stand: The Parties, They Were a-Changin' with Goldwater

When Lyndon Johnson signed the Civil Rights Act in July, he feared that he was signing away the South for the Democratic Party. The fear proved to be well-founded in the Deep South.

South Carolina senator Strom Thurmond announced in a speech broadcast to eight southern states that he was again leaving the party,[13] becoming a Republican, and supporting Goldwater. Thurmond denounced the Democrats as a party that had "abandoned the people." Sporting a gold lapel pin featuring a Republican elephant wearing Goldwater's trademark black-rimmed glasses, Thurmond called upon other southerners (referring, of course, only to those with pale complexions) to join him, elect Goldwater, and make the Republicans a "party which supports freedom, justice, and constitutional government."[14]

The day after Thurmond's announcement, the senator introduced Goldwater at rallies in South Carolina and other southern states. Goldwater told southern Democrats that "their fathers up in heaven would say 'Thank God' if they left the national Democratic party."[15] Confederate flags were prominently displayed at his appearances in the Deep South.

The irony in this shift of white southerners to Goldwater because of his vote against the Civil Rights Act is that Goldwater's views on race were not at all like those of the segregationists he attracted. Goldwater was a member of the NAACP and an opponent of segregation. He had been persuaded to vote against the civil rights bill by two members of his "brain trust"—both of whom would later become major national figures on the political right: William Rehnquist and Robert Bork. They convinced the candidate to oppose the Civil Rights Act on constitutional grounds. When Goldwater cast his vote against the Civil Rights Act, he was described by associates as "a shaken man afraid he was signing his political death warrant [but] convinced that the Constitution offered him no other honorable choice."[16]

None of this was known to the candidate's racist base. They saw only the "no" vote, not the non-racist reasoning that had led to it. All that mattered was that Lyndon Johnson was for the "niggers" and Barry Goldwater was against *them*—and so, for *us*. They had found their Great White Hope.

Four years earlier, Lyndon Johnson had correctly analyzed what had been happening in the South for decades and has continued to happen ever since. "If you can convince the lowest white man he's better than the best colored man, he won't notice you're picking his pocket. Hell, give him somebody to look down on, and he'll empty his pockets for you."[17] LBJ's assessment then still applies to all too many struggling white people today.

LBJ made the Democratic Party the Party of Lincoln and, in so doing, drove the racists and haters into what was rapidly becoming the Anti-Lincoln Party. This process would culminate in 2016. The 1964 Goldwater vote was heavily concentrated in the Deep South, especially in the majority-black counties (where, in this pre–Voting Rights Act era, scarcely any African Americans were permitted to vote).

The five most ardently segregationist states of the Deep South

—Mississippi, Alabama, South Carolina, Louisiana, and Georgia (all of which except Georgia had gone for Thurmond in 1948)—dramatically switched from their traditional Democratic allegiance to Goldwater. This switch reflects how many white people in the region had concluded that the party of white supremacy had changed its name from "Democratic" to "Republican." The vote for Goldwater in the Deep South ranged from an astounding 87 percent in Mississippi to 54 percent in Georgia. Outside the South, however, Goldwater had little appeal. He eked out a one-point win in his home state of Arizona. Johnson swept the rest of the West, along with everywhere else, including taking 52 percent of the vote in the South as a whole, one point more than Kennedy had won in the region in 1960,[18] indicating that he must have received a considerably larger share of the votes in the rest of the South.

The 1964 Republican campaign had lived and died in Dixie.

"We Must Either Love Each Other, or We Must Die": The "Daisy Girl" Spot

About a week after Goldwater's nomination, Johnson's press secretary, George Reedy, told the president that he thought Goldwater's "big weakness is that people think he's pretty reckless." Reedy suggested using Goldwater's vote against the Nuclear Test Ban Treaty in a way that would "get this thing down to some gut things: Mothers that are worried about having radio-active poison in their kids' milk. Men that are worried about becoming sterile. Uh, give them some thoughts about maybe kids being born with two heads and things like that."[19]

The Johnson campaign pursued this line of attack and the result was what is still widely considered to be

"Peace, Little Girl" (Daisy Girl Spot), LBJ campaign commercial, September 1964.[20]

the most famous political television commercial in history: "The Daisy Girl." The one-minute spot aired only once, on the evening of Labor Day, the traditional starting point for fall campaigns. It begins with a little girl counting the petals as she pulls them off a daisy. As she nears ten, she looks up in a startled way and a stern male voice reverses her counting order, counting down "10, 9, 8 . . ." as the camera zooms in for an extreme closeup on one of the girl's eyes. At the end of the countdown, a thermonuclear blast detonates in her eye and, as the blast fills the whole screen, President Johnson's voice-over comes on saying, "These are the stakes—to make a world in which *all* of God's children can live, or go into the dark. We must either love each other, or we must die." The spot concludes with an announcer's voice-over instructing, "Vote for President Johnson on November 3rd. The stakes are too high for you to stay home."

The impact of the Daisy Girl spot was enormous. It was played repeatedly on news broadcasts—an estimated 40 million people saw it. The Republicans' loud reaction amplified the effects. "This ad implies that Senator Goldwater is a reckless man and Lyndon Johnson is a careful man," Republicans complained after its only airing. That, of course, was the point. "The shriek of Republican indignation fastened the bomb message on [the Republicans] more tightly than any calculation could have expected," Theodore White wrote the next year."[21] Now, the Democratic version of Goldwater's campaign slogan became: "In Your Heart You Know He Might [blow up the world]."

The admen working for Johnson portrayed Goldwater and anyone who would vote for him as madmen, freeing the president to take the high road and run at his level one of the most positive campaigns the nation had ever seen. Having demonstrated his toughness in August by lying about the Gulf of Tonkin incident and ordering the bombing of North Vietnam, President Johnson was able to use a larger lie in the fall to present himself as the candidate who would maintain peace. "We are not about to send American boys nine or ten thousand miles away from home to do what Asian boys ought to be doing for themselves," the president proclaimed in a speech at Akron in October.[22] In fact, he was preparing to do just that.

"Well Hello, Lyndon . . . You're Lookin' Swell, Lyndon"*: The Johnson Campaign

> We're in favor of a lot of things,
> and we're against mighty few!
> —Lyndon B. Johnson impromptu
> campaign talk, Providence, Rhode
> Island (September 28, 1964)[23]

In 1964, Lyndon Johnson was able to sail through the election campaign as a conquering hero. The emerging sentiments of the sixties, a desire to complete the mission people thought John F. Kennedy had been on when he was gunned down, the attractiveness of his own optimistic "can do" message, distaste for extremism, and Goldwater's self-destructive statements contributed to his victory.

During a stop in Providence in late September, Johnson was energized by a sea of people. He grabbed a bullhorn, climbed on top of a car and shouted a statement that perfectly captured the positive, optimistic spirit of liberalism at its 1964 peak: "We're in favor of a lot of things and against mighty few."[24] While that position is open to justifiable criticism, it contrasts favorably with the negative politics in which candidates concentrate on what they're *against* that has dominated the American public square for much of the time since.

The most significant speech the president made during the 1964 campaign was at the Jung Hotel in New Orleans in early October. It came three weeks after Barry Goldwater's swing through Dixie and at a time when it seemed clear that white people across much of the Deep South were abandoning LBJ and his party to support the Republican candidate because they believed him to be a segregationist.

While New Orleans hardly qualified as the "belly of the beast" of Deep South racism—that appellation was the tightly held property of nearby Mississippi—Lyndon Johnson was in hostile territory. His political advisers warned him against saying anything on civil rights. As

---

* President Johnson chose as his 1964 campaign song a takeoff on the title song from the Broadway musical *Hello Dolly!*, which in a version recorded by Louis Armstrong had reached number one on the *Billboard* chart in May.

he had done when he insisted on highlighting the civil rights bill in his address to the nation five days after President Kennedy's assassination, Johnson rejected the counsel. "I am going to repeat here . . . what I have said in every state that I have appeared in," he told a huge, inter-racial crowd that met him at the train station. "As long as I am your president, I am going to be president of *all* the people." In his speech at the Jung later that evening, LBJ made an impassioned plea to fellow southerners to change their racist course. Speaking of his vision for the American future, the president declared, "We are not going to lose that tomorrow in divisions over things of the past."

"The people that would use us and destroy us first divide us. . . . And all these years they have kept their foot on our necks by appealing to our animosities and dividing us." Directly addressing what held the South back, Johnson proclaimed: "I am not going to let them build up the hate and try to buy my people by appealing to prejudice." Then he departed from his prepared text to give what could only be characterized as a revival sermon. He quoted what Texas Senator Joseph W. Bailey had once said to Sam Rayburn about the cause of the region's plight. Bailey was originally from Mississippi (in his remarks, Johnson named neither Bailey nor the state), and he told Rayburn that he wished he could go back there and "make them one more Democratic speech. . . . The poor old State, they haven't heard a Democratic speech in thirty years." By this point, Johnson had his arms raised up and he was shouting. "All they ever hear at election time is 'Negro, Negro, Negro.'" (He pronounced the word "nigra.") That, of course, was precisely what was being said in the Deep South in 1964—and what would be said implicitly in later years down to the present, to woo white people away from the Democratic Party. Johnson would have none of it. "It is time for all of us to follow the Golden Rule," he said in New Orleans. "It is time for all of us to have a little trust and a little faith in each other, and to try to find some areas that we can agree on so we can have a united program."[25]

Here was Lyndon Johnson at his finest, reflecting the best in Amer-ica. And, for that brief shining moment in 1964, it was reflective of most of America outside the Deep South. "The New Orleans speech was courageous—and, most especially, *courageous politics*," top aide Horace Busby said to Johnson afterwards. "Overnight, they [the press] are speaking of you—as once of FDR—as the 'master,' 'the champ.'"[26]

The huge, cheering crowds that swelled around him as the campaign progressed allowed LBJ to begin to feel the love of the public he had always craved. It was, though, almost certainly more their fear of Goldwater and their love of the Democratic policies than it was personal affection for Johnson that the crowds were expressing.

Passing Clouds in LBJ's Blue Skies

Nobody should accept corruption in positions
of public trust as a way of life.
—Barry Goldwater, campaign
commercial (October 1964)[27]

Apart from the Vietnam/"soft on communism" issue, which Johnson had neutralized with bombs in early August, and the concern over the possibility of "white backlash," the only potential worries LBJ had during the campaign came from scandals involving his associates.

An investigation of his former protégé Bobby Baker, which had been on the verge of sinking Johnson around midday on November 22, 1963, but was paused by the news from Dallas, had resumed a few months later. Baker was called to testify in February 1964 and exercised his Fifth Amendment right against self-incrimination.[28] Although the Senate, controlled by Democrats, tried to end the investigation, in September President Johnson felt obliged to call upon the FBI to look into one of the allegations.[29] The investigation was sure to take months and no findings would be publicized until well after the election, but it provided fodder for the Republican campaign.

The cloud of another Johnson associate, Billie Sol Estes, also hung in the president's mostly sunny skies during the 1964 campaign. The West Texas con man had been arrested by the FBI on charges of fraud in 1962 and convicted the following year.[30] No evidence was found of Lyndon Johnson being involved in wrongdoing in connection with Estes, but his name added to the questionable associations that tarnished the president.[31]

Goldwater's attempts to stir fears over corruption, crime, race, and declining morality and pin them to his opponent got him nowhere in

1964, but they proved to be the outline for a strategy his party would employ with great success in future years.

◆◆◆

While the Baker and Estes problems were failing to have much of a negative effect, a potentially much larger threat to Johnson arose less than a month before Election Day. On October 7, the president's long-time aide and closest confidant (Johnson had called him as his "vice president in charge of everything"[32]), Walter Jenkins, was arrested in the men's room of the Washington YMCA, where police had drilled peepholes that enabled them to catch men engaged in sexual acts with each other. Jenkins was booked on a disorderly conduct charge and paid a $50 fine. President Johnson was told of the arrest soon after it occurred and tried to keep the story from becoming public.

Over the following days, however, people in the Republican National Committee, who had presumably been told of the incident by someone in the Washington police department, began to circulate rumors of Jenkins's arrest on a "morals charge." A reporter for the *Washington Star* found the police record and, on October 14, the paper's managing editor called the White House for comment. Jenkins went to see Johnson counsel Abe Fortas, who checked him into a hospital while Fortas and Clark Clifford went around Washington asking editors not to publish the story. In the course of this undertaking, they learned that Jenkins had also been arrested in 1959 in the same YMCA on the charge of "disorderly conduct (pervert)."[33] Late in the afternoon, Fortas called the president, who was in New York to speak that night at the Alfred E. Smith Dinner, to inform him of the situation.

Johnson's relatively calm reaction to the news in Fortas's call (though he did say in a voice that sounded like he meant it, "I just can't *believe* this!"[34]) supports the suspicion that he already knew of the incident. Yet, it also seems that the president, who liked to shore up his insecure masculinity by repeating J. Edgar Hoover's oft-stated comment on homosexuals, "You can spot one by the way they walk,"[35] had enormous sympathy for Jenkins and didn't see him as a "pervert."

At 6 p.m., Dean Burch, the RNC chair, issued a statement referring to "a report sweeping Washington that the White House is desperately trying to suppress a major news story affecting the national security."[36] As the president found that many others knew about the incident and there would be no way to keep the lid on it, he said to Fortas that "the Presidency is at stake. It's not important what happens to me or Walter. I don't believe that we can know this and sit around on it and do nothing. I think we just build it up that way."[37] Johnson insisted that Jenkins had been set up by Republicans, a charge that rings hollow, but agreed with his advisers that Jenkins had to resign.[38] Bill Moyers replaced him.

While Johnson was concerned that the Jenkins arrest might provide fuel for the Goldwater campaign's themes of morality and character, he was almost certainly more concerned about the possibility of the contents of Jenkins's safe falling into unfriendly hands. The safe contained information about Johnson's private life, as well as those of many other political allies and opponents, probably along with cash and records of secret donations. The president was asking the FBI to begin an immediate investigation in order to be able to be assured that no security breach had happened as a result of Jenkins's sexual preferences, which might have opened him to being blackmailed by foreign agents. ("It is axiomatic that sexual deviates are susceptible to blackmail," an article on Jenkins in *Time* said.[39]) LBJ wanted to be sure that the safe was cleaned out before FBI agents got to it, since he didn't want J. Edgar Hoover to have the information it contained to use against him.[40]

Republicans were elated by the Jenkins story. As people in the Goldwater campaign saw it, in Theodore White's words, "Here, if ever, was demonstration of [Goldwater's] charge of 'moral decay, of sickness of soul, of bestiality in Babylon.'"[41] GOP operatives quickly began churning out buttons and bumper stickers. As Democrats had amended Goldwater's slogan, "In your heart, you know he's right," into a variety of damning versions, Republicans now came up with takes on Johnson's slogan, "All the Way with LBJ." Bumper stickers read "ALL THE WAY WITH LBJ, BUT DON'T GO NEAR THE YMCA" and "EITHER WAY WITH LBJ."[42]

But the Jenkins incident turned out to have little effect on the election, in part because most people in the media were less eager to exploit such stories than their counterparts would be in later years. (Walter

Trohan, the Washington bureau chief of the *Chicago Tribune*, for example, told Fortas that he couldn't "bring himself to write a story like this about a man who has got six children."[43]) Another element was that, in sharp contrast to the Republicans who were gleeful about the potential for the Jenkins "scandal" to harm Johnson's campaign, Barry Goldwater himself refused to say anything about it. Off the record, he remarked to reporters, "What a way to win an election. Communists and cocksuckers."[44]

In addition to those factors, three major international stories almost immediately diverted public attention to far more important matters. On October 16, the morning after newspapers reported the Jenkins arrest, their banner headlines announced that Nikita Khrushchev had been deposed as Soviet leader.[45] A *New York Times* story with a small headline below the Soviet leadership change report summarized the remarkably short life span of the Jenkins affair as a factor in the election. After referring to the surging hopes of the Goldwater camp in the morning, the story speculated that "the possible anti-Johnson impact of the Jenkins disclosure might be nullified by the effect of an international crisis upon the voters."[46]

LBJ's "luck" in this regard was continuing even as the papers with that assessment were being printed. In the wee hours of the morning (Washington time) of October 16, China exploded its first atomic bomb.[47] And, in the midst of those two momentous world events, the Labour Party unseated the Conservative government in Great Britain, making Harold Wilson the new prime minister.[48] The times, they were a-changin' around the world, and for most Americans that fact overshadowed a men's-room arrest of a top presidential aide—even in a time of great prejudice against homosexuals.

The fear of the Red Chinese, as they were invariably called in the United States at that time, having the bomb made Goldwater's loose talk about using "nukes" all the more terrifying to many voters. "Suddenly," as historian Rick Perlstein has written of this moment, "the nation was interested in little more than having a steady hand on the tiller."[49] "Perhaps the most amazing of all events of the campaign of 1964," Theodore White wrote of the Jenkins matter, "is that the nation faced the fact fully—and shrugged its shoulders."[50] Though the gay rights movement would not take flight until five years later, that reaction suggests that the times were also beginning to change at least a bit in attitudes on that front in 1964.

"The Maximum of Individual Freedom": Ronald Reagan Delivers "The Speech"

Freedom has never been so fragile.
—Ronald Reagan
(October 27, 1964)

The one bright spot in the dismal Republican campaign was to come near its end. A week before the election, a filmed speech by movie and television actor Ronald Reagan in support of Goldwater was televised nationally. In retrospect, one of the most significant legacies of 1964 would be Reagan's political career. It was the confluence that year of the Free Speech Movement and "The Speech" on freedom that started him on his way to the presidency.

Reagan, who had once been on the left fringes of the New Deal and an ardent supporter of Franklin Roosevelt, had been moving to the right since the late 1940s, had joined "Democrats for Nixon" in 1960, and officially become a Republican in 1962. As a spokesman for General Electric from 1954 to 1962, Reagan had been giving essentially the same speech to business and conservative audiences for years. People in those circles in Southern California had come to refer to it simply as "The Speech."[51]

Goldwater was unable to attend a $1,000-a-plate California dinner for his campaign and Reagan replaced him.[52] When Reagan's speech was over, the wealthy Southern California men who put it on got the idea to ask him to do "The Speech" in a television studio to make what turned out to be a half-hour commercial. The Goldwater "brain trust" opposed it, but the candidate himself endorsed using it.[53]

It is not hyperbole to say that Barry Goldwater begat Ronald Reagan. Reagan's nationally televised speech of October 27, 1964, on behalf of Goldwater's doomed candidacy, was, in the accurate assessment of David Broder and Steve Hess, "the most successful national political debut since William Jennings Bryan electrified the 1896 Democratic

Ronald Reagan delivering televised speech, "A Time for Choosing," October 27, 1964.

Convention with the 'Cross of Gold' speech.'"[54] Ronald Reagan's theme was freedom, the theme that prevailed across the ideological spectrum in the sixties. "Freedom has never been so fragile," he asserted. "If we lose freedom here, there's no place to escape to."

Pointing to an enemy that held the potential to shift the traditional populist hostility of the hinterlands from Wall Street and the financial elite to Washington and another sort of elite, he posed the fundamental question as "whether we abandon the American Revolution and confess that a little intellectual elite in a far-distant capital can plan our lives for us better than we can plan them ourselves." Labeling "man's age-old dream" as "the maximum of individual freedom consistent with order," Reagan said the choice was to move in that direction "or down to the ant heap of totalitarianism" and warned that "those who would sacrifice freedom for security have embarked on this downward path." He identified the enemy as "those who ask us to trade our freedom for the soup kitchen of the welfare state."[55]

On this late October day in 1964, Ronald Reagan pushed most of the buttons that he and others would press with so much political effect in later decades: taxes, debt, waste, no-win wars, misused foreign aid, impersonal, far-away government bureaucracy . . . often making the points with a humor that Goldwater never projected. Here, clearly, was the Messenger to deliver the Gospel According to William F. Buckley Jr.

Reagan's address was officially titled "A Time for Choosing." A week later, Americans overwhelmingly chose a different definition of freedom, but Reagan's speech turned out to be much more a harbinger of the future that would emerge by the later 1970s than was Johnson's landslide victory. As an actor, Reagan was able to put a smiling human face on an ideology that Goldwater had presented with all its ugliness showing.[56] Reagan's appealing persona would, in following years, make the message persuasive to millions of Americans, with consequences for wealth and income concentration and middle-class decline that are a major part of the landscape of the 2020s.

After the Republican election debacle, the wealthy Californians who had chosen Reagan to speak for Goldwater began pushing Reagan as the front man for their political revolution. Joan Didion would later describe this "small group of industrialists and entrepreneurs" as the men who "financed, as a venture in risk capital, Ronald Reagan's appearances in both Sacramento and Washington."[57] Few other risk capital ventures have ever returned greater profits than this one did over the coming decades and down to the present.

Yet the shift in the American people's choice from Johnson's vision toward Reagan's between 1964 and later years was much more the result of Johnson's actions and failures (and, ironically, Nixon's[58]) than it was of either the inherent superiority of the "conservative" vision of freedom or the power of Reagan's rhetoric. The people who would call themselves movement conservatives were able to take over the Republican Party in 1964 but not the country. That would come later, and only after they had lost the GOP itself back to Nixon for a time.

Decades later, following the two-term presidency of a man who is the sum of all the fears of the Goldwater Movement in 1964—a man who is biracial with a Muslim name and an international upbringing—the heirs of those who supported Goldwater and Reagan have come back with a vengeance. Trumpism is the old vinegar of the Goldwater movement in a new bottle. Donald Trump managed to sell enough of that old vinegar—corporate "freedom" is good for everyone, making the rich ever richer will "trickle down" to those below, the poor are the problem, government intervention is evil, and, of course, racism—in 2016 to win a narrow Electoral College victory and then to reverse much of what Johnson accomplished in 1964–1965. In 2020, constant lies, spewing of hate, and voter suppression proved insufficient for him to prevail. But, stoking hatred with the sort of Big Lie that Adolf Hitler had advocated, the election had been stolen from him, Trump instigated a violent insurrection that invaded the Capitol on January 6, 2021, in an attempt to overturn the election and end democracy. It failed, but a large majority of Republicans refused to condemn it and the division that was evident in 1964 remains a major battle line in the 2020s.

The Anticlimax:
"Johnson Swamps Goldwater"

"I doubt that there has ever been so many people
seeing so many things alike on decision day.
                              —Lyndon B. Johnson
                              (November 5, 1964)[59]

The *New York Times* summarized the extraordinary result of the 1964 election with an economy of words in its banner headline: "JOHNSON SWAMPS GOLDWATER."[60]

The combination of fear of Goldwater and approval of the liberal social programs Johnson was pushing as components of the Great Society delivered the largest popular vote mandate in the history of contested American presidential elections. Apart from Republicans, Johnson won every demographic group—sex, race, education, occupation, age, religion, politics, region, and union membership—analyzed by the Gallup organization. The only two categories among whom his margin of victory was at all close were the South and people with college degrees, both of which he carried with 52 percent support. Johnson also outperformed John Kennedy's showing four years earlier among every measured segment of the electorate except Catholics and Independents.

LBJ carried most groups within the national electorate by huge margins. Examples include: 60 percent of men and 62 percent of women (up from 52 and 49, respectively for JFK); 59 percent of white voters and 94 percent of "nonwhite" voters (up from 49 and 68 for JFK); 68 percent in the East, 61 percent in the Midwest, and 60 percent in the West (up from 53, 48, and 49 for JFK).[61]

Johnson's winning of 60 percent of men and 59 percent of white voters is particularly striking in retrospect. No Democratic presidential nominee has carried a majority of white men since Johnson won them by a very large margin in 1964.[62] The huge increase in LBJ's share of the "nonwhite" vote while he was simultaneously winning a landslide among white voters indicates that the racial party realignment that grew out of the mid-sixties occurred first as the positive movement of black voters to the Democratic Party. Only later did the Democratic Party see the negative movement of white voters outside the Deep South away from it. The latter was less a response against the Civil Rights Act than it was a reaction to other developments, such as the Watts Uprising the following year.

Even the largest popular vote repudiation in the history of American presidential elections does not indicate the extent of Goldwater's defeat. He received 27 million votes, but a later poll found that only six million of the people who had voted for him were pro-Goldwater. The rest cast their ballots for him only out of loyalty to the Republican Party.[63]

Seeking the Dark Lining in the Silver Cloud of Victory: Election Night and the Day After

> Love. That's why he did everything. That's why he went into politics. . . . He wanted all the voters to love him, too. Guess all he really wanted out of life was love.
> —Jedediah Leland, speaking of Charles Foster Kane, *Citizen Kane* (1941)

Never one who was able to calm his internal demons or to take any lasting reassurance from an electoral victory, no matter how overwhelming, Lyndon Johnson could not manage to bring himself to savor the greatest landslide in the history of United States presidential elections even through election night.

At his moment of triumph Johnson thought of Walter Jenkins and again showed, in private, his apparent tolerance for homosexuality, which was still anathema to the vast majority of Americans. When Bill Moyers told the president that he had called Jenkins, Johnson sought to be sure that his love and support were conveyed to his longtime friend. "Tell him we just love him more than anything in the world," Johnson instructed.[64]

In his long-established routine of campaigns, LBJ fell into exhaustion even before the polls closed. "Well, I just fell apart," he told Moyers by phone. "My back's hurting. My head's hurting. I'm aching all over. I've got a headache—I don't know what I'm going to do. I've been in bed *all* day long." [65] He yawned before saying, "I'm afraid of Vietnam." [66]

By midday on Wednesday, hours after he had achieved an unprecedented triumph, Lyndon Baines Johnson was being gripped by the demons of insecurity that always haunted him. As historian Michael Beschloss has nicely put it, Johnson was "angry and resentful, seizing whatever black lining might exist within the silver cloud of victory." [67]

The most gratifying aspect of the sweeping victory for Lyndon Johnson must have been that his 61.1 percent of the popular vote outdid even the 60.8 percent his idol, Franklin D. Roosevelt, had received in 1936. Democrats gained two seats in the Senate for a 68–32 majority and 36 seats in the House for a 295–140 majority, Now, with huge margins in Congress, LBJ could go on to try to outdo FDR in legislation and social reform, as well.

There were, however, warning signs even in the election returns. One of the most ominous was that on Election Day, as California voters were choosing Lyndon Johnson over Barry Goldwater with nearly 60 percent of the vote, they approved, by an even larger margin (65.4 percent in favor), Proposition 14 striking down the state's Rumford Fair Housing Act, passed in 1963, which prohibited property owners from discriminating against buyers or renters on the basis of race. [68]

That was an indication that the times that were a-changin' in so many ways in 1964 could change again in a different direction. The public's love that Johnson had so long sought and that he experienced on Election Day would, over the next few years, be transformed into widespread hate.

19

"No More a Man's World Than It Is a White World"

Women and Their Positions

November 1964

Mary King (left) and Casey Hayden (right).

Assumptions of male superiority are as widespread and deep rooted and every much as crippling to the woman as the assumptions of white supremacy are to the Negro.
> —SNCC Position Paper
> (November 1964)[1]

After fighting alongside men in a radical movement to correct a grievous wrong, the women then woke up and wondered, 'What about us?'
> —Susan Brownmiller,
> *In Our Time* (1999)[2]

W OMEN WHO WORKED IN the civil rights movement to assist others in gaining freedom from oppression and injustice were already inclined to shed established gender roles. They came together with men, many of whom were not so predisposed, in one of the more pregnant convergences of the sixties. The offspring issuing from this union would be a feminism considerably more radical than that envisioned by Betty Friedan—born, perhaps a bit prematurely, in Waveland, Mississippi, in the fall of 1964.

Sex and race were intertwined. Each was a very long-standing and powerful hierarchical division. "Right order" as it was defined in American society required that men and white people remain firmly on top and that their position not be challenged. Confronting racial hierarchy was bound to lead to questions about the sexual hierarchy, as had happened more than a century before when the nineteenth-century women's movement arose out of abolitionism.

The Mississippi Summer Project of 1964 provided an incubator for a radical women's movement. Forty percent of the project's volunteers were women. A substantial majority of those women were white. They had been brought up in the age of what Friedan had the year before named "the Feminine Mystique." While those who sought to join a nonviolent army and go off to a dangerous land were already rejecting traditional gender roles,[3] nonviolence and social reform were traditionally seen as more feminine. In that regard, it was the men in the Summer Project who were going against their expected gender roles, which may have made some of them more intent on maintaining traditional roles for women. When male volunteers sang "black and white together," they meant on a basis of equality: together horizontally. Many of them were not ready to sing "pink and blue together," at least not if "together" was taken to imply equality.

"Many people who are very hip to the implications of the racial caste system, even people in the movement," Casey Hayden and Mary King would write a year after they anonymously broached the subject at Waveland, "don't seem to see the sexual caste system, and, if it's raised they respond with: 'That's the way it's supposed to be. There are biological differences.' Or with other statements that sound like a white segregationist confronted with integration."[4] For their part, the men against whom the Freedom Movement was struggling were adamant champions of the established roles in both race and sex.

The issue of interracial sex was the most explosive of all, but it is essential to realize that the taboo was not on intercourse between the races but on a particular version of it. Sexual relations between white men and black women constituted no threat to "right order"; on the contrary, they reinforced it. Putative superiors "screwing" putative inferiors was in keeping with the established system of dominance. A white man having sex with a black woman also served to reinforce the order by reminding black men that they could not protect "their women," and so were not men at all.

But a black man having sex with a white woman would overturn all order. Worse, from the perspective of insecure white men, it would mean that it was *they* who could not control "their women" and so were not "real men." It would constitute nothing less than the end of the world as they knew it and so it must be prevented at all costs.[5]

Mississippi in 1964 has accurately been described as "obsessed" with interracial sex.[6] Fears about the breakdown of segregation were often put in terms of the paramount need to protect white women from black men and prevent the "mongrelization" of the white race. It should not be missed in this context that white men had been "mongrelizing" the black race for centuries by impregnating black women— often forcibly and always through sexual assault in terms of power relationships—during and long after slavery. The lighter complexions of most African Americans in comparison with Africans are the result of this form of interracial sex. As the poet Caroline Randall Williams pointed out in 2020, she and millions of other African Americans today have "rape-colored skin."[7] Virtually all their white ancestors from the era of enslavement—and most for a long time thereafter— were rapists.[8]

The arrival in Mississippi in the summer of 1964 of a few hundred young white women who would live among the black population was akin to throwing a match into the arid sagebrush that filled the heads of many white males in the state and far beyond. Mississippi segregationists made the prospect of sex between black men and white women a major part of their attack on the Summer Project.[9]

Psychological Emasculation and Views of Women

A man's most easily accessible symbol of
freedom is a woman.
—Ralph Ellison,
Invisible Man (1952)[10]

It may be surprising that people who were "hip to" the evils of racism
would not also recognize and be against sexism, but many did not. The
reasons are complicated, but in one sense also straightforward.

The model for all other dominance/subordination relationships,
the oldest, deepest form of asserting supremacy, is the contention
that males are superior to females. Across the vast sweep of recorded
human history, the primary means to belittle a man has been to declare
him to be like a woman and place him in the social position of a
woman. That was done through enslavement and continued in the
racist hierarchy of Jim Crow after the "peculiar institution" formally
ended. African American men were denied all the socially accepted
attributes of being a "man." These include the "three P's" of being
a provider, a protector, and a procreator. Enslaved men could not be
providers for their families. They could not protect "their women,"
who were subject to the sexual desires of white enslavers, of being
sold away, and having their children sold. To be "the Man" was to be
in a position of authority. To be a "man" was to be "free." Being a
woman has for a very long time meant *not* being free.[11]

Enslavement and racism entailed symbolic emasculation. "They
[Muslims from elsewhere] had not been aware that [the plight of the
black man in America] . . . was a psychological castration," Malcolm X
pointed out after his 1964 pilgrimage.[12] A black man who ignored the
rules that prohibited him from acting as a man risked severe punishment, up to and including lynching. All this meant that the desire to
be seen as a man, the generally accepted definition of which included
being dominant over women, was especially important for many black
males. Given the extraordinarily long history of the axiomatic equation of *woman* with *inferior*, for a man to accept equality with women
seemed to identify himself as an inferior. White men had, purpose-
fully, stripped black men of the socially defined symbols and roles of

men, and some black men sought to assert their "manhood" by putting themselves above women.

"A man's most easily accessible symbol of freedom is a woman," a black veteran in Ralph Ellison's 1952 novel *Invisible Man* declares.[13] That statement has much wider applicability to men in general, but it was especially the case with black men who had for so long been in what was classified as the female position. The desire—the perceived *need*—to insist that women are subordinate to men was evident among many of the prominent black men seeking freedom for themselves. "The word *man* means master," Cassius Clay opined in 1963. "Women don't take over nothing, unless man lets them. The animals, the trees, the chickens, everything was put here for man. I see women leading men to the dance floor. That's wrong. The man should lead the woman. The man is the master."[14]

Becoming Men by Acting like Women?:
Sex and Nonviolent Resistance

Nonviolent resistance was and is an extraordinarily nonconformist approach. It was an unconventional way for those on the bottom of the racial hierarchy to challenge those with all the conventional power. It provided a paradoxical way for men to become "men"—free human beings—by acting, to some degree at least, like women.

That the modern civil rights movement in America was generally seen as having started with a woman sitting down and thereby standing up "like a man" is highly symbolic. The movement was based on what would generally be seen as a feminine approach: nonviolent resistance rather than violent confrontation was a means available to those with less raw power than their opponents. Nonviolent resistance was a means of acting by *not* acting.[15]

The relationship between nonviolent resistance and "being a man" had been a central question for the civil rights movement since its inception in the wake of Rosa Parks's courageous act of defiance. During his speech to the mass meeting at which the Montgomery Improvement Association was founded and the bus boycott organized, Alabama NAACP leader E. D. Nixon echoed the association of freedom with manhood. "We've worn aprons all our lives," Nixon said.

"It's time to take the aprons off. . . . If we're gonna be mens, now's the time to be mens."[16]

If nonviolent resistance is perceived as unmanly, it is not weak. "This method is nonaggressive physically, but strongly aggressive spiritually," Martin Luther King Jr. argued.[17] Still, Malcolm X was disdainful of the approach. "It's not so good to refer to what you're going to do as a sit-in. That right there castrates you," Malcolm said in Detroit in April 1964. "Think of the image of someone sitting. An old woman can sit . . . a coward can sit, anything can sit. Well, you and I been sitting long enough and it's time for us today to start doing some standing and some fighting to back that up."[18] Implying that nonviolent resisters were cowards is absurd, but in a male market that believed violence is "manly," the case for nonviolence was a difficult item to sell.

◆ ◆ ◆

The equation *man = freedom* was enshrined in the nation's founding Declaration, which proclaimed that all men are equal and free. The tricky part is figuring out what it means to be a man. Crèvecoeur's 1782 question—"What then is the American, this new man?"[19]—proved to be much more than a rhetorical one. It has been one of the issues around which much of American history has revolved. And it certainly was the issue around which the freedom movements of 1964 and the rest of the sixties revolved: Are males who are not white "men"? Are women "men"? Are those who oppose war "men"? Are males whose sexual preference is other males "men"?

Being a "man" was a constant struggle for middle-class white males emasculated by corporations, for young white males emasculated by a puritanical society, and for black males emasculated by enslavement and racism. But being a man was also a constant struggle for southern white men, who were emasculated by their region's history: their ancestors had lost a war. And, at least in the American popular mind, no other Americans had ever lost a war. That's quite a blow to the manhood, even for later generations. Now the damned Yankees were trying to tell them they had to stop emasculating black males and accept them as their equals.

Some black men emasculated by racism, the society, and economy sought, for a time, to prove their "manhood" through traditionally female means, though many others, especially after 1964, went in the other direction and asserted their "manhood" through traditionally male means.

It is a delicious irony that "unmanly" nonviolence was used to confront and ultimately overthrow a racial/sexual hierarchy that was based in substantial part on the sexual fears of white males. Beyond that irony, the civil rights movement's emphasis on nonviolent resistance was an important aspect of its relationship with the women's movement. This philosophy/tactic provided an alternate means of resistance for those for whom violent resistance was not an option. Women are, on average, weaker in the physical areas most useful in engaging in violence and, again on average, they seem to be somewhat less prone to resort to it.

Nonviolence, like the teachings of Jesus out of which it grew either directly or indirectly, through Gandhi, was a particularly feminine philosophy. The civil rights movement showed women that it was possible to succeed in bringing about change through means that were both consistent with women's traditions and with their lack of the usual instruments of power.

Freedom Sisters[20]

Shit! I asked for volunteers and they sent
me white women.
> —SNCC field secretary, Meridian,
> Mississippi (summer 1964)[21]

In her memoir of her years in the freedom struggles, first for black people and then for women, Susan Brownmiller, a writer and a somewhat older (she was twenty-nine in 1964) Summer Project volunteer, addressed the paradox that constituted a ticking time bomb in the Freedom Movement:

"SNCC was cast in the image of a young, fearless black male, *a concept that may have been necessary for its time*, but its corollary was that women of both races were expected to occupy a lesser role [emphasis added]."[22]

Men who had been denied all the symbols of manhood felt a need to assert their superiority over women, as other men did. Yet they were working in a movement dedicated to freedom and equality with a large number of women, at least some of whom were likely to notice the contradiction. Several women—including but by no means limited to Ella Baker, Rosa Parks, Diane Nash, and Fannie Lou Hamer—had already played major roles in the movement.

Two of the white women who were working in Mississippi that summer were among those who began to notice the inconsistency in the treatment of women as subordinates rather than equals by men who were ready to put their lives on the line to help end black subordination. Sandra ("Casey") Cason grew up in East Texas and had become involved in the movement when she joined sit-ins to desegregate restaurants in Austin in 1960. That summer she attended the National Student Association Congress in Minneapolis, where she made an impression with a speech in which she declared: "I cannot say to a person who suffers injustice, 'Wait.' And having decided that I cannot urge caution, I must stand with him." It was at this NSA gathering that she met Tom Hayden, whom she would marry the next year. (They divorced in 1962, but Casey kept the last name.) In October 1960, she attended the second SNCC organizing conference and began working with Ella Baker. Cason was among the first white southerners in the movement. In 1963, she moved to Mississippi.[23] The movement was, she later recalled, "exciting, liberating, spicy, when we were young and in the South."[24]

Casey Hayden became friends with Mary King, who joined the struggle at the age of twenty-two in 1962, when she met, among others, John Lewis, Ella Baker, and Julian Bond. King joined SNCC in Atlanta and was sent to Mississippi at the time of the Freedom Vote in 1963. She returned to the state for the 1964 Summer Project, in which she worked on communications for the effort. "Mary and I were the golden girls," Hayden later said, "and nothing could touch us." The certainty that they were on the side of right pushed away fear. "The freedom of absolute right action—this is where it was safe." They were part of the Beloved Community; they had "simply dropped race."[25]

But, by the end of the summer, it was becoming apparent to many in the movement that dropping race was easier said than done. It was also becoming plain to Casey Hayden, Mary King, and some other women in SNCC that sex and gender could not be simply dropped either.

During the 1964 Summer Project, King and Hayden "studied the French existentialists in their evening hours." They found that passages in Simone de Beauvoir's *The Second Sex*[26] "spoke to them so directly that they began pressing the book on others." Some in the movement started to see the two women as "undisciplined sentimentalists 'on a Freedom high.'"[27]

After the Summer Project ended, James Forman invited members of the SNCC staff to write position papers to be discussed at a week-long SNCC "reassessment" conference meeting to be held in November in Waveland, on the Mississippi Gulf Coast. "We are a boat in the middle of the ocean," Bob Moses explained. The boat "has to be rebuilt in order to stay afloat. It also has to stay afloat in order to be rebuilt."[28]

Inspired in part by the study of Beauvoir's arguments and in part by her own experiences and observations in the Freedom Movement, Mary King decided to submit a paper dealing with the position of women in SNCC.[29] She was, she recalled years later, "shaken with doubt" when she sat down at her typewriter. "The issue was enormous," and she was afraid. "The reaction, I was convinced, would be one of ridicule." King's later remark revealed how groundbreaking raising the issue was: "Within the framework of the civil rights movement and the fields of human rights and civil liberties at the time—*women's rights had no meaning and indeed did not exist* [emphasis added]."[30]

She gathered evidence and talked with several other women in SNCC. After she had completed a draft of the paper, she consulted with Casey Hayden, who agreed to join with her and made some additions to the draft.[31] The paper that emerged was not an attack on SNCC; it was an attempt to apply the group's philosophy more broadly. Recognizing the personhood and equality of women was something that should flow inevitably from the principles on which SNCC was founded and operated. And, King said, "sooner or later" she and Casey "would have to reveal our new awareness as political beings who were concerned with the status of women, if we were to be honest with ourselves and with each other."[32] Even so, they were fearful of the reaction from their male colleagues, and they requested that their names as the paper's authors be withheld.

◆◆◆

The reaction when the paper was distributed at the Waveland meeting confirmed the authors' fears. King described it as "crushing criticism"—and their anonymity didn't last long. "People quickly figured out who had written it. Some mocked and taunted us." King says that the paper was disdained by most, but there were several women at the meeting who supported them, as did, significantly, Bob Moses and a few other SNCC men.[33]

As Elizabeth Cady Stanton and her colleagues had done with the 1848 Seneca Falls "Declaration of Sentiments," King and Hayden wrote in a form similar to the Declaration of Independence with its laying out of evidence of what the men in 1776 had termed "a long train of abuses" to justify the need for the revolution they were proposing. King and Hayden began by citing several examples of the problems faced by women in the movement.

Among the instances they enumerated were the all-male composition of key committees and leadership, the listing of people in one Mississippi project as "three girls," an apology issued by the SNCC office in Atlanta for the appointment of a woman as interim project director of an important Mississippi project, a list of attorneys working for the Movement in Mississippi that had following one name "(girl)," and that even the most "capable, responsible, and experienced women who are in leadership positions can expect to have to defer to a man on their project for final decision making."

King and Hayden said that "the list could continue as far as there are women in the movement," but that most women in the movement didn't talk about such things, because these women's issues were not "discussable . . . strange to some, petty to others, laughable to most."

"The woman in SNCC," they asserted, "is often in the same position as that token Negro hired in a corporation." The problem stemmed from the same sources that led to the average white person not realizing that "he assumes he is superior. And naturally he doesn't understand the problem of paternalism. So too the average SNCC worker finds it difficult to discuss the woman problem because of the assumptions of male superiority. Assumptions of male superiority are as widespread and deep rooted and every much as crippling to the woman as the assumptions of white supremacy are to the Negro."

The analysis that King and Hayden were presenting was revolutionary. The links they were seeing between racism and sexism were the beginning of the serious analysis of the unquestioned assumption of male supremacy as the model upon which all other unequal relationships are based. They were digging all the way down to uncover the causes of the wreck of human history of which Adrienne Rich would write a few years later.[34]

While decidedly more radical than *The Feminine Mystique*, the SNCC position paper dealt with some of the issues Friedan had raised. "It needs to be made know[n] that many women in the movement are not 'happy and contented' with their status." Hayden and King were also aware of the sort of problems women faced that had been brought up in "You Don't Own Me" several months before. "So too, many women, in order to be accepted by men, on men's terms, give themselves up to that caricature of what a woman is—unthinking, pliable, an ornament to please the man."

The hopes of Hayden and King for short-term accomplishments flowing from their raising of the topic were modest. "What can be done? Probably nothing right away. Most men in this movement are probably too threatened by the possibility of serious discussion on this subject," they wrote. "Many women are as unaware and insensitive to this subject as men, just as there are many Negroes who don't understand they are not free or who want to be part of white America. They don't understand that they have to give up their souls and stay in their place to be accepted."

The paper's authors were more hopeful that they might be starting something for the longer run. "Maybe the only thing that can come out of this paper is discussion—amidst the laughter—but still discussion. (Those who laugh the hardest are often those who need the crutch of male supremacy the most.)" They hoped to "start the slow process of changing values and ideas so that all of us gradually come to understand that this is no more a man's world than it is a white world."[35]

Laughter and the Crutch of Male Supremacy: "What is the position of women in SNCC"?

The position of women in SNCC is prone!
—Stokely Carmichael
(November 1964)[36]

A joke that Stokely Carmichael (later Kwame Ture) made one evening at Waveland came to be even more remembered than the King-Hayden paper—and gave that paper a good deal more attention than it might otherwise have received. A group of the attendees took a gallon of wine out on a pier and sought to alleviate the tensions of the meeting. Among those in the group were Casey Hayden, Mary King, and Carmichael.

Under a bright moon, with the small waves of the Mississippi Gulf Coast lapping at the pier and the wine easing tensions and loosening

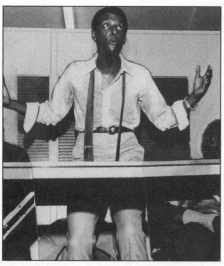

Stokely Carmichael in 1965.

tongues, Carmichael, an inveterate jokester, launched into one of his trademark monologues (those who knew him well in those days say he could have been a standup comic). After poking fun at many other targets, he turned his attention to the "anonymous" paper on women. Looking straight at Mary King, he shouted, "What is the position of women in SNCC?" Grinning broadly, he proclaimed: "The position of women in SNCC is prone!" Carmichael laughed uproariously and the women joined him. King saw it as him poking fun at his own attitudes; actually, he was among the males at the gathering who were most responsive to the points raised in the paper.[37]

Other women who were present also dismissed the comment as not serious. "Stokely made a joke, because he did not know how to keep his mouth shut," Sheila Michaels said. "It did not reflect his point of view. . . . Stokely loved strong women. . . . It is small-minded to single him out because he could not ever resist running his mouth & sometimes ran on to dry ground while his mouth kept moving."[38]

Carmichael's comment became infamous, which was an injustice to him. He was among the males in SNCC who were most supportive of women's equality. He happily worked alongside women. But his joke was not inaccurate in reflecting the views of many other men in the movement, where the reflexive belief in male superiority was nearly as widespread as it was in the larger society. Lawrence Guyot of SNCC, for example, was an admirable and heroic man as a champion of racial equality, but he took the position that women should step back and let men take the leadership.[39]

It is often in reaction to such statements as Carmichael's that movements for social change arise and grow, and as "The position of women in SNCC is prone" statement spread widely over the ensuing years, it outraged many women and motivated them to prove it wrong in its applicability to the larger society. And, since the joking statement had been in reaction to the King-Hayden paper, it served to increase the impact of what they had written.

It's a Girl!
Her Name Is "Women's Liberation"

> Objectively, the chances seem slim that we could
> start a movement based on anything as distant to
> general American thought as a sex-caste system.
> —Casey Hayden and Mary King,
> "A Kind of Memo"
> (November 1965)[40]

In the months that followed their SNCC paper, Casey Hayden and Mary King continued to explore the issue. During that time, more women were becoming receptive to the questions that the authors had raised in the paper, and open discussion of them was increasing.[41] Now more confident that they were onto something important, in the fall of 1965 they composed—this time with Hayden writing the first draft—what they called "A Kind of Memo" and sent it to thirty-two women around the country who were activists in SNCC, along with a few in SDS and antiwar organizations.[42] A vast majority of the thirty-two addressees had "a shared history in the freedom movement," historian Michelle Moravec found in a study published in 2017. "Sixteen black women, twelve white women, and one Latina all had strong ties to SNCC. Only three white women among the addressees were active in SDS."[43]

A later version published in *Liberation* in April 1966 was titled "Sex and Caste: A Kind of Memo."[44] Along with its 1964 forerunner, the document became foundational in the more radical side of the developing feminist movement.[45]

Hayden and King made it clear that their insights about the situation of women grew directly out of the principles of SNCC: "Having learned from the movement to think radically about the personal worth and abilities of people whose roles in society had gone unchallenged before, a lot of women in the movement have begun trying to apply those lessons to their own relations with men." They and other women in the movement had found themselves "trying to break out of very deeply learned fears, needs, and self-perceptions, and of what happens when we try to replace them with concepts of people and freedom learned from the movement and organizing." In seeking to understand their own oppression, they had talked almost exclusively with other women because, they wrote, "very few men can respond non-defensively, since the whole idea is either beyond their comprehension or threatens and exposes them. The usual response is laughter." The women argued that deeply ingrained ideas had taught women to think "about ourselves" in terms of those expectations and "to feel silly rather than trust our inner feelings." They described the consequence as "the straitjacketing of both sexes."

Their expectations for what would come of what they were saying were restrained. They hoped that they might stimulate women starting "to talk with each other more openly than in the past and create a community of support." In a particularly significant passage, Hayden and King said, "The very fact that the country can't face, much less deal with, the questions we're raising justifies real efforts at dialog within the movement and with whatever liberal groups, community women, or students might listen."

The closing Hayden and King chose for their letter was entirely appropriate:

"FREEDOM,
Casey and Mary"[46]

This remarkable document, this "kind of memo"—"this thing," as they called it near the end of the original letter—contained much of what would come to be known a few years later as Women's Liberation. Most of the meaningful slogans of the women's liberation movement that emerged in 1967 and the following years are implicit (and in some cases, explicit) in what Hayden and King wrote: "The Personal is Political"; "Women's Liberation Is Human Liberation"; "Sisterhood is Powerful"; "Free Our Sisters; Free Ourselves"; "Consciousness Raising." When they wrote, "all the problems between men and women and all the problems of women functioning in society as equal human beings are among the most basic that people face," they were coming close to the key insight about human history that the assumption that male is superior to female is the model upon which all other hierarchical, dominant/subordinate relationships are based. Remove the word *among* from the sentence and they are there. Similarly, when they said the issue they were raising is "a radicalizing question," if they had changed the indefinite article *a* to the definite *the*, they would have had it exactly right.[47] In those insights, they were presaging the conclusions of such feminist classics of a few years later as the 1969 "Redstockings Manifesto" and Robin Morgan's 1970 "Goodbye to All That."[48]

King and Hayden were revealing parallels that many of the leading male figures in the struggle for African American freedom failed to see. Beginning in 1964, the "Freedom Sisters" performed an invaluable service to humanity by exposing what was hiding in plain sight and remained unseen by so many others who sought dramatic change.

The Hayden-King memo was responsible for stimulating the discussions among many of the women who were key in founding Women's Liberation. Robin Morgan, one of the most important women in the new movement, joined a New York group after hearing "A Kind of Memo" discussed on a radio program in New York.[49] At gatherings of radical organizations, women began to notice that many of their male comrades seemed to identify with the problems of every oppressed category of people—except women. "They had all this empathy for the Vietnamese, and for black Americans," one woman pointed out, "but they didn't have much empathy for the women in their lives; not the women they slept with, not the women they shared office space with, not the women they fought at demonstrations with. So our first anger and fury was directed against men of the left."[50]

Sara Evans and Susan Brownmiller are among the historians of feminism who have concluded King and Hayden were the founders of the Women's Liberation Movement and that movement grew directly out of SNCC and the Mississippi Freedom Summer.[51]

20

Nonviolence and Violence

Year-end in Oslo and Saigon

December 1964

*Martin Luther King Jr. receiving
Nobel Peace Prize, Oslo,
December 10, 1964.*

*Wreckage from bombing of Brinks Hotel,
Saigon, December 1964.*

These are the most hopeful times since Christ
was born in Bethlehem
> —Lyndon B. Johnson, lighting the
> White House Christmas tree
> (December 18, 1964)[1]

A MERICA WAS AT A crossroads in 1964. In both civil rights and Viet-. nam, the question was which road to take—that of nonviolence or violence.

Nineteen sixty-four's last month began with the Rolling Stones' "Time Is on My Side" at number six, its peak on the Billboard Hot 100, and President Johnson realizing more than ever before that time was *not* on his side in Vietnam. He held a two-and-a-half-hour meeting with top advisers on December 1 to discuss proposals for expanding the war. When newsmen entered the Cabinet Room afterward, the president appeared to be considering allowing Ambassador Maxwell Taylor to have a news conference. But Defense Secretary Robert McNamara was overheard whispering to Johnson, "It would be impossible for Max to talk with these people without leaving the impression that the situation is going to hell."[2]

The plain fact as calendar 1964 was drawing to a close was that the "situation in Vietnam" *was*, from an American perspective, going to hell. A story about Vietnam was on page one of the *New York Times* on nearly every day of 1964's last month. Yet, what Johnson said at the White House tree-lighting was in most other respects accurate— hope abounded. Estimates announced in the year's last week indicated that the American economy, as measured by gross national product, had grown by a then-astounding $40 billion in 1964. "The American economy has become so big that it is beyond the imagination to comprehend," a European diplomat said. "But now on top of size, you are getting rapid growth as well. It is a situation of fundamental power unequaled in the history of the world."[3]

But Vietnam was threatening more by the day to undermine that extraordinary hope.

To almost all President Johnson's top advisers, there was no acceptable alternative to escalating the war. They believed that pulling out would be a sign of American weakness and decline. The only notable exception was Undersecretary of State George Ball, who had attempted to begin a realistic discussion of the situation by writing a memo early in October. Ball concluded his memorandum with a truth that his colleagues in the Johnson administration refused to admit: "It remains to be proved that in terms of U.S. prestige and our world position, we would risk less or gain more through enlarging the war than through searching for an immediate political solution that would avoid deeper U.S. involvement." He sent the memorandum to Defense Secretary Robert McNamara, National Security Advisor McGeorge Bundy, and Secretary of State Dean Rusk. Their response was the equivalent of putting their fingers in their ears while humming loudly.

"Bob McNamara in particular seemed shocked that anyone would challenge the verities in such an abrupt and unvarnished manner and implied that I had been imprudent in putting such doubts on paper," Ball recalled. "My colleagues were dead set against the views I presented and uninterested in the point-by-point discussion I had hoped to provoke. They regarded me with benign tolerance; to them my memorandum seemed merely an idiosyncratic diversion from the only relevant problem: how to win the war."[4]

A Nobel Prize for the Civil Rights Movement

I believe that unarmed truth and unconditional love
will have the final word in reality. This is why right
temporarily defeated is stronger than evil triumphant.
                                    —Martin Luther King Jr.
                                    (December 10, 1964)[5]

Nonviolence and the civil rights movement briefly took the spotlight from Vietnam on December 10, when Martin Luther King Jr. was awarded the Nobel Peace Prize in Oslo and gave one of his many memorable speeches. At thirty-five years old, King was at the time the youngest person ever selected for the prize.

King's acceptance speech was written and delivered with the sermon-like quality for which his oratory was known. Making plain that he believed in the promise of America—the values to which the nation has aspired even while often falling far short of practicing them—King said, "I accept this award today with an abiding faith in America and an audacious faith in the future of mankind." In a particularly memorable sentence, King said he refused "to accept the view that mankind is so tragically bound to the starless midnight of racism and war that the bright daybreak of peace and brotherhood can never become a reality." His moral optimism was further reflected in his declaration, "Civilization and violence are antithetical concepts."

It was a moment at the close of the year in which the sixties began that highlighted the best of what is associated with the era. The Jesus/ Gandhi/Martin Luther King Jr./Jim Lawson/John Lewis approach of nonviolence, of refusing to employ the barbaric methods of your opponents, of trying to convert them to your beliefs and practices, stands in stark contrast to military methods. What nonviolent resistance does is change the operative idea from "they're doing it to us" to "we're *not* going to do it to them." It is seeking freedom by freeing ourselves of the methods of those who deny us freedom.

But it was also a time when reactions in the White House and Pentagon to events on the other side of the globe were laying the groundwork for some of the worst of what we remember from the sixties.

Seismic Movement along the Sixties Cultural Fault Lines: Lenny Bruce, *Goldfinger*, and *The Pawnbroker*

Six days after Dr. King spoke in Oslo, Lenny Bruce entered a New York courtroom for the denouement of his long-running struggle along the emerging battle lines in the sixties cultural war.

A remarkable group of young comics who arose in the 1950s and early 1960s constituted an important, often overlooked element in the rebellious cultural forces that would fuel the sixties. Beneath the placid surface of the fifties, these comedians were bringing satire to an audience beyond the readers of *The New Yorker* and other enclaves of the Eastern elite.[6] A growing fraction of that satire consisted of political and social commentary, and this antiestablishment comedy was as much a part of the seeding of the sixties as were the Beats and rock 'n' roll.

The satirical comics gestated in the same underground (often literally) milieu that produced other cultural subversives of the pre-sixties: the small clubs in San Francisco, Greenwich Village, and Chicago in which jazz, blues, and folk musicians and Beat poets were holding forth. Among the ones with a cutting edge were Mort Sahl, Sid Caesar, the team of Mike Nichols and Elaine May, Chicago's Second City, Tom

Lehrer, Steve Allen, Lenny Bruce, and eventually Joan Rivers, Dick Gregory, and Woody Allen.

All of them rebelled in various ways against the conformity of the McCarthy Era, but Lenny Bruce was the one who went the farthest in challenging norms—and laws—and foreshadowing the sixties. He talked about topics that were not supposed to be mentioned in "mixed company," and he did so in public performances. He talked about drugs. He talked about religious hypocrites. He talked about politics. And when he talked, he sometimes used words that were banned.[7]

Bruce was often profane, earning him the title of "sick comic," but what his audiences most appreciated about him was that he was brutally honest in a time when that character trait was in short supply in public life. He exposed and opposed hypocrisy, which was coming to be seen by a large segment of postwar American youth as the most unforgiveable sin.

Lenny Bruce was brought to the attention of a much larger American public in April 1959, when Steve Allen gave him a national television gig on his NBC variety show. "Ladies and gentlemen," Allen said in introducing him, "here is the very shocking comedian, the most shocking comedian of our time . . . Lenny Bruce!"[8]

Bruce's growing fame placed him in the sights of the custodians of public morality. His defiant use of words classified as obscene brought him into escalating trouble with the law, and in the first years of the 1960s, authorities in Los Angeles, San Francisco, and Chicago arrested him for violating obscenity laws.[9]

Early in 1964, Bruce took his act back to New York, where he thought he would not be harassed by police and prosecutors. In March, he booked a series of performances at the Café Au Go Go in Greenwich Village. In decline both physically and artistically, with little in the way of new material, he resorted to some of his raunchiest stories, including those that had led to his arrests in California and Illinois. On March 31 and April 1, undercover agents from the Manhattan district attorney's office attended the shows, took notes, and, on the second night, made an audio recording. The DA's office presented the evidence to a grand jury and quickly obtained an indictment for the violation of a statute prohibiting "obscene, indecent, immoral, and impure dram, play, exhibition, and entertainment . . . which would tend to the corruption of the morals of youth and others."[10] Right before his scheduled performance on April 3, Bruce was arrested.

Many observers believe that the mistake the comic made was less in using "bad words" than in disparaging organized religion in his performances in cities in which a substantial portion of the police, prosecutors, and judges were conservative Catholics. That was certainly the case in New York.[11]

Forceful protest from New York's intellectual and cultural community was rapid and widespread. Woody Allen, James Baldwin, Richard Burton, Bob Dylan, Allen Ginsberg, Joseph Heller, Norman Mailer, Paul Newman, George Plimpton, Susan Sontag, Elizabeth Taylor, John Updike, and Gore Vidal were among the more than eighty notables who signed a petition calling for Bruce to "be allowed to perform free from censorship or harassment."[12]

At the trial, which began in mid-June, a few days before Schwerner, Chaney, and Goodman vanished in Mississippi, the defense presented experts from the New York media, who said Bruce's show did not offend "local community standards," and various literary and art critics, who assured the court of the social significance of the defendant's humor and that Bruce's use of vulgarity was artistically justified.[13] One of the most powerful witnesses was Dorothy Kilgallen, a newspaper columnist and television personality who always appeared prim and proper. Kilgallen told the court that she considered Bruce to be "a brilliant satirist, perhaps the most brilliant that I have ever seen." His "social commentary, whether I agree with it or not," Kilgallen testified, "is extremely valid and important, and I have enjoyed his acts on several occasions." The following exchange between one of Bruce's attorneys, Martin Garbus, and Kilgallen is especially memorable as a sign of how the times were changing in 1964:

> GARBUS: Miss Kilgallen, in the transcripts the words "motherfucker," "cocksucker," "fuck," "shit," "ass" are found, isn't that correct?
> KILGALLEN: Yes.
> GARBUS: Is there an artistic purpose in the use of language as set forth in these transcripts in evidence?

KILGALLEN: In my opinion there is.

GARBUS: In what way?

KILGALLEN: Well, I think that Lenny Bruce, as a
nightclub performer, employs these words the way James
Baldwin or Tennessee Williams or playwrights employ
them on the Broadway stage—for emphasis or because
that is the way that people in a given situation would talk.
They would use those words.[14]

Though what transpired in the courtroom clearly portended a more
open and free future, when the verdict was finally announced on
November 4, the three-judge court ruled against Bruce, 2–1. Bruce
pleaded that his career not be taken away from him, saying that his
words were being "locked up."[15]

On December 16, Bruce arrived at the courtroom for sentencing.
Like his performances and his life, his attire (a blue-striped T-shirt
and blue jeans) was not conventional for such occasions. The judge
allowed him to make a statement and Bruce entered into an hour-
long monologue in which he gave several reasons why his conviction
was unjust. The judge imposed a sentence of "four months in the
workhouse."[16]

The comic remained free on bond as his appeal of the conviction
was made. He would never see either the inside of the workhouse or
the vindication of the appellate court's overturning of his conviction.
After the trial, he fell ever deeper into despair and died of a morphine
overdose at his home in the Hollywood Hills in August 1966.[17] In a
telling episode of the sixties division between the emerging youth culture and traditionalists, the LAPD left Bruce's naked, bloated body,
with a syringe in his arm, lying on the floor and allowed photographers
to record the humiliating scene.[18]

◆ ◆ ◆

Another indication from the world of entertainment that the times
were a-changin' came with the American premiere of the third James
Bond movie, *Goldfinger*, on December 21. The female lead was named
"Pussy Galore." American censors insisted that promotional material

employed in the United States not use her first name, but they reluctantly accepted the name's inclusion in the film.[19]

Another film made in 1964 and released in April 1965 played a major role in the breakdown of the Motion Picture Production Code, a set of self-censorship rules adopted in 1934 that would not approve the depiction of anything that might lower "moral standards."[20] Sidney Lumet's *The Pawnbroker* was denied the MPAA's seal—normally a prerequisite for a movie to be screened—which censors withheld because of scenes in which two of the actresses' breasts were fully exposed (for a total of less than five seconds) and another scene that they deemed "unacceptably sex suggestive and lustful." After the movie was released without the seal, the MPAA backed down and granted approval in exchange for a minuscule reduction in the length of time the exposed breasts appeared. Although the association's appeals board granted an exception for the film, it insisted that the action would not set a precedent.[21] The reality was that the retreat heralded the end for the code. Having for the first time placed, as it were, its seal of approval on bare breasts, the MPAA's censoring powers were crumbling and moviegoers would soon be treated to views of other body parts and their interactions with those of partners. The National Catholic Office for Motion Pictures (née the Legion of Decency) took the opposite approach and refused to reverse its classification of *The Pawnbroker* as "condemned." Standing firm proved to be as detrimental to the authority of the Catholic censors as backing down was to the MPAA.[22]

After the MPAA retreated on *The Pawnbroker*, it announced that the code would undergo the first revision in its thirty-five-year existence. The censors insisted that the updated code would "seek to preserve a firm ban on indecent acts and offensive language in films while abolishing some of the 'archaic' specifics of the old code."[23] Within a few years the surrender of the code would be unconditional.

◆

An Unwelcome Christmas Message from Saigon

[The South Vietnamese military will not fight] to
carry out the policy of any foreign country.
—General Nguyen Khanh
(December 22, 1964)[24]

In the week that calendar 1964 reached its end, the Beatles' "I Feel
Fine" was number one on the *Billboard* Hot 100. Surely the title
reflected how many Americans felt, but where things were headed as
the sixties picked up steam could better be seen on the opposite side
of the planet.

As December wound down, the conditions that would eventually
lead to a defeat for the United States on the international stage were
escalating alarmingly. On December 20, a group of South Vietnamese
military commanders overthrew the country's civilian provisional legislature. Ambassador Maxwell Taylor warned the military leaders that
unless "the fabric of legal government" was restored promptly, the
United States might have to reconsider its position of close alliance
with Saigon in the anti-Communist war."[25]

The South Vietnamese government, then headed by Gen. Nguyen
Khanh, rejected the American demands. Johnson's government
responded by warning that "American support was based on the maintenance of a government free of 'improper interference' by military
leaders in Saigon."[26] Khanh urged South Vietnamese leaders to take
an open anti-American stance, saying that United States aid was not
necessary for South Vietnam. Here was one of the many opportunities
for the United States to get out of Vietnam before it was too late.

On Christmas Eve, the Viet Cong sent a message making plain
that the times might not be as hopeful for America and the world as
Lyndon Johnson had said they were less than a week earlier. Two Viet
Cong operatives who had studied the habits of South Vietnamese officers disguised themselves in Army of the Republic of [South] Vietnam
(ARVN) uniforms, placed a bomb in a car, set a timing device for it
to go off during happy hour for the Americans, and drove it into a
parking garage under Saigon's Brinks Hotel, called by the Americans

the Brink Bachelor Officers Quarters. The blast killed two Americans and injured more than fifty people. An entire wing of the building was severely damaged.[27]

The Brinks bombing was intended to show the Americans that they could not depend on their South Vietnamese allies to provide them with protection and so the Americans should leave Southeast Asia. President Johnson considered a retaliatory bombing of North Vietnam but decided against it for the moment.

During the last week of 1964, Democratic Senator Frank Church of Idaho called for a major change of course on US policy in Southeast Asia. Declaring that the United States should not have intervened in the area after the French were defeated in 1954, Church suggested that the region be neutralized. He said (rightly, as it turned out) that the idea that extending bombing into North Vietnam could save the situation in the South was "folly."[28]

Lyndon Johnson had been right in the spring when he assessed that a full-scale American war in Vietnam would be an unwinnable disaster. Yet, Johnson's insecurities would not let him bring himself to seize, while it was still possible, the opportunity that General Khanh offered him and withdraw with the cover of saying that's what South Vietnam wanted.

Therein lay much of the worst of the dawning sixties.

21

"Unmatched in the History of Freedom"

The Rest of the Long 1964 and the Lasting Impact of the Year

Legacies of 1964

We have achieved a unity of interest among our
people that is unmatched in the history of freedom.
                    —Lyndon B. Johnson, State of the
                    Union Address (January 4, 1965)[1]

A FEW DAYS AFTER THE end of calendar 1964, there seemed little reason to question the president's assertion that the nation had reached a lasting consensus on its proper direction. Johnson's approval rating *among Republicans* was an astonishing 74 percent.[2]

"I'm sick of all these people who talk about the things we can't do," Johnson had told carryover Kennedy adviser Richard Goodwin the previous March when Goodwin was summoned into a White House bathroom while the leader of the free world was seated on the toilet defecating. "Hell, we're the richest country in the world, the most powerful. We can do it all."[3] Johnson said at the time that he would wait until after the election to bring his full program to fruition. Now, with overwhelming Democratic majorities in both houses of Congress, Johnson would continue to build the legacy of outdoing Lincoln and Franklin Roosevelt that he sought for himself. "We would sit around in the White House and ask each other, 'What needs to be done?'" Goodwin later told me as he recalled early 1965. "We should be able to pass anything we want to."[4]

And pass legislation they did: providing federal aid to local schools through the Elementary and Secondary Education Act in April; giving children from deprived backgrounds a chance to catch up through Project Head Start in May; providing healthcare for the elderly and the poor through the creation of Medicare and Medicaid in the Social Security Amendments in July; protecting the right to vote of all citizens through the Voting Rights Act in August; providing for low income housing assistance in the Housing and Urban Development Act in August; establishing federal patronage of culture with the National Foundations on the Arts and Humanities Act in September; in October abolishing quotas favoring immigrants from Europe in the Immigration and Nationality Act and eliminating national origin, race, and ancestry as bases for being allowed to enter the United States—a law that would have substantial effects over the following decades in altering the ethnic makeup of the United States; seeking to limit air and water pollution through the Motor Vehicle Pollution Control Act in October and the Water Quality Act in November; and increasing federal funding for universities, along with making available to students scholarships and low-interest loans and setting up a Teacher Corps to go into low-income area schools in urban and rural America in the

Higher Education Act in November. For anyone who was keeping score, it was a remarkable set of progressive achievements.

LBJ *was* keeping score. He carried a card in his jacket pocket on which he checked off items on his agenda. Nearly everything that the Johnson administration proposed in 1965 was enacted. Johnson had achieved his ambition of outdoing FDR in expanding the role of the government in uplifting the people and assuring equal treatment for all and ensuring a revolutionary transformation of America by doing so. Yet, even before the autumn leaves of the Great Society agenda had fallen into Johnson's basket, the "unity of interest," the consensus that the president had celebrated in January, had begun to fracture, largely because of events in the rice paddies, villages, and jungles of Vietnam and in the streets of Los Angeles.

In this concluding chapter, I'll complete my account of the "Long 1964" by looking in some detail at the unfolding, mostly in the first half of 1965, of the two issues that would tear the nation apart in the sixties and far beyond: Vietnam and race. Then I'll discuss, more briefly, some of the many other legacies of 1964 that shaped both the sixties and subsequent American history to the present.

"My Answer Is Yes. But My Judgment Is No": Into the Tragic Vietnam Vortex

> All right. We'll just go with it. We know what we're walking into. . . . My answer is yes. But my judgment is no.
> —Lyndon Johnson
> (March 6, 1965)[5]

The table had been set in 1964 for a full-fledged American war in Vietnam. In the first half of 1965, President Johnson and the "best and the brightest" advisers whom he had inherited from Jack Kennedy seated themselves and the American nation at that table and began to ingest the toxins being served.

In his State of the Union Address on January 4, 1965, Johnson raised a question that was much on his mind: "Why are we there [in

Vietnam]?" His answer: "First, because a friendly nation has asked us for help against the Communist aggression." He asserted that a second reason was that "our own security is tied to the peace of Asia." Knowing what was likely to sell in the American market, at least in the short term, LBJ packaged his war in a wrapper labeled *freedom*. "What is at stake," Johnson avowed, "is the cause of freedom and in that cause America will never be found wanting."[6]

Despite Johnson's confidence that the United States had the capacity to "do it all" on domestic problems, including winning the War on Poverty, his private view of the prospects in Vietnam was "can't do." Yet, over the first seven months of 1965, the president agonized about Vietnam, rejecting several proposals and opportunities to get out before it was too late. Realizing that the war was unwinnable, he kept blowing past all the warning signs, choosing at each fork in the road the one that would lead ever deeper into one of the worst tragedies in American history.

♦ ♦ ♦

Lyndon Johnson had decided against a strong immediate response to the Christmas Eve Brinks bombing and other enemy attacks in the last week in 1964. Through the early weeks of 1965, he and his military advisers weighed the possible consequences of launching a large-scale bombing campaign against North Vietnam. The next major event in Vietnam came on February 7, 1965. The Viet Cong launched an attack on Camp Holloway, at Pleiku in the Central Highlands, killing nine and wounding more than a hundred Americans.[7] After quickly retaliating with three airstrikes on targets in North Vietnam, Johnson worked with Defense Secretary Robert McNamara and others on a plan for a vastly larger air campaign.

Within a week, the president had approved a plan, "Operation Rolling Thunder," for a sustained and widespread bombing campaign in the north. It would wind up lasting from March 1965 to the beginning of November 1968. During Rolling Thunder, American planes dropped approximately *863,000 tons* of bombs on North Vietnam—more than the total dropped in either the Korean War or the war in the Pacific during World War II. More than nine hundred American aircraft were lost. The air campaign was a large escalation in the American participation in the war, but Johnson rejected advice to give a major speech on it because he feared it would undermine his Great Society legislation and raise questions he didn't want to address about where such an escalation might lead.

A few days after LBJ gave tentative approval to the bombing campaign, Vice President Hubert Humphrey sent him a detailed memorandum calling for the beginning of an American exit strategy from the conflict in Southeast Asia. "It is always hard to cut losses," Humphrey said. "But the Johnson Administration is in a stronger position to do so than any administration in this century. 1965 is the year of minimum political risk for the Johnson administration."[8] Johnson's reaction was not positive. "I want to negotiate more than any man in the world!" he said to National Security Advisor McGeorge Bundy the next day. "But I don't think my wanting to negotiate is necessarily the best way to win the girl."[9]

Johnson remained agonizingly torn over Vietnam policy. "Now we're off to bombing these people," he said to McNamara on February 26. "We're over that hurdle. I don't think anything is going to be as bad as losing, and I don't see any way of winning."[10] On March 6, the president would agree to land thousands of Marines in Da Nang to protect the American planes engaged in Rolling Thunder. That evening at dinner, he said to his wife, "I can't get out, and I can't finish it with what I have got. And I don't know what the hell to do!"[11]

On March 8, two battalions—3,500 United States Marines—came ashore on a beach at Da Nang. Filming made it appear to be like a World War II landing on a Japanese-held South Pacific island. The reality was that, behind the cameras, there were beautiful Vietnamese women awaiting the Americans with leis.

The introduction of regular American combat troops—the previous US forces in country, numbering fewer than twenty-five thousand by the end of 1964, were classified as "advisers"—was another major escalation in the United States presence in Vietnam. The American land war in Southeast Asia was beginning. But, from the American perspective, there was no improvement in the situation over the next few months, leading Johnson and his men to confront the final decision on whether to go "all in" or cut their losses and get out. Even at this point, there were voices speaking strongly against this misadventure. "As I analyze the pros and cons of placing any considerable number of Marines in Da Nang," General Maxwell Taylor, the US ambassador to South Vietnam, cabled from Saigon, "I develop grave reservations as to the wisdom and necessity of doing so."[12]

Undersecretary of State George Ball continued to be the strongest advocate within the administration for sanity on Vietnam. On July 1, he sent the president a memorandum that predicted what would happen if the United States sent an additional eighty thousand troops to Vietnam. He powerfully made the case that the costs of getting out in mid-1965 would be far less than those of staying in.

"No one can assure you that we can beat the Viet Cong," Ball wrote, "no matter how many hundred thousand *white, foreign* (U.S.) troops we deploy." Ball emphasized how difficult it would be for white foreigners to win a guerrilla war among Asians "in a jungle terrain." He argued that the decision Johnson was about to make was of immense importance. "Once we suffer large casualties, we will have started a well-nigh irreversible process," he maintained, the only alternatives would be sending ever more troops in to try to achieve American objectives or face national humiliation. "I think that humiliation would be more likely than the achievement of our objectives—even after we have paid terrible costs."

"If we act before we commit a substantial U.S. [force] to combat in South Vietnam," Ball wrote, "we can, by accepting some short-term costs, avoid what may well be a long-term catastrophe."[13] His foresight was 20/20.

On July 8, President Johnson brought in the "wise men," ten leading former foreign policy officials, including Dean Acheson and Clark Clifford. With little specific information on the situation in Southeast Asia, they told Johnson that he had no choice other than to expand the war. Ball was incensed. "You goddamned old bastards," he yelled at Acheson and another "wise man" after the meeting. "You remind me of nothing so much as a bunch of buzzards sitting on a fence and letting young men die. You don't know a goddamned thing about what you're talking about. . . . You just sit there and say these irresponsible things!"[14] But Ball's critique was never heard by Johnson, who took the unanimous position of the "experts" as a validation of the policy of escalation toward which he was leaning.

"Vietnam is getting worse every day," LBJ said to Lady Bird that night. "I have the choice to go in with great casualty lists or to get out with disgrace. It's like being in an airplane and I have to choose between crashing the plane or jumping out. I do not have a parachute."[15] In fact, he had refused several parachutes that had been available to him, including General Khanh's December 1964 statement that South Vietnam didn't want or need American aid.

On July 28, Johnson announced that the number of US troops would be increased to 125,000 "almost immediately" and that "additional forces would be needed later and would be sent as requested."[16]

With that decision, Lyndon B. Johnson put the American Vietnam plane on automatic pilot on a course to crash and burn. By October 1965, there were 200,000 American troops in Vietnam. Ultimately, the number would peak at more than 542,000 at the end of 1968. More than 58,000 Americans and three million Vietnamese would die. This monumental mistake would tear the United States into bitterly opposed factions—a division that remains today—and would play a significant part in the vast increase in drug use by Americans.

From Selma to Watts and Beyond: "A Turning Point in Man's Unending Search for Freedom"

This damn world is shifting and changing so fast. I got 38 percent of these young Negro boys out on the streets. They've got no school to go to and no job. And by God, I'm just *scared to death* what's going to happen in June and July.

—Lyndon B. Johnson
(March 23, 1965)[17]

The outlook on race, the other principal issue of the sixties that would shatter the nation's "unity of interest," appeared much better than was the case for Vietnam through the first half of 1965. While the president was firmly committed to achieving unimpeded voting by all African Americans, he was hesitant to press for a federal voting rights act early in the year. Reflecting on how long it had taken to break the southern filibuster against the civil rights bill the previous year and assuming another Senate filibuster on a voting rights bill, LBJ wanted to delay the measure until after Congress enacted his other major "Great Society" legislation.[18] Martin Luther King Jr., however, didn't believe in waiting. He had written a book, published in July 1964, titled *Why We Can't Wait*.[19] King planned a campaign to force voting legislation by demonstrating to the American public the continuing brutality of southern authorities against black people seeking to vote.

MLK's adviser James Bevel chose Selma, Alabama, for the site of the voting rights campaign. King's aide Andrew Young called Selma—where less than 1 percent of the black voting-age population was registered—the "most oppressive" city in the South.[20] A black businesswoman in Selma, Amelia Boynton, had a sign on her office wall that summed up the situation: A VOTELESS PEOPLE IS A HOPELESS PEOPLE.[21] The county's sheriff, Jim Clark, was no more capable of declining his assigned role as the brutal, bigoted "lawman" in King's Selma drama than Bull Connor had been in King's 1963 morality play in Birmingham. Sheriff Clark stated his position on racial equality succinctly on a lapel pin: NEVER.[22] King announced a march from Selma to the state capitol in Montgomery to begin on Sunday, March 7.

When John Lewis and other marchers reached the Edmund Pettus Bridge crossing the Alabama River on that fateful Sunday, a large force of state troopers and Sheriff Clark's men met them. Pettus had been a general in the enslavers' rebellion against the United States and a "grand dragon" of the Ku Klux Klan. What ensued befit the name on the bridge. Lewis and others decided to kneel and pray, but before they could bend their knees, the defenders of white dominance viciously attacked them, using nightsticks, whips, barbed wire wrapped around rubber tubing, tear gas, and the hooves of their horses trampling peaceful demonstrators.[23] John Lewis was the first to go down, struck by a club that fractured his skull. Ruthless beating and stomping and gassing continued. The savage and unprovoked violence inflicted on people seeking to vote horrified news crews on the scene. White residents of Selma cheered and whooped as they watched black heads being smashed.[24] Only two years after the outcry against the images of Bull Connor's dogs and firehoses in Birmingham had led President Kennedy to call for a civil rights bill, police engaged in vicious acts in front of television cameras, reflecting a nearly total "We don't give a damn" attitude. Their actions were televised nationally that night. The day came to be known as "Bloody Sunday."

John Lewis being beaten by Selma police on Bloody Sunday, March 7, 1965.

Even in his wounded condition, John Lewis linked the two main issues facing the nation. "I don't see how President Johnson can send troops to Vietnam," Lewis said, "and not send them to Selma, Alabama."[25] Johnson quickly condemned the police brutality and said he would introduce a voting rights bill in the coming days. On March 15, LBJ appeared before a joint session of Congress and a national television audience and delivered a stunning speech.

"I speak tonight for the dignity of man and the destiny of democracy," Johnson began. Like Lexington and Concord and Appomattox, he asserted, Selma constituted "a turning point in man's unending search for freedom." "There is no Negro problem," the president declared. "There is no Southern problem. There is no Northern problem. There is only an American problem."

"There is no issue of States rights or national rights," LBJ proclaimed. "There is only the struggle for human rights." "Their cause must be our cause too," Johnson affirmed. "Because it is not just Negroes, but really it is all of us, who must overcome the crippling legacy of bigotry and injustice." Then this southern Democrat paused before startling almost everyone by raising his arms and declaring: "And we shall overcome."

"The American Negro," Johnson said, "has called upon us to make good the promise of America. And who among us can say that we would have made the same progress were it not for his persistent bravery, and his faith in American democracy? . . .

"I want to be the President who helped to end hatred among his fellow men and who promoted love among the people of all races and all regions and all parties," Johnson declared as he came almost to the end of his speech. "I want to be the President who helped to end war among the brothers of this earth."[26]

That's the Lyndon B. Johnson we would remember were it not for Vietnam.

Martin Luther King and John Lewis cried as they watched the speech on television together.[27] It was Lyndon Johnson's finest hour.[28] Unfortunately for him—and the nation and world—his expression of his desire to help "to end war among brothers on earth" came exactly one week after he had landed American Marines at Da Nang.

By early July, the Voting Rights bill had won overwhelming approval in both houses of Congress. Johnson triumphantly signed it into law on August 6 in a Capitol Rotunda ceremony staged beneath Trumbull's painting of Cornwallis surrendering at Yorktown for the purpose of sending a message that the forces of racism were finally defeated.[29] He referred to the incongruity at the base of American history that has now come to be known by the shorthand of 1619 and 1776. Noting that "the first Negroes had arrived at Jamestown" in chains three and a half centuries before, the president asserted that the nation was finally striking "away the last major shackle of those fierce and ancient bonds. Today the Negro story and the American story fuse and blend." "Today is a triumph for freedom," Johnson proclaimed, "as huge as any victory that has ever been won on any battlefield."[30] The situation in Vietnam was getting worse, but the prospects for improving race relations looked rosy.

That outlook changed markedly only five days later.

"Burn, Baby! Burn!"—Watts

Watts, August 1965.

> They couldn't call me a boy anymore. I was
> respected as a man. . . . It was a free feeling.
> —Paul Williams, participant
> in 1965 Watts Uprising[31]

On the evening of August 11, 1965, a young black man, Marquette Frye, was arrested for DWI in the Watts neighborhood of South Central Los Angeles. A subsequent altercation in which someone pushed his mother began a conflict that would play a significant role in bending the course of American history. During the initial confrontation, one of the black people remarked, "It's just like Selma."[32] A rumor quickly spread that a policeman had kicked a pregnant woman. Crowds of local African Americans began throwing objects at the police and unrest spread across a growing area of Watts. Someone shouted "Burn, baby! Burn!" and the Watts uprising had its slogan, which would be adopted in later uprisings in the 1960s.[33]

The next day, Los Angeles police chief William Parker said the event was an insurgency, likened the participants to the Viet Cong, and called for bringing in the National Guard. Ultimately, more than thirteen thousand members of the Guard were deployed in Watts. Street battles, burning buildings, and looting continued in the neighborhood for six days. The death toll was thirty-four. More than a thousand were injured. Nearly four thousand arrests were made.[34] It was at the time the worst rioting in the United States since the New York anti-draft riots in 1863.

The underlying causes of the Watts Uprising were many; some of them long antedated 1964, and others dated from 1964 and the first half of 1965. Among the most significant was the long-term abuse of people of color by the Los Angeles Police Department. Nearly all the police (200 of 205) assigned to Watts, were white.[35] Police in the City of Angels used a radio salute at the beginning of a shift in which they were going into African American neighborhoods: "LSMFT." The well-known acronym was the slogan of Lucky Strike cigarettes: "Lucky Strike Means Fine Tobacco." It had a different meaning in the LAPD: "Let's Shoot a Mother Fucker Tonight."[36]

Like their brothers and sisters in the South and almost everyone else in sixties America, African Americans in Los Angeles and other cities wanted freedom. The sort of freedom they sought and the tactics they would use to try to get it differed from those of the civil rights movement, but the courage and determination of SNCC, Dr. King, John Lewis, and others in the South inspired them and showed that change was possible.

Malcolm X had also roused the young African Americans in Watts. He had made an exhilarating speech against police brutality in Los Angeles in 1962,[37] which addressed their experience and goals much more directly than Martin Luther King Jr. did. Black youth left Malcolm's Los Angeles speech proclaiming, "We have a leader now."[38] Selma also had an impact on residents of Watts. They saw police brutality by white cops against black Americans and black people refusing to back down. That impressed many urban African Americans: *If they can do it, why can't we?*

And, while the Voting Rights Act itself meant little to African Americans living in Los Angeles and other cities outside the South, President Johnson's March 15 televised speech calling for that legislation did resonate with some people in those areas. When LBJ said, "The real hero of this struggle is the American Negro," who "awakened the conscience of this Nation" with actions "designed to provoke change," calling "upon us to make good the promise of America" through "his persistent bravery," it stirred African Americans who faced different manifestations of bigotry along with police brutality to think that they, too, should take action—and that their actions might succeed.[39]

On June 4, almost exactly halfway between his March 15 address to Congress and the outbreak of the Watts Uprising, President Johnson gave the commencement speech at Howard University. Speaking to the graduates of the historically black university, he went farther in calling for the end to injustice and for the establishment of genuine equality than he ever had before.

He began the speech by talking of the centrality of revolution in the history of the United States. "Nothing," the president declared, "is more freighted with meaning for our own destiny than the revolution of the Negro American. In far too many ways American Negroes have been another nation: deprived of freedom, crippled by hatred, the doors of opportunity closed to hope."

After recounting several examples of genuine progress over the preceding few years, Johnson proclaimed: "But freedom is not enough. You do not wipe away the scars of centuries by saying: Now you are free to go where you want, and do as you desire, and choose the leaders you please." It was not enough, the president said, "just to open the gates of opportunity. All our citizens must have the ability to walk through those gates. . . . We seek not just freedom but opportunity. We seek not just legal equity but human ability, not just equality as a right and a theory but equality as a fact and equality as a result."[40]

LBJ's words on June 4 were even more startling and radical and full of idealistic promise than what he had said in his voting rights speech in March. They speak to what might have been after all that began in 1964 and indicated how great the potential for a better America was before Watts and the major escalation of the war in Vietnam.

The events in Watts were incomprehensible to almost everyone in white America. *War* breaking out on the streets of an American city, seemingly without warning—and in a city where African Americans were generally thought to be better off than in most other places in the United States. Lyndon Johnson was taken aback by the uprising coming immediately on the heels of his signing of the Voting Rights Act into law. "How is it possible," he asked, "after all we've accomplished? How could it be? Is the world topsy-turvy?"[41] "Negroes will end up pissing in the aisles of the Senate and make fools of themselves, the way they had" during Reconstruction, LBJ said to his newly appointed special assistant, Joseph Califano, on Sunday morning.[42] (Johnson had presumably gotten his distorted images of "Black Reconstruction" from *Birth of a Nation*.)

Americans saw what happened in Watts in as radically different ways as they would the verdict in the O. J. Simpson trial three decades later. Many of the participants in the 1965 events in Watts saw them as a positive development. "If you ever felt you had some human rights, that's when you had some," recalled Paul Williams, a Watts-born resident who was seventeen at the time of the uprising. "They couldn't call me a Negro anymore. They couldn't call me a boy anymore. I was respected as a man."[43] To much of white America, watching the uprising on television was horrifying. Reporters spoke of "orgies" of violence, looting, and burning.[44]

With his March and June speeches in 1965, Lyndon Johnson embraced the cause of African Americans. He even seemed to be claiming leadership in this new American revolution. He sanctioned the actions of black protestors. In Watts, that protest ceased to be nonviolent, and many white Americans saw Johnson and liberal policies in general as major contributors to racial violence.

The willingness of many white people to go along with improvement for the lives of African Americans fell precipitously in the wake of Watts. So did white support for Johnson, his Great Society, and liberalism in general. Always politically perceptive, Johnson predicted while the riots were going on that one of the main beneficiaries would be Ronald Reagan.[45]

Though it had been preceded by the riots in the summer of 1964, Watts was the prototype for the "long, hot summer" of ghetto uprisings in subsequent years of the sixties in Newark, Detroit, and several other cities in 1967 and scores of cities following the murder of Martin Luther King in 1968.

The Rapid Erosion of the Democratic Coalition

Although it was not yet evident as Lyndon Johnson swept to his landslide election victory, America had begun to unravel in the summer of

1964. The fault lines within the dominant Democratic coalition were beginning to crack. In pushing through the Civil Rights Act, Johnson was putting at great risk the support of an important, if incongruent, portion of the New Deal coalition: white southerners.

Then in August, at the Democratic National Convention in Atlantic City, the split between traditional liberal pragmatists and young idealistic activists began in earnest over the issue of seating the Mississippi Freedom Democratic Party delegates. That division expanded swiftly thereafter, particularly over the war in Southeast Asia.

Another major component of the New Deal coalition, working-class white Americans outside the South, were pleased with the social programs of the Great Society but were angered over black rioting, beginning with Watts. Later, many would become even more angered about "unpatriotic" antiwar protestors, hippies, women's liberation, drug use, and so on. During Richard Nixon's 1968 campaign and subsequent presidency, the slogan "law and order," became emblematic of what he claimed was a "silent majority" opposed to what was identified as "the sixties," such as questioning authority, opposition to an American war, urban rioting, and "sex, drugs, and rock 'n' roll." Republicans would echo the slogan, with its authoritarian overtones, in 2020 and beyond.

In November 1968, nearly ten million middle- and working-class whites voted for third-party candidate George Wallace, who captured more than 13 percent of the vote, as Richard Nixon narrowly defeated Democratic nominee Hubert Humphrey. Following that victory, Nixon fleshed out a "Southern Strategy" by which he and other Republicans could combine the 1968 Wallace voters with his own and create a solid majority that was evident in Nixon's huge victory in 1972 and only temporarily interrupted in the wake of the Watergate scandal. What held that majority together and continues to fuel the right wing in America is opposition to most of what was associated with the sixties since 1964.

Running for the presidency in 1980, Ronald Reagan fully embraced the Southern Strategy that had been introduced in the Goldwater campaign in 1964 and elaborated by Nixon in 1968 and 1972. Reagan launched his general election campaign in Neshoba County, Mississippi, proclaiming, "I believe in states' rights." At a place known across the nation for the 1964 murder of civil rights workers by Klansmen associated with local government, Reagan pledged to "restore to states and local governments the power that properly belongs to them." The code was unmistakable, and the white crowd of 10,000 cheered wildly.[46] Reagan's presidency would be a turning point away from the achievement of a fairer social contract that began in 1964 and toward the extreme concentration of wealth and power at the very top from which we suffer today.

The anti-sixties attitude of many middle Americans persisted in 2016 and 2020 to be exploited by the faux patriotism and allusions to the good old days of the fifties put forth by Donald Trump. Trump and his followers adopted the blatant racism that had first burst forth among Republicans in the Goldwater campaign and was the main fuel for George Wallace. They readily recycled Nixon's "law and order" theme and Reagan's campaign slogan "Make America Great Again." A large part of what Trump ran on amounted to a repudiation of 1964 and the ensuing years. Almost all the themes of the Trump movement and the Republican Party of today were set forth in the film *Choice*, made for the Goldwater campaign in 1964, that I discussed in the introduction.[47]

"People Got to Be Free": Rock 'n' Roll

> But "Like a Rolling Stone" changed it all.
> —Bob Dylan, *Playboy* interview (1966)[48]

The revolution in rock that would produce its greatest era had burst forth in 1964 with the British Invasion, especially in its second wave. A strong case can be and often has been made that rock came of age during the late spring and early summer of 1965. The songs that *Rolling Stone* rated in 2004 as the two best rock songs ever were composed and recorded within a few weeks of each other at that time.[49]

According to the generally accepted creation story of the song chosen as number two on that list, in April or early May 1965, Keith Richards awoke one morning to find that a blank tape he had put into a recorder had spooled through to the end. When he rewound and played it, he heard a three-note guitar riff followed a few chords and his sleepy voice singing the words, "I can't get no satisfaction." Apparently, he had awakened during the night with it in his head and quickly recorded the snippet. Sitting by the pool at a Clearwater, Florida, hotel on May 6, Mick Jagger completed the song by writing most of the lyrics.[50] "(I Can't Get No) Satisfaction" was released on June 6 (coincidentally, the day before the *Griswold* decision was announced). The song, combining an attack on advertising and consumerism's constant effort to prevent satisfaction in order to continue selling things with the traditional blues/rock theme of seeking sexual satisfaction, became the Stones' first number one song in the United States and, ultimately, the most recognizable song in rock history.

Ten days after the Rolling Stones' release of "Satisfaction," Bob Dylan recorded the song *Rolling Stone* picked as number one in the Rock Era: "Like a Rolling Stone." That's a lot of occurrences of "Rolling Stone" in one sentence, but that's the way it was in the late spring of 1965.

Dylan hadn't been getting much satisfaction of late, either, and the songs have more in common than is usually noticed. Speaking powerfully about freedom in many of his songs, Dylan had come in his early twenties to be widely seen as the spokesman for an emerging generation. He was an icon of both the folk music revival and protest, focused on civil rights but also opposing war. In July 1965, he seemingly took a turn in a radically different direction and a different meaning of freedom.

Though most of his fans were taken by surprise when a new, unfamiliar Dylan emerged that month, the singer had by then been moving away from his public image for at least a year. By mid-1964, he had concluded that being categorized took away his freedom. "Me, I don't want to write *for* people anymore," Dylan told writer Nat Hentoff in the summer of 1964. "You know—be a spokesman." He said that the only organization he felt "a part of spiritually" was SNCC. "What's wrong is how few people are free," he declared. "Most people walking around are tied down to something that doesn't let them really *speak.*"[51]

Distressed with where he was, where he was going, and where the world was heading in the spring of 1965, Dylan later said, "I found myself writing this song, this story, this long piece of vomit about twenty pages long, and out of it I took 'Like a Rolling Stone' and made it as a single."[52]

The song seems to be addressed to a woman who previously had a secure place but now was adrift. Many of the lines, though, could as easily be interpreted as being about Dylan himself.

He was telling his followers that he had no answers to offer them—maybe that there were no answers. "I don't believe in anything. I don't see anything to believe in," Dylan said to a reporter in 1965. "But 'Like a Rolling Stone' changed it all," Dylan said in a *Playboy* interview in 1966. "I mean it was something that I myself could dig. It's very tiring having other people tell you how much they dig you if you yourself don't dig you."[53]

"Like a Rolling Stone" was, like so much else in this period, about *freedom*. But it didn't paint a rosy picture of what being free means. According to Dylan's lyrics, it means having no possessions, no home, no direction in which to go. This message was similar to that delivered four years later by Kris Kristofferson in "Me and Bobby McGee": "Freedom's just another word for nothin' left to lose."

At least superficially, Dylan's rejection of being labeled "the voice of his generation" seems similar to the way in which two champions of bottom-up decision-making, Bob Moses and Mario Savio—both of whom were in the process of vanishing from the public scene—had rebuffed the role of being "leader."[54] On April 26, 1965, at the end of a speech before a student gathering in Sproul Plaza, Savio made a startling announcement. "Lest I feel that I'm deserving of the charge of Bonapartism[55]—which I might be moved to accuse myself of—I'd like to wish you good luck and goodbye."[56] Moses had resigned from SNCC two months before because, he later said, he had become "too strong, too central, so that people who did not need to, began to lean on me, to use me as a crutch."[57] Dylan had distilled this outlook to three words in a song he recorded in January and released on his album *Bringing It All Back Home* in March, "Subterranean Homesick Blues": "Don't follow leaders."[58]

Five days after the release of "Like a Rolling Stone," Dylan "went electric" for the first time in public at the 1965 Newport Folk Festival. Nearly 100,000 fans waited expectantly for their hero's performance.[59] "You know him. He's yours," the woman introducing him shouted to the screaming fans.[60] But the man who walked onstage wearing a black leather jacket and carrying an *electric* guitar wasn't someone the audience knew. Nor was he "theirs," which he made abundantly clear both in the lyrics of "Like a Rolling Stone" and in his performance that night.

Bob Dylan goes electric at 1965 Newport Folk Festival.

As soon as he came out on stage, there were boos and some people yelled, "Get rid of the electric guitar!"[61] Dylan opened with a searing performance of "Maggie's Farm," itself a declaration of his independence from others' expectations. In the film of the performance, boos and jeers at the end of the song can readily be heard, at least as plentiful as cheers, as they can after the second song in the set, "Like a Rolling Stone."[62]

Accounts of the reactions to Dylan's electric performance by the keepers of the folk tradition conflict. Pete Seeger, who was the emcee that night, was widely reported to be irate at the electronics, saying, "If I had an axe, I'd cut the cable!"[63] Seeger frequently denied the story[64] but later agreed that he said those words. He insisted, though, that his anger was over the sound system distorting Dylan's words and making them inaudible, not that he was using amplifiers.[65]

The revolution in music that had been begun in 1964 by the Beatles and Rolling Stones was brought to its zenith in mid-1965 by the Stones and Dylan. The way was now open for the most creative and powerful period in the history of rock. Everything from Monterey Pop and *Sgt. Pepper* in 1967 through Woodstock and Altamont in 1969 and far beyond, would follow from the musical revolution of 1964–1965.

"I'm Free":
The Dawn of an "Anything Goes" Culture

All three of the sixties triumvirate of "sex, drugs, and rock 'n' roll" were part of the move toward not only the elusive goal of "freedom" but also individualism and the complete focus on the self—hedonism.

What Dylan was doing with his songs—most powerfully in "Like a Rolling Stone"—and his electric set at Newport was best stated by musician Robbie Robertson: "This was the rebel rebelling against the rebellion."[66] In moving from acoustic folk and protest music to electronic rock 'n' roll, Dylan was going from the political to the personal, from the social to the subjective: from *we* to *me*. "Me, I'm cool," he had told Hentoff several months before. "All I can do is be me," he continued. "I can't tell them how to change things, because there's only one way to change things, and that's to cut yourself off from all the chains."[67]

A young man who had been into trying to help black people to get "white freedom," joining in singing "*We* shall overcome," was now going his own way, turning to another conception of freedom, one that was individual rather than societal and was being expressed concurrently by the chief evangelists of black freedom to young white people with the words "*I* can't get no satisfaction." Jagger and Richards would proclaim this personal meaning of freedom more boldly in a song recorded in September titled simply, "I'm Free": "'Cause I'm free any old time to get what I want, yes I am."[68]

The modern trend toward a culture and society of "anything goes" was clearly underway in the Long 1964. Eventually, that movement would come to encompass even many of the "conservatives" who had fought a culture war against it for more than forty years.

Besides the Lenny Bruce case and the struggle over *The Pawnbroker*, 1964 had seen two other major developments in the direction of freer expression. The Supreme Court's decision in *Jacobellis* v. *Ohio*, announced on June 22, 1964, reversed the conviction of a movie theater manager for screening a 1958 French film *Les Amants* (*The Lovers*), which contains an explicit love scene that the lower courts deemed obscene. The Justices were divided in their reasoning, but six of them agreed that the film was not obscene and its showing was protected by the Constitution.[69]

On the same June 1964 day that the *Jacobellis* ruling was handed down, the high court ruled in *Grove Press, Inc.* v. *Gerstein* that the 1934 Henry Miller novel *Tropic of Cancer*—about which a member of the

Pennsylvania Supreme Court had said, is "not a book. It is a cesspool, an open sewer, a pit of putrefaction, a slimy gathering of all that is rotten in the debris of human depravity"[70]—is protected by the First Amendment.[71]

In the area of censorship, the times they were a-changin' rapidly. By 1967, the Motion Picture Association of America's Production Code had been relegated to history's dustbin.

The Collapse of Trust in Government

One of the most dramatic and lasting changes following 1964 was the collapse of the American people's trust in the federal government. The peak of such trust in the years since the question began to be polled in 1958 came in October 1964, as Lyndon Johnson was campaigning on fighting a war against poverty and building a Great Society. At that point, 77 percent of Americans polled said that they believed that they could trust the government in Washington always or most of the time. Perhaps even more striking is that in 1964 there was only a small gap on the question between Democrats and Republicans: 80 percent of Democrats and 74 percent of Republicans trusted their government that fall.

The precipitous decline in the public's trust of Washington began in 1965 and was closely associated with Vietnam and racial division following Watts. Four years after the 77 percent peak, trust had fallen to 62 percent in October 1968, shortly before Richard Nixon's narrow election victory. It was down to 53 percent on the eve of Nixon's huge reelection victory in 1972. Then, as the cover-up of the Watergate scandal unraveled, trust in government fell sharply, reaching 36 percent in late 1974 after Nixon resigned and Gerald Ford pardoned him.[72]

The decline in trust in Washington was not yet over. During the presidency of Jimmy Carter, it bottomed out—up until that time—at 27 percent early in 1980, as the Iranian hostage crisis continued to be unresolved. Few would question President Carter's 1978 statement that the federal government had become like a foreign country to many American citizens. In 1980, Ronald Reagan ran against what he disdainfully pronounced as the "gub-mint"—and won in a landslide.

In his inaugural address, President Reagan declared that government was the problem, not the solution.

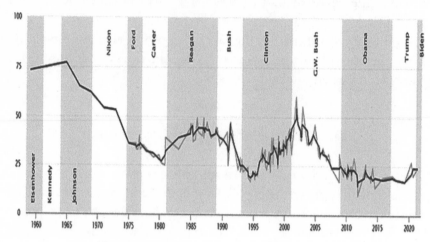

Trust in the Federal Government, 1958–2021.

Apart from a brief spike following the Persian Gulf War in 1991, a steady climb during the prosperity of Bill Clinton's presidency, and a short-lived rally-round-the-flag surge to 60 percent right after the attacks of September 11, 2001, trust in Washington has remained at levels often far below half of what it was in 1964. In 2019, it had sunk to a trifling 17 percent, the second-lowest level of trust in the federal government in the six decades on record, and scarcely one-fifth of the 1964 high. The number ticked up slightly in 2020 and in the spring of President Biden's first year climbed to 24 percent but plunged to an all-time low of 5 percent among "conservative Republicans."[73]

There can be no doubt that one of the most significant, deleterious, and long-lasting consequences of the events set in motion in 1964, particularly the American war in Vietnam and a decade of an astounding level of presidential lying by Lyndon Johnson and Richard Nixon, has been an extraordinary loss of trust in government.

And yet, government accomplished much good in the years from 1964 forward. It is true that some of the programs created in the whirlwind of Great Society legislation in 1964 and '65 were rushed through without sufficient consideration of how—or even *if*—they would work. Some of them did not work as intended. On the whole, though, those programs were successful.

How well did the programs work collectively? "From 1963 when Lyndon Johnson took office until 1970 as the impact of his Great Society programs were felt," Special Assistant to the President Johnson Joseph A. Califano Jr., pointed out in 1999, "the portion of Americans living below the poverty line dropped from 22.2 percent to 12.6 percent, the most dramatic decline over such a brief period in" the twentieth century.[74]

Before Medicare, more than half of all Americans sixty-five and older had no health insurance. After Medicare was well established, the number of uninsured seniors became negligible. Medicare is also associated with a dramatic drop in the percentage of seniors living in poverty. In 1959, 35.2 percent of the elderly were below the poverty line. Social Security had greatly reduced the number of seniors living in poverty since the 1930s, and improvements in that system played a major part, along with Medicare, in the remarkable further reduction in senior poverty, down to 8.9 percent in 2009—*75 percent lower* than before 1964.[75]

The Best of the Sixties Legacy

The legacies of the sixties that arrived in 1964 are mixed, but, on balance, they are positive. Before 1964, America was "great" for straight white men, particularly if they were at least fairly well-off financially, but not so much for anyone else.

The worst of the sixties is the hedonism on which the counterculture and the consumer culture came together, though almost always without realizing that they had done so. By the 1970s and 80s, while still attacking drugs and sexual freedom for culture war political purposes and imprisoning people of color for drug use,[76] many of those in authority tacitly accepted that young white Americans could have much "black freedom"—"sex, drugs and rock 'n' roll"—because it wasn't a fundamental threat to their power and wealth (indeed, much money was to be made from hedonism), whereas the sort of freedom sought by SNCC, SDS, and FSM would overthrow that power. "Sex, drugs and rock 'n' roll" leave most people as consumers, not with power.

While promoting self-centeredness themselves, Republicans have run against the excessive self-indulgence of some of the youth of the later 1960s and early 1970s. Much as the Republicans had run against the Rebels of the 1860s for the rest of the nineteenth century by "waving the bloody shirt"—reminding voters that the enslavers who rebelled against the United States were Democrats—the realigned Republican Party ran against the rebels of the 1960s for the rest of the twentieth century (and now well into the twenty-first) by what could be termed waving the tie-dyed shirt.[77]

The reality was that both of those tactics were diversions to gain voters' support for what the GOP was about in both eras: furthering the interests of corporations, greed, and wealth.[78] In their exploitation of the divisions that arose after 1964, they obscured the best of the sixties: the civil rights and peace movements, the expansion of compassionate government and the social contract, diversity, and equality.

Far, far greater diversity has been achieved in America since 1964. The nation has* also become substantially more democratic. Vastly more women, people of color, and LGBTQ people have gained prominent places in government, business, and across the society. Following the Voting Rights Act, there have been huge increases in minority voting. One striking example: by the early 1970s, Mississippi had the most African American elected officials—not only per capita, but in absolute numbers—of any state. It is obvious that, the gains notwithstanding, African Americans have yet to achieve genuine equal treatment, as is reflected in another of the modern legacies of the movement of the sixties, the growing awareness of police brutality publicized by such organizations as Black Lives Matter.[79]

The second wave of feminism that arose in 1963–1964 spread along two different rapidly growing rivers—one of middle-class actions led by the National Organization for Women flowing from *The Feminine Mystique*, and the other bursting up from the wellspring of the treatment of women in the Mississippi Summer Project and "Sex and Caste: A Kind of Memo."[80] While the latter, which came to be called Women's Liberation, scared men, much as the Black Power movement

---

* The appropriate tense is in question at this writing, as there has been a powerful move against democracy under Donald Trump and by his party following his defeat in the 2020 presidential election.

did white people during the same period, it also laid the groundwork for great advances, broadening human rights issues to include reproductive rights, sexual harassment, and problems in the workplace. Its successes would include, among many others, the legalization of abortion, first by some states and then nationwide with the *Roe v. Wade* Supreme Court decision in 1973 and the #MeToo movement that took off in 2017. At the time of this writing in 2021, all these advancements for women are endangered by the Trumpist "Republicans." The Supreme Court, with three Trump appointees, appears poised to deny women control over their bodies. When the Violence against Women Act Reauthorization Act of 2021 came up in the House, Democrats voted 215–0 in favor and Republicans 172–29 against.[81] As for sexual harassment, Donald Trump "won" in 2016 after a recording of him bragging about grabbing some women and forcing himself on others became public.

The eruption of consciousness of historical deprivation of rights also spread to other groups, including Latinos and homosexuals. The former had an active movement in the mid-1960s that came into the public eye in 1966, when the United Farm Workers, led by Cesar Chavez and Dolores Huerta, promoted a nationwide boycott of grapes grown in areas of California where Chicano pickers were on strike. Meanwhile, the Immigration and Nationality Act of 1965 was quietly laying the foundation for future struggles over the place of Hispanics in the United States. The gay rights movement was not triggered until a ruthless police raid on a gay bar, the Stonewall Inn, in Greenwich Village in June 1969. Such police treatment of homosexuals was nothing new, but this time the targets fought back. Six days of protests and violent confrontations with cops ensued, and the gay rights movement was born.[82]

◆ ◆ ◆

The increase in democracy and diversity occurred on many fronts. The 1964 Supreme Court case of *Reynolds v. Sims*,[83] which established the one-person, one-vote concept in legislative apportionment, was among the significant advances in democracy in 1964. Reforms agreed to as part of the compromise over the Mississippi Freedom

Democratic Party at the 1964 Democratic National Convention facilitated the achievement of both diversity and more democracy within the Democratic Party.

Over the years since, the Democratic Party has continued to embrace diversity and democracy, while the Republicans have gone decisively in the other direction. By 2016, the contrast between the parties in this regard had become a chiaroscuro painting. Half of the Democratic delegates were nonwhite, while 94 percent of Republican delegates were non-Hispanic whites. Less than 1 percent of the GOP delegates were black, the lowest percentage of African American delegates at a Republican convention since 1912.[84]

This stark difference between the parties on the nature of America—a diverse, welcoming nation embodying the spirit of Emma Lazarus's poem on the Statue of Liberty or an exclusive, monochromatic nation of racially based nationalism, "blood and soil," as the Nazis called it—was already evident in 1964. The latter was, of course, nothing new then. There is a long history of "already here" Americans—either descendants of immigrants or immigrants themselves—vigorously opposing the entrance of "different" people into the United States. But it was in 1964 that this white nationalism became a feature of the erstwhile Party of Lincoln. The identification of the Republican Party with this ideology was fortified when Richard Nixon chose to unite his supporters with those of George Wallace, was confirmed under Ronald Reagan, and became the party's identity with Donald Trump. In the 2020s such modern ethnonationalist authoritarians as Vladimir Putin in Russia and Viktor Orbán in Hungary have been taken as models by Trumpists in the United States.[85]

As a presidential candidate in 1992, Bill Clinton pledged to have "a cabinet that looks more like America."[86] In contrast, Donald Trump's policies seemed to aim at creating an American people who look more like his Cabinet, the meetings of which appeared to take place in an all-white country club at which Dr. Ben Carson was a waiter who had mistakenly taken a seat.

◆◆◆

More than a half century after 1964 launched the sixties, the fundamental questions of that time continue to rip Americans apart: what sort of a nation the United States should be, pluralist or "singularist"; whether we should embrace diversity and equality for all or seek to return to being "a white man's country"; whether we should be compassionate and welcoming to "Your huddled masses yearning to breathe free, / The wretched refuse" of the rest of the world or build walls intended to keep them out; whether to espouse tolerance or intolerance, more or less democracy; whether women are people who own their bodies or property in which a government can mandate that fetuses must be allowed to develop against a woman's will. All these questions center on the meaning of *freedom* and who gets to have it.

It had seemed that with the victory of Barack Obama in 2008, the good part of the sixties had finally triumphed over the bad, that "*We shall overcome*" had won out over "*I shall overindulge.*" With the demographic changes that are remaking the United States, the victory of a biracial candidate and all the cultural implications that went with it seemed to be the death knell for the political forces that had been running against the sixties for four decades. Yet, a sharp reaction by many white males to seeing the nation under the leadership of "them," enabled the forces advocating "Make America white- and male-dominated again" to take power in 2016 through the Electoral College even while losing by more than three million votes.

Among the consequences in the short term was a multifaceted effort by the administration of Donald Trump to reverse everything Obama did, but also to undo all the progress made in 1964 and the decade that followed. The years 2017 to 2020 saw a pace of destruction that rivaled the pace of Lyndon Johnson's construction of "the Great Society" in 1964–1965. The destruction was achieved mostly through administrative actions by right-wing heads of executive branch agencies rather than by legislative actions. The era of reform in 1964–1965 was nearly matched by an "era of deform" in Trump's time in office. This period of regression aimed to wipe out the fruits of the period of progression in the long 1964.

But if the American constitutional republic survives, the prognosis for the complete recovery of the best legacies of 1964 and the subsequent sixties is excellent, both because of the demographic momentum and the reaction against the "anti-sixties" excesses of the Trump party.

◆◆◆

Most of the issues facing and dividing Americans in the 2020s can be reduced to this question: Should we return to what 1964 was all about or should we seek to bury the accomplishments that began to be achieved then and make the United States again the sort of "white man's country" it still was, to a large extent, in the 1950s and early 1960s?

The first of those paths would mean moving farther away from the terrible legacy of 1619 and toward fulfilling and modernizing the vision of 1776: treating all people as equals, lessening poverty; expanding the middle class; reining in corporate dominance and a top-heavy distribution of wealth and income; using antitrust laws to foster competition; accepting and utilizing science; living in a world of fact; defining medical care as a right, not a privilege for those who can afford it; balancing police protection with ending police racism and brutality; assuring equality for all, including women and LGBTQ people; recognizing that women are people, not property, and their bodies belong to them; freedom of thought and expression; no censorship; dealing with our history honestly; continuing to build a diverse and inclusive society; moving rapidly toward a green economy and counteracting climate change; showing that government can work for the benefit of all; completing the building of the sort of fair economy—capitalism with checks and balances—that was started during the New Deal and greatly furthered in 1964–1965; and securing the nation's status as a constitutional republic grounded in democratic participation by all.

The second path would mean moving back away from the vision of 1776: denying that all people are equals, growing poverty; countenancing a stagnating and shrinking middle class; continuing and accelerating the trends that began around 1980 toward ever-greater concentration of wealth and income at the very top; accepting domination by monopolistic corporations; rejecting and ignoring science; living in a world of "alternative facts"; saying that medical care should only be available to those who have financial resources; overlooking police mistreatment of people of color; increasing inequality, including returning women and people of color to the subordinated status in which they lived prior to 1964; treating women's bodies as property over which they do not have control; book banning; whitewashing our history; curbing diversity and inclusion; continuing a carbon-based energy system and ignoring climate change; opposing government regulation for the public good; enhancing corporate dominance; and overturning the reforms made under FDR and LBJ—all of which could only be accomplished by undermining the constitutional republic and moving away from full democratic participation.

What would the United States look like if the second path prevails? In his 2013 book, *Average Is Over*, economist Tyler Cowen, one of the leading architects of the radical right agenda directed by billionaire Charles Koch and others, described the future he seeks for America: "wage polarization," "recreating a Mexico-like or Brazil-like environment" with "partial shantytowns" and poor water quality. "Some version of Texas—and then some—is the future for a lot of us," Cowen proclaims. "It is frightening, but it is exciting also."[87]

To rebalance the system along the lines of what was happening in 1964 or to further unbalance it along the lines of what it was before that year? That is the question facing the American people in the 2020s.

Whichever way that question is answered in the short term, if democracy survives the anti-/ante-1964 forces are sure to be on the losing side in the longer term. It is, as historian Heather Cox Richardson commented after the 2020 Census findings were released, "unlikely that an increasingly urbanizing, multicultural nation will continue to accept being governed by an ever-smaller white, rural minority"[88]—or, we might add, by an alliance of billionaires, misogynists, and white supremacists.

Will the chance come again for the losers of the past forty years to win? Dylan reminds us that we should beware of speaking too soon, because "the wheel's still in spin / And there's no tellin' who that it's namin'"[89] At the time of this writing, no one can say to what degree, if any, Joe Biden's attempt to bend the trajectory of American history will succeed. To whatever extent it does, it will be reviving the spirit of 1964.

ACKNOWLEDGMENTS

T HIS PROJECT BEGAN LONG ago, and I have discussed the sixties—
and 1964 in particular—with and benefited from the thoughts
and knowledge of people far too numerous to include in a few pages
of acknowledgments.

The origins of this book date back, appropriately, to 1964. As
one who was born on the cutting edge of the postwar baby boom, I
spent my childhood in the happy daze of the 1950s in Matawan, New
Jersey. My earliest memory from the news was mention of the siege
of the exotic-sounding Dien Bien Phu (which, decades later, I would
visit several times), My parents were of a now-extinct species: liberal
Republicans. I was brought up in an atmosphere that condemned racism. My mother told me in the late 1950s that I could marry whomever
I wanted: "A Jewish girl, a Negro girl . . ." She said I should be aware
of the problems we would face if I followed the latter course, but it
would be all right with her. *That* was extraordinarily liberal in the 1950s.

I completed my senior year in high school and started college in
1964, and was already fascinated by what was going on, especially in
the civil rights movement, politics, music, and sports. In the years leading up to 1964, I was impacted by photos of the white racist reaction
against black students integrating Central High School in Little Rock
and the sit-in movement, was horrified by the film of Bull Connor's
dogs and water cannons attacking young demonstrators in Birmingham, and was captivated by the new music, especially the girl groups.
The assassination of John F. Kennedy was announced on our school's
intercom while I was taking an American history test. Though I was
at first dismayed at the idea that Lyndon Johnson was president, his
civil rights and social and economic programs soon turned me into an
enthusiastic supporter, until Vietnam changed all that a few years later.
Over the year-plus that followed JFK's death—what I now identify
as the Long 1964—I was in awe of what young people were doing
to achieve freedom for African Americans in the South. I was an

aficionado of Bob Dylan, Joan Baez, and Peter, Paul and Mary, caught up in Beatlemania, a great admirer of Cassius Clay and delighted when he defeated Sonny Liston in February, among the first American fans of the Rolling Stones when *England's Newest Hitmakers* came out in May. I traveled in August to Atlantic City for a day of the Democratic National Convention and talked on the boardwalk with some of the delegates of the Mississippi Freedom Democratic Party. In the fall, I began classes at Rutgers and frequently talked late into the night with new friends in my dorm about what was going on in the world beyond the campus as we drank beer, played cards, and listened to the Stones' rendition of "I'm a King Bee." I became a history major and learned an invaluable lesson about how widespread prejudice is when I brought a girl from home to a fraternity rush party and we were ostracized because she is Jewish. Had I not brought her to the party, I probably would have unknowingly joined a fraternity populated by bigots, and there's no telling what different turns my life might have taken, so I thank her and those who blackballed me.

As the decade progressed (and regressed), I saw the Rolling Stones perform in person in 1966 (I've been to several of their performances in recent years, and they are much better now), turned strongly against the American war in Vietnam, and attended the Pentagon March in 1967. For the most part, I remained on the civil rights/antiwar/ political strand of the freedom swirl, even in the late sixties when the counterculture definition of freedom had become the lead partner in that dance. My life has been substantially shaped by the 1960s, but when it comes to the "if it feels good, do it" hedonism of the decade's later years, I was more *in* the sixties than *of* the "sixties." Another way to put that, it occurs to me, is to say I was and remain much more of the Long 1964 than of the "sixties," in the sense of the images that are most often associated with that word.

In 1973, I began my teaching career at a remarkable beacon of light in Mississippi, Millsaps College. My experiences there have been wonderful. My colleagues and students have been major contributors to what I am today. I could not have spent my career at a better institution.

In the years since the mid-seventies, I have had many experiences that advanced my understanding of this book's subject. Most important among them were a four-day retrospective on Mississippi's Freedom

Summer that I organized at Tougaloo and Millsaps Colleges in 1979; seven trips I have led to Vietnam and Cambodia since 2009; and a cross-disciplinary American culture course on "The Sixties" that I have taught every other year for more than three decades. I see teaching and writing as extensions of each other, and I have often been enlightened by insights from students far too numerous to list here.

Many people with whom I have interacted over the decades since the early 1960s have contributed to my understanding of 1964 and how it relates to us in the 2020s: high school and college friends, participants in and interpreters of the events of the time, colleagues, and students in my courses.

I owe incalculable debts to my mentors, particularly Lawrence W. Levine, Charles W. Forcey, Lloyd Gardner, and Joan Wallach Scott, and to historian and other academic and writer friends who have advanced my thinking, including Joyce Appleby, Alexander Bloom, Clayborne Carson, Bill Chafe, John Dittmer, Ralph Eubanks, Jeanne Middleton Hairston, David Halberstam, Dan Hise, Bill Leuchtenburg, T. W. Lewis, James Loewen, C. Leigh McInnis, Leslie McLemore, Elaine Tyler May, Neil McMillen, Willie Morris, Paul Murray, Judy Page, James T. Patterson, Charles Sallis, Arthur Schlesinger Jr., Harvard Sitkoff, Patricia Sullivan, Studs Terkel, Milton Viorst, and Eudora Welty.

Among the participants in events in 1964 and since with whom I have had illuminating discussions are: Ella Baker, Joe Biden, Unita Blackwell, Julian Bond, Ernst Borinski, Harry Bowie, Anne Braden, Guy Carawan, George Carlin, John Chancellor, Ramsey Clark, Bill Clinton, Hillary Rodham Clinton, Robert Coles, Paul Cowan, Mario Cuomo, Barbara Dane, Dave Dennis, Annie Devine, John Doar, John Emmerich, Betty Friedan, James Forman, Richard Goodwin, Dick Gregory, Lawrence Guyot, Fred Harris, Tom Hayden, Aaron Henry, Jesse Jackson, Ted Kennedy, Coretta Scott King, Edwin King, Jeanette King, Anthony Lewis, John Lewis, Al Lowenstein, Staughton Lynd, Bill Minor, Anne Moody, Bob Moses, Joan Trumpauer Mulholland, Perry Nussbaum, John O'Neal, Willie (Wazir) Peacock, Claude Ramsay, Joe Rauh, Anne Romaine, John Salter, Bernie Sanders, Pete Seeger, Charles Sherrod, Hazel Brannon Smith, Margaret Chase Smith, Ted Sorensen, Michael Thelwell, Son Thomas, Bennie Thompson, Mary Travers, Jimmy Travis, Hollis Watkins, William Winter, and Bob Zellner.

Friends I made in Vietnam and Cambodia, particularly Phuc Pham, Duc Tran, Ll Ly, Nguyen Duc Phu, and Rathana Keo provided me with insights into some of the effects far beyond the borders of the United States of the decisions Lyndon Johnson made in 1964 that would undermine all that he achieved in that extended year.

I also offer thanks to a few people whom I never met but who have inspired me deeply, either through their courageous actions or their extraordinary writing abilities: Joan Didion, Fannie Lou Hamer, James Lawson, Tim O'Brien, and Mario Savio.

Special thanks to Heather Cox Richardson because of all she does on an almost-daily basis to keep us deeply informed, vigilant, motivated, sane, and at least a little hopeful in times that endanger the achievements of 1964—and those of the 1930s, the 1860s, and the 1770s.

My writing career was significantly helped by my longtime editor and friend Edward T. "Ned" Chase. I greatly thank Amy Cherry of W. W. Norton and my then agent David Hendin for putting up with my years-long attempts to write a comprehensive history of the whole decade of the 1960s before I finally realized that the reason no one has done it is that adequately addressing that remarkable era's culture, social movements, politics, and war and showing how they continue greatly to influence us today would require a volume of at least two thousand pages. I ultimately decided to narrow my focus to the long year in which the era arrived.

The book has been substantially improved by the diligent efforts of my agent, Don Fehr, and my editor, Cal Barksdale. I give large thanks to both.

As always, my greatest thanks go to my amazing family: my parents, Edward and Ruth McElvaine, our "children"—all now beyond an age for which that word seems appropriate—Kerri, Lauren, Allison, and Brett, our grandchildren, Evan, Anna, and Ian, and our son-in-law, Brian. It was only in the concluding stages of this book that, through DNA analysis, I discovered my biological family. My birth mother, Annabelle Louise Compher, and my still unknown biological father contributed nothing to the book but my genetic makeup, but I'm grateful for that. My previously unknown-to-me half-sisters—Carol,

Barb, Candy, and Cris—had nothing to do with the book, but they are already adding to my happiness.

As always, my greatest, beyond-repayment, debt is owed to the woman I met less than a year after the Long 1964 came to a close and have been with ever since, the love of my life, Anne.

Robert S. McElvaine
Clinton, Mississippi
January 2022

PERMISSIONS
ACKNOWLEDGMENTS

NOTES

PREFACE

1   Robert A. Caro, *The Years of Lyndon Johnson: The Passage to Power* (New York: Knopf, 2012), 536–37.

2   Nancy MacLean, *Democracy in Chains: The Deep History of the Radical Right's Stealth Plan for America* (New York: Viking, 2017), 233.

3   MacLean, *Democracy in Chains*, 175.

4   Peter Baker, "Biden Makes Case to Vastly Expand Government Role," *New York Times*, April 29, 2021.

5   *People* v. *Bruce* (1964) http://law2.umkc.edu/faculty/projects/ftrials/bruce/brucecourtdecisions.html

6   David Maraniss, "Patterns of Denial Joined to the Appetites of Power," *Washington Post*, January 26, 1998.

7   *Griswold v. Connecticut*, 381 U.S. 479 (1965).

8   Arthur H. Miller, "Political Issues and Trust in Government: 1964–1970," *American Political Science Review*, vol. 68, no. 3 (September 1974), 953.

9   Pew Research Center, "Public Trust in Government, 1958–2021." May 17, 2021. https://www.pewresearch.org/politics/2021/05/17/public-trust-in-government-1958-2021/

10 Ronald Reagan, News Conference, August 12, 1986. https://www.reaganfoundation.org/ronald-reagan/reagan-quotes-speeches/news-conference-1/

11 William Jefferson Clinton, State of the Union Address, January 23, 1996. https://clintonwhitehouse4.archives.gov/WH/New/other/sotu.html

12 "The Times They Are a-Changin'" (lyrics by Bob Dylan, 1963; Warner Brothers, 1964/Special Rider Music, 1991, 1992).

13 "The 500 Greatest Songs of All Time," *Rolling Stone*, 963 (December 2004).

INTRODUCTION

1   John Winthrop, *A Modell of Christian Charity* (1630), Collections of the Massachusetts Historical Society (Boston, 1838), 3rd series 7:31–48, 40. http://history.hanover.edu/texts/winthmod.html.

2   Norman Mailer, "The White Negro," *Dissent*, vol. 4 (Spring, 1957); reprinted in Mailer, *Advertisements for Myself* (New York: Putnam, 1959), 337–58.

3   Nathaniel Hawthorne, "The May-Pole of Merry Mount" (1836), in
     Hawthorne, *Twice-Told Tales* (1837; London: J. M. Dent, 1911), 39.
4   William Bradford, *Of Plymouth Plantation* (1620–1647), ed. by Harvey Wish
     (New York: Capricorn Books, 1962), 141.
5   Robert S. McElvaine, "The Red, the Blue and the Gray," *Washington Post*,
     February 8, 2009.
6   Christopher Lasch, *Haven in a Heartless World: The Family Besieged* (New York:
     Basic Books, 1977).
7   Daniel Bell, *The Cultural Contradictions of Capitalism* (New York: Basic Books,
     1976).
8   Among the numerous examples of this fact is Caroline Randall Williams, "You
     Want a Confederate Monument? My Body Is a Confederate Monument," *New
     York Times*, June 26, 2020.
9   Jack Kerouac, *On the Road* (New York: Viking, 1957); Mailer, "The White
     Negro."
10   "Me and Bobby McGee" (1969, lyrics by Kris Kristofferson).
11   Ernest Dichter, as quoted in Vance Packard, *The Hidden Persuaders* (New York:
     David McKay, 1957), 263.
12   Tom Wicker, "Convention Ends," *New York Times*, July 17, 1964.
13   Tom Wolfe, "The 'Me' Decade and the Third Great Awakening," *New York*,
     August 23, 1976.
14   See Robert S. McElvaine, *The Great Depression: America, 1929–1941* (New York:
     Times Books, 1984), 196–223.
15   Leslie A. Fiedler, "The New Mutants," *Partisan Review*, Fall 1965, 516, 521.

CHAPTER 1

1   "The Times They Are a-Changin'" (lyrics by Bob Dylan, Warner Brothers,
     1963, 1964/Special Rider Music, 1991, 1992).
2   "A Change is Gonna Come" (1963, lyrics and music by Sam Cooke).
3   Kurt Andersen, *Evil Geniuses—The Unmaking of America: A Recent History* (New
     York: Random House, 2020), 23.
4   "The 1619 Project," *New York Times Magazine*, August 14, 2019; "We Respond
     to the Historians Who Critiqued the 1619 Project, *New York Times*, December
     20, 2019; Conor Friedersdorf, "1776 Honors American Diversity in a Way
     1619 Does Not," *The Atlantic*, January 6, 2020; Nikole Hannah-Jones, *The 1619
     Project: A New Origin Story* (New York: One World, 2021).
5   Michael G. Kammen, *People of Paradox: An Inquiry Concerning the Origins of
     American Civilization* (New York: Knopf, 1972).
6   Nikole Hannah-Jones, "Our Democracy's Ideals Were False When They Were
     Written. Black Americans Have Fought to Make Them True," *New York Times
     Magazine*, Aug. 14, 2019.

7   Langston Hughes, "Let America Be America Again," *Esquire*, July 1936, reprinted in *The Collected Poems of Langston Hughes*, edited by Arnold Rampersad with David Roessel New York: Knopf, 1994).

8   Vann R. Newkirk II, "When America Became a Democracy," *Atlantic*, March 2021, 28–59.

9   Dylan, "The Times They Are a-Changin'."

10   Bob Dylan, September 1963, as quoted in Clinton Heylin, *Bob Dylan: Behind the Shades Revisited* (New York: HarperCollins, 2003), 126.

11   Zora Neale Hurston, *Their Eyes Were Watching God* (New York: Lippincott, 1937; Perennial, 1990), 55.

12   In an honors thesis he wrote under my direction, Andrew Marion makes a persuasive case that even the first Woody Guthrie–like Bob Dylan was a fiction created by Dylan as part of a plan to make himself a rock star. Andrew Marion, "The Dylans They Are a-Changin'," Millsaps College 2013.

13   Pete Seeger, letter to Charles Seeger, "A Certain Independent Originality," 1967, in Pete Seeger, with Rob Rosenthal and Sam Rosenthal, *Pete Seeger in His Own Words* (London: Paradigm, 2012), 320.

14   "It Ain't Me Babe" (lyrics by Bob Dylan, Warner Brothers, 1964/Special Rider Music, 1991).

15   "With God on Our Side" (lyrics by Bob Dylan, Warner Brothers, 1963/Special Rider Music, 1991).

16   Dylan, "The Times They Are a-Changin'."

17   Svetlana Boym, *The Future of Nostalgia* (New York: Basic, 2001).

18   Nick Bryant, *When America Stopped Being Great: A History of the Present* (London: Bloomsbury Continuum, 2021), 3.

19   Anne Applebaum, *Twilight of Democracy: The Seductive Lure of Authoritarianism* (New York: Doubleday, 2020), 74–75.

20   "Bill Clinton Honors LBJ at Civil Rights Summit," *USA Today*, April 9, 2014.

21   Rick Perlstein, *Before the Storm: Barry Goldwater and the Unmaking of the American Consensus* (New York: Hill and Wang, 2001), 384.

22   As quoted in Perlstein, *Before the Storm*, 428.

23   Nelson Rockefeller, as quoted in Jon Margolis, *The Last Innocent Year: America in 1964* (New York: William Morrow, 1999), 23.

24   Gary Donaldson, *Liberalism's Last Hurrah: The Presidential Campaign of 1964* (Armonk, NY: M. E. Sharpe, 2003), 274.

25   Sabrina Tavernise and Robert Gebeloff, "Census Shows Sharply Growing Numbers of Hispanics, Asian and Multiracial Americans, *New York Times*, August 12, 2021.

26   Andersen, *Evil Geniuses*, 266n. Emphasis in original.

27   As quoted in Jen Kirby, "Trump Wants Fewer Immigrants from 'Shithole Countries' and More from Places Like Norway," *Vox*, January 11, 2018. https://www.vox.com/2018/1/11/16880750/trump-immigrants-shithole -countries-norway

28　Paul Weyrich. https://www.youtube.com/watch?v=8GBAsFwPglw

29　"Trump Says Republicans Would 'Never' Be Elected Again if It Was Easier to Vote," *Guardian*, March 30, 2020. https://www.theguardian.com/us-news/2020/mar/30/trump-republican-party-voting-reform-coronavirus.

30　Brennan Center for Justice, "Voting Rights Roundup: October 2021." https://www.brennancenter.org/our-work/research-reports/voting-laws-roundup-october-2021

31　Voting Rights Lab, "A Threat to Our Democracy: Election Subversion in the 2021 Legislative Session, September 29, 2021. 20210924 VRL: Election Subversion Report (votingrightslab.org); Heather Cox Richardson, *Letters from an American*, September 30, 2021. https://heathercoxrichardson.substack.com/p/september-30-2021

32　"To Pass H.R. 6400, The 1965 Voting Rights Act," July 9, 1965. https://www.govtrack.us/congress/votes/89-1965/h87; "To Pass S. 1564, An Act to Enforce the Fifteenth Amendment to the Constitution of the United States, May 26, 1965. https://www.govtrack.us/congress/votes/89-1965/s78

33　"By a Vote of 98-0, Senate Approves 25-Year Extension of Voting Rights Act," *New York Times*, July 21, 2006.

34　Carl Hulse, "Democrats Search for Path on Voting Rights amid Republican Blockade," *New York Times*, October 20, 2021; Heather Cox Richardson, *Letters from an American*, October 20, 2021. https://heathercoxrichardson.substack.com/p/october-20-2021

35　Samuel G. Freedman, "The First Days of the Loaded Political Image," *New York Times*, September 1, 1996.

36　"Politics: Most Disappointing," *Time*, October 30, 1964.

37　A wonderful irony in the film is that the people making it must have found a clip of children reciting the Pledge from some time prior to 1954, when, at the urging of President Eisenhower (who was seeking the Ultimate Ally in the struggle against communism), "under God" was added. In the film, the kids recite the original version: "one nation, indivisible, with liberty and justice for all."

38　*Choice* (1964, produced by F. Clifton White and Russ Walton.) https://www.youtube.com/watch?v=xniUoMiHm8g

39　Theodore H. White, *The Making of the President—1964* (New York: Atheneum, 1969), 333n.

40　Perlstein, *Before the Storm*, 484–96.

41　Robert Dallek, *Flawed Giant: Lyndon Johnson and His Times, 1961–1973* (New York: Oxford University Press, 1998), 178–79.

42　Freedman, "The First Days of the Loaded Political Image."

43　Kurt Andersen neatly characterizes it as this "OMG-decadence-black-people-chaos film." Andersen, *Evil Geniuses*, 45.

44　Perlstein, *Before the Storm*, x.

45　Jon Margolis, *The Last Innocent Year: America in 1964—The Beginning of the "Sixties"* (New York: William Morrow, 1999).

46 James T. Patterson, *The Eve of Destruction: How 1965 Transformed America* (New York: Basic Books, 2012).

47 Margolis, *The Last Innocent Year*, vii.

48 James W. Loewen, *Lies My Teacher Taught Me: Everything Your American History Textbook Got Wrong* (New York: New Press, 1995).

49 "Michele de Cuneo's Letter on the Second Voyage, 28 October 1495," in Samuel Eliot Morison, ed., *Journals and Other Documents on the Life and Voyages of Christopher Columbus* (New York: Heritage Press, 1963), 209–14.

50 "30 Receive Freedom Medal at White House," *New York Times*, September 15, 1964.

51 "What Did You Learn in School Today?" (lyrics by Tom Paxton, BMG Rights Management, 1964).

52 John Adams to Benjamin Rush, April 4, 1790. https://founders.archives.gov /documents/Adams/99-02-02-0903

53 See Heather Cox Richardson, *The End of Reconstruction: Race, Labor, and Politics in the Post–Civil War North* (Cambridge, MA: Harvard University Press, 2004).

54 Robert S. McElvaine, "Birthers, Then and Now," *Huffington Post*, February 8, 2015. https://www.huffpost.com/entry/birthers-then--now_b_6641084

55 Henry Steele Commager, "A Shadow Stretched Across Our History for a Hundred Years" (a review of Willie Lee Rose, *Rehearsal for Reconstruction: The Port Royal Experiment* (Indianapolis and New York: Bobbs-Merrill, 1964), *New York Times Book Review*, September 13, 1964.

56 W. E. B. Du Bois, *Black Reconstruction in America, 1860–1880* (New York: Harcourt, Brace and Howe, 1935).

57 In addition to Rose's *Rehearsal for Reconstruction*, see Kenneth M. Stamp, *The Era of Reconstruction, 1865–1877* (New York: Knopf, 1965).

58 "Trump's '1776 Report' Defends America's Founding on the Basis of Slavery and Blasts Progressivism," *New York Times*, January 18, 2021; "Trump's 1776 Commission Critiques Liberalism in Report Derided by Historians," *New York Times*, January 18, 2021.

59 *FP Insider*, January 21, 2021. https://foreignpolicy.com/2021/01/21/1776 -project-desperate-search-enemies-identity-politics-unamerican/

60 "On Day 1, Biden Moves to Undo Trump's Legacy," *New York Times*, January 20, 2021.

61 Heather Cox Richardson, *Letters from an American*, October 16, 2021. https://heathercoxrichardson.substack.com/p/october-16-2021

62 Carl Oglesby, "Let Us Shape the Future," November 27, 1965. https://www.sds-1960s.org/sds_wuo/sds_documents/oglesby_future.html

63 *Easy Rider* (1969, directed by Dennis Hopper, Columbia).

CHAPTER 2

1 Anne Moody, *Coming of Age in Mississippi* (New York: Dial, 1968; New York: Dell, 1971), 354.

2   Ted Reardon, as quoted in Ted Sorensen, *Counselor: A Life at the Edge of History* (New York: HarperCollins, 2008), 368.

3   John F. Kennedy, November 22, 1963, as quoted in Kenneth O'Donnell and David F. Powers, *"Johnny, We Hardly Knew Ye"* (Boston: Little, Brown, 1970), 11.

4   David Talbot, *Brothers: The Hidden History of the Kennedy Years* (New York: Simon & Schuster, 2007), 260.

5   Edwin Walker, as quoted in Robert Dallek, *An Unfinished Life: John F. Kennedy, 1917–1963* (Boston: Little, Brown, 2003), 693.

6   Jan Jarboe Russell, *Lady Bird: A Biography of Mrs. Johnson* (New York: Simon & Schuster, 1999; Lanham, MD: Rowman & Littlefield, 2004), 207–8.

7   Robert A. Caro, *The Years of Lyndon Johnson: The Passage to Power* (New York: Knopf, 2012), 149–56.

8   Vincent Bugliosi, *Reclaiming History: The Assassination of President John F. Kennedy* (New York: Norton, 2007).

9   Robert Dallek, *Flawed Giant: Lyndon Johnson and His Times, 1961–1973* (New York: Oxford University Press, 1998), 52.

10   LBJ, as quoted in Joseph A. Califano, *The Triumph and Tragedy of Lyndon Johnson* (New York: Simon and Schuster, 1991), 295.

11   Evan Thomas, Robert Kennedy: His Life (New York: Simon & Schuster, 2000), 284.

12   "The effectiveness of Public Law 102-526, the President John F. Kennedy Assassination Records Collection Act of 1992: Hearing before the Legislation and National Security Subcommittee of the Committee on Government Operations, House of Representatives, One Hundred Third Congress, first session, November 17, 1993." http://www.archive.org/stream /effectivenessofp00unit/effectivenessofp00unit_djvu.txt.

13   Harris Poll, reported in "66% in Poll Accept Plot View," *New York Times*, May 30, 1967.

14   Philip Shenon, "Who Killed John Kennedy? After 25 Years, More Theories than Certainty," *New York Times*, November 18, 1988.

15   Jacqueline Kennedy, speaking with Theodore White, November 29, 1963, "Camelot Documents," Theodore H. White Papers, John F. Kennedy Presidential Library; Theodore H. White, *In Search of History: A Personal Adventure* (New York: Harper & Row, 1978), 523.

16   Dick Cheney, interviewed on *Meet the Press*, NBC, September 14, 2003. http://www.msnbc.msn.com/id/3080244/.

17   Caro, *Passage to Power*, 342.

18   Ben Bradlee, *A Good Life: Newspapering and Other Adventures* (New York: Simon & Schuster, 1995), 261.

19   Ken Ringle, "The Day a Generation's Spirit Died," *Washington Post*, November 22, 2003.

20   Jacqueline Kennedy, speaking with Theodore White, November 29, 1963, "Camelot Documents," Theodore H. White Papers, John F. Kennedy Presidential Library; Theodore H. White, *In Search of History: A Personal Adventure* (New York: Harper & Row, 1978), 523.

21 Theodore H. White, "For President Kennedy: An Epilogue," *Life*, December 6, 1963.

22 "The Impossible Dream" (1964, lyrics by Joe Darion, music by Mitch Leigh).

23 Dallek, *Unfinished Life*, 708.

24 Barack Obama, *Dreams from My Father: A Story of Race and Inheritance* (1995; New York: Crown, 2007), 25–26.

25 Daniel Patrick Moynihan, November 22, 1963, as quoted in Godfrey Hodgson, *The Gentleman from New York: Daniel Patrick Moynihan: A Biography* (Boston: Houghton Mifflin, 2000), 85.

26 "Leader of the Pack" (1964, George "Shadow" Morton, Jeff Barry, Ellie Greenwich).

27 Theodore Sorensen, as quoted in Dallek, *Unfinished Life*, 631.

28 Tom Wicker, as quoted in Vincent Bugliosi, *Four Days in November: The Assassination of John F. Kennedy* (New York: Norton, 2007), 154.

29 Allan Kozinn, "They Came, They Sang, They Conquered," *New York Times*, February 6, 2004.

30 Sorensen, *Counselor*, 191.

31 Theodore H. White, *The Making of the President, 1960* (New York: Atheneum, 1962), 298.

32 White, *Making of the President, 1960*, 331.

33 Dallek, *Unfinished Life*, 225.

34 Steven D. Stark, *Meet the Beatles: A Cultural History of the Band that Shook Youth, Gender, and the World* (New York: HarperEntertainment, 2005), 30–33.

35 Elaine Tyler May, "Explosive Issues: Sex, Women, and the Bomb," in Lary May, *Recasting America: Culture and Politics in the Age of the Cold War* (Chicago: University of Chicago Press, 1989), as quoted in Stark, *Meet the Beatles*, 3–4.

CHAPTER 3

1 Franklin D. Roosevelt, as quoted in Robert Dallek, *Lone Star Rising: Lyndon Johnson and His Times, 1908–1960* (New York: Oxford University Press, 1991), 161.

2 Lyndon B. Johnson to advisers at LBJ Ranch, 1958, as quoted in Robert A. Caro, *The Years of Lyndon Johnson: The Passage to Power* (New York: Knopf, 2012), 12.

3 John F. Kennedy, speaking of Lyndon Johnson, to Newton Minow, as quoted in Ted Sorensen, *Counselor: A Life at the Edge of History* (New York: Harper, 2008), 241.

4 *Julius Caesar*, Act 1, scene ii.

5 George Reedy, *Lyndon B. Johnson: A Memoir* (New York: Andrews and McMeel, 1982), 9, as quoted in Samuel Walker, *Presidents and Civil Liberties from Wilson to Obama: A Study of Poor Custodians* (Cambridge and New York: Cambridge University Press, 2012), 240.

6   Unnamed LBJ aide, as quoted in Laurence Stern, "Johnson 'Totally Immersed' in His Job," *Milwaukee Sentinel,* July 1, 1965. http://news.google.com/ newspapers?nid=1368&dat=19650701&id=2MMVAAAAIBAJ&sjid= QREEAAAAIBAJ&pg=7506,58020

7   Hubert Humphrey, as quoted in Joy Hakim, *All the People* (New York: Oxford University Press, 2003), 109.

8   Rainer Maria Rilke, *Letters to a Young Poet.*

9   Horace Richards, as quoted in Robert A. Caro, *The Years of Lyndon Johnson: The Path to Power* (New York: Knopf, 1982), 156.

10 Hugh Sidey, *A Very Personal Presidency: Lyndon Johnson in the White House* (New York: Atheneum, 1968, 22–23.

11 Doris Kearns, *Lyndon Johnson and the American Dream* (New York: Harper & Row, 1976), 15.

12 Rebekah Baines Johnson, as quoted in Caro, *Path to Power,* 95.

13 Caro, *Path to Power,* 160.

14 Robert Dallek, *Flawed Giant: Lyndon Johnson and His Times, 1961–1973* (New York: Oxford University Press, 1998), 280–81.

15 For a full discussion of the effects of masculine insecurity on male leaders, see Robert S. McElvaine, *Eve's Seed: Biology, the Sexes, and the Course of History* (New York: McGraw-Hill, 2001).

16 Kearns, *Lyndon Johnson and the American Dream,* 24.

17 Kearns, *Lyndon Johnson and the American Dream,* 22–23.

18 Kearns, *Lyndon Johnson and the American Dream,* 33.

19 Kearns, *Lyndon Johnson and the American Dream,* 38.

20 Caro, *Path to Power,* 156.

21 Caro, *Passage to Power,* 314.

22 Caro, *Path to Power,* 110–11.

23 David Halberstam, *The Best and the Brightest* (New York: Random House, 1972), 531.

24 Dallek, *Lone Star Rising,* 559.

25 Hubert Humphrey, *The Education of a Public Man: My Life in Politics* (Garden City, NY: Doubleday, 1976), 307–8.

26 For a full discussion of this central metaphor in the unfolding of human history, see McElvaine, *Eve's Seed.*

27 LBJ, as quoted in Eric Alterman, *When Presidents Lie: A History of Official Deception and Its Consequences* (New York: Penguin, 2005), 181.

28 LBJ, as quoted in Larry L. King, "Machismo in the White House: LBJ and Vietnam," *American Heritage,* vol. 27, August 1976, 99. Caro, *Path to Power,* 155.

29 Dallek, *Flawed Giant,* 408.

30 Caro, *Path to Power,* 155.

31 Jerome Doolittle, "The Member from Johnson City," *Bad Attitudes,* June, 2000. http://www.badattitudes.com/Organ.html

32 Dallek, *Flawed Giant,* 491.

33 King, "Machismo in the White House," 100.

34 Kearns, *Lyndon Johnson and the American Dream*, 251.

35 Tim O'Brien, *The Things They Carried* (New York: Houghton Mifflin, 1990; Penguin, 1991), 48–49, 54–55, 63.

36 Kearns, *Lyndon Johnson and the American Dream*, 25.

37 Kearns, *Lyndon Johnson and the American Dream*, 45.

38 *The American Experience: The Presidents: Lyndon Johnson* (PBS, 2008). http://www.pbs.org/wgbh/americanexperience/features/transcript/lbj-transcript/

39 Kenneth Rexroth, *The Alternative Society: Essays from the Other World* (New York: Herder and Herder, 1970), 121.

40 LBJ, as quoted in Dallek, *Flawed Giant*, 160.

41 Dallek, *Flawed Giant*, 186.

42 Caro, *Path to Power*, 198; Stanley Karnow, *Vietnam: A History* (New York: Viking, 1983; rev. ed.: Penguin, 1997), 372.

43 Kearns, *Lyndon Johnson and the American Dream*, 41.

44 Caro, *Path to Power*, 218–19.

45 Caro, *Path to Power*, 294.

46 Robert Dallek, *Lyndon B. Johnson: Portrait of a President* (New York: Oxford University Press, 2004), 27.

47 Dallek, *Portrait of a President*, 31.

48 Dallek, *Portrait of a President*, 34.

49 Caro, *Path to Power*, 446–49.

50 Franklin D. Roosevelt, as quoted in Dallek, *Lone Star Rising*, 161.

51 LBJ, as quoted in Kearns, *Lyndon Johnson and the American Dream*, 201.

52 Caro, *Passage to Power*, 87.

53 Robert F. Kennedy, as quoted in Arthur M. Schlesinger Jr., *A Thousand Days: John F. Kennedy in the White House* (Boston: Houghton Mifflin), 56.

54 A good review of the events that day can be found in Caro, *Passage to Power*, 109–43.

55 Bobby Baker, *Wheeling and Dealing: Confessions of a Capitol Hill Operator* (New York: Norton, 1978), 130.

56 Caro, *Passage to Power*, 129.

57 John Nance Garner, as quoted in Carol Felsenthal, *Power, Privilege, and the Post: The Katherine Graham Story* (New York: Seven Stones Press, 1999), 175.

58 LBJ, as quoted by Clare Boothe Luce, in Ralph G. Martin, *A Hero for Our Time: An Intimate Story of the Kennedy Years* (New York: Random House, 1984), 170.

59 Jack Conway, as quoted in Dallek, *Lone Star Rising*, 579.

60 LBJ, as quoted in Caro, *Passage to Power*, 205.

61 LBJ, as quoted in Caro, *Passage to Power*, 165.

62 Caro, *Passage to Power*, 159–75.

63 LBJ, as quoted in Kearns, *Lyndon Johnson and the American Dream*, 164.

64 Caro, *Passage to Power*, 201–205.

CHAPTER 4

1 Horace Busby, as quoted in Robert A. Caro, *The Years of Lyndon Johnson: The Passage to Power* (New York: Knopf, 2012), 332.

2 Caro, *Passage to Power*, 319.

3 Jeff Shesol, *Mutual Contempt: Lyndon Johnson, Robert Kennedy and the Feud that Defined a Decade* (New York: Norton, 1998), 114–115.

4 Lyndon Baines Johnson, *The Vantage Point: Perspectives on the Presidency, 1963–1969* (New York: Holt, Rinehart and Winston, 1971), 18.

5 Johnson, *The Vantage Point*, 21.

6 LBJ, as quoted in Hugh Sidey, *A Very Personal Presidency: Lyndon Johnson in the White House* (New York: Atheneum, 1968), 86.

7 LBJ, as quoted in Sidey, *Very Personal Presidency*, 86.

8 LBJ, as quoted in Doris Kearns, *Lyndon Johnson and the American Dream* (New York: Harper & Row, 1976), 177.

9 LBJ, as quoted in Kearns, *Lyndon Johnson and the American Dream*, 343.

10 LBJ, as quoted in Caro, *Passage to Power*, 372.

11 LBJ, as quoted in Kearns, *Lyndon Johnson and the American Dream*, 178.

12 LBJ, as quoted in Kearns, *Lyndon Johnson and the American Dream*, 340–41.

13 Dallek, *Flawed Giant*, 236.

14 Sidey, *Very Personal Presidency*, 40–41.

15 "President Speaks," *New York Times*, November 26, 1963.

16 Caro, *Passage to Power*, 486.

17 "Off the Record Remarks of President Johnson to a Group of Governors of the United States Present in Washington to Attend the Funeral of John F. Kennedy, held in the Executive Office Building, 8:20 pm., Monday, November 25, 1963," as quoted in Caro, *Passage to Power*, 420–21.

18 Caro, *Passage to Power*, 601.

19 Caro, *Passage to Power*, 602.

20 Lady Bird Johnson, as quoted in William Manchester, *The Glory and the Dream: A Narrative History of America, 1932–1972* (Boston: Little, Brown, 1974), 1010.

21 Robert Dallek, *Flawed Giant: Lyndon Johnson and His Times, 1961–1973* (New York: Oxford University Press, 1998), x.

22 LBJ, as quoted by Abe Fortas in Merle Miller, *Lyndon: An Oral Biography* (New York: Putnam, 1980; Ballantine, 1981), 411.

23 Lyndon B. Johnson, "Address Before a Joint Session of the Congress," November 27, 1963. http://www.presidency.ucsb.edu/ws/index.php?pid=25988.

24 "The Times They Are a-Changin'" (lyrics by Bob Dylan, Warner Brothers, 1963, 1964)

25 Russell Long, as quoted in Caro, *Passage to Power*, 469.

26 Orville Freeman and Richard Russell, as quoted in Caro, *Passage to Power*, 465.

27 MLK, as quoted in Nick Kotz, *Judgment Days: Lyndon Baines Johnson, Martin Luther King Jr., and the Laws that Changed America* (Boston: Houghton Mifflin Harcourt, 2006), 67.

28 Caro, *Passage to Power*, 539.

29 LBJ, November 23, 1963, as quoted by Walter Heller. Caro, *Passage to Power*, 539–40.

30 Lyndon B. Johnson, "Annual Message to Congress on the State of the Union," January 8, 1964. https://www.presidency.ucsb.edu/documents/annual-message-the-congress-the-state-the-union-25

31 Caro, *Passage to Power*, 548.

32 LBJ, as quoted in Kearns, *Lyndon Johnson and the American Dream*, 340.

33 LBJ, as quoted in Tom Wicker, *JFK and LBJ: The Influence of Personality on Politics* (New York: William Morrow, 1968), 205.

CHAPTER 5

1 *Dr. Strangelove, or: How I Learned to Stop Worrying and Love the Bomb* (1964; directed by Stanley Kubrick; Columbia).

2 http://vault.fbi.gov/louie-louie-the-song/louie-louie-the-song/view

3 http://tvaholics.blogspot.com/2012/10/classic-tv-ratings-and-rankings-1963-64.html

4 *Dr. Strangelove*.

5 Bosley Crowther, "Kubrick Film Presents Sellers in 3 Roles," *New York Times*, January 30, 1964.

6 As quoted in Loudon Wainwright, "The Strange Case of Strangelove," *Life*, March 13, 1964.

7 Rick Perlstein, *Before the Storm: Barry Goldwater and the Unmaking of the American Consensus* (New York: Hill & Wang, 2001; New York: Nation Books, 2009), 283.

8 *2001: A Space Odyssey* (1968, directed by Stanley Kubrick, MGM).

9 Sen. Richard Russell (D, GA), remarks in the Senate during debate on the antiballistic missile, October 2, 1968, *Congressional Record*, vol. 114, 29175.

10 James T. Patterson, *Grand Expectations: The United States, 1945–1971* (New York: Oxford University Press, 1996), 498.

11 JFK, as quoted in Robert Dallek, *An Unfinished Life: John F. Kennedy, 1917–1963* (Boston: Little Brown, 2003), 547.

12 Timothy Naftali and Philip D. Zelikow, eds., *The Presidential Recordings: John F. Kennedy: The Great Crises, vol. II: September-October 21, 1962* (New York: Norton, 2001), 578–98.

13 LBJ, October 27, 1962, as quoted in Ted Sorensen, *Counselor: A Life at the Edge of History* (New York: Harper, 2008), 304.

14 Robert F. Kennedy, *Thirteen Days: A Memoir of the Cuban Missile Crisis* (New York: Norton, 1969), 98.

15 May and Zelikow, *Kennedy Tapes*, 264.

16 JFK and Castro, as quoted in Michael Beschloss, *Crisis Years: Kennedy and Khrushchev, 1960–1963* (New York: Edward Burlingame, 1991), 549, 543.

17 Curtis LeMay, as quoted in Martin Walker, *The Cold War: A History* (revised ed., New York: Macmillan, 1995), 179.
18 Sorensen, *Counselor*, 289. Emphasis added.
19 "Fluoridation is the most monstrously conceived and dangerous Communist plot we have ever had to face," Ripper proclaims. Fluoridation actually was labeled as a Communist plot by many right-wingers.
20 Sorensen, *Counselor*, 296.
21 JFK, September 7, 1960, Eugene, OR, quoting Henry David Thoreau. JFK Link http://www.jfklink.com/speeches/jfk/sept60/jfk070960_eugene02.html.
22 Joan Didion, "John Wayne: A Love Song," *Saturday Evening Post*, 1965, in Didion, *Slouching Towards Bethlehem* (New York: Macmillan, 1968), 31.
23 *Easy Rider* (1969, directed by Dennis Hopper, Columbia).
24 *Midnight Cowboy* (1969, directed by John Schlesinger, United Artists).
25 David Halberstam, *The Best and the Brightest* (New York: Random House, 1972), 531.

CHAPTER 6

1 Frank Rich, "Ticket to Ride," *New York Times*, November 18, 1995.
2 Steven D. Stark, *Meet the Beatles: A Cultural History of the Band that Shook Youth, Gender, and the World* (New York: HarperEntertainment, 2005), 27.
3 Ed Sullivan, as quoted in Laurel Sercombe, "'Ladies and Gentlemen …' The Beatles: The Ed Sullivan Show, CBS TV, February 9, 1964," in Ian Inglis, *Performance and Popular Music: History, Place and Time* (Farnham, UK: Ashgate Publishing, 2007), 6.
4 Allan Kozinn, "They Came, They Sang, They Conquered," *New York Times*, February 6, 2004.
5 Jonathan Gould, *Can't Buy Me Love: The Beatles, Britain, and America* (New York: Three Rivers, 2007), 1.
6 Stark, *Meet the Beatles*, 154.
7 Joel Whitburn, *The Billboard Hot 100 Charts: The Sixties* (Menonomee Falls, WI: Record Research, 1990).
8 Rich, "Ticket to Ride."
9 Tony Carricker, as quoted in Stark, *Meet the Beatles*, 27.
10 "Don't Worry, Be Happy" (1988, lyrics by Bobby McFerrin).
11 George Martin, as quoted in Stark, *Meet the Beatles*, 128.
12 "Glad All Over" (1963, written by Dave Clark and Mike Smith).
13 "Needles and Pins" (1964, written by Sonny Bono and Jack Nitzsche).
14 "Bad to Me" (1963, written by John Lennon and Paul McCartney).
15 "World Without Love" (1964, written by John Lennon and Paul McCartney).
16 "Don't Let the Sun Catch You Crying" (1964, written by Gerry Marsden, Freddie Marsden, Les Chadwick, and Les Maguire).

17 "A Summer Song" (1964, written by Chad Stewart, Clive Metcalfe and Keith Noble).

18 David Hajdu, *Positively 4th Street: The Lives and Times of Joan Baez, Bob Dylan, Mimi Baez Fariña, and Richard Fariña* (New York: Macmillan, 2002), 197.

19 Stark, *Meet the Beatles*, 60–65, 149–50.

20 Joyce Maynard, *Looking Back: A Chronicle of Growing Up Old in the Sixties* (1973, iUniverse, 2003), 34.

21 Marcy Lanza, as quoted in Stark, *Meet the Beatles*, 153.

22 *A Hard Day's Night* (1964, directed by Richard Lester, United Artists).

23 "All in the Family Theme" ("Those Were the Days") (1969, written by Koo Joseph).

24 Jeanne Maglaty, "When Did Girls Start Wearing Pink?" Smithsonianmag.com, April 7, 2011. https://www.smithsonianmag.com/arts-culture/when-did-girls-start-wearing-pink-1370097/; Jo B. Paoletti, *Pink and Blue: Telling the Boys from the Girls in America* (Bloomington: Indiana University Press, 2012).

25 Jack Kerouac, *On the Road* (New York: Viking, 1957), 180.

26 Norman Mailer, "The White Negro," *Dissent*, vol. 4 (Spring, 1957); reprinted in Mailer, *Advertisements for Myself* (New York: Putnam, 1959), 340.

27 David Halberstam, *The Fifties* (New York: Villard Books, 1993; Ballantine, 1994), 464.

28 "I'm Ready" (1959, written by Fats Domino, Al Lewis, and Sylvester Bradford).

29 Sam Phillips, as quoted in Peter Guralnick, *Feels Like Going Home: Portraits in Blues and Rock 'n' Roll* (Hachette Digital, 2012).

30 John Lennon, August 28, 1965, as quoted in Jane Ellen Wayne, *The Leading Men of MGM* (New York: Da Capo, 2006), 386.

31 Guralnick, *Last Train to Memphis*, 110.

32 Susan J. Douglas, *Where the Girls Are: Growing Up Female with the Mass Media* (New York: Times Books, 1993), 84.

33 Guralnick, *Last Train to Memphis*, 43.

34 Guralnick, *Last Train to Memphis*, 81.

35 Lennon, as quoted in Wayne, *Leading Men of MGM*, 386.

36 See Charlotte Greig, *Will You Still Love Me Tomorrow?: Girl Groups from the 50s on* (London: Virago Press, 1989).

37 Douglas, *Where the Girls Are*, 84.

38 Douglas, *Where the Girls Are*, 97.

39 John Lennon, as quoted in Tim Riley, *John Lennon: The Man, the Myth, the Music—The Definitive Biography* (New York: Hyperion, 2011).

40 Robert Shelton, *No Direction Home: The Life and Music of Bob Dylan.* (Milwaukee: Backbeat Books. 2010), 38.

41 Veronica "Ronnie" Bennett Spector, as quoted in Riley, *John Lennon*.

42 Douglas, *Where the Girls Are*, 95.

43 Stark, *Meet the Beatles*, 155.

44 Albert Grossman, as quoted Stark, *Meet the Beatles*, 27.

45 Sercombe, "'Ladies and Gentlemen . . .' The Beatles," 12.
46 Stark, *Meet the Beatles*, 37–38.
47 See, for example, "Singers: The Unbarbershopped Quartet," *Time*, February 21, 1964.
48 George Martin, as quoted in Stark, *Meet the Beatles*, 129.
49 Paul McCartney, as quoted in *The Beatles Anthology* (San Francisco: Chronicle Books, 2000), 101.
50 "Baby It's You" (1961, written by Burt Bacharach, Luther Dixon, and Mack David).
51 "Please Mr. Postman" (1961, written by George Dobbins, William Garrett, Freddie Gorman, Brian Holland, and Robert Bateman).
52 "She Loves You" (1963, written by John Lennon and Paul McCartney).
53 Elaine Tyler May, as quoted in Stark, *Meet the Beatles*, 29.
54 Barbara Ehrenreich, Elizabeth Hess, and Gloria Jacobs, *Re-making Love: The Feminization of Sex* (New York: Anchor/Doubleday, 1986), 34.
55 Ehrenreich, Hess and Jacobs, *Re-making Love*, 11.

CHAPTER 7

1 "You Don't Own Me" (1963, written by John Madara and Dave White).
2 "Chapel of Love" (1964; written by Jeff Barry, Ellie Greenwich, and Phil Spector).
3 "Wives and Lovers" (1963, written by Burt Bacharach and Hal David, Sony/ATV Music Publishing LLC).
4 "Stand By Your Man" (1968, written by Tammy Wynette and Billy Sherrill).
5 "It's My Party" (1963; written by Walter Gold, John Gluck Jr., and Hern Weiner).
6 "You Don't Own Me" (1963; written by John Madara, and David White Tricker).
7 "I Saw Her Standing There" (1963, written by John Lennon and Paul McCartney).
8 Betty Friedan, "I Say: Women are People Too!" *Good Housekeeping*, September 1960), 59–61, 161–62.
9 Betty Friedan, *The Feminine Mystique* (New York: Norton, 1963), 22.
10 Friedan, "I Say: Women are People Too!" 59–61, 161–62.
11 *Newsweek*, March 7, 1960, as quoted in Friedan, *Feminine Mystique*, 14.
12 Friedan, *Feminine Mystique*, 20–22.
13 Paul Foley, "Whatever Happened to Women's Rights?" *Atlantic Monthly*, March 1964.
14 Foley, "Whatever Happened to Women's Rights?"
15 Harriet Ann Jacobs, *Incidents in the Life of a Slave Girl* (1861; Indo-European Publishers, 2010), 228.
16 Toni Morrison, *Sula* (New York: Knopf, 1973; reprint: Plume, 1982), 83.

17 Deirdre McGowan, "They Did Own Me," March 29, 2004, paper written for Liberal Studies 5000, "Oh! Freedom: America in the 1960s," Millsaps College.

18 Adlai Stevenson, 1955, as quoted in Friedan, *Feminine Mystique*, 60–61.

19 David Halberstam, *The Fifties* (New York: Villard Books, 1993; Ballantine, 1994), 597.

20 Deborah Siegel, *Sisterhood Interrupted: From Radical Women to Girls Gone Wild* (New York: Macmillan, 2007), 77.

21 Harry S Truman, 1945, as quoted in James T. Patterson, *Grand Expectations: The United States, 1945–1971* (New York: Oxford University Press, 1996), 35.

22 "The Pill" (2003, *American Experience*, PBS). http://www.pbs.org/wgbh/amex /pill/timeline/timeline2.html

23 John F. Kennedy, remarks upon signing the Equal Pay Act into law, June 10, 1963. http://www.presidency.ucsb.edu/ws/?pid=9267

24 *American Women: Report of the President's Commission on the Status of Women*, 1963.

25 Katharine St. George, February 8, 1964, as quoted in *Congressional Record* 110, Pt. 2 (February 8, 1964), 2581.

26 *New York Times*, January 28, 1964.

27 Howard Smith, February 8, 1964, as quoted in *Congressional Record* 110, Pt. 2 (February 8, 1964), 2577.

28 *New York Times*, February 9, 1964.

29 Martha Griffiths, as quoted in Jo Freeman, *We Will Be Heard: Women's Struggles for Political Power in the United States* (Lanham, MD: Rowman & Littlefield, 2008), 181.

30 Katharine St. George, February 8, 1964, as quoted in *Congressional Record* 110, Pt. 2 (February 8, 1964), 2581.

31 Lyndon B. Johnson, news conference, February 1, 1964. http://www. presidency.ucsb.edu/ws/?pid=26055

32 Jo Freeman, *The Politics of Women's Liberation* (New York: Longman, 1975), 53–54.

33 "We'll Sing in the Sunshine" (1963; written by Gale Garnett).

CHAPTER 8

1 Cassius Clay, at press conference the morning after he won the World Heavyweight Boxing Championship, as quoted in Robert Lipsyte, "Clay Discusses His Future, Liston and Black Muslims," *New York Times*, February 27, 1964.

2 Malcolm X, *Malcolm X Speaks* (George Breitman, ed.) (New York: Merit Publishers, 1965), 51.

3 David Remnick, *King of the World: Muhammad Ali and the Rise of an American Hero* (New York: Random House, 1998), 158.

4 Muhammad Ali, as quoted in Alex Haley, Foreword, *Autobiography of Malcolm X* (New York: Grove Press, 1965), 35.

5   Ferdie Pacheco, as quoted in Randy Roberts and Johnny Smith, *Blood Brothers: The Fatal Friendship between Muhammad Ali and Malcolm X* (New York: Basic Books, 2016), ix.

6   Gerald Early, *The Culture of Bruising: Prizefighting, Literature and Modern American Culture* (New York: Ecco Press, 1994), 246.

7   Haley, Foreword, *Autobiography of Malcolm X*, 17.

8   C. Eric Lincoln, *The Black Muslims in America* (Boston: Beacon, 1963), 10–15.

9   *Autobiography of Malcolm X*, 79.

10 Anna Malaika Tubbs, *The Three Mothers: How the Mothers of Martin Luther King Jr., Malcolm X, and James Baldwin Shaped the Nation* (New York: Flatiron Books, 2021), 120.

11 *Autobiography of Malcolm X*, 118.

12 *Autobiography of Malcolm X*, 497.

13 *Autobiography of Malcolm X*, 497.

14 Roberts and Smith, *Blood Brothers*, 29.

15 https://www.youtube.com/watch?v=GsOR6wGcG9M

16 Roberts and Smith, *Blood Brothers*, 34.

17 Haley, Foreword, *Autobiography of Malcolm X*, 54.

18 Randy Roberts and Johnny Smith, "The Branding of Muhammad Ali," *New Republic*, June 4, 2016.

19 As quoted in Horn, "Who Made Me—Is Me!" 42.

20 Lamont Johnson, as quoted in Remnick, *King of the World*, 82.

21 Remnick, *King of the World*, 87.

22 Jack Olsen, *Black Is Best: The Riddle of Cassius Clay* (New York: Dell, 1967), 140.

23 Roberts and Smith, *Blood Brothers*, 18.

24 Cassius Clay, as quoted in Huston Horn, "Who Made Me—Is Me!" *Sports Illustrated*, September 25, 1961, 47.

25 Remnick, *King of the World*, xiii.

26 *Ebony*, March 1963, as quoted in Thomas Hauser, *Muhammad Ali: His Life and Times* (New York: Simon & Schuster, 1991), 81.

27 Remnick, *King of the World*, 125.

28 George Kimball and John Schulian, eds., *At the Fights: American Writers on Boxing* (New York: Library of America, 2011).

29 Sonny Liston, as quoted in W. K. Stratton, *Floyd Patterson: The Fighting Life of Boxing's Invisible Champion* (Boston: Houghton Mifflin Harcourt, 2012), 146.

30 Cassius Clay, as quoted in Hauser, *Muhammad Ali: His Life and Times*, 58.

31 Hauser, *Muhammad Ali: His Life and Times*, 58–59.

32 Alex Haley, "An Interview with Cassius Clay," *Playboy*, October 1964. http://www.alexhaley.com/alex_haley_cassius_clay_interview.htm

33 *Autobiography of Malcolm X*, 414.

34 *Autobiography of Malcolm X*, 413.

35 Ferdie Pacheco, as quoted in Roberts and Smith, *Blood Brothers*, Preface.

36 Roberts and Smith, *Blood Brothers*, Preface.

37 Ferdie Pacheco, as quoted in Remnick, *King of the World*, 165.

38 Kevin Boyle, *The Shattering: America in the 1960s* (New York: Norton, 2021), 127.

39 "Malcolm X Scores Kennedy and U.S.," *New York Times*, December 2, 1963.

40 *Autobiography of Malcolm X*, 410–11.

41 *Malcolm X: Make It Plain* (PBS American Experience, 1994) http://www.pbs .org/wgbh//amex/malcolmx/filmmore/pt.html

42 *Autobiography of Malcolm X*, 413–16.

43 Remnick, *King of the World*, 169.

44 Roberts and Smith, *Blood Brothers*, 158.

45 *Autobiography of Malcolm X*, 417.

46 Elijah Muhammad, as quoted in Roberts and Smith, *Blood Brothers*, 171.

47 Cassius Clay, "A Song of Myself" (1964). http://www.monologues.co.uk /Celebrity/Song_of_Myself.htm

48 Haley, "Interview with Cassius Clay."

49 Haley, "Interview with Cassius Clay."

50 Sonny Liston, as quoted in Roberts and Smith, *Blood Brothers*, 151.

51 Remnick, *King of the World*, 177.

52 "Hysterical Outbursts at Weigh-In Cost Clay $2,500," *New York Times*, February 26, 1964; Remnick, *King of the World*, 178–82.

53 Haley, "Interview with Cassius Clay."

54 Haley, "Interview with Cassius Clay."

55 Lipsyte, "Clay Is Exultant."

56 The 2020 film *One Night in Miami* is a fictionalized version of this gathering.

57 Jim Brown, as quoted in Hauser, *Muhammad Ali: His Life and Times*, 106; Roberts and Smith, *Blood Brothers*, 200.

58 "Clay Says He Has Adopted Islam Religion and Regards It as a Way to Peace," *New York Times*, February 28, 1964.

59 Lipsyte, "Clay Discusses His Future"; Remnick, *King of the World*, 206–7.

60 Roberts and Smith, *Blood Brothers*, Preface.

61 Cassius Clay, as quoted in "Clay Says He Has Adopted Islam."

62 Gerald Eskenazi, "World Boxing Group Threatens to Lift Clay's Title," *New York Times*, March 23, 1964.

63 Floyd Patterson, as quoted in Gay Talese, "Patterson Gears Body and Mind for Day of Victory over Clay, *New York Times*, March 22, 1964.

64 Elijah Muhammad, as quoted in Taylor Branch, *Pillar of Fire: America in the King Years, 1963–65* (New York: Simon & Schuster, 1998), 251.

65 *Louisville Courier-Journal*, March 8, 1964, as quoted in Roberts and Smith, *Blood Brothers*, 221.

66 Cassius Clay, as quoted in Tom Wolfe, "The Marvelous Mouth," *Esquire*, October 1963, 192.

67 Muhammad Ali and Hannah Yasmeen Ali, *The Soul of a Butterfly: Reflections on Life's Journey* (New York: Simon & Schuster, 2004), 84.

68 Roberts and Smith, *Blood Brothers*, 218.

69 Muhammad Ali, as quoted in Remnick, *King of the World*, 214.

70 Remnick, *King of the World*, 215.

71 Haley, "Interview with Cassius Clay."

72 "Muhammad Ali in Ghana," *Sports Illustrated*, June 1, 1964.

73 *Autobiography of Malcolm X*, 457.

74 Hauser, *Muhammad Ali: His Life and Times*, 112.

75 *Autobiography of Malcolm X*, 479.

76 Malcolm X, as quoted in Don Atyeo and Felix Dennis, *The Holy Warrior: Muhammad Ali* (London: Bunch Books, 1975), 53.

77 Malcolm X, "The Ballot or the Bullet," Cleveland, Ohio, April 3, 1964. http://www.edchange.org/multicultural/speeches/malcolm_x_ballot.html

78 Goldman, *Death and Life of Malcolm X*, 165.

79 *Autobiography of Malcolm X*, 433.

80 *Autobiography of Malcolm X*, 447.

81 Roberts and Smith, *Blood Brothers*, 247.

82 *Autobiography of Malcolm X*, 483.

83 Louis Farrakhan, *Muhammad Speaks*, December 4, 1964, as quoted in *New York Times*, March 13, 1994.

84 Zak A. Kondo, *Conspiracys: Unraveling the Assassination of Malcolm X* (Washington, DC: Nubia Press, 1993), 170.

85 *Muhammad Speaks*, April 10, 1964. http://www.columbia.edu/cu/ccbh/mxp/images/sourcebook_img_111.jpg

86 *New York Times*, November 22, 2021.

87 El-Hajj Malik El-Shabazz (Malcolm X), "Prospects for Freedom in 1965," Militant Labor Forum, New York, January 7, 1965. *Malcolm X Speaks*, 148.

88 "The Murder of Malcolm X," *New York Post*, February 22, 1965, as quoted in Russell J. Rickford, *Betty Shabazz, Surviving Malcolm X: A Remarkable Story of Survival and Faith before and after Malcolm X* (Naperville, IL: Sourcebooks, 2005), 247.

89 Robert Lipsyte, as quoted in Remnick, *King of the World*, 156–57.

90 Roberts and Smith, *Blood Brothers*, 103–4.

91 *Pittsburgh Courier*, Feb 2, 1963; Roberts and Smith, *Blood Brothers*, 105–6.

92 Jerry Izenberg, *Once There Were Giants: The Golden Age of Heavyweight Boxing* (New York: Skyhorse Publishing, 2017).

93 Eldridge Cleaver, *Soul on Ice* (New York: McGraw-Hill, 1968), 92.

94 Remnick, *King of the World*, 158.

95 Robert Lipsyte, "The Beatles and Clay Spar a Fast Roundalay," *New York Times*, February 19. 1964; George Varga, "Beatles Were a Knockout for Muhammad Ali in 1964," *Miami Herald*, June 4, 2016. http://www.miamiherald.com/news/nation-world/national/article81828347.html; Roberts and Smith, *Blood Brothers*, 168–69.

96 "Cassius Cuts a Disk, a Caper and a Defeated Sonny Liston," *New York Times*, March 4, 1964.

97 "Advertising: 'Greatest'—but Can He Sell/" *New York Times*, February 27, 1964.

98   Lawrence W. Levine, *Black Culture and Black Consciousness: Afro-American Folk Thought from Slavery to Freedom* (New York: Oxford University Press, 1977), 349–50.

99   Mike Rubin, "Muhammad Ali: 4 Ways He Changed America," *Rolling Stone*, June 5, 2016. http://www.rollingstone.com/culture/news/muhammad-ali-4 -ways-he-changed-america-20160605

100 Preezy da Kid, "Did Muhammad Ali Give Birth to Hip-Hop 50 Years Ago Today," *Uproxx*, February 25, 2014. http://uproxx.com/smokingsection /muhammad-ali-february-25th-1964-spirit-hip-hop/

101 Angus Batey, "Muhammad Ali's Influence Ran Deep through Rap's Golden Age," *The Guardian*, June 6, 2016. https://www.theguardian.com/music /musicblog/2016/jun/06/muhammad-ali-influence-rap-golden-age

102 "SNCC Position Paper: On Vietnam," January 6, 1966. http://www2.iath .virginia.edu/sixties/HTML_docs/Resources/Primary/Manifestos/SNCC _VN.html

103 Muhammad Ali, as quoted in Rubin, "Muhammad Ali: 4 Ways He Changed America."

104 Stefan Fatsis, "No Vietcong Ever Called Me Nigger," *Slate*, June 8. 2016. http://www.slate.com/articles/sports/sports_nut/2016/06/did_muhammad _ali_ever_say_no_viet_cong_ever_called_me_nigger.html

105 Jerry Izenberg, "A Year Later, Looking Back at How Muhammad Ali Was Remembered," *Newark Star-Ledger*, June 3, 2017. http://www.nj.com/sports /index.ssf/2017/06/a_year_later_looking_back_at_how_muhammad_ali_was. html

106 Ossie Davis, Eulogy at the Funeral of Malcolm X.

107 M. S. Handler, "Negro Factions Are Considering a United Front," *New York Times*, July 29, 1964.

108 *Autobiography of Malcolm X*, 489.

109 *Autobiography of Malcolm X*, 488.

110 http://content.time.com/time/magazine/article/0,9171,988496,00.html

111 *Autobiography of Malcolm X*, 496.

112 Dick Gregory, as quoted in Goldman, *Death and Life of Malcolm X*, 23.

113 Ali, *Soul of a Butterfly*, 85.

CHAPTER 9

1   Will Rogers, as quoted in Paula McSpadden Love, *The Will Rogers Book* (Waco, TX: Texian Press, 1972), 119.

2   Lyndon Johnson telephone conversation with Richard Russell, June 11, 1964, in Michael R. Beschloss, ed., *Taking Charge: The Johnson White House Tapes, 1963– 1964* (New York: Simon & Schuster, 1997), 402.

3   LBJ, as quoted in Doris Kearns, *Lyndon Johnson and the American Dream* (New York: Harper & Row, 1976), 251–52.

4   Ho Chi Minh, as quoted in Stanley Karnow, *Vietnam: A History* (New York: Viking, 1983; rev. ed.: Penguin, 1997), 169.
5   William Safire, "On Language: Free World," *New York Times Magazine*, August 31, 2008.
6   David Halberstam, *The Best and the Brightest* (New York: Random House, 1972), 329–31.
7   Ho Chi Minh, as quoted in Stanley Karnow, *Vietnam: A History* (New York: Viking, 1983; rev. ed.: Penguin, 1997), 169.
8   Pham Van Dong, as quoted in Karnow, *Vietnam*, 220, 345.
9   Norodom Sihanouk, Nov. 11, 1967, as quoted in Philip Short, *Pol Pot: Anatomy of a Nightmare* (New York: Macmillam, 2007), 181.
10 Graham Greene, *The Quiet American* (London, Heinemann, 1955; Penguin, 2004), 52.
11 Greene, *Quiet American*, 86.
12 Greene, *Quiet American*, 10.
13 Greene, *Quiet American*, 171.
14 Greene, *Quiet American*, 78.
15 Greene, *Quiet American*, 168.
16 Greene, *Quiet American*, 52.
17 Greene, *Quiet American*, 144.
18 Robert Stone, Introduction to Greene, *Quiet American*, xvii.
19 Greene, *Quiet American*, 166.
20 LBJ in telephone conversation with McGeorge Bundy, May 26, 1964, in Beschloss, ed., *Taking Charge*, 372.
21 Theodore C. Sorensen and Arthur Schlesinger Jr., "What Would J.F.K. Have Done?" *New York Times*, December 4, 2005.
22 LBJ, as quoted in Gayle B. Montgomery, James W. Johnson and Paul Manolis, *One Step from the White House: The Rise and Fall of Senator William F. Knowland* (Berkeley and Los Angeles: University of California Press, 1998), 170.
23 As quoted in Karnow, *Vietnam*, 340–41.
24 Lyndon B. Johnson, *The Vantage Point: Perspectives of the Presidency, 1963–1969* (New York: Holt, Rinehart and Winston, 1971), 63.
25 LBJ, as quoted in Charles A. Stevenson, *Warriors and Politicians: Civil-Military Relations under Stress* (New York: Routledge, 2006), 53.
26 LBJ, telephone conversation with John Knight, February 3, 1964, as quoted in Robert A. Caro, *The Years of Lyndon Johnson: The Passage of Power* (New York: Knopf, 2012), 534.
27 NSC Action Memorandum 288, March 17, 1964, Karnow, *Vietnam*, 358.
28 LBJ in telephone conversation with McGeorge Bundy, May 26, 1964, in Beschloss, *Taking Charge*, 372.
29 LBJ telephone conversation with Richard Russell, June 11, 1964, in Beschloss, *Taking Charge*, 401–2. Emphasis added.
30 LBJ telephone conversation with Richard Russell, June 11, 1964, in Beschloss, *Taking Charge*, 403.

31   Kearns, *Lyndon Johnson and the American Dream*, 253.
32   Tim O'Brien, *The Things They Carried* (New York: Houghton Mifflin, 1990; Penguin, 1991), 48–49, 63.

CHAPTER 10

1   Keith Richards, *Life* (New York: Little, Brown, 2010), 159.
2   Paul McCartney, as quoted in David Remnick, "Paul McCartney Doesn't Really Want to Stop the Show," *New Yorker*, October 11, 2021.
3   Philip Norman. *Mick Jagger* (New York: Ecco, 2012), 163.
4   http://www.songfacts.com/detail.php?id=413
5   http://www.songfacts.com/detail.php?id=413
6   Joyce Maynard, *Looking Back: A Chronicle of Growing Up Old in the Sixties* (Garden City, NY: Doubleday, 1973), 35.
7   Richards, *Life*, 159.
8   Alan Clayson, *Mick Jagger: The Unauthorized Biography* (London: Sanctuary, 2005), 22.
9   Clayson, *Jagger*, 26.
10   Citizens' Council of Greater New Orleans circular, as quoted in Timothy E. Scheurer, *American Popular Music: The Age of Rock* (Madison: University of Wisconsin, 1990), 171.
11   Bruce Watson, *Freedom Summer: The Savage Season that Made Mississippi Burn and Made America a Democracy* (New York: Viking, 2010), 201.
12   "How Whites Feel About a Painful America," *Newsweek*, October 21, 1963, 44–51.
13   Kerouac, *On the Road*, 115.
14   Kerouac, *On the Road*, 180.
15   *Gooch* and *goochie* were regional slang terms used for *vagina*. This appears to be the source of "hoochie coochie man" as one who could readily get into that part of the anatomy of numerous women.
16   Richards, *Life*, 109–10.
17   Kerouac, *On the Road*, 4.
18   I am indebted to my former student Lizz Gardner for pointing me toward some of these insights in her journal of December 2004.
19   Kerouac, *On the Road*, 180.
20   For a deeper and more contemporary exploration of this phenomenon, see Greg Tate, *Everything But the Burden: What White People Are Taking from Black Culture* (New York: Random House, 2003).
21   Norman Mailer, *Advertisements for Myself* (New York: Putnam, 1959), 23.
22   "The Pilgrim, Chapter 33" (1971; written by Kris Kristofferson).
23   Richards, *Life*, 149–51.
24   Mick Jagger, Dora Lowenstein, and Philip Dodd, *According to the Rolling Stones*. San Francisco: Chronicle Books, 2003), 42; Stanley Booth, *The True Adventures of the Rolling Stones* (1984; Chicago: Chicago Review Press, 2000), 140.

25 "I'm a King Bee" (1957, written by James Moore [Slim Harpo]).

26 As quoted in Clayson, *Jagger*, 47.

27 Eric Easton to Paul Drew, May 26, 1964. https://garyrocks.wordpress.com/2015/01/25/eric-easton-hopes-the-rolling-stones-will-be-accepted-by-the-american-public/

28 Richards, *Life*, 167, 170, 166.

29 "Moves Like Jagger" (2011, lyrics by Adam Levine, Benny Blanco, Ammar Malik and Shellback).

30 Norman. *Mick Jagger*, 147.

31 Norman, *Mick Jagger*, 146.

32 Richards, *Life*, 8, 153.

33 Steven D. Stark, *Meet the Beatles: A Cultural History of the Band that Shook Youth, Gender, and the World* (New York: HarperEntertainment, 2005), 155.

34 Richards, *Life*, 161.

35 As quoted in Watson, *Freedom Summer*, 113.

36 *Magic Trip: Ken Kesey's Search for a Kool Place* (2011, directed by Alex Gibney and Alison Ellwood, Magnolia Pictures).

37 *Magic Trip*; Stephen Holden, "Stoned Archive: Wild Ride of the Merry Pranksters," *New York Times*, August 4, 2011; Dominck Cavallo, *A Fiction of the Past: The Sixties in American History* (New York: St. Martin's, 1999), 110–12; "LSD Road Trip," *Witness History*, BBC https://www.bbc.co.uk/sounds/play/p0253hsr

38 Richards, *Life*, 151.

39 Rolling Stones on *The Hollywood Palace*, ABC, June 13, 1964. http://retronewser.com/2014/06/03/the-rolling-stones-tape-first-american-tv-appearance-50-years-ago-today-june-3-1964/

40 "I Just Want to Make Love to You" (1954, written by Willie Dixon).

41 Norman, *Mick Jagger*, 148.

42 Graham Gordon, *Rebels with a Cause: The Secret History of the Original Rolling Stones* (independently published, 2017), 99–100; Norman, *Mick Jagger*, 149–51.

43 Richards, *Life*, 163.

44 Booth, *True Adventures of the Rolling Stones*, 157–59; "The Rolling Stones, the Glasgow Fair, and a Riot in Blackpool," *The Scotsman*, June 7, 2018. https://www.scotsman.com/arts-and-culture/rolling-stones-glasgow-fair-and-riot-blackpool-284178;.

45 Norman, *Mick Jagger*, 159.

46 *Ed Sullivan Show*, CBS, February 23, 1964. http://www.youtube.com/watch?v=Ft5YC31PDqw.

47 Rolling Stones, "Time Is on My Side," *Ed Sullivan Show*, October 25, 1964. https://www.youtube.com/watch?v=Wiho7GoubFM

48 Jessica Damiano, "Rolling Stones on 'Ed Sullivan': All Hell Breaks Loose," *Newsday*, October 25, 2011. http://www.newsday.com/entertainment/pop-cult-1.811972/rolling-stones-on-ed-sullivan-all-hell-breaks-loose-1.3271090.

49 The Official Ed Sullivan Site. http://www.edsullivan.com/artists/the-rolling-stones/

50 Robert Gore-Langton, "The Original Bad Boys of Rock," *Express*, July 12, 2012. http://www.express.co.uk/posts/view/332351/The-original-bad-boys-of-rock

51 Rolling Stones, "Let's Spend *Some Time* Together," *Ed Sullivan Show*, CBS, January 15, 1967. http://www.youtube.com/watch?v=6tjs3utYrSY

52 Joel Whitburn, *The Billboard Hot 100 Charts: The Sixties* (Menonomee Falls, WI: Record Research, 1990).

53 T.A.M.I. was sometimes said to stand for "Teenage Awards Music International."

54 Norman, *Mick Jagger*, 161.

55 *T.A.M.I. Show* (1964, directed by Steve Binder, AIP).

56 Geoffrey Cannon, as quoted in http://www.discoogle.com/wiki/Wyman,_Bill.

57 Tom Wolfe, as quoted in Stark, *Meet the Beatles*, 156.

58 Richards, *Life*, 181.

CHAPTER 11

1 Michael Schwerner, May 1964, as quoted in William Bradford Huie, *Three Lives for Mississippi* (New York: WWC Books, 1965; reprint: Jackson: University Press of Mississippi, 2000), 73.

2 Lawrence W. Levine, *Black Culture and Black Consciousness* (New York: Oxford University Press, 1977), 329.

3 John Lewis, as quoted in Jon Meacham, *His Truth Is Marching On: John Lewis and the Power of Hope* (New York: Random House, 2020), 56.

4 John Lewis, as quoted in Milton Viorst, *Fire in the Streets: America in the 1960s* (New York: Simon & Schuster, 1979), 104.

5 James Lawson, eulogy at funeral of John Lewis, July 30, 2020. https://www.youtube.com/watch?v=YOxpSPT5PnI.

6 Ella Baker, as quoted in Meacham, *His Truth Is Marching On*, 61.

7 Bob Moses, as quoted in Godfrey Hodgson, *America in Our Time: From World War II to Nixon—What Happened and Why* (Garden City, NY: Doubleday, 1976; New York: Vintage, 1978), 207.

8 Robert Moses, with Charles E. Cobb Jr., *Radical Equations: Civil Rights from Mississippi to the Algebra Project* (Boston: Beacon, 2001, 2002), 44.

9 Aaron Henry, as quoted in Chris Myers Asch, *The Senator and the Sharecropper: The Freedom Struggles of James O. Eastland and Fannie Lou Hamer* (Chapel Hill: University of North Carolina, 2011).

10 John Dittmer, *Local People: The Struggle for Civil Rights in Mississippi* (Urbana and Chicago: University of Illinois Press, 1994), 200.

11 Clayborne Carson, *In Struggle: SNCC and the Black Awakening of the 1960s* (Cambridge, MA: Harvard University Press, 1981), 98.

12 Edwin King, as quoted in Dittmer, *Local People*, 204.

13 Dave Dennis, as quoted in Dittmer, *Local People*, 205.

14 Willie Peacock, remarks at the "Freedom Summer Reviewed" conference, Tougaloo College and Millsaps College, October 30–November 2, 1979.

15 Bob Moses and Fannie Lou Hamer, as quoted in Dittmer, *Local People*, 209.

16 James Forman, *The Making of Black Revolutionaries* (Washington, DC: Open Head, 1985), 385.

17 Bob Moses, as quoted in James Atwater, "'If We Can Crack Mississippi . . .'," *Saturday Evening Post*, July 25, 1964, 16.

18 Dave Dennis, as quoted in Howell Raines, *My Soul Is Rested: Movement Days in the Deep South Remembered* (New York: Putnam, 1977, Penguin, 1983), 274.

19 Mao Zedong, as quoted in A. J. Langguth, *Our Vietnam: The War, 1954–1975* (New York: Simon & Schuster, 2000), 118.

20 Moses, *Radical Equations*, 38.

21 Willie (Wazir) Peacock, interview, July 2001, Veterans of the Civil Rights Movement. http://www.crmvet.org/tim/timhis62.htm#1962–4.

22 Bob Moses, as quoted in Sally Belfrage, *Freedom Summer* (New York: Viking, 1965), 10.

23 Belfrage, *Freedom Summer*, 3. (Belfrage was in the second training group, which arrived a week later, on June 21, but the experience with song was the same with the group that arrived on June 14.)

24 Bob Moses, June 14, 1964, as quoted in Seth Cagin and Philip Dray, *We Are Not Afraid: The Story of Goodman, Schwerner, and Chaney and the Civil Rights Campaign for Mississippi* (New York: Macmillan, 1988), 30.

25 Paul Johnson Jr., June 1964, as quoted in Belfrage, *Freedom Summer*, 21.

26 William J. Simmons, interview, November 8, 1985, for *Eyes on the Prize: America's Civil Rights Years* (produced by Blackside, Inc.). Henry Hampton Collection, Washington University Film and Media Archive. http://digital. wustl.edu/cgi/t/text/text-idx?c=eop;cc=eop;rgn=main;view=text;idno=s im0015.1044.097.

27 Bruce Watson, *Freedom Summer: The Savage Season that Made Mississippi Burn and Made America a Democracy* (New York: Viking, 2010), 146.

28 Letter to Turner Catledge, quoted in Cagin and Dray, *We Are Not Afraid*, 15.

29 Walter Cronkite, "Mississippi 1964: Civil Rights and Unrest," June 16, 2005. National Public Radio. http://www.npr.org/templates/story/story. php?storyId=4706688.

30 Cagin and Dray, *We Are Not Afraid*, 39.

31 Cagin and Dray, *We Are Not Afraid*, 19, 38.

32 Dittmer, *Local People*, 251.

33 Bob Moses, June 22, 1964, as quoted in Belfrage, *Freedom Summer*, 11.

34 Len Holt, *The Summer That Didn't End* (New York: Morrow, 1965), 264.

35 Martin Popper, as quoted in "Lynching of Chaney, Schwerner & Goodman," Civil Rights Movement Veterans. http://www.crmvet.org/tim/tim64b. htm#1964csg.

36 Claude Sitton, "3 in Rights Drive Reported Missing," *New York Times*, June 23, 1964.

37   Associated Press, "Charred Hulk of Car Spurs Intense Search," *New Haven Register*, June 24, 1964.
38   Ellen Barry, "Killen Guilty of Manslaughter in 1964 Civil Rights Slayings," *Los Angeles Times*, June 22, 2005.
39   Governor Paul Johnson Jr., July 13, 1964, as quoted in Cagin and Dray, *We Are Not Afraid*, 370.
40   "Mississippi: God Bless Everyone," *Time*, January 31, 1964.
41   Dittmer, *Local People*, 276.
42   Letter from Tchula, Mississippi, July 16, 1964, in Elizabeth Sutherland Martínez, *Letters from Mississippi* (New York: McGraw-Hill, 1965; Brookline, MA: Zephyr Press, 2002), 218.

CHAPTER 12

1   Bob Moses, as quoted in Seth Cagin and Philip Dray, *We Are Not Afraid: The Story of Goodman, Schwerner, and Chaney and the Civil Rights Campaign for Mississippi* (New York: Macmillan, 1988), 30.
2   Richard Russell and LBJ, as quoted in Robert Dallek, *Flawed Giant: Lyndon Johnson and His Times, 1961–1973* (New York: Oxford University Press, 1998), 112.
3   LBJ, as quoted in Bill Moyers, "What a Real President Was Like," *Washington Post*, November 13, 1988; Bill Moyers, *Moyers on America: A Journalist and his Times* (2004; New York: Anchor, 2005), 197.
4   James Farmer in *The American Experience: The Presidents: Lyndon Johnson* (PBS, 2008). http://www.pbs.org/wgbh/americanexperience/features/transcript/lbj-transcript/
5   Roger Wilkins in *The American Experience: The Presidents: Lyndon Johnson* (PBS, 2008). http://www.pbs.org/wgbh/americanexperience/features/transcript/lbj-transcript/
6   LBJ, as quoted in Doris Kearns, *Lyndon Johnson and the American Dream* (New York: Harper & Row, 1976), 54.
7   As quoted in Randall Woods, *LBJ: Architect of American Ambition* (New York: Simon & Schuster, 2007), 411–412.
8   Dallek, *Flawed Giant*, 116.
9   Robert D. Loevy, "A Brief History of the Civil Rights Act of 1964," in David C. Kozak and Kenneth N. Ciboski, editors, *The American Presidency* (Chicago, IL: Nelson Hall, 1985), 411–419.
10   LBJ, as quoted in Scott Barbour, *Lyndon B. Johnson* (Farmington Hills, MI: Greenhaven Press, 2001), 127.
11   George Wallace, as quoted in Allen J. Matusow, *The Unraveling of America: A History of Liberalism in the 1960s* (New York: Harper & Row, 1984), 139.
12   "Wallace Considers Primaries in North," *New York Times*, January 11, 1964.
13   *New York Times*, April 9, 1964; May 6, 1964.

14 Lyndon Baines Johnson, *The Vantage Point: Perspectives on the Presidency, 1963–1969* (New York: Holt, Rinehart and Winston, 1971), 159.

15 Loevy, "Brief History of the Civil Rights Act."

16 Hubert Humphrey, as quoted in Merle Miller, *Lyndon: An Oral Biography* (New York: Putnam, 1980), 369.

17 Johnson, *Vantage Point*, 159.

18 Humphrey, as quoted in Miller, *Lyndon*, 368.

19 Humphrey, as quoted in Woods, *LBJ: Architect of American Ambition*, 474.

20 Woods, *LBJ: Architect of American Ambition*, 474.

21 Loevy, "Brief History of the Civil Rights Act."

22 LBJ, as quoted in Woods, *LBJ: Architect of American Ambition*, 475.

23 Dallek, *Flawed Giant*, 113–14.

24 Woods, *LBJ: Architect of American Ambition*, 477.

25 Everett Dirksen, as quoted in Dallek, *Flawed Giant*, 119.

26 Dallek, *Flawed Giant*, 120.

27 Russell, as quoted in Miller, *Lyndon*, 450.

28 It is more than mere coincidence that every Democrat who won a presidential election in the forty-four years from the passage of the 1964 Civil Rights Act to Barack Obama's victory in 2008 was from the South: Johnson, Jimmy Carter, Bill Clinton, and Al Gore (yes; he won the 2000 election).

29 Lee White, as quoted in Dallek, *Flawed Giant*, 120.

30 Transcript of President Johnson's Address on the Civil Rights Bill, *New York Times*, July 3, 1964.

31 Bruce Watson, *Freedom Summer: The Savage Season that Made Mississippi Burn and Made America a Democracy* (New York: Viking, 2010), 132.

32 LBJ, as quoted in Dallek, *Flawed Giant*, 120.

33 Dallek, *Flawed Giant*, 121.

34 James Bevel, as quoted in Diane McWhorter, *Carry Me Home: Birmingham, Alabama, The Climactic Battle of the Civil Rights Revolution* (New York: Simon & Schuster, 2001), 361.

35 LBJ, in *The American Experience: The Presidents: Lyndon Johnson* (PBS, 2008). http://www.pbs.org/wgbh/americanexperience/features/transcript/lbj-transcript/

36 Dallek, *Flawed Giant*, 83.

37 LBJ, March 1964, as quoted in Richard Goodwin, *Remembering America: A Voice from the Sixties* (Boston: Little Brown, 1988), 257.

38 Michael Janeway, *The Fall of the House of Roosevelt: Brokers of Ideas and Power from FDR to LBJ* (New York: Columbia University Press, 2004), Chapter 1.

39 Michael Harrington, *The Other America* (New York: Macmillan, 1962).

40 Matusow, *Unraveling of America*, 107–19.

41 Johnson, *Vantage Point*, 74.

42 Matusow, *Unraveling of America*, 123.

43 Dallek, *Flawed Giant*, 75.

44   LBJ, Remarks upon Signing the Economic Opportunity Act, August 20, 1964. http://www.presidency.ucsb.edu/ws/?pid=26452#axzz2h4FbN900

45   Dallek, *Flawed Giant*, 80–81.

46   LBJ, "The Great Society," Commencement Address, University of Michigan, May 22, 1964. http://www.pbs.org/wgbh/americanexperience/features /primary-resources/lbj-michigan/

47   Dallek, *Flawed Giant*, 82–83.

48   Barbara Benson, Brooklyn, NY, letter to the editor, July 20, 1964 "Why Harlem Negroes Riot," *New York Times*, July 22, 1964.

49   Lyndon Johnson telephone conversation with Richard Russell, June 11, 1964, in Michael R. Beschloss, ed., *Taking Charge: The Johnson White House Tapes, 1963–1964* (New York: Simon & Schuster, 1997), 402.

50   Fred C. Shapiro and James W. Sullivan, *Race Riots, New York, 1964* (New York: Crowell, 1964). 4.

51   Paul L. Montgomery and Francis X. Clines, "Thousands Riot in Harlem Area; Scores Are Hurt," *New York Times*, July 19, 1964.

52   Shapiro and Sullivan, *Race Riots, New York, 1964*, 50.

53   Benson, letter to the editor, *New York Times*, July 22, 1964.

54   George Reedy in conversation with LBJ, July 20, 1964, in Beschloss, *Taking Charge*, 459.

55   Statement by the President," *New York Times*, July 22, 1964.

56   "Brooklyn Riots Continue; Police Shoot 2 as Looters," *New York Times*, July 23, 1964.

57   "The North: Doing No Good," *Time*, September 4, 1964.

58   Elizabeth Hinton, *America on Fire: The Untold History of Police Violence and Black Rebellion since the 1960s*. New York: Liveright, 2021.

59   Theodore H. White, *The Making of the President–1964* (New York: Atheneum, 1965), 234.

60   Rick Perlstein, *Nixonland: The Rise of a President and the Fracturing of America* (New York: Scribner, 2008), 3–19.

CHAPTER 13

1   Bob Moses, as quoted in Bruce Watson, *Freedom Summer: The Savage Season that Made Mississippi Burn and Made America a Democracy* (New York: Viking, 2010), 73.

2   Patricia R. Schroeder, *Robert Johnson, Mythmaking, and Contemporary American Culture* (Urbana: University of Illinois Press, 2004), 36–39.

3   Sylvie, letter written from Oxford, Ohio, June 24, 1964, in Elizabeth Sutherland Martínez, *Letters from Mississippi* (New York: McGraw-Hill, 1965; Brookline, MA: Zephyr Press, 2002), 32.

4   Robert Coles, *Farewell to the South* (Boston: Little, Brown, 1972), 246–47, 269

5   Watson, *Freedom Summer*, 101–102.

6   James Forman, interview with Doug McAdam, August 29, 1985, as quoted in
     McAdam, *Freedom Summer*, 40.

7   McAdam, *Freedom Summer*, 35, 292–93 n. 1.

8   *Washington Post*, June 25, 1964.

9   "Mississippi: Allen's Army," *Newsweek*, February 24, 1964.

10   Watson, *Freedom Summer*, 53–54. The "rape gang" story was reported in the
     Tupelo Journal, June 19. 1964.

11   Letter from unnamed volunteer, quoted in John Dittmer, *Local People: The
     Struggle for Civil Rights in Mississippi* (Urbana and Chicago: University of Illinois
     Press, 1994), 246.

12   Sally Belfrage, *Freedom Summer* (New York: Viking, 1965), 28.

13   James Forman, June 1964, as quoted in Belfrage, *Freedom Summer*, 25.

14   Bob Moses, June 1964, as quoted in Belfrage, *Freedom Summer*, 10.

15   Belfrage, *Freedom Summer*, 22.

16   Sara M. Evans, *Personal Politics: The Roots of Women's Liberation in the Civil Rights
     Movement and the New Left* (New York: Knopf, 1979, Vintage, 1980), 60.

17   Dave Dennis, as quoted in Dittmer, *Local People*, 249,

18   Watson, *Freedom Summer*, 211.

19   Watson, *Freedom Summer*, 238.

20   As quoted in Sutherland Martínez, *Letters from Mississippi*, 41.

21   Robert Miles, June 1964, as quoted in Watson, *Freedom Summer*, 59.

22   Charles Cobb, as quoted in Dittmer, *Local People*, 259.

23   Jane Stembridge, "Notes on Teaching in Mississippi," as quoted in Susie
     Erenrich, *Freedom is a Constant Struggle: An Anthology of the Mississippi Civil Rights
     Movement* (Montgomery, AL: Black Belt Press, 1999), 110.

24   Dittmer, *Local People*, 258–59.

25   MLK, July 21, 1964, Greenwood, Miss., as quoted in Watson, *Freedom Summer*,
     183.

26   Watson, *Freedom Summer*, 219–20

27   Watson, *Freedom Summer*, 180–81.

28   Mary King, *Freedom Song: A Personal History of the 1960s Civil Rights Movement*
     (New York: Morrow, 1987), 307–8.

29   MLK, July 21, 1964, Greenwood, Miss., as quoted in Watson, *Freedom Summer*,
     183.

30   Watson, *Freedom Summer*, 188.

31   Only a few years earlier, when racism was not the major issue it had become
     by 1964, Mississippians had been crowned Miss America two years in a row: in
     1958, Mary Ann Mobley was chosen as Miss America 1959 and in 1959 Lynda
     Mead took the crown for 1960.

32   BBC online, "1964: Poitier Breaks New Ground with Oscar Win."
     http://news.bbc.co.uk/onthisday/hi/dates/stories/april/13/
     newsid_2524000/2524235.stm; Aram Goudsouzian, *Sidney Poitier: Man, Actor,
     Icon* (Chapel Hill: University of North Carolina, 2004), 216–17.

33   Harry Belafonte, as quoted in Goudsouzian, *Sidney Poitier*, 224.

34   Watson, *Freedom Summer*, 218–19.

35   Sidney Poitier, as quoted in Goudsouzian, *Sidney Poitier*, 224.

36   Watson, *Freedom Summer*, 226.

37   Don Whitehead, *Attack on Terror: The FBI against the Ku Klux Klan in Mississippi* (New York: Funk & Wagnalls, 1970), 6–8.

38   Dittmer, *Local People*, 251.

39   The characterization was made by Oliver Emmerich, editor of the McComb *Enterprise-Journal*, who suffered a beating for denouncing the local terrorists, *New York Times*, April 2, 1978. Dittmer, *Local People*, 268.

40   Rick Perlstein, *Before the Storm: Barry Goldwater and the Unmaking of the American Consensus* (New York: Hill & Wang, 2001; New York: Nation Books, 2009), 363.

41   Watson, *Freedom Summer*, 190.

42   Watson, *Freedom Summer*, 138.

43   Chris Williams, as quoted in Watson, *Freedom Summer*, 23.

44   Pam Parker, letter to parents, June 30, 1964, as quoted in Doug McAdam, *Freedom Summer* (New York: Oxford University Press, 1988), 72.

45   I experienced this phenomenon myself a decade and a half later when I organized a fifteen-year retrospective conference on Freedom Summer, "Freedom Summer Reviewed," held over a four-day period at the end of October and beginning of November 1979, at Tougaloo and Millsaps colleges. Dozens of participants from the 1964 Summer Project were there, and the old differences flared anew on several occasions. Each time, though, someone would start singing a freedom song, everyone would join in, and harmony would be restored.

46   Dittmer, *Local People*, 264.

47   Dittmer, *Local People*, 368 ff.

CHAPTER 14

1   Barry Goldwater, Acceptance Speech, San Francisco, July 16, 1964. http:// www.washingtonpost.com/wp-srv/politics/daily/may98/goldwaterspeech .htm.

2   Theodore H. White, *The Making of the President—1964* (New York: Atheneum, 1965), 216–17.

3   M. Stanton Evans, et al., "The Sharon Statement," September 11, 1960. http://www.oac.cdlib.org/view?docId=kt5q2nb12s&brand=oac4&doc .view=entire_text

4   Heather Cox Richardson, *Letters from an American*, December 30, 2020. https:// heathercoxrichardson.substack.com/p/december-30-2020

5   Goldwater, as quoted in Jonathan Martin Kolkey, *The New Right, 1960–1968 with an Epilogue, 1969–1980* (Lanham, MD: University Press of America, 1983), 184.

6   Nancy MacLean, *Democracy in Chains: The Deep History of the Radical Right's Stealth Plan for America* (New York: Viking, 2017), 151; James M. Buchanan, *The Limits of Liberty: Between Anarchy and Leviathan* (Chicago: University of Chicago Press, 1975).

7   MacLean, *Democracy in Chains*, 118.

8   Richard Hofstadter, *Anti-Intellectualism in American Life* (New York: Knopf, 1963).

9   The practice of calling ideas that have no factual basis "theories" has helped them to gain traction. A theory in science has been substantially tested and sustained by evidence. "Conspiracy theories" are the opposite: crackpot beliefs that are accepted as articles of faith.

10 Richard Hofstadter, "The Paranoid Style in American Politics," *Harper's*, November 1964.

11 Richard M. Nixon, Address to the American People, September 23, 1952. http://www.presidency.ucsb.edu/ws/index.php?pid=24485

12 Heather Cox Richardson, *Letter from an American*, February 9, 2020. https://heathercoxrichardson.substack.com/p/february-9-2020

13 Allan J. Lichtman, *White Protestant Nation: The Rise of the American Conservative Movement* (New York: Grove, 2008), 240.

14 MacLean, *Democracy in Chains*, 46–71.

15 Stuart Stevens, *It Was All a Lie: How the Republican Party Became Donald Trump* (New York: Knopf, 2020), 85.

16 William F. Buckley Jr., as quoted in Rick Perlstein and Edward H. Miller, "The John Birch Society Never Left," *New Republic*, March 8, 2021.

17 In fact, many of those behind the scenes in this movement then—and even more in later decades down to the present—understood themselves not to be conservatives at all. They identified as radical right-wing revolutionaries. They adopted the term *conservative* as a misleading marketing label because they believed that they needed to hide their true intentions from a public that would reject them. See MacLean, *Democracy in Chains*, 140–41.

18 Evans, et al., "Sharon Statement."

19 Richard Rovere, *The Goldwater Caper* (New York: Harcourt, Brace & World, 1965), 46.

20 Stephen Shadegg, *Barry Goldwater: Freedom Is His Flight Plan* (New York: Fleet Publishing, 1962).

21 Barry Goldwater, as quoted in Rovere, *Goldwater Caper*, 4.

22 Barry Morris Goldwater, *The Conscience of a Conservative* (1960; Princeton, NJ: Princeton University Press, 2007), 15.

23 Rovere, *Goldwater Caper*, 29.

24 Rovere, *Goldwater Caper*, 42.

25 Heather Cox Richardson, *Letters from an American*, August 9, 2021. https://heathercoxrichardson.substack.com/p/august-9-2021

26 Barry Goldwater, as quoted in Adam Clymer, "Barry Goldwater, Conservative and Individualist, Dies at 89," *New York Times*, May 29, 1998.

27   "Goldwater's Remarks to the Press," *New York Times*, July 17, 1964.

28   Barry M. Goldwater, *Why Not Victory? A Fresh Look at American Foreign Policy* (New York: McGraw-Hill, 1962), 24.

29   Goldwater, as quoted in Rovere, *Goldwater Caper*, 51.

30   Rovere, *Goldwater Caper*, 51.

31   "Goldwater's Remarks to the Press," *New York Times*, July 17, 1964.

32   Gladwin Hill, "Nixon Denounces Press as 'Biased,'" *New York Times*, November 8, 1962.

33   Gladwin Hill, "Mrs. Rockefeller Received Divorce; 2 Sons With Her," *New York Times*, March 17, 1962.

34   "Many in G.O.P. Say Marriage Would Hurt Rockefeller in 1964," *New York Times*, May 3, 1963.

35   Norman Mailer, "In the Red Light: A History of the Republican Convention in 1964," *Esquire*, November, 1964, reprinted in *Norman Mailer, Cannibals and Christians* (New York: Dell, 1967), 6–45.

36   Clymer, "Goldwater . . . Dies at 89."

37   Anthony Leviero, "Final Vote Condemns McCarthy, 67–22," *New York Times*, December 3, 1954.

38   Barry Goldwater, 1957, as quoted in Clymer, "Goldwater . . . Dies at 89."

39   Goldwater, as quoted in Bart Barnes, "Barry Goldwater, GOP Hero, Dies at 89," *Washington Post*, May 30, 1998.

40   Goldwater, as quoted in Chalmers Roberts, "Goldwater Backs Army Cuts Abroad: Would Give NATO Commanders Power to Use A-Weapons," *Washington Post*, October 25, 1963.

41   Dylan chose the song as the one he would sing on what would have been his first appearance on the *Ed Sullivan Show* in May 1963. Sullivan himself liked the song, but CBS executives feared legal problems and told Dylan at the rehearsal he would have to sing another song. Dylan refused and walked off the set, an action that garnered him much favorable publicity. Val Adams, "Satire on Birch Society Barred from Ed Sullivan's TV Show," *New York Times*, May 14, 1963.

42   Erick Trickey, "Long Before QAnon, Ronald Reagan and the GOP Purged John Birch Extremists from the Party," *Washington Post*, January 15, 2021.

43   John A. Stormer, *None Dare Call It Treason* (Florissant, MO: Liberty Bell Press, 1964).

44   James Reston, "Goldwater Says He'll Run to Give Nation a 'Choice,'" *New York Times*, January 4, 1964.

45   Mailer, "In the Red Light: A History of the Republican Convention in 1964."

46   Dwight Eisenhower, as quoted in White, *The Making of the President—1964*, 200.

47   "TV Reporter, Still Broadcasting, Is Ousted from Convention Floor," *New York Times*, July 15, 1964; "Television: Iron Chancellor," *Time*, August 2, 1971.

48   Lyle Johnston, *"Good Night, Chet": A Biography of Chet Huntley* (Jefferson, NC: McFarland, 2003), 70.

49   Tom Wicker, "Platform Voted . . . Rockefeller Booed," *New York Times*, July 15, 1964; Mailer, "In the Red Light."

50 When David Rockefeller founded the Trilateral Commission in 1973, it was immediately identified by right-wing extremists as the center of the internationalist conspiracy.

51 Rick Perlstein, *Before the Storm: Barry Goldwater and the Unmaking of the American Consensus* (New York: Hill & Wang, 2001), 6.

52 This sort of paranoia and belief in conspiracies, which was common among the core of the Goldwater supporters in 1964, has continued to be a persistent feature on the American right. A few later examples include the belief that spread among right-wing "militia" groups that men in black helicopters were coming to impose a "New World Order" and the belief that arose in 2015 that the American military was preparing a takeover of Texas by building tunnels under abandoned Walmarts. The latter conspiracy belief became so widespread that Texas governor Greg Abbott instructed the Texas National Guard to be on watch for an invasion by *American* troops. And Alex Jones's repulsive claim that the 2012 Sandy Hook massacre of Connecticut school children was a green screen hoax perpetrated for the purpose of "taking away our guns," Pizzagate (the fake story that Hillary Clinton was running a child sex slave operation out of the basement of a DC pizza parlor that didn't even have a basement), the innumerable made-of-whole-cloth stories spread by Donald Trump, and QAnon, with its fantasy of a cabal of Democrats, Hollywood elites, Jews, and Q-knows-who that are pedophile cannibals from whom Trump would "save us."

53 Tom Wicker, "Vote is 883 to 214," *New York Times*, July 16, 1964.

54 Goldwater, Acceptance Speech, July 16, 1964.

55 Tom Wicker, "Scranton Beaten on Rights Move as Republican Convention Opens," *New York Times*, July 14, 1964.

56 Telephone conversation between LBJ and Bill Moyers, July 17, 1964, Michael Beschloss, *Taking Charge: The Johnson White House Tapes, 1963–1964* (New York: Simon & Schuster, 1997), 456.

57 Jackie Robinson, as quoted in the *Pittsburgh Courier*, July 23, 1964. Taylor Branch, *Pillar of Fire: America in the King Years, 1963–65* (New York: Simon & Schuster, 1998), 404.

58 MacLean, *Democracy in Chains*, xv–xxi.

59 Murray Rothbard, as quoted in MacLean, *Democracy in Chains*, 140.

60 LBJ, "Remarks upon signing the Civil Rights Bill, July 2, 1964."

61 George Fleming, as quoted in Branch, *Pillar of Fire*, 404.

62 Jackie Robinson, as quoted in the *Pittsburgh Courier*, July 23, 1964. Branch, *Pillar of Fire*, 404.

63 MacLean, *Democracy in Chains*, 89.

64 Allen J. Matusow, *The Unraveling of America: A History of Liberalism in the 1960s* (New York: Harper & Row, 1984), 137.

65 Barry Goldwater in an interview in *U.S. News & World Report*, October 22, 1962.

66 Kurt Andersen, *Evil Geniuses: The Unmaking of America* (New York: Random House, 2020), 44.

67   Rick Perlstein, *Nixonland: The Rise of a President and the Fracturing of America* (New York: Scribner, 2008), 5.

CHAPTER 15

1   Jim Stockdale and Sybil Stockdale, *In Love and War: The Story of a Family's Ordeal and Sacrifice During the Vietnam Years* (New York: Harper & Row, 1984), 21.
2   Joseph Heller, *Catch-22* (New York: Simon & Schuster, 1961, S&S Classic Edition, 1999).
3   Lyndon Johnson telephone conversation with Richard Russell, June 11, 1964, in Michael R. Beschloss, ed., *Taking Charge: The Johnson White House Tapes, 1963– 1964* (New York: Simon & Schuster, 1997), 402.
4   Gallup Poll, July 13, 1964. http://rangevoting.org/GallupPolls1964.txt
5   Barry Goldwater, Acceptance Speech, San Francisco, July 16, 1964. http:// www.washingtonpost.com/wp-srv/politics/daily/may98/goldwaterspeech .htm.
6   Edwin E. Moïse, *Tonkin Gulf and the Escalation of the Vietnam War* (Chapel Hill: University of North Carolina Press, 1996), 29.
7   Summary of a Meeting, the White House, June 10, 1964, *Foreign Relations of the United States, 1964–1968, Volume 1: Vietnam, 1964*. Document 210. http:// history.state.gov/historicaldocuments/frus1964-68v01/d210
8   LBJ telephone conversation with Robert Anderson, August 3, 1964, 9:46 a.m., in Beschloss, *Taking Charge*, 493–94.
9   Moïse, *Tonkin Gulf*, 60–62.
10   Moïse, *Tonkin Gulf*, 56–59.
11   Robert J. Hanyok, "Skunks, Bogies, Silent Hounds, and the Flying Fish: The Gulf of Tonkin Mystery, 2–4 August 1964," *Cryptologic Quarterly*, Winter 2000/ Spring 2001. http://www.nsa.gov/public_info/_files/gulf_of_tonkin/articles /rel1_skunks_bogies.pdf
12   Gen. Nguyen Dinh Uoc, paraphrased in David K. Shipler, "Robert McNamara and the Ghosts of Vietnam," *New York Times Magazine*, August 10, 1997.
13   LBJ telephone conversation with Robert Anderson, August 3, 1964, 9:46 a.m., in Beschloss, *Taking Charge*, 493–94.
14   LBJ telephone conversation with Robert McNamara, August 3, 1964, 10:20 a.m., in Beschloss, *Taking Charge*, 495.
15   Tim O'Brien, *The Things They Carried* (Boston: Hough Mifflin, 1990), 80.
16   It was later shown that these intercepts were misrepresented, mishandled, misinterpreted, and misconstrued. A 2000 NSA historical study found that only those intercepts "that supported the claim that the communists had attacked the two destroyers [were] given to administration officials." The objective was to tell the administration what it wanted to hear: that there had been a deliberate attack on US ships. "Yet, in order to substantiate that claim, all of the relevant SIGINT could not be provided to the White House and the Defense and intelligence officials. The conclusion that would be drawn from

a review of all SIGINT evidence would have been that the North Vietnamese not only did not attack, but were uncertain as to the location of the [American] ships." The NSA historical study found that "the handful of SIGINT reports which suggested that an attack had occurred contained severe analytic errors, unexplained translation changes, and the conjunction of two unrelated messages into one translation. This latter product would become the Johnson administration's main proof of the 4 August attack." Robert J. Hanyok, "Skunks, Bogies, Silent Hounds, and the Flying Fish: The Gulf of Tonkin Mystery, 2–4 August 1964," *Cryptologic Quarterly*, Winter 2000/Spring 2001.

17 Moïse, *Tonkin Gulf*, 209.
18 LBJ telephone conversation with McNamara, August 4, 1964, 11:06 a.m., in Beschloss, *Taking Charge*, 498.
19 Editorial Note on meetings held on August 4, 1964, *Foreign Relations of the United States, 1964–1968, Volume 1: Vietnam, 1964*. Document 276. http://history.state.gov/historicaldocuments/frus1964-68v01/d276
20 Editorial Note on meetings held on August 4, 1964.
21 Gareth Porter, *Perils of Dominance: Imbalance of Power and the Road to the Vietnam War* (Berkeley and Los Angeles: University of California Press, 2004), 194–99.
22 Editorial Note on meetings held on August 4, 1964.
23 McGeorge Bundy, as quoted in Moïse, *Tonkin Gulf*, 209.
24 George Ball, 1976 or 1977, as quoted in Moïse, *Tonkin Gulf*, 99.
25 Beschloss, *Taking Charge*, 500.
26 LBJ telephone conversation with McNamara, August 4, 1964, 5:09 p.m., in Beschloss, *Taking Charge*, 500.
27 "Notes of the Leadership Meeting, White House," August 4, 1964, 6:45 p.m., *Foreign Relations of the United States, 1964–1968, Volume 1: Vietnam, 1964*. Document 280. http://history.state.gov/historicaldocuments/frus1964-68v01/d280.
28 Richard Eder, "Aiken Suggests U.S. Say It Has Won the War," *New York Times*, October 20, 1966.
29 "Notes of the Leadership Meeting," August 4, 1964.
30 "Summary Notes of the 538th Meeting of the National Security Council," August 4, 1964, 6:15–6:40 p.m., *Foreign Relations of the United States, 1964–1968, Volume 1: Vietnam, 1964*. Document 278. http://history.state.gov/historicaldocuments/frus1964-68v01/d278
31 Stockdale's plane was later shot down over North Vietnam in 1965 and he was held in Hanoi as a prisoner of war. He would be the vice-presidential running mate of independent candidate H. Ross Perot in 1992.
32 Stockdale and Stockdale, *In Love and War*, 21.
33 Hanyok, "Skunks, Bogies, Silent Hounds, and the Flying Fish."
34 Tom Mintier, "Two Former Enemies Meet in Friendship," CNN, November 9, 1995. http://www.cnn.com/WORLD/9511/vietnam_mcnamara/11-09/

35 Moïse, *Tonkin Gulf*, 139–42.

36 LBJ, as quoted in George Ball, *The Past Has Another Pattern* (New York: Norton, 1982), 379.

37 LBJ, as quoted in "Freedom of Information Then and Now," *Now*, PBS, March 17, 2006.

38 Cartha DeLoach, telephone conversation with LBJ, August 4, 1964, 8:01 p.m., in Beschloss, *Taking Charge*, 501–502.

39 Telephone conversation between Governor Paul B. Johnson Jr., and LBJ, August 4, 1964, 9:35 p.m.; lbj_wh6408_06_4711, http://millercenter.org/scripps/archive/presidentialrecordings/johnson/1964/08_1964.

40 President's Daily Diary, August 4, 1964.

41 Telephone conversation between LBJ and Robert McNamara, August 4, 1964, 9:15 p.m. http://www.gwu.edu/~nsarchiv/NSAEBB/NSAEBB132/tapes.htm.

42 Telephone conversation between Barry Goldwater and LBJ, August 4, 1964, 10:06 p.m., in Beschloss, *Taking Charge*, 504; lbj_wh6408_06_4715-1, http://millercenter.org/scripps/archive/presidentialrecordings/johnson/1964/08_1964.

43 Lyndon B. Johnson, Radio and Television Address to the American People Following Renewed Aggression in the Gulf of Tonkin, August 4, 1964. http://www.presidency.ucsb.edu/ws/?pid=26418

44 Joint Resolution of Congress H.J. RES 1145 August 7, 1964. http://avalon.law.yale.edu/20th_century/tonkin-g.asp.

45 Sen. Ernest Gruening and Sen. Wayne Morse, Senate Debate on Gulf of Tonkin Resolution, August 7, 1964. http://vietnam.vassar.edu/overview/doc9.html.

46 *Washington Post* editorial, reprinted in "Opinion of the Week: At Home and Abroad," *New York Times*, August 9, 1964.

47 McNamara, telephone conversation with LBJ, August 6, 1964, 12:46 p.m., in Beschloss, *Taking Charge*, 507.

48 LBJ, as quoted in Robert Dallek, *Lyndon B. Johnson: Portrait of a President* (New York: Oxford University Press, 2005), 179.

49 LBJ, telephone conversation with Gov. Paul B. Johnson Jr., August 4, 1964, 9:35 p.m.; lbj_wh6408_06_4711, http://millercenter.org/scripps/archive/presidentialrecordings/johnson/1964/08_1964.

50 LBJ telephone conversation with Paul Johnson.

51 George F. Will, "JFK, The Conservative," *Washington Post*, November 21, 2013.

52 LBJ, September 18, 1964, as quoted in Porter, *Perils of Dominance*, 202.

53 LBJ, as quoted in Porter, *Perils of Dominance*, 202.

54 Stanley Karnow, *Vietnam: A History* (New York: Viking, 1983; rev. ed.: Penguin, 1997), 350.

CHAPTER 16

1 Fannie Lou Hamer, August 22, 1964, as quoted in Kay Mills, *This Little Light of Mine: The Life of Fannie Lou Hamer* (Lexington: University Press of Kentucky, 2007), 121.

2 John Lewis with Michael D'Orso, *Walking with the Wind: A Memoir of the Movement* (New York: Simon & Schuster, 1998), 291.

3 LBJ, telephone conversation with Hale Boggs and Carl Albert, August 8, 1964, in Michael R. Beschloss, *Taking Charge: The Johnson White House Tapes, 1963–1964* (New York: Simon & Schuster, 1997), 510.

4 John Dittmer, *Local People: The Struggle for Civil Rights in Mississippi* (Urbana and Chicago: University of Illinois Press, 1994), 281.

5 Bob Moses, as quoted in Dittmer, *Local People*, 282.

6 Dittmer, *Local People*, 283.

7 J. Edgar Hoover, as quoted in Nick Kotz, *Judgment Days: Lyndon Johnson, Martin Luther King, and the Laws that Changed America* (Boston: Houghton Mifflin, 2005), 199.

8 LBJ, telephone conversation with Walter Reuther, August 9, 1964, in Beschloss, *Taking Charge*, 510–11.

9 "Democrats to Open Mississippi Parley," *New York Times*, July 28, 1964.

10 Dittmer, *Local People*, 273.

11 LBJ telephone conversation with Sen. Hubert Humphrey, August 14, 1964, in Beschloss, *Taking Charge*, 516.

12 LBJ telephone conversation with Roy Wilkins, August 15, 1964, in Beschloss, *Taking Charge*, 517.

13 Tom Wicker, "President Bars Kennedy, Five Others from Ticket," *New York Times*, July 31, 1964.

14 LBJ, telephone conversation with Richard Russell, August 24, 1964, in Beschloss, *Taking Charge*, 525.

15 LBJ, telephone conversation with Walter Jenkins, August 25, 1964, in Beschloss, *Taking Charge*, 532.

16 Kotz, *Judgment Days*, 199.

17 William Sullivan, as quoted in Jeff Shesol, *Mutual Contempt: Lyndon Johnson, Robert Kennedy, and the Feud that Defined a Decade* (New York: Norton, 1998), 217.

18 *Intelligence Activities and the Rights of Americans, Book II: Final Report of the Select Committee to Study Governmental Operations, United States Senate* (Washington: Government Printing Office, 1976), 117–19. http://www.aarclibrary.org/publib/church/reports/book2/html/ChurchB2_0067a.htm

19 Dittmer, *Local People*, 292.

20 John Connally to LBJ, August 1964, as quoted in Dittmer, *Local People*, 290.

21 Fannie Lou Hamer, as quoted in Nan Robertson, "Mississippian Relates Struggle of Negro in Voter Registration," *New York Times*, August 24, 1964.

22 Fannie Lou Hamer, Testimony before the Credentials Committee, Democratic National Convention, Atlantic City. August 22, 1964.

American Rhetoric website. http://www.americanrhetoric.com/speeches/fannielouhamercredentialscommittee.htm

23 Kate Clifford Larson, *Walk with Me: A Biography of Fannie Lou Hamer* (New York: Oxford University Press, 2021), 178.

24 Robertson, "Mississippian Relates Struggle of Negro in Voter Registration."

25 Fannie Lou Hamer, as quoted in Keisha N. Blain, *Until I Am Free: Fannie Lou Hamer's Enduring Message to America* (Boston: Beacon, 2021), 86.

26 That, of course, is exactly what happened in the Deep South in 1964 and across the South (and to a somewhat lesser extent, other regions) in the years to come.

27 "Text of Democratic Party Platform's Domestic Section as Approved by Committee," *New York Times*, August 25, 1964.

28 Telephone conversation between LBJ and Russell, August 24, 1964, in Beschloss, *Taking Charge*, 524.

29 Dittmer, *Local People*, 289–90.

30 Annie Devine, August 23, 1964, as quoted in Wesley C. Hogan, *Many Minds, One Heart: SNCC's Dream for a New America* (Chapel Hill: University of North Carolina Press, 2007), 192.

31 Milton Viorst, *Fire in the Streets: America in the 1960s* (New York: Simon & Schuster, 1979), 256.

32 Hubert Humphrey, as quoted in Larson, *Walk with Me*, 181.

33 Author's interview with Rev. Edwin King, September 9, 1997.

34 Fannie Lou Hamer, as quoted in Larson, *Walk with Me*, 181.

35 Hubert Humphrey, as quoted in Jim Dann, *Challenging the Mississippi Firebombers: Memories of Mississippi, 1964–65* (Montreal: Baraka Books, 2013), 119; Larson, *Walk with Me*, 182.

36 LBJ, as quoted in Taylor Branch, *Pillar of Fire: America in the King Years, 1963–1965* (New York: Simon & Schuster, 1998), 473.

37 It should be noted that the combination of his insecurities about his own abilities, his fear of Robert Kennedy defeating him, and the separation of the Vietnam issue from his political fortunes that brought Johnson to the point of considering retirement in August 1964 is strikingly similar to the mix of factors that would lead him to step aside in March 1968.

38 LBJ, telephone conversation with Walter Reuther, August 25, 1964, in Beschloss, *Taking Charge*, 534.

39 Bob Moses, August 25, 1964, as quoted in Marshall Frady, *Martin Luther King Jr.: A Life* (New York: Penguin, 2002), 148–49.

40 "Texts of Convention Committee Report and Mississippi Statement," *New York Times*, August 26, 1964.

41 Bayard Rustin, August 26, 1964, as paraphrased in James Forman, *The Making of Black Revolutionaries* (New York: Macmillan, 1972; Seattle: University of Washington Press, 1997), 392.

42 Fannie Lou Hamer, as quoted in Lani Guinier, "No Two Seats: The Elusive Quest for Political Equality," *Virginia Law Review*, vol. 77, no. 8 (November 1991), 1413n.

43 Bob Moses, August 25, 1964, as quoted in Frady, *Martin Luther King Jr.: A Life*, 148–49.

44 R. W. Apple Jr., "Kennedy Gets an Ovation; Recalls Ideals of Brother," *New York Times*, August 28, 1964; Beschloss, *Taking Charge*, 541n.

45 Anthony Lewis, "Plank Spurning Extremists Completes Platform Draft," *New York Times*, August 25, 1964.

46 Mary C. Brennan, *Turning Right in the Sixties: The Conservative Capture of the GOP* (Chapel Hill: University of North Carolina Press, 1995), 95.

47 Richard H. Rovere, "Big Pumpkin on the Boardwalk: A Letter from Atlantic City," August 28, 1964, in Rovere, *The Goldwater Caper* (New York: Harcourt, Brace & World, 1965), 129–30.

48 Telephone conversation between LBJ and Walter Reuther, August 24, 1964, in Beschloss, *Taking Charge*, 526.

49 Rovere, "Big Pumpkin on the Boardwalk," 129–30.

50 Lewis and D'Orso, *Walking with the Wind*, 291.

51 Joyce Ladner, as quoted in Dittmer, *Local People*, 302.

52 Tom Wicker, "Mississippi Delegates Withdraw," *New York Times*, August 26, 1964.

53 Vincent Harding, as quoted in Sally Belfrage, *Freedom Summer* (New York: Viking, 1965), 7.

54 Viorst, *Fire in the Streets*, 235.

55 Julian Bond, Introduction to in Elizabeth Sutherland Martínez, *Letters from Mississippi* (New York: McGraw-Hill, 1965; Brookline, MA: Zephyr Press, 2002), xi.

56 Vincent Harding, as quoted in Sally Belfrage, *Freedom Summer*, 7.

57 Letter from Tchula, MS, August 30, 1964, in Sutherland Martínez, *Letters from Mississippi*, 56.

58 Cleveland Sellers, with Robert Terrell, *The River of No Return: The Autobiography of a Black Militant and the Life and Death of SNCC* (Jackson: University Press of Mississippi, 1990), 111.

59 MLK, August 22, 1964, as quoted in Branch, *Pillar of Fire*, 460.

CHAPTER 17

1 Mario Savio, June 1964, as quoted in Robert Cohen, *Freedom's Orator: Mario Savio and the Radical Legacy of the 1960s* (New York: Oxford University Press, 2009), 52.

2 Mario Savio to Cheryl Stevenson, July 3, 1964, as quoted in Cohen, *Freedom's Orator*, 55, 432. Even as he was so sanguine about the possibilities for positive change, Savio was wary of the possible effects of another of the major forces developing in 1964. "But what about Vietnam?" he wrote in the same letter. That was a month before the Gulf of Tonkin.

3 Hal Draper, *Berkeley: The New Student Revolt* (New York: Grove Press, 1965, 2009), 3.

4 Cohen, *Freedom's Orator*, 222.
5 Rennie Davis, as quoted in Milton Viorst, *Fire in the Streets: America in the 1960s* (New York: Simon and Schuster, 1979), 176.
6 Mario Savio, "An End to History," *Humanity, An Arena of Critique and Commitment*, No. 2, December 1964. http://www.fsm-a.org/stacks/endhistorysavio.html.
7 Savio, "An End to History."
8 Draper, *Berkeley: The New Student Revolt*, 15.
9 *Time*, October 17, 1960.
10 Viorst, *Fire in the Streets*, 279.
11 David Horowitz, *Student* (New York: Ballantine Books, 1962), 15.
12 Draper, *Berkeley: The New Student Revolt*, 4.
13 Clark Kerr, *The Uses of the University* (1963; Cambridge, MA: Harvard University Press, 2001), 66, 78.
14 Kerr, *Uses of the University*, 22–29.
15 John Kenneth Galbraith, *American Capitalism: The Concept of Countervailing Power* (Boston: Houghton Mifflin, 1952).
16 Katherine A. Towle, letter to student organizations, September 14, 1964. http://fsm-a.org/stacks/chron_ca_monthly.html
17 Viorst, *Fire in the Streets*, 285.
18 Draper, *Berkeley: The New Student Revolt*, 28–29.
19 Towle, letter to student organizations, September 14, 1964.
20 Michael Rossman, *The Wedding within the War* (Garden City, NY: Doubleday, 1965), in Alexander Bloom and Wini Breines, eds., *Takin' It to the Streets: A Sixties Reader* (New York: Oxford University Press, 1995; second edition, 2003), 82.
21 Draper, *Berkeley: The New Student Revolt*, 36.
22 Joseph Heller, *Catch-22* (New York: Simon & Schuster, 1961, S&S Classic Edition, 1999), 375.
23 Jackie Goldberg, as quoted in Cohen, *Freedom's Orator*, 101.
24 Savio, as quoted in Cohen, *Freedom's Orator*, 96.
25 Lawrence Levine, as quoted in Cohen, *Freedom's Orator*, 187.
26 Savio, as quoted in Cohen, *Freedom's Orator*, 88.
27 Parker Donham, "Mario Savio," *Harvard Crimson*, December 15, 1964.
28 Cohen, *Freedom's Orator*, 103.
29 John Steinbeck, *The Grapes of Wrath* (New York: Viking, 1939; Penguin, 1992), 152.
30 Cohen, *Freedom's Orator*, 99.
31 Clark Kerr, *The Gold and the Blue: A Personal Memoir of the University of California, 1949–1967* (Berkeley: University of California Press, 2003), vol. 2, 195–96; Draper, *Berkeley: The New Student Revolt*, 50.
32 Draper, *Berkeley: The New Student Revolt*, 50–51; Rossman, *The Wedding within the War*, 85.
33 "How a Sermon Cooled Rebels," *San Francisco Examiner*, October 3, 1964.
34 Draper, *Berkeley: The New Student Revolt*, 60–62.

35 Kerr, *The Gold and the Blue*, vol. 2, 199.

36 Kerr, *The Gold and the Blue*, vol. 2, 197.

37 Kerr, *The Gold and the Blue*, vol. 2, 198.

38 Cohen, *Freedom's Orator*, 119–20.

39 Joan Baez, as quoted in Draper, *Berkeley: The New Student Revolt*, 67.

40 Kerr, *The Gold and the Blue*, vol. 2, 200.

41 Jack Weinberg, as quoted in Tom Brokaw, *Boom! Voices of the Sixties* (New York: Random House, 2007), 593.

42 Savio, as quoted in Cohen, *Freedom's Orator*, 140.

43 Beverly A. Potter and Mark J. Estren, *Question Authority to Think for Yourself* (Oakland, CA: Ronin, 2012), 22, 97.

44 William H. Chafe, *Civilities and Civil Rights: Greensboro, North Carolina, and the Black Struggle for Freedom* (New York: Oxford University Press, 1980), 8.

45 Weinberg, as quoted in James Benet, "Growing Pains at UC," *San Francisco Chronicle*, November 15, 1964.

46 Paul Galloway, "Radical Redux," *Chicago Tribune*, November 16, 1990. http://articles.chicagotribune.com/1990-11-16/features/9004050125_1_jack-weinberg-california-gubernatorial-candidate-berkeley; Cohen, *Freedom's Orator*,131.

47 Fact Finding Committee of Graduate Political Scientists, "The Berkeley Free Speech Controversy, Preliminary Report," December 13, 1964. http://www.fsm-a.org/stacks/GradStudentReport.html.

48 Draper, *Berkeley: The New Student Revolt*, 68.

49 Kerr, as quoted in Ben Williams, "'Reds on Campus'—UC's Kerr," *San Francisco Examiner*, October 3, 1964.

50 Ed Montgomery, "Free Speech Unrest May Spread," *San Francisco Chronicle*, November 27, 1964.

51 Mao Zedong, "Problems of War and Strategy" (November 6, 1938). https://www.marxists.org/reference/archive/mao/works/red-book/ch05.htm

52 Cohen's paraphrase of Savio, Cohen, *Freedom's Orator*, 143.

53 Ralph J. Gleason, "The Tragedy at the Greek Theater," *San Francisco Chronicle*, December 9, 1964. http://www.fsm-a.org/stacks/R_Gleason.html

54 Cohen, *Freedom's Orator*, 148.

55 *Daily Californian*, October 15, 1964.

56 Ralph J. Gleason, "On the Town: Songs Born of the UC Berkeley Rebellion," *San Francisco Chronicle*, November 23, 1964.

57 Cohen, *Freedom's Orator*, 173. The use of the word *atrocity* for the suspension of student protestors (and Goldberg was far from the only one in the FSM to use the word) points to the question of the validity of the contention that the fight of the students was the same as that of blacks in the South. While the disciplinary actions can readily be termed outrageous, they were hardly in the same league with the beatings and murders that black people and others in the Freedom Movement in the Deep South faced. The latter were genuine atrocities.

58　Mario Savio, Address on Steps of Sproul Hall, December 2, 1964. http://www.americanrhetoric.com/speeches/mariosaviosproulhallsitin.htm

59　Cohen, *Freedom's Orator*, 179.

60　Savio, Sproul Hall Address, December 2, 1964.

61　Cohen, *Freedom's Orator*, 194.

62　Kerr, *The Gold and the Blue*, vol. 2, 212.

63　Cohen, *Freedom's Orator*, 196–97.

64　Carolyn Anspacher, "Students Call Police Brutal," *San Francisco Chronicle*, December 4, 1964.

65　Gleason, "Tragedy at the Greek Theater." His reference was to the battle over integration on the campus of the University of Mississippi just over two years earlier.

66　Wallace Turner, "796 Students Arrested as Police Break Up Sit-in at U of California," *New York Times*, December 4, 1964.

67　Mario Savio, letter to his family, from Santa Rita Jail, December 4, 1964; "December 4, 1964 Letter by Mario Savio while Detained in Santa Rita Jail," *Daily Californian*, November 14, 2011. http://www.dailycal.org/2011/11/14/dec-4-1964-letter-by-mario-savio-while-detained-in-santa-rita-jail/

68　Kerr, *The Gold and the Blue*, vol. 2, 215.

69　"Demonstrators Out of Jail; Pickets March," *Berkeley Daily Gazette*, December 4, 1964.

70　Kerr, *The Gold and the Blue*, vol. 2, 215.

71　Wallace Turner, "Berkeley Parley Upset as Police Grab Student," *New York Times*, December 8, 1964.

72　Sheila (no last name given), message in Mario Savio memorial book, December 8, 1996, as quoted in Cohen, *Freedom's Orator*, 223.

73　Savio, Letter from Santa Rita Prison.

74　Gleason, "Tragedy at the Greek Theater."

75　Marvin Garson, "Catch-801," in Bloom and Breines, *Takin' It to the Streets*, 94–95.

76　Mervin D. Field, "The UC Student Protests: California Poll," in Seymour Martin Lipset and Sheldon S. Wolin, eds., *The Berkeley Student Revolt* (Garden City, NY: Anchor Books, 1965), 199.

77　The reference is to the title of the first history of the 1960s, William L. O'Neill, *Coming Apart: An Informal History of America in the 1960s* (Chicago: Quadrangle, 1971).

78　M. H. Lund, Oakland, CA, to Gov. Pat Brown, December 5, 1964, as quoted in Cohen, *Freedom's Orator*, 219.

79　Elizabeth Hinton, *America on Fire: The Untold History of Police Violence and Black Rebellion since the 1960s*. New York: Liveright, 2021.

80　Kerr, *The Gold and the Blue*, vol. I, 260.

81　Wallace Turner, "Kerr is Resigning at U. of California; Aide also Leaving," *New York Times*, March 10. 1965.

82　Kerr, *The Gold and the Blue*, vol. I, 260.

83 Cohen, *Freedom's Orator*, 221.

84 Barbara Garson, "Freedom Is a Big Deal," in Bloom and Breines, *Takin' It to the Streets*, 95–96.

CHAPTER 18

1 Lyndon B. Johnson, Concluding speech of 1964 campaign, Pasadena, Texas, November 2, 1964. http://www.presidency.ucsb.edu/ws/?pid=26712

2 Editorial, "The Johnson Landslide," *New York Times*, November 4, 1964.

3 John William Middendorf, II, *A Glorious Disaster: Barry Goldwater's Presidential Campaign and the Origins of the Conservative Movement* (New York: Basic Books, 2006), 55.

4 Rick Perlstein, *Before the Storm: Barry Goldwater and the Unmaking of the American Consensus* (New York: Hill & Wang, 2001; New York: Nation Books, 2009), 282.

5 Rick Perlstein, *Nixonland: The Rise of a President and the Fracturing of America* (New York: Scribner, 2008), 62.

6 Allen J. Matusow, *The Unraveling of America: A History of Liberalism in the 1960s* (New York: Harper & Row, 1984), 131.

7 William L. O'Neill, *Coming Apart: An Informal History of America in the 1960s* (Chicago: Quadrangle, 1971), 108.

8 Perlstein, *Before the Storm*, 333.

9 O'Neill, *Coming Apart*, 109.

10 Theodore H. White, *The Making of the President—1964* (New York: Atheneum, 1969), 323.

11 Barry Goldwater, 1961, as quoted in "The Conservative Progression: Goldwater to Bush," *The Sixties: The Years that Shaped a Generation* (PBS). http://www.pbs.org/opb/thesixties/topics/politics/legacy.html (accessed September 19, 2009).

12 "Saw, Eastern Seaboard." http://www.youtube.com/watch?v=i4bXPHBBJ58.

13 Thurmond had had split with the Democrats in 1948 when the party adopted a very modest civil rights plank and become the presidential candidate of the States Rights ("Dixiecrat") Party, but later returned.

14 Claude Sitton, "Thurmond Break Is Made Official," *New York Times*, September 17, 1964.

15 Charles Mohr, "Thurmond Joins Goldwater Drive," *New York Times*, September 18, 1964.

16 Perlstein, *Before the Storm*, 363. It is fascinating to notice the similarity of the political fears of Barry Goldwater and Lyndon Johnson when the former voted against and the latter signed the Civil Rights Act of 1964. Goldwater feared that he was signing his political death warrant by voting against the bill, and Johnson feared that he was delivering "the South to the Republican Party for a long time to come" by signing it into law.

17   Lyndon B. Johnson, 1960, remark to Bill Moyers, quoted in Moyers, "What a Real President Was Like," *Washington Post*, November 13, 1988.

18   Gallup, "Vote by Groups, 1960–1964." http://www.gallup.com/poll/9454 /election-polls-vote-groups-19601964.aspx

19   George Reedy, telephone conversation with LBJ, July 20, 1964. Lyndon Baines Johnson Presidential Library and Museum (WH6407.11 / 4286). http://www .conelrad.com/daisy/audio.php#george.

20   https://www.loc.gov/item/mbrs01185386/

21   White, *Making of the President—1964*, 322.

22   LBJ, speech at Akron University, October 21, 194. http://www.presidency. ucsb.edu/vietnam/shownews.php?newsid=11

23   LBJ, September 28, 1964, as quoted in White, *Making of the President—1964*, 366.

24   LBJ, September 28, 1964, as quoted in White, *Making of the President—1964*, 366.

25   Lyndon B. Johnson, speech at the Jung Hotel, New Orleans, October 9, 1964. http://millercenter.org/president/speeches/detail/3526; White, *Making of the President—1964*, 363–64; Robert Dallek, *Flawed Giant: Lyndon Johnson and His Times, 1961–1973* (New York: Oxford University Press, 1998), 182–83.

26   Horace Busby, as quoted in Dallek, *Flawed Giant*, 183.

27   "Dowager," Goldwater campaign ad, October 1964. http://www .livingroomcandidate.org/commercials/1964

28   Arthur Krock, "In the Nation," *New York Times*, February 21, 1964.

29   Editorial, "More on Bobby Baker," *New York Times*, September 3, 1964.

30   "Estes Sentenced to 15-Year Term," *New York Times*, April 16, 1963.

31   Dallek, *Flawed Giant*, 39–40.

32   LBJ, as quoted in Michael Beschloss, *Reaching for Glory: Lyndon Johnson's Secret White House Tapes, 1964–1965* (New York: Simon & Schuster, 2002), 54.

33   Max Frankel, "President's Aide Quits on Report of Morals Charge," *New York Times*, October 15, 1964.

34   LBJ telephone conversation with Abe Fortas, October 14, 1964, Miller Center Presidential Recordings – Lyndon Johnson (WH6410.08) http://web2 .millercenter.org/lbj/audiovisual/whrecordings/telephone/conversations /1964/lbj_wh6410_08_5876.mp3

35   Perlstein, *Before the Storm*, 491.

36   Frankel, "President's Aide Quits."

37   LBJ telephone conversation with Clark Clifford and Abe Fortas, 8:02 p.m., October 14, 1964, in Beschloss, *Reaching for Glory*, 61.

38   Perlstein, *Before the Storm*, 489–91.

39   "The Senior Staff Man," *Time*, October 23, 1964.

40   Beschloss, *Reaching for Glory*, 57n.

41   White, *Making of the President—1964*, 369.

42   Perlstein, *Before the Storm*, 493.

43   Beschloss, *Reaching for Glory*, 63.

44   Barry Goldwater, as quoted in Dallek, *Flawed Giant*, 181.

45   Henry Tanner, "Khrushchev Ousted from Top Posts . . . ," *New York Times*, October 16, 1964.

46   Tom Wicker, "Johnson Denies Jenkins Cover-Up . . . ," *New York Times*, October 16, 1964.

47   Seymour Topping, "China Tests Atomic Bomb, Asks Summit Talk on Ban; Johnson Minimizes Peril," *New York Times*, October 17, 1964.

48   Sydney Gruson, "Wilson Is Prime Minister; Labor Has 4-Seat Margin," *New York Times*, October 17, 1964.

49   Perlstein, *Before the Storm*, 493.

50   White, *Making of the President - 1964*, 368.

51   Perlstein, *Before the Storm*, 499.

52   Perlstein, *Before the Storm*, 499.

53   Perlstein, *Before the Storm*, 500.

54   As quoted in review of Perlstein, *Before the Storm*, *New York Times*, April 1, 2001.

55   Ronald Reagan, "A Time for Choosing," televised address, October 27, 1964. http://www.americanrhetoric.com/speeches/ronaldreaganatimeforchoosing .htm; https://www.youtube.com/watch?v=qXBswFfh6AY

56   Louis Menand, "He Knew He Was Right," *New Yorker*, March 26, 2001.

57   Joan Didion, "In the Realm of the Fisher King," (1989), reprinted in Didion, *After Henry* (New York: Simon & Schuster, 1992), 31.

58   Robert S. McElvaine, "Why the Debacle Shouldn't Hearten Liberals,' *New York Times*, December 9, 1986.

59   "Johnson Victory Speech," *New York Times*, November 4, 1964.

60   Tom Wicker, "Johnson Swamps Goldwater," *New York Times*, November 4. 1964.

61   Gallup, "Vote by Groups, 1960–1964."

62   Jackie Calmes, "Democrats Try Wooing Ones Who Got Away: White Men," *New York Times*, March 2, 2014.

63   Menand, "He Knew He Was Right."

64   https://allthewaywithlbj.com/lbjs-election-analysis/

65   http://allthewaywithlbj.com/lbjs-election-analysis/

66   As quoted in Perlstein, *Before the Storm*, 512.

67   Beschloss, *Reaching for Glory*, 119.

68   Perlstein, *Nixonland*, 11.

CHAPTER 19

1   Anonymous [Casey Hayden and Mary King], Position Paper ["The Position of Women in SNCC"], SNCC meeting, Waveland, Mississippi, November 1964. http://www.crmvet.org/docs/6411w_us_women.pdf.

2   Susan Brownmiller, *In Our Time: Memoir of a Revolution* (New York: Dial Press, 1999), 11.

3   Doug McAdam, *Freedom Summer* (New York: Oxford University Press, 1988), 43.

4   Casey Hayden and Mary King, "A Kind of Memo," November 18, 1965. http://womhist.alexanderstreet.com/SNCC/doc101.htm.

5   The irrational hatred of Barack Obama on the part of a substantial minority of Americans from 2008 onward surely had a lot to do with the fact that he is the sum of all the fears of such people: the product of a black man and a white woman.

6   Bruce Watson, *Freedom Summer: The Savage Season that Made Mississippi Burn and Made America a Democracy* (New York: Viking, 2010), 229.

7   Caroline Randall Williams, "You Want a Confederate Monument? My Body Is a Confederate Monument," *New York Times*, June 26, 2020.

8   Almost all biracial children born during slavery were the products of white men and women who were legally their "property." A white mistress giving birth to a partly black child would have been greeted as the opposite of a "blessed event."

9   John Dittmer, *Local People: The Struggle for Civil Rights in Mississippi* (Urbana and Chicago: University of Illinois Press, 1994), 263.

10   Ralph Ellison, *Invisible Man* (New York: Modern Library, 1952), 153.

11   Robert S. McElvaine, *Eve's Seed: Biology, the Sexes, and the Course of History* (New York: McGraw-Hill, 2001), 352 and passim.

12   *Autobiography of Malcolm X* (New York: Grove Press, 1965), 452.

13   Ellison, *Invisible Man*, 153.

14   Robert Daley, "Cassius Clay: A Wise Man Can Act the Fool," *New York Times*, June 13, 1963.

15   James T. Patterson, *Grand Expectations: The United States, 1945–1974* (New York: Oxford university Press, 1996), 401.

16   E. D. Nixon, as quoted in Taylor Branch, *Parting the Waters: America in the King Years, 1954–63* (New York: Simon & Schuster, 1988), 136.

17   Martin Luther King Jr., "The Power of Nonviolence," speech at Berkeley, California, June 4, 1957, in James Melvin Washington, ed., *A Testament of Hope: The Essential Writings of Martin Luther King Jr.*, (San Francisco: HarperSanFrancisco, 1991), 12.

18   Malcolm X, speech in Detroit, April 12, 1964. http://americanradioworks .publicradio.org/features/blackspeech/mx.html

19   J. Hector St. John de Crèvecoeur, *Letters from an American Farmer* (1782; New York: Penguin, 1981), 69.

20   This is the title Andrew Young, in his Foreword, suggested for Chapter 12 of Mary King's *Freedom Song: A Personal History of the 1960s Civil Rights Movement* (New York: William Morrow, 1987).

21   Brownmiller, In Our Time, 12.

22   Brownmiller, *In Our Time*, 12.

23   https://snccdigital.org/people/casey-hayden/

24 Casey Hayden, Preface to Mary King, *Freedom Song: A Personal Story of the 1960s Civil Rights Movement* (New York: William Morrow, 1987), 7.

25 Hayden, Preface to King, *Freedom Song*, 8.

26 Simone de Beauvoir, *The Second Sex* (1952; New York: Knopf, 1953).

27 Brownmiller, *In Our Time*, 13.

28 Bob Moses, as quoted in "SNCC's Waveland Conference." https://snccdigital.org/events/snccs-waveland-conference/

29 Brownmiller, *In Our Time*, 13.

30 King, *Freedom Song*, 443.

31 King, *Freedom Song*, 444.

32 King, *Freedom Song*, 445.

33 King, *Freedom Song*, 450.

34 Adrienne Rich, "Diving into the Wreck" (1972) https://www.poets.org/poetsorg/poem/diving-wreck.

35 SNCC Position Paper (name withheld by request), November 1964. http://www.crmvet.org/docs/6411w_us_women.pdf

36 Sabina Peck, "The Only Position for Women in SNCC is Prone," *History in the Making,* vol. 1, no. 1. https://historyitm.files.wordpress.com/2013/08/peck.pdf.

37 King, *Freedom Song*, 451–52.

38 Sheila Michaels, 12/28/2013. "Women, SNCC, and Stokely, An Email Dialog, 2013–14." http://www.crmvet.org/disc/women2.htm.

39 Peck, "The Only Position for Women in SNCC is Prone."

40 Casey Hayden and Mary King, "A Kind of Memo," November 18, 1965. http://womhist.alexanderstreet.com/SNCC/doc101.htm

41 King, Freedom Song, 454.

42 King, Freedom Song, 443–45, 456–58.

43 Michelle Moravec, "Revisiting 'A Kind of Memo' from Casey Hayden and Mary King," *Women in Social Movements in the United States, 1600–2000*, March 2017. http://womhist.alexanderstreet.com/SNCC/revisiting.htm#en5

44 Casey Hayden and Mary King, "Sex and Caste: A Kind of Memo," *Liberation,* April 1966, 35–36. http://www.crmvet.org/docs/sexcaste.pdf

45 SNCC Digital Gateway. https://snccdigital.org/people/casey-hayden/

46 Hayden and King, "A Kind of Memo."

47 McElvaine, *Eve's Seed*, 349.

48 "Redstockings Manifesto" (1969) http://www.redstockings.org/index.php/rs-manifesto; Robin Morgan, "Goodbye to All That" (1970) http://faculty.atu.edu/cbrucker/Amst2003/Texts/Goodbye.pdf.

49 Brownmiller, *In Our Time*, 14–16.

50 As quoted in Maurice Isserman, "The Not-So-Dark and Bloody Ground: New Works on the 1960s," *American Historical Review*, October 1989, 1000–1; James T. Patterson, *Grand Expectations: The United States, 1945–1974* (New York: Oxford University Press, 1996), 645.

51   Sara Evans, *Personal Politics: The Roots of Women's Liberation in the Civil Rights Movement and the New Left* (New York: Knopf, 1979), 155; Brownmiller, *In Our Time*, 13–15.

CHAPTER 20

1   Lyndon B. Johnson, December 18, 1964, as quoted in Rick Perlstein, *Nixonland: The Rise of a President and the Fracturing of America* (New York: Scribner, 2008), 6.

2   "Johnson Directs Taylor to Press Vietnam on War," *New York Times*, December 2, 1964.

3   "US Economy is Up; Added Gains Seen," *New York Times*, December 26, 1964.

4   George Ball Memorandum, October 5, 1964; George W. Ball, "Top Secret: The Prophecy the President Rejected," *Atlantic*, July 1972, 36–49; http://www.presidency.ucsb.edu/vietnam/showdoc.php?docid=24

5   Martin Luther King's Acceptance Speech, on the occasion of the award of the Nobel Peace Prize in Oslo, December 10, 1964. https://www.nobelprize.org/nobel_prizes/peace/laureates/1964/king-acceptance_en.html

6   Gerald Nachman, *Seriously Funny: The Rebel Comedians of the 1950s and 1960s* (New York: Pantheon, 2003).

7   Fred Kaplan, "1959: Sex, Jazz and Datsuns," *New York*, May 31, 2009. http://nymag.com/nymag/features/57058/index3.html

8   Kaplan, "1959."

9   "Obscenity Case Files: *People v. Bruce*." http://cbldf.org/about-us/case-files/obscenity-case-files/people-v-bruce-the-lenny-bruce-trial/

10   Doug Linder, "The Trials of Lenny Bruce." http://law2.umkc.edu/faculty/projects/ftrials/bruce/bruceaccount.html

11   Richard Corliss, "A Tribute to Lenny Bruce," *Time*, August 10, 2006. http://content.time.com/time/arts/article/0,8599,1225432,00.html

12   Linder, "Trials of Lenny Bruce."

13   "Obscenity Case Files: *People v. Bruce*."

14   Linder, "Trials of Lenny Bruce."

15   Linder, "Trials of Lenny Bruce."

16   "Obscenity Case Files: *People v. Bruce*."

17   Linder, "Trials of Lenny Bruce."

18   Corliss, "A Tribute to Lenny Bruce."

19   Tricia Jenkins, "James Bond's 'Pussy' and Anglo-American Cold War Sexuality," *Journal of American Culture*, vol. 28 (3), September 2005, 309–17.

20   Bosley Crowther, "Screen; 'The Pawnbroker' Opens on Three Screens,' *New York Times*, April 21, 1965.

21   A. H. Weiler, "Board Gives Seal to 'Pawnbroker,'" *New York Times*, March 29, 1965.

22 Mark Harris, *Pictures at a Revolution: Five Movies and the Birth of the New Hollywood* (New York: Penguin, 2008), 175–76.

23 Peter Bart, "Hollywood's Morality Code Undergoing First Major Revision in 35 Years," *New York Times*, April 7, 1965.

24 Peter Grose, "Khanh Spurns 'Foreign' War Aims," *New York Times*, December 23, 1964.

25 Peter Grose, "Saigon Military Uprising Denounced by U.S. Aides," *New York Times*, December 21, 1964.

26 John W. Finney, "U.S. Warns Vietnamese Military Help Is Based on Free Civil Rule," *New York Times*, December 23, 1964; Grose, "Khanh Spurns 'Foreign' War Aims."

27 Peter Grose, "Terrorists Bomb Saigon Quarters of U.S. Officers," New York Times, December 25, 1964; "Saigon Security Tightened by U.S. after Explosion," *New York Times*, December 26, 1964.

28 "Senator Church Sees Need for a Major Shift on Asia," *New York Times*, December 27, 1964.

CHAPTER 21

1 Lyndon B. Johnson, Annual Message to Congress on the State of the Union, January 4, 1965. http://www.presidency.ucsb.edu/ws/?pid=26907

2 Rick Perlstein, *Before the Storm: Barry Goldwater and the Unmaking of the American Consensus* (New York: Hill & Wang, 2001), 307.

3 LBJ, March 1964, as quoted in Richard Goodwin, *Remembering America: A Voice from the Sixties* (Boston: Little Brown, 1988), 257.

4 Author's interview with Richard Goodwin, July 8, 1985, Bourne, Massachusetts.

5 LBJ, telephone conversation with Robert McNamara, March 6, 1965, in Michael Beschloss, *Reaching for Glory: Lyndon Johnson's Secret White House Tapes, 1964–1965* (New York: Simon & Schuster, 2001), 215.

6 Johnson, Annual Message to Congress, January 4, 1965.

7 Seymour Topping, "Seven G.I.'s Slain, 80 Wounded in Vietcong Raid," *New York Times*, February 7, 1965.

8 Memorandum from Vice President Humphrey to President Johnson, February 17, 1965. http://www.presidency.ucsb.edu/vietnam/showdoc.php?docid=64

9 LBJ, telephone conversation with McGeorge Bundy, February 18, 1965, in Beschloss, *Reaching for Glory*, 184.

10 LBJ, telephone conversation with Robert McNamara, February 26, 1965, in Beschloss, *Reaching for Glory*, 194.

11 LBJ, February 7, 1965, as quoted in Lady Bird Johnson's tape-recorded diary, in Beschloss, *Reaching for Glory*, 216.

12 Kevin Boyle, *The Shattering: America in the 1960s* (New York: Norton, 2021), 183.

13 Memorandum for the President from George Ball, "A Compromise Solution in South Vietnam," July 1, 1965. https://www.mtholyoke.edu/acad/intrel /pentagon4/doc260.htm

14 George Ball, July 8, 1965, as quoted in Robert Dallek, *Flawed Giant: Lyndon Johnson and His Times, 1961–1973* (New York: Oxford University Press, 1998), 273.

15 Lyndon Johnson, July 8, 1965, as quoted in Nick Kotz, *Judgment Days: Lyndon Baines Johnson, Martin Luther King Jr., and the Laws that Changed America* (Boston: Houghton Mifflin, 2005), 354.

16 John D. Pomfret, "No Reserve Call; Additional Troops Will Be Senate as Needed, President Says," *New York Times*, July 29, 1965.

17 LBJ, telephone conversation with Sen. John McClellan, March 23, 1964, in Beschloss, *Reaching for Glory*, 237.

18 James T. Patterson, *The Eve of Destruction: How 1965 Transformed America* (New York: Basic Books, 2012), 72.

19 Martin Luther King Jr., *Why We Can't Wait* (New York: Harper & Row, 1964).

20 Ari Berman, "Jim Crow II," *Nation*, October 22, 2013.

21 Jon Meacham, *His Truth Is Marching On: John Lewis and the Power of Hope* (New York: Random House, 2020), 188.

22 Patterson, *Eve of Destruction*, 70.

23 Patterson, *Eve of Destruction*, 79.

24 Meacham, *His Truth Is Marching On*, 196–99.

25 Roy Reed, "Alabama Police Use Gas and Clubs to Rout Negroes," *New York Times*, March 8, 1965.

26 Lyndon B. Johnson, Special Message to Congress: "The American Promise," March 15, 1965. http://www.lbjlibrary.org/lyndon-baines-johnson/speeches -films/president-johnsons-special-message-to-the-congress-the-american-promise

27 Robert A. Caro, "When LBJ said, 'We Shall Overcome,'" *New York Times*, August 28, 2008; Meacham, *His Truth Is Marching On*, 206.

28 At least up until that moment. A strong case can be made that his commence-ment address at Howard University eleven weeks later was an even finer hour for LBJ.

29 Boyle, *The Shattering*, 198.

30 Lyndon B. Johnson, "Remarks on the Signing of the Voting Rights Act," August 6, 1965. https://millercenter.org/the-presidency/presidential -speeches/august-6-1965-remarks-signing-voting-rights-act

31 Paul Williams, as quoted in Milton Viorst, *Fire in the Streets: America in the 1960s* (New York: Simon & Schuster, 1979), 339.

32 Patterson, *Eve of Destruction*, 180.

33 Robert Conot, *Rivers of Blood, Years of Darkness: The Unforgettable Classic Account of the Watts Riot* (New York: William Morrow, 1968), 232.

34 Kotz, *Judgment Days*, 343.

35 Patterson, *Eve of Destruction*, 181.

36   Lewis C. Poteet and Aaron J. Poteet, *Cop Talk: A Dictionary of Police Slang* (Bloomington, IN: iUniverse, 2000), 126.

37   Malcolm X, speech in Los Angeles, May 5, 1962. https://www.youtube.com/watch?v=3-ZiqTFB3JQ

38   Viorst, *Fire in the Streets*, 323.

39   LBJ, "American Promise," March 15, 1965.

40   LBJ, Commencement Address at Howard University, "To Fulfill these Rights," June 4, 1965. http://www.presidency.ucsb.edu/ws/?pid=27021

41   Robert Dallek, *Flawed Giant*, 223.

42   LBJ, as quoted in Joseph A. Califano, *The Triumph and Tragedy of Lyndon Johnson: The White House Years* (New York: Simon & Schuster, 1991, 2015), 51–52.

43   Paul Williams, as quoted in Viorst, *Fire in the Streets*, 339.

44   Patterson, *Eve of Destruction*, 183.

45   Lou Cannon, *Reagan* (Putnam, 1982), 162.

46   Douglas E. Kneeland, "Reagan Campaigns at Mississippi Fair," *New York Times*, August 4, 1980.

47   *Choice* (1964, produced by F. Clifton White and Russ Walton.) https://www.youtube.com/watch?v=xniUoMiHm8g

48   Bob Dylan, *Playboy* interview, 1966, reprinted in Jonathan Cott, ed., *Bob Dylan: The Essential Interviews* (New York: Wenner Books, 2006; Simon & Schuster, 2017), 104.

49   "The 500 Greatest Songs of All Time," *Rolling Stone*, December 9, 2004.

50   Andrew Leahey, "Behind the Song: 'Satisfaction,'" *American Songwriter*, March 9, 2012. http://americansongwriter.com/2012/03/behind-the-song-i-cant-get-no-satisfaction/; Jay Cridlin, "50 Years Ago, the Rolling Stones Song 'Satisfaction' Was Born in Clearwater," *Tampa Bay Times*, May 1, 2015. http://www.tampabay.com/things-to-do/music/50-years-ago-the-rolling-stones-song-satisfaction-was-born-in-clearwater/2227921

51   Bob Dylan, as quoted in Nat Hentoff, "The Crackin' Shakin' Breakin' Sounds," *New Yorker*, Oct 24, 1964. https://www.newyorker.com/magazine/1964/10/24/the-crackin-shakin-breakin-sounds

52   Mark Polizzotti, *Highway 61 Revisited* (New York: Continuum, 2006), 32.

53   Bob Dylan, *Playboy* interview, 1966, 104.

54   Robert Cohen, *Freedom's Orator: Mario Savio and the Radical Legacy of the 1960s* (New York: Oxford University Press, 2009), 136.

55   Savio's speech was delivered five days before the first show on Dylan's England tour, during which Dylan's disillusion with his role and the fans who were worshipping him led him to begin to compose the long poem from which he would take the lyrics for "Like a Rolling Stone." It is interesting to note that just after Savio was saying he might deserve the charge of Bonapartism and was escaping from it, Dylan would write the lines *You used to be so amused / At Napoleon in rags and the language that he used*, presumably in reference to the way his adoring fans viewed him. It is highly unlikely that Dylan was aware to Savio's speech and picked up the negative Bonaparte image from it, but it is

fascinating that both of these public figures who had become unhappy with their fame turned, within a matter of days, to the same historical image of what they thought they had become and what they sought to escape.

56 Mario Savio, April 26, 1965, as quoted in Clark Kerr, *The Gold and the Blue: A Personal Memoir of the University of California, 1949–1967* (Berkeley: University of California Press, 2003), vol. I, 265.

57 "Bob Moses, Crusader for Civil Rights and Math Education, Dies at 86," *New York Times*, July 25, 2021.

58 "Subterranean Homesick Blues" (1965, Lyrics by Bob Dylan, © Special Rider Music).

59 Jess Righthand, "July 25, 1965: Dylan Goes Electric at the Newport Folk Festival," Smithsonian.com, July 23, 2010. https://www.smithsonianmag.com /smithsonian-institution/july-25-1965-dylan-goes-electric-at-the-newport-folk -festival-114743/

60 Shmoop, "Like a Rolling Stone—Meaning." https://www.shmoop.com/like-a -rolling-stone/meaning.html.

61 Greil Marcus, *Like a Rolling Stone: Bob Dylan at the Crossroads* (New York: PublicAffairs, 2006), 32.

62 Bob Dylan Live at Newport Folk Festival. https://www.youtube.com/watch ?time_continue=16&v=G8yU8wk67gY

63 David King Dunaway, *How Can I Keep from Singing: Pete Seeger* (New York: McGraw-Hill, 1981), 245–48.

64 As he did to me when he saw that I had written "Pete Seeger . . . was so outraged that he considered cutting Dylan's cables" in my book *What's Left?—A New Democratic Vision for America* (Holbrook, MA: Adams, 1996), 72.

65 Pete Seeger, in *No Direction Home* (2005, Martin Scorsese, Paramount).

66 Robbie Robertson, as quoted in Shmoop, "Like a Rolling Stone."

67 Bob Dylan, as quoted in Hentoff, "Crackin' Shakin' Breakin' Sounds."

68 "I'm Free" (1965, Lyrics by Mick Jagger and Keith Richards).

69 *Jacobellis* v. *Ohio* 378 US 184 (1964).

70 *Commonwealth* v. *Robin* 421 Ps 70 (1966). https://law.justia.com/cases /pennsylvania/supreme-court/1966/421-pa-70-0.html

71 *Grove Press, Inc.* v. *Gerstein* 378 US 577 (1964)

72 Pew Research Center, "Public Trust in Government, 1958–2021." May 17, 2021. https://www.pewresearch.org/politics/2021/05/17/public-trust-in -government-1958-2021/

73 Pew, "Public Trust in Government, 1958–2021."

74 Joseph A. Califano Jr., "What Was Really Great About the Great Society," *Washington Monthly*, October 1, 1999.

75 http://www.politifact.com/wisconsin/statements/2011/aug/25/ron-kind/us -rep-ron-kind-says-thanks-medicare-75-fewer-seni/

76 "We could arrest their leaders, raid their homes, break up their meetings, and vilify them night after night on the evening news," top Nixon aide John Ehrlichman admitted in 1994. "Did we know we were lying about the drugs?

Of course we did." As quoted in Dan Baum, "Legalize It All, *Harper's*, April 2016.

77   Robert S. McElvaine, "'Everyday People' Turns Forty—and the 'Good Sixties' Triumph," *Huffington Post*, December 30, 2008. https://www.huffingtonpost.com/entry/everyday-people-turns-for_b_147162.html

78   On the post-Reconstruction era, see Heather Cox Richardson, *The Death of Reconstruction: Race, Labor, and Politics in the Post–Civil War North, 1865–1901* (Cambridge, MA: Harvard University Press, 2001).

79   Elizabeth Hinton, *America on Fire: The Untold Story of Police Violence and Black Rebellion since the 1960s*. (New York: Liveright, 2021).

80   Casey Hayden and Mary King, "Sex and Caste: A Kind of Memo," *Liberation*, April 1966, 35–36. http://www.crmvet.org/docs/sexcaste.pdf

81   https://clerk.house.gov/Votes/202186.

82   Martin Duberman, *Stonewall: The Definitive Story of the LGTBQ Uprising that Changed America*. New York: Plume, 2019).

83   *Reynolds v. Sims 377 US 533 (1964)*.

84   https://www.vox.com/2016/7/29/12295830/republican-democratic-delegates-diversity-nonwhite

85   See Anne Applebaum, *Twilight of Democracy: The Seductive Lure of Authoritarianism* (New York: Doubleday, 2020) and Benjamin Novak and Michael M. Grynbaum, "Conservative Fellow Travelers," *New York Times*, August 7, 2021.

86   Thomas L. Friedman, "The Transition," *New York Times*, November 13, 1992.

87   Tyler Cowen, *Average Is Over: Powering America Beyond the Age of the Great Stagflation* (New York: Dutton, 2013), 229–41; Nancy MacLean, *Democracy in Chains: The Deep History of the Radical Right's Stealth Plan for America* (New York: Viking, 2017), 213.

88   Heather Cox Richardson, *Letters from an American*, August 13, 2021. https://heathercoxrichardson.substack.com/p/august-13-2021

89   Dylan, "The Times They Are a-Changin'."

BIBLIOGRAPHY

Ali, Muhammad, and Hannah Yasmeen Ali. *The Soul of a Butterfly: Reflections on Life's Journey.* New York: Simon & Schuster, 2004.

Alterman, Eric. *When Presidents Lie: A History of Official Deception and Its Consequences.* New York: Penguin, 2005.

Andersen, Kurt. *Evil Geniuses: The Unmaking of America: A Recent History.* New York: Random House, 2020.

Applebaum, Anne. *Twilight of Democracy: The Seductive Lure of Authoritarianism.* New York: Doubleday, 2020.

Asch, Chris Myers. *The Senator and the Sharecropper: The Freedom Struggles of James O. Eastland and Fannie Lou Hamer.* Chapel Hill: University of North Carolina Press, 2011.

Atyeo, Don, and Felix Dennis. *The Holy Warrior: Muhammad Ali.* London: Bunch Books, 1975.

Ball, George. *The Past Has Another Pattern.* New York: Norton, 1982.

Barbour, Scott. *Lyndon B. Johnson.* Farmington Hills, MI: Greenhaven Press, 2001.

Beauvoir, Simone de. *The Second Sex.* 1952; New York: Knopf, 1953.

Belfrage, Sally. *Freedom Summer.* New York: Viking, 1965.

Bell, Daniel. *The Cultural Contradictions of Capitalism.* New York: Basic Books, 1976.

Bell, Jack. *Mr. Conservative: Barry Goldwater.* Garden City, NY: Doubleday, 1962.

Beschloss, Michael R., *Crisis Years: Kennedy and Khrushchev, 1960–1963.* New York: Edward Burlingame, 1991.

Beschloss, Michael R., ed. *Reaching for Glory: Lyndon Johnson's Secret White House Tapes, 1964–1965.* New York: Simon & Schuster, 2002.

———. *Taking Charge: The Johnson White House Tapes, 1963–1964.* New York: Simon & Schuster, 1997.

Blain, Keisha N. *Until I Am Free: Fannie Lou Hamer's Enduring Message to America.* Boston: Beacon, 2021.

Booth, Stanley. *The True Adventures of the Rolling Stones*. New York: Vintage, 1985; Chicago: Chicago Review Press, 2000.

Boyle, Kevin. *The Shattering: America in the 1960s*. New York: Norton, 2021.

Boym, Svetlana. *The Future of Nostalgia*. New York: Basic, 2001.

Bradford, William. *Of Plymouth Plantation* (1620–1647). ed. by Harvey Wish. New York: Capricorn Books, 1962.

Bradlee, Ben. *A Good Life: Newspapering and Other Adventures*. New York: Simon & Schuster, 1995.

Branch, Taylor. *Parting the Waters: America in the King Years, 1954–63*. New York: Simon & Schuster, 1988.

———. *Pillar of Fire: America in the King Years, 1963–65*. New York: Simon & Schuster, 1998.

Brennan, Mary C. *Turning Right in the Sixties: The Conservative Capture of the GOP*. Chapel Hill: University of North Carolina Press, 1995.

Brokaw, Tom. *Boom! Voices of the Sixties*. New York: Random House, 2007.

Brownmiller, Susan. *In Our Time: Memoir of a Revolution*. New York: Dell, 1999.

Bryant, Nick. *When America Stopped Being Great: A History of the Present*. London: Bloomsbury Continuum, 2021.

Buchanan, James M. *The Limits of Liberty: Between Anarchy and Leviathan*. Chicago: University of Chicago Press, 1975.

Bugliosi, Vincent. *Four Days in November: The Assassination of John F. Kennedy*. New York: Norton, 2007.

———. *Reclaiming History: The Assassination of President John F. Kennedy*. New York: Norton, 2007.

Cagin, Seth., and Philip Dray. *We Are Not Afraid: The Story of Goodman, Schwerner, and Chaney and the Civil Rights Campaign for Mississippi*. New York: Macmillan, 1988.

Califano, Joseph A. *The Triumph and Tragedy of Lyndon Johnson*. New York: Simon and Schuster, 1991.

Caputo, Philip. *A Rumor of War*. New York: Henry Holt, 1977.

Caro, Robert A. *The Years of Lyndon Johnson: The Passage to Power*. New York: Knopf, 2012.

———. *The Years of Lyndon Johnson: The Path to Power*. New York: Knopf, 1982.

Carson, Clayborne. *In Struggle: SNCC and the Black Awakening of the 1960s.* Cambridge, MA: Harvard University Press, 1981.

Cavallo, Dominck. *A Fiction of the Past: The Sixties in American History.* New York: St. Martin's, 1999.

Chafe, William H. *Civilities and Civil Rights: Greensboro, North Carolina, and the Black Struggle for Freedom.* New York: Oxford University Press, 1980.

————. *Never Stop Running: Allard Lowenstein and American Liberal Activism.* New York: Basic Books, 1993.

Clayson, Alan. *Mick Jagger: The Unauthorized Biography.* London: Sanctuary, 2005.

Cohen, Robert. *Freedom's Orator: Mario Savio and the Radical Legacy of the 1960s.* New York: Oxford University Press, 2009.

Coles, Robert. *Farewell to the South.* Boston: Little, Brown, 1972.

Conot, Robert. *Rivers of Blood, Years of Darkness: The Unforgettable Classic Account of the Watts Riot.* New York: William Morrow, 1968.

Coontz, Stephanie. *A Strange Stirring:* The Feminine Mystique *and American Women at the Dawn of the 1960s.* New York: Basic Books, 2011.

Cott, Jonathan, ed. *Bob Dylan: The Essential Interviews.* New York: Wenner Books, 2006; Simon & Schuster, 2017.

Cowen, Tyler. *Average Is Over: Powering America Beyond the Age of the Great Stagflation.* New York: Dutton, 2013.

Crèvecoeur, J. Hector St. John de. *Letters from an American Farmer.* 1782; New York: Penguin, 1981.

Dallek, Robert. *Flawed Giant: Lyndon Johnson and His Times, 1961–1973.* New York: Oxford University Press, 1998.

————. *Lyndon B. Johnson: Portrait of a President* (New York: Oxford University Press, 2004.

Dann, Jim. *Challenging the Mississippi Firebombers: Memories of Mississippi, 1964–65.* Montreal: Baraka Books, 2013.

Davis, Mike and Jon Weiner. *Set the Night on Fire: L.A. in the Sixties.* (New York: Verso, 2020).

Dickstein, Morris. *Gates of Eden: American Culture in the Sixties.* New York: Basic Books, 1977.

Didion, Joan. *After Henry.* New York: Simon & Schuster, 1992.

————. *Slouching Towards Bethlehem.* New York: Farrer, Straus & Giroux, 1968.

Dittmer, John. *Local People: The Struggle for Civil Rights in Mississippi.* Urbana: University of Illinois Press, 1994.

Donaldson, Gary. *Liberalism's Last Hurrah: The Presidential Campaign of 1964.* Armonk, NY: M.E. Sharpe, 2003.

Douglas, Susan J. *Where the Girls Are: Growing Up Female with the Mass Media.* New York: Times Books, 1994.

Draper, Hal. *Berkeley: The New Student Revolt.* New York: Grove Press, 1965, 2009.

Duberman, Martin. *Stonewall: The Definitive Story of the LGTBQ Uprising that Changed America.* New York: Plume, 2019.

Du Bois, W. E. B. *Black Reconstruction in America, 1860–1880.* New York: Harcourt, Brace and Howe, 1935.

Dunaway, David King. *How Can I Keep from Singing: Pete Seeger.* New York: McGraw-Hill, 1981.

Early, Gerald. *The Culture of Bruising: Prizefighting, Literature and Modern American Culture.* New York: Ecco Press, 1994.

Ehrenreich, Barbara, Elizabeth Hess, and Gloria Jacobs, *Re-making Love: The Feminization of Sex.* New York: Anchor/Doubleday, 1986.

Ellison, Ralph. *Invisible Man.* New York: Modern Library, 1952.

Erenrich, Susie. *Freedom Is a Constant Struggle: An Anthology of the Mississippi Civil Rights Movement.* Montgomery, AL: Black Belt Press, 1999.

Evans, Sara M. *Personal Politics: The Roots of Women's Liberation in the Civil Rights Movement and the New Left.* New York: Knopf, 1979, Vintage, 1980.

Felsenthal, Carol. *Power, Privilege, and the Post: The Katherine Graham Story.* New York: Seven Stones Press, 1999.

Feminist Revolution. New Paltz, NY: Redstockings, 1975.

FitzGerald, Frances. *America Revised: What History Textbooks Have Taught Our Children about their Country and Why Those Textbooks Have Changed in Different Decades.* Boston: Atlantic-Little Brown, 1979.

———. *Fire in the Lake: The Vietnamese and the Americans in Vietnam.* Boston: Little Brown, 1972.

Forman, James. *The Making of Black Revolutionaries.* Washington, DC: Open Head, 1985.

Frady, Marshall. *Martin Luther King Jr.: A Life.* New York: Penguin, 2002.

———. *Wallace.* New York: World Publishing, 1968.

Freeman, Jo. *The Politics of Women's Liberation*. New York: Longman, 1975.

———. *We Will Be Heard: Women's Struggles for Political Power in the United States*. Lanham, MD: Rowman & Littlefield, 2008.

Friedan, Betty. *The Feminine Mystique*. New York: Norton, 1963.

Galbraith, John Kenneth. *American Capitalism: The Concept of Countervailing Power*. Boston: Houghton Mifflin, 1952.

Gardner, Lloyd C. *Pay Any Price: Lyndon Johnson and the Wars for Vietnam*. Chicago: Ivan R. Dee, 1995.

Garrow, David J. *Bearing the Cross: Martin Luther King Jr. and the Southern Christian Leadership Conference*. New York: William Morrow, 1986.

———. *Protest at Selma: Martin Luther, Jr., and the Voting Rights Act of 1965*. New Haven: Yale University Press, 1978.

Gitlin, Todd. *The Sixties: Years of Hope, Days of Rage*. New York: Bantam, 1987.

Glaude, Eddie S., Jr. *Begin Again: James Baldwin's America and Its Urgent Lessons for Our Own*. New York: Crown, 2020.

Goldman, Peter. *The Death and Life of Malcolm X*. New York: Harper & Row, 1973.

Goldwater, Barry M. *Why Not Victory? A Fresh Look at American Foreign Policy*. New York: McGraw-Hill, 1962.

Goodwin, Richard. *Remembering America: A Voice from the Sixties*. Boston: Little Brown, 1988.

———. *The Conscience of a Conservative*. 1960; Princeton, NJ: Princeton University Press, 2007.

Gordon, Graham. *Rebels with a Cause: The Secret History of the Original Rolling Stones*. Independently published, 2017.

Goudsouzian, Aram. *Sidney Poitier: Man, Actor, Icon*. Chapel Hill: University of North Carolina Press, 2004.

Gould, Jonathan. *Can't Buy Me Love: The Beatles, Britain, and America*. New York: Three Rivers, 2007.

Greene, Graham. *The Quiet American*. London: Heinemann, 1955; Penguin, 2004.

Greig, Charlotte. *Will You Still Love Me Tomorrow?: Girl Groups from the 50s on*. London: Virago Press, 1989.

Guralnick, Peter. *Feels Like Going Home: Portraits in Blues and Rock 'n' Roll*. Hachette Digital, 2012.

———. *Last Train to Memphis: The Rise of Elvis Presley*. New York: Back Bay Books, 1995.

Hajdu, David. *Positively 4th Street: The Lives and Times of Joan Baez, Bob Dylan, Mimi Baez Fariña, and Richard Fariña*. New York: Macmillan, 2002.

Hakim, Joy. *All the People*. New York: Oxford University Press, 2003.

Halberstam, David. *The Best and the Brightest*. New York: Random House, 1972.

———. *The Fifties*. New York: Villard Books, 1993.

Hannah-Jones, Nikole. *The 1619 Project: A New Origin Story*. New York: One World, 2021.

Harrington, Michael. *The Other America*. New York: Macmillan, 1962.

Harris, Mark. *Pictures at a Revolution: Five Movies and the Birth of the New Hollywood*. New York: Penguin, 2008.

Hauser, Thomas. *Muhammad Ali: His Life and Times*. New York: Simon & Schuster, 1991.

Heller, Joseph. *Catch-22*. New York: Simon & Schuster, 1961, S&S Classic Edition, 1999.

Hendrickson, Paul. *Sons of Mississippi: A story of Race and Its Legacy*. New York: Knopf, 2003.

Herr, Michael. *Dispatches*. New York: Knopf, 1977.

Heylin, Clinton. *Bob Dylan: Behind the Shades Revisited*. New York: HarperCollins, 2003.

Hinton, Elizabeth. *America on Fire: The Untold Story of Police Violence and Black Rebellion since the 1960s*. New York: Liveright, 2021.

Hodgson, Godfrey. *America in Our Time: From World War II to Nixon— What Happened and Why*. New York: Doubleday, 1976.

———. *The Gentleman from New York: Daniel Patrick Moynihan: A Biography*. Boston: Houghton Mifflin, 2000.

Hofstadter, Richard. *Anti-Intellectualism in American Life*. New York: Knopf, 1963.

Hogan, Wesley C. *Many Minds, One Heart: SNCC's Dream for a New America*. Chapel Hill: University of North Carolina Press, 2007.

Huie, William Bradford *Three Lives for Mississippi*. New York: WWC Books, 1965; reprint: Jackson: University Press of Mississippi, 2000.

Humphrey, Hubert. *The Education of a Public Man: My Life in Politics*. Garden City, NY: Doubleday, 1976.

Intelligence Activities and the Rights of Americans, Book II: Final Report of the Select Committee to Study Governmental Operations, United States Senate. Washington: Government Printing Office, 1976.

Izenberg, Jerry. *Once There Were Giants: The Golden Age of Heavyweight Boxing.* New York: Skyhorse Publishing, 2017.

Jagger, Mick, Dora Lowenstein, and Philip Dodd, *According to the Rolling Stones.* San Francisco: Chronicle Books, 2003.

Janeway, Michael. *The Fall of the House of Roosevelt: Brokers of Ideas and Power from FDR to LBJ.* New York: Columbia University Press, 2004.

Johnson, Lyndon Baines. *The Vantage Point: Perspectives of the Presidency, 1963–1969.* New York: Holt, Rinehart, and Winston, 1971.

Johnston, Lyle. *"Good Night, Chet": A Biography of Chet Huntley.* Jefferson, NC: McFarland, 2003.

Jones, Landon Y. *Great Expectations: America and the Baby Boom Generation.* New York: Coward, McCann & Geoghegan, 1980.

Kammen, Michael G. *People of Paradox: An Inquiry Concerning the Origins of American Civilization.* New York: Knopf, 1972.

Karnow, Stanley. *Vietnam: A History.* New York: Viking, 1983; rev. ed.: Penguin, 1997.

Kearns, Doris. *Lyndon Johnson and the American Dream.* New York: Harper & Row, 1976.

Kennedy, Robert F. *Thirteen Days: A Memoir of the Cuban Missile Crisis.* New York: Norton, 1969.

Kerouac, Jack. *On the Road.* New York: Viking, 1957.

Kerr, Clark. *The Gold and the Blue: A Personal Memoir of the University of California, 1949–1967.* Berkeley: University of California Press, 2003.
———. *The Uses of the University.* 1963; Cambridge, MA: Harvard University Press, 2001.

Kimball, George, and John Schulian, eds. *At the Fights: American Writers on Boxing.* New York: Library of America, 2011.

King, Martin Luther, Jr. *Why We Can't Wait.* New York: Harper & Row, 1964.

King, Mary. *Freedom Song: A Personal History of the 1960s Civil Rights Movement.* New York: Morrow, 1987.

Kolkey, Jonathan Martin. *The New Right, 1960–1968 with an Epilogue, 1969–1980.* Lanham, MD: University Press of America, 1983.

Kondo, Zak A. *Conspiracys: Unraveling the Assassination of Malcolm X*. Washington, DC: Nubia Press, 1993.

Kotz, Nick. *Judgment Days: Lyndon Baines Johnson, Martin Luther King Jr., and the Laws that Changed America*. Boston: Houghton Mifflin Harcourt, 2006.

Kozak, David C., and Kenneth N. Ciboski, eds. *The American Presidency*. Chicago, IL: Nelson Hall, 1985.

Langguth, A. J. *Our Vietnam: The War, 1954–1975*. New York: Simon & Schuster, 2000.

Larson, Kate Clifford. *Walk with Me: A Biography of Fannie Lou Hamer*. New York: Oxford University Press, 2021.

Lasch, Christopher. *Haven in a Heartless World: The Family Besieged*. New York: Basic Books, 1977.

Levine, Lawrence W. *Black Culture and Black Consciousness: Afro-American Folk Thought from Slavery to Freedom*. New York: Oxford University Press, 1977.

Lewis, John, with Michael D'Orso. *Walking with the Wind: A Memoir of the Movement*. New York: Simon & Schuster, 1998.

Lichtman, Allan J. *White Protestant Nation: The Rise of the American Conservative Movement*. New York: Grove, 2008.

Lincoln, C. Eric. *The Black Muslims in America*. Boston: Beacon, 1963.

Lipset, Seymour Martin, and Sheldon S. Wolin, eds. *The Berkeley Student Revolt*. Garden City, NY: Anchor Books, 1965.

Loewen, James W. *Lies My Teacher Taught Me: Everything Your American History Textbook Got Wrong*. New York: New Press, 1995.

MacLean, Nancy. *Democracy in Chains: The Deep History of the Radical Right's Stealth Plan for America*. New York: Viking, 2017.

Mailer, Norman. *Advertisements for Myself*. New York: Putnam, 1959.

Manchester, William. *The Glory and the Dream: A Narrative History of America, 1932–1972*. Boston: Little, brown, 1974.

Marcus, Greil. *Like a Rolling Stone: Bob Dylan at the Crossroads*. New York: PublicAffairs, 2006.

Margolis, Jon. *The Last Innocent Year: America in 1964*. New York: William Morrow, 1999.

Martin, Ralph G. *A Hero for Our Time: An Intimate Story of the Kennedy Years*. New York: Random House, 1984.

Martínez. Elizabeth Sutherland. *Letters from Mississippi: Personal Reports from Civil Rights Volunteers of the 1964 Freedom Summer.* Brookline, MA: Zephyr Press, 2002.

Marwick, Arthur. *The Sixties: Cultural Revolution in Britain, France, Italy, and the United States, c. 1958–c. 1974.* New York: Oxford University Press, 1998.

Matusow, Allen J. *The Unravelling of America: A History of Liberalism in the 1960s.* New York: Harper & Row, 1984.

Mayer, Jane. *Dark Money: The Hidden History of the Billionaires Behind the Rise of the Radical Right.* New York: Doubleday, 2016.

Maynard, Joyce. *Looking Back: A Chronicle of Growing Up Old in the Sixties.* 1973, iUniverse, 2003.

McAdam, Doug. *Freedom Summer.* New York: Oxford, 1988.

McElvaine, Robert S. *Eve's Seed: Biology, the Sexes, and the Course of History.* New York: McGraw-Hill, 2001.

———. *The Great Depression: America, 1929–1941.* New York: Times Books, 1984.

———. *What's Left?: A New Democratic Vision for America.* Holbrook, MA: Adams, 1996.

McWhorter, Diane. *Carry Me Home: Birmingham, Alabama, The Climactic Battle of the Civil Rights Revolution.* New York: Simon & Schuster, 2001.

Meacham, Jon. *His Truth Is Marching On: John Lewis and the Power of Hope.* New York: Random House, 2020.

———. *The Soul of America: The Battle for Our Better Angels.* New York: Random House, 2018.

Medved, Michael, and David Wallechinsky, *What Really Happened to the Class of '65?* New York: Random House, 1976.

Middendorf, John William II. *A Glorious Disaster: Barry Goldwater's Presidential Campaign and the Origins of the Conservative Movement.* New York: Basic Books, 2006.

Miller, Merle. *Lyndon: An Oral Biography.* New York: Putnam, 1980; Ballantine, 1981.

Mills, Kay. *This Little Light of Mine: The Life of Fannie Lou Hamer.* Lexington: University Press of Kentucky, 2007.

Moïse, Edwin E. *Tonkin Gulf and the Escalation of the Vietnam War.* Chapel Hill: University of North Carolina Press, 1996.

Montgomery, Gayle B., James W. Johnson, and Paul Manolis. *One Step from the White House: The Rise and Fall of Senator William F. Knowland.* Berkeley and Los Angeles: University of California Press, 1998.

Moody, Anne. *Coming of Age in Mississippi.* New York: Dial, 1968; New York: Dell, 1971.

Morgan, Robin, comp., *Sisterhood is Powerful: An Anthology of Writings from the Women's Liberation Movement.* New York: Random House, 1970.

Morison, Samuel Eliot, ed. *Journals and Other Documents on the Life and Voyages of Christopher Columbus.* New York: Heritage Press, 1963.

Moses, Robert, with Charles E. Cobb, Jr. *Radical Equations: Civil Rights from Mississippi to the Algebra Project.* Boston: Beacon, 2001, 2002.

Moyers, Bill. *Moyers on America: A Journalist and his Times.* 2004; New York: Anchor, 2005.

Nachman, Gerald. *Seriously Funny: The Rebel Comedians of the 1950s and 1960s.* New York: Pantheon, 2003.

Naftali, Timothy and Philip D. Zelikow, eds. *The Presidential Recordings: John F. Kennedy: The Great Crises, vol. II: September–October 21, 1962.* New York: Norton, 2001.

Norman, Philip. *Mick Jagger.* New York: Ecco, 2012.

O'Brien, Tim. *The Things They Carried.* Franklin Library, 1990; New York: Broadway Books, 1998.

O'Donnell, Kenneth, and David F. Powers. *"Johnny, We Hardly Knew Ye".* Boston: Little Brown, 1970.

O'Neill, William L. *Coming Apart: An Informal History of America in the 1960s.* Chicago: Quadrangle, 1971.

Obama, Barack. *Dreams from My Father: A Story of Race and Inheritance.* 1995; New York: Crown, 2007.

Olsen, Jack. *Black Is Best: The Riddle of Cassius Clay.* New York: Dell, 1967.

Packard, Vance. *The Hidden Persuaders.* New York: David McKay, 1957.

Paoletti, Jo B. *Pink and Blue: Telling the Boys from the Girls in America.* Bloomington: Indiana University Press, 2012.

Patterson, James T. *An Unfinished Life: John F. Kennedy, 1917–1963.* Boston: Little, Brown, 2003.

———. *Grand Expectations: The United States, 1945–1974.* New York: Oxford University Press, 1996.

————. *The Eve of Destruction: How 1965 Transformed America*. New York: Basic Books, 2012.

Perlstein, Rick. *Before the Storm: Barry Goldwater and the Unmaking of the American Consensus*. New York: Hill and Wang, 2001.

————. *Nixonland: The Rise of a President and the Fracturing of America*. New York: Scribner, 2008.

Polizzotti, Mark. *Highway 61 Revisited*. New York: Continuum, 2006.

Porter, Gareth. *Perils of Dominance: Imbalance of Power and the Road to the Vietnam War*. Berkeley and Los Angeles: University of California Press, 2004.

Poteet, Lewis C. and Aaron J. Poteet. *Cop Talk: A Dictionary of Police Slang*. Bloomington, IN: iUniverse, 2000.

Potter, Beverly A. and Mark J. Estren. *Question Authority to Think for Yourself*. Oakland, CA: Ronin, 2012.

Raines, Howell. *My Soul Is Rested: Movement Days in the Deep South Remembered*. New York: Putnam, 1977, Penguin, 1983.

Reedy, George. *Lyndon B. Johnson: A Memoir*. New York: Andrews and McMeel, 1982.

Remnick, David. *King of the World: Muhammad Ali and the Rise of an American Hero*. New York: Random House, 1998.

Rexroth, Kenneth. *The Alternative Society: Essays from the Other World*. New York: Herder and Herder, 1970.

Richards, Keith. *Life*. New York: Little, Brown, 2010.

Richardson, Heather Cox. *The End of Reconstruction: Race, Labor, and Politics in the Post–Civil War North*. Cambridge, MA: Harvard University Press, 2004.

Rickford, Russell J. *Betty Shabazz, Surviving Malcolm X: A Remarkable Story of Survival and Faith before and after Malcolm X*. Naperville, IL: Sourcebooks, 2005.

Riley, Tim. *John Lennon: The Man, the Myth, the Music—The Definitive Biography*. New York: Hyperion.

Roberts, Randy and Johnny Smith. *Blood Brothers: The Fatal Friendship between Muhammad Ali and Malcolm X*. New York: Basic Books, 2016.

Rose, Willie Lee Rose. *Rehearsal for Reconstruction: The Port Royal Experiment*. Indianapolis and New York: Bobbs-Merrill, 1964.

Rossman, Michael. *The Wedding within the War*. Garden City, NY: Doubleday, 1965.

Rovere, Richard. *The Goldwater Caper.* New York: Harcourt, Brace & World, 1965.

Russell, Jan Jarboe. *Lady Bird: A Biography of Mrs. Johnson.* New York: Simon & Schuster, 1999; Lanham, MD: Rowman & Littlefield, 2004.

Scheurer, Timothy E. *American Popular Music: The Age of Rock.* Madison: University of Wisconsin, 1990.

Schlesinger, Arthur M., Jr. *A Thousand Days: John F. Kennedy in the White House.* Boston: Houghton Mifflin, 1965.

———. *Robert Kennedy and His Times.* Boston: Houghton Mifflin, 1978.

Schroeder, Patricia R. *Robert Johnson, Mythmaking, and Contemporary American Culture.* Urbana: University of Illinois Press, 2004.

Seeger, Pete., with Rob Rosenthal and Sam Rosenthal, *Pete Seeger in His Own Words.* London: Paradigm, 2012.

Sellers, Cleveland, with Robert Terrell. *The River of No Return: The Autobiography of a Black Militant and the Life and Death of SNCC.* Jackson: University Press of Mississippi, 1990.

Shadegg, Stephen. *Barry Goldwater: Freedom Is His Flight Plan.* New York: Fleet Publishing, 1962.

———. *What Happened to Goldwater? The Inside Story of the 1964 Republican Campaign.* New York: Holt, Rinehart and Winston, 1965.

Shapiro, Fred C. and James W. Sullivan. *Race Riots, New York, 1964.* New York: Crowell, 1964.

Sheehan, Neil. *A Bright Shining Lie: John Paul Vann and America in Vietnam.* New York: Random House, 1988.

Sheffield, Rob. *Dreaming the Beatles: The Love Story of One Band and the World.* New York: Dey Street Books, 2017.

Shelton, Robert. *No Direction Home: The Life and Music of Bob Dylan.* Milwaukee: Backbeat Books. 2010.

Shesol, Jeff. *Mutual Contempt: Lyndon Johnson, Robert Kennedy and the Feud that Defined a Decade.* New York: Norton, 1998.

Short, Philip. *Pol Pot: Anatomy of a Nightmare.* New York: Macmillan, 2007.

Sidey, Hugh. *A Very Personal Presidency: Lyndon Johnson in the White House.* New York: Atheneum, 1968.

Siegel, Deborah. *Sisterhood Interrupted: From Radical Women to Girls Gone Wild.* New York: Macmillan, 2007.

Silver, James W. *Mississippi: The Closed Society.* New York: Harcourt, Brace and World, 1964.

Sorensen, Theodore C. *Counselor: A Life at the Edge of History.* New York: HarperCollins, 2008.

———. *Kennedy.* New York: Harper & Row, 1965.

Stamp, Kenneth M. *The Era of Reconstruction, 1865–1877.* New York: Knopf, 1965.

Stark, Steven D. *Meet the Beatles: A Cultural History of the Band that Shook Youth, Gender, and the World.* New York: HarperEntertainment, 2005.

Stevens, Stuart. *It Was All a Lie: How the Republican Party Became Donald Trump.* New York: Knopf, 2020.

Stevenson, Charles A. *Warriors and Politicians: Civil-Military Relations under Stress.* New York: Routledge, 2006.

Stockdale, Jim, and Sybil Stockdale. *In Love and War: The Story of a Family's Ordeal and Sacrifice During the Vietnam Years.* New York: Harper & Row, 1984.

Stormer, John A. *None Dare Call It Treason.* Florissant, MO: Liberty Bell Press, 1964.

Stratton, W. K. *Floyd Patterson: The Fighting Life of Boxing's Invisible Champion.* Boston: Houghton Mifflin Harcourt, 2012.

Sullivan, Patricia. *Justice Rising: Robert Kennedy's America in Black and White.* Cambridge, MA: Belknap. 2021.

Talbot, David. *Brothers: The Hidden History of the Kennedy Years.* New York: Simon & Schuster, 2007.

Tate, Greg. *Everything But the Burden: What White People Are Taking from Black Culture.* New York: Random House, 2003.

Thomas, Evan. *Robert Kennedy: His Life.* New York: Simon & Schuster, 2000.

Tubbs, Anna Malaika. *The Three Mothers: How the Mothers of Martin Luther King Jr., Malcolm X, and James Baldwin Shaped the Nation.* New York: Flatiron Books, 2021.

Viorst, Milton. *Fire in the Streets: America in the 1960s.* New York: Simon & Schuster, 1979.

Walker, Martin. *The Cold War: A History,* revised ed. New York: Macmillan, 1995.

Walker, Samuel. *Presidents and Civil Liberties from Wilson to Obama: A Study of Poor Custodians*. Cambridge and New York: Cambridge University Press, 2012.

Ward, Geoffrey, and Ken Burns. *Vietnam: An Intimate History*. New York: Knopf, 2017.

Washington, James Melvin, ed. *A Testament of Hope: The Essential Writings of Martin Luther King Jr*. San Francisco: HarperSanFrancisco, 1991.

Watkins, Hollis, with C. Leigh McInnis. *Brother Hollis: The Sankofa of a Movement Man*. Clinton, MS: Sankofa Southern Publishing, 2015.

Watson, Bruce. *Freedom Summer: The Savage Season that Made Mississippi Burn and Made America a Democracy*. New York: Viking, 2010.

Wayne, Jane Ellen. *The Leading Men of MGM*. New York: Da Capo, 2006.

Whitburn, Joel. *The Billboard Hot 100 Charts: The Sixties*. Menonomee Falls, WI: Record Research, 1990.

White, Theodore H. *In Search of History: A Personal Adventure*. New York: Harper & Row, 1978.

———. *The Making of the President, 1960*. New York: Atheneum, 1962.

———. *The Making of the President, 1964*. New York: Atheneum, 1969.

Whitehead, Don. *Attack on Terror: The FBI against the Ku Klux Klan in Mississippi*. New York: Funk & Wagnalls, 1970.

Wicker, Tom. *JFK and LBJ: The Influence of Personality on Politics*. New York: William Morrow, 1968.

Wilkerson, Isabel, *Caste: The Origins of Our Discontents*. New York: Random House, 2020.

Woods, Randall. *LBJ: Architect of American Ambition*. New York: Simon & Schuster, 2007.

X, Malcolm. *Malcolm X Speaks* (George Breitman, ed.). New York: Merit Publishers, 1965.

X, Malcolm, with Alex Haley, *Autobiography of Malcolm X*. New York: Grove Press, 1965.

Zellner, Bob, with Constance Curry. *The Wrong Side of Murder Creek: A White Southerner in the Freedom Movement*. Montgomery: New South Books, 2008.

Zinn, Howard. *SNCC: The New Abolitionists*. Boston: Beacon, 1964.

ILLUSTRATION CREDITS

INTRODUCTION

Freedom Now: Warren K Leffler/PhotoQuest/Getty Images

CHAPTER 1

Dylan, Times portrait, January 64: Michael Ochs Archives/Getty Images
LBJ, 1964: Central Press/Getty Images

CHAPTER 2

JFK casket: Photo by © Wally McNamee/CORBIS/Corbis via Getty Images
Beatles departing London for NY, February 2, 1964: Photo by © Wally McNamee/CORBIS/Corbis via Getty Images

CHAPTER 3

FDR shakes hands with young LBJ, Governor Allred of Texas in between. Galveston, Texas on May 12, 1937: National Archives: National Archives

CHAPTER 4

LBJ delivers State of the Union, January 1964: Photo by © CORBIS/Corbis via Getty Images

CHAPTER 5

Dr Strangelove: Photo by Sunset Boulevard/Corbis via Getty Images

CHAPTER 6

Beatles first appearance on Ed Sullivan: Photo by Michael Ochs Archives/Getty Images

CHAPTER 7

Lesley Gore, 1964: Photo by Keystone/Getty Images
Ava Gardner holding copy of *Feminine Mystique* at an airport: Photo by Nigel Dobinson/Getty Images

CHAPTER 8

Malcolm X and Cassius Clay outside the Trans-Lux Newsreel Theater in New York in 1964: AP photo
Clay and Beatles, February 1964: Bettmann/Getty Images

CHAPTER 9

LBJ with VN advisers, March 1964: Photo by Abbie Rowe/PhotoQuest/Getty Images

CHAPTER 10

James Brown and Mick Jagger at TAMI 1964: Courtesy of the Bob Bonis Archive
Rolling Stones 1964 Tour Poster, San Bernadino History and RR Museum: San Bernadino Railroad Museum
Gather No Moss: Photo by John Kisch Archive/Getty Images:
Policemen holding back Rolling Stones fans in NYC, June 1 1964: Photo by William Lovelace/Daily Express/Getty Images

CHAPTER 11

FBI Poster of Missing Civil Rights Workers: Public domain
SNCC logo: Public domain
Bob Moses: SNCC Digital Gateway: Matt Herron/Take Stock/TopFoto
MLK holding photos of Schwerner, Chaney, and Goodman: Bett-
    mann/Getty Images

CHAPTER 12

LBJ signs Civil Rights Act: Photo by Hulton Archive/Getty Images
White Party supporters of George Wallace: Photo by FPG/Archive
    Photos/Getty Images
Girls Fleeing from Police During 1964 Bedford-Stuyvesant Riot: Bet-
    tmann/Getty Images

CHAPTER 13

Bob Moses KKK Wanted Poster: Public domain

CHAPTER 14

YAF-Goldwater: Bettmann/Getty Images
Civil Rights Activists dressed as Klansmen for Goldwater, San Fran-
    cisco, 1964:
Photo by Warren K. Leffer, Library of Congress

CHAPTER 15

Gulf of Tonkin retaliation: Bettmann/Getty Images

CHAPTER 16

Fannie Lou Hamer testifying at DNC Credentials Committee: Bett-
    mann/Getty Images
Mississippi Freedom Party delegates at DNC: Bettmann/Getty Images
Goldwater billboard with Dem Response: Bettmann/Getty Images

CHAPTER 17

Mario Savio speaking to FSM crowd: Bettmann/Getty Images
Mario Savio and Joan Baez: Photo by © Ted Streshinsky/CORBIS/
Corbis via Getty Images

CHAPTER 18

LBJ campaigning in Austin: Bettmann/Getty Images
Daisy Girl: Library of Congress
Reagan televised speech, "A Time for Choosing": Ronald Reagan Pres-
idential Library

CHAPTER 19

Mary King: SNCC Digital Gateway: George Ballis/Take Stock/
TopFoto
Casey Hayden: SNCC Digital Gateway: Matt Herron/Take Stock/
TopFoto
Stokeley Carmichael: Photo by Afro American Newspapers/Gado/
Getty Images

CHAPTER 20

MLK receives Nobel Prize, December 4, 1964: Photo by Keystone/
Getty Images
After Brink bombing, Saigon, December 1964: Bettmann/Getty
Images

CHAPTER 21

Legacies of 1964: Woodstock ticket-ordering brochure: Photo by
Blank Archives/Getty Images; Trump supporters hold "Stop the
Steal" rally: Photo by Jon Cherry/Getty Images; Jimi Hendrix
performs onstage at Monterey Pop Festival, June 18, 1967: Photo
by Michael Ochs Archives/Getty Images; Legalize Weed march in
New York City, July 10, 1999: Photo by Bill Tompkins/ Michael

Ochs Archives/Getty Images; President Donald Trump stands in the colonnade: Photo by Mark Wilson/Getty Images; Republican presidential candidate Donald Trump delivers remarks: Photo by Win McNamee/Getty Images; Cambodia after the genocide: Photo by Shaul Schwarz/Getty Images; white power demonstrators: Photo by Underwood Archives/Getty Images; demonstrator at Rally for Women's Lives: Photo by Mark Reinstein/Corbis via Getty Images; nation reacts to Derek Chauvin trial verdict (Black Lives Matter): Photo by Sarah Silbiger/Getty Images; carrying wounded comrade: Bettmann/Getty Images; President Nixon points to a reporter: Bettmann/Getty Images; Nancy Pelosi holds gavel as Speaker of the House: Photo by Win McNamee/Getty Images; Barack Obama campaigns: Photo by Ethan Miller/Getty Images; Ronald Reagan giving campaign speech: Photo by © Wally McNamee/CORBIS/Corbis via Getty Images; newly married couple has their bridal photos taken: Photo by George Rose/Getty Images; War Criminal–Pentagon march: Bettmann/Getty Images; women's liberation parade: Bettmann/Getty Images; attendees at Woodstock Music & Arts Festival: Photo by Warner Bros/Michael Ochs Archives/Getty Images;

John Lewis being beaten at Selma: Bettmann/Getty Images

Armed National Guardsmen in streets of Watts, August 1965: Photo by Hulton Archive/Getty Images

Bob Dylan goes electric at Newport 1965: Alice Ochs/Michael Ochs Archives/Getty Images

Trust in Government, 1958–2021: Pew Research

INDEX

Abbott, Greg, 398n52
Acheson, Dean, 334
Adams, Abigail, 4
Adams, John, 25
Aiken, George, 238
Ali, Muhammad. *See* Clay,
   Cassius
Allen, Steve, 323
Allen, Woody, 323–324
Alvarez, Everett, Jr., 242
American Dream, 75
"American Pie" (McLean), 37
Andersen, Kurt, 12, 19
Anderson, Robert, 234, 238
Another Side of Bob Dylan
   (Dylan), 15
*Anti-Intellectualism in American
   Life* (Hofstadter), 212
Applebaum, Anne, 17
Average Is Over (Cowen), 357

Bacharach, Burt, 94
Baez, Joan, 276–277
Baker, Bobby, 52
Baker, Ella, 165, 310
Baldwin, James, 324
Ball, George, 237, 240, 320, 334
Beach Boys, The, 159
Beatles, The, 29, 68, 108, 144–145,
   150–151, 157–160, 327, 347

A Hard Day's Night (film), 81,
   83, 92
Beatlemania, 36–37, 71, 89–92
and British Invasion, 79–83,
   89–92
and Cassius Clay, 126–128
on *Ed Sullivan Show*, 79, 80,
   103, 126
and Elvis Presley, 87–88
first visit to America, 36–38
"I Feel Fine," 327
"I Want to Hold Your Hand,"
   36–37, 68, 80–82
Sgt Pepper, 347
"She Loves You," 80, 91
See also Harrison, George;
   Lennon, John; McCartney,
   Paul; Starr, Ringo
Belafonte, Harry, 205
Bell, Daniel, 6
Bennett, Ronnie. *See* Spector,
   Ronnie
Benson, Barbara, 191–193
Benson, Harry, 126–127
Berry, Chuck, 151, 157, 159
Beschloss, Michael, 302
Bevel, James, 186, 336
Biden, Joe, *xii, xvi,* 17
Billboard, 37, 80–81, 90, 95, 102,
   158, 191, 320, 327

439